THE TIMES
WORLD
MYTHOLOGY

First published in 2002 by
Times Books, London
77-85 Fulham Palace Road
Hammersmith, London W6 8JB

The HarperCollins website address is
www.fireandwater.com

Printed and bound in Italy

British Library Cataloguing in Publication Data
A catalogue record for this book is available from
the British Library

ISBN 0 00 71 3139 9

General Editor
William G.Doty
Chair of Religious Studies and professor
of Humanities, University of
Alabama/Tuscaloosa, USA.

Contributors
See pages 4–5

Editorial and Design Team for Flame Tree
Jennifer Bishop, Michelle Clare, Vicky Garrard,
Dave Jones, Julia Rolf, Nick Wells,
Polly Willis, Tom Worsley

Editorial and Design Team for HarperCollins
Martin Brown, Ceire Clark, Philip Parker

THE TIMES WORLD MYTHOLOGY

General Editor: William G.Doty

TIMES BOOKS

London

Contributors

DR WILLIAM G. DOTY
General Editor, Introduction
William G. Doty is Chair of Religious Studies and Professor of Humanities at the University of Alabama/Tuscaloosa, USA. He is a prolific writer, translator and editor who has published 14 books and over 70 essays in a wide range of journals on subjects including religious studies, anthropology, psychology, classics and art criticism. Recent publications include *Myths of Masculinity* (Crossroad, 1993) and *Mythography: The Study of Myths and Rituals* (University of Alabama Press, 1986. 2nd ed. 1997). He is currently editor of *Mythosphere: A Journal for Image, Myth, and Symbol*, published by Gordon and Breach.

LOREN AUERBACH
Northern Europe
Loren Auerbach specialized in Old English and Old Icelandic at King's College London, where she gained a Masters degree. She recently co-authored the Northern European volume of the prestigious Time Life Books series *Myth and Mankind*, and wrote the chapter on Northern Europe for the Paragon *Encyclopedia of World Mythology* (Dempsey Parr, 1999).

NORMAN BANCROFT-HUNT
North America
Norman Bancroft-Hunt graduated from Kingston School of Art with a degree in Graphic Design, but has since concentrated on studying Native American cultures. He is the author of numerous books about the Native Americans, is a Fellow of the Royal Anthropological Institute and holds a Doctorate in Historical and Theoretical Studies from the University of London.

MIRANDA BRUCE-MITFORD
Southeast Asia
Miranda Bruce-Mitford is a tutor and lecturer on Southeast Asian art at the British Museum. Author of the *Illustrated Book of Signs and Symbols*, she has contributed to a number of encyclopedias and other publications dealing with the art, religion and mythology of Asia.

DR RAY DUNNING
The Celts, Central and Eastern Europe
Ray Dunning has a special interest in non-Mediterranean European mythologies and has contributed to many books, writing on Celtic, Norse and Central and Eastern European mythologies. He has taught art and art history for many years and his illustrations appear in books on mythology and the ancient world. He is currently Head of the Department of Design Studies at Kingston College.

DR JAMES H. GRAYSON
Korea
James H. Grayson, an anthropologist and Methodist minister who lived in Korea for 16 years, is Reader in Modern Korean Studies and Dean of the Faculty of Social Sciences at the University of Sheffield. His most recent book is *Myths and Legends from Korea: An Annotated Compendium of Ancient and Modern Materials* (Curzon, 2001). A previous book, *Korea: A Religious History* (Oxford, 1989), will be republished soon by Curzon.

STEPHEN HODGE
Japan
Stephen Hodge is a linguist in Japanese and an author with a specialist knowlege of Japanese culture.

MARK NUTTALL
The Arctic Regions
Mark Nuttall is Professor of Social Anthropology at the University of Aberdeen and specializes in the peoples and cultures of the Arctic and North Atlantic. His research interests include human-environment relationships; kinship, identity and the person; the sustainable uses of living marine resources, and the impacts of climate change on the Arctic regions.

PROFESSOR JAMES RIORDAN
Greece, Africa
James Riordan is Emeritus Professor at the University of Surrey and Honorary Professor at both Stirling and Hong Kong Universities. He has published several books on myths and folklore, including Heracles and Jason and the Argonauts from Ancient Greece, and Yoruba myths from Africa. He has also gathered tales among the natives of North America and Siberia.

DR NICHOLAS J. SAUNDERS
Caribbean, Central and South America
Nicholas J. Saunders studied archaeology at the universities of Sheffield and Southampton, and anthropology at Queens' College Cambridge. He has held teaching and research posts in the USA, Trinidad, Jamaica, Argentina and Mexico. He is currently Lecturer in Material Culture at University College London, specializing in pre-Columbian archaeology and anthropology.

TADEUSZ SKORUPSKI
Tibet
Tadeusz Skorupski has studied in Poland, Canada, Italy and Great Britain. He holds degrees in philosophy, theology and Buddhist Studies. The main focus of his academic research is on Indo-Tibetan Buddhism, especially doctrines, literature, rituals and iconography. He currently teaches Buddhism at the School of Oriental and African Studies, University of London.

RACHEL STORM
Rome
Rachel Storm has studied and written about mythology and religion since the 1980s. She is the author of three books in the area and has contributed to a number of encyclopedias, as well as to national and international magazines and newspapers.

DR JAMES F. WEINER
Australia, Oceania
James F. Weiner is a Visiting Fellow at the Department of Anthropology, Research School of Pacific and Asian Studies, Australian National University. He has done extensive fieldwork in both Papua New Guinea and in Queensland, Australia and has written and edited many books on the social life of the Foi and other Papua New Guinea peoples.

DR ROY WILLIS
Egypt, Ancient Near East
Roy Willis is a social anthropologist with extensive field experience in Central-East Africa. He is the author of books on animal symbolism, pre-colonial African history, African 'spirit' healers and numerous other scholarly publications. He is the editor of *World Mythology* (Duncan Baird, 1993) and is currently a research fellow at Edinburgh University.

Contents

Introduction

There are dozens of reference works devoted to 'world mythologies'. Many are quite compendious and quite useful. Almost all of them are collections of snippets of myths from various cultures and few provide much socio-cultural information about the stories. Generally they regard myths as belonging primarily to the literary long ago, by societies seen as vanishing if not vanished.

The *Times World Mythology* is not only compendious, and certainly useful, but its features stand out in contrast to those just described. First, it does not just retell stories, mythical narratives, yet again, but recognizes many forms of the mythological. Second, it provides social and cultural information about the myth-makers, their societies and their stories, and it surveys the primary sources of the mythologies. Third, while it recognizes that many myths do refer to events of yore, many of them remain viable and vital today in many cultures. They remain living cultural materials that are constantly changing as they are

Aboriginal religion gives great importance to fertility and there are a number of myths concerning the regeneration of the cosmos. There are various beings associated with fertility cults across Australia; the Rainbow Serpent shown in this painting represents fertility rites in the Central Desert and Northern Territory.

transmitted, and contributors are sensitive to transmission-transformation over time. And fourth, the entries written entirely fresh for this volume by outstanding scholarly authorities acknowledge intimate and profound ties between the stories of myths and the practice of rituals.

These writers understand that myths have consequences, that they are part of the ideological substructures of cultures – they are foundational to the social structures, and hence cannot be comprehended without looking at their reception and repetition within modern-day communities. Etymological derivation is less crucial than historical usages, so that mythologies are usually considered to be stories of and about the suprahuman.

Various sections track contemporary ethnological findings, while others refer to contemporary issues such as representations of gender – for instance, the role of goddesses in several cultures, of the matriarchy in Japan, and fertility deities in Northern Europe, the Caribbean, Australia and Oceania.

The range of cultures studied is truly worldwide. The encyclopedia includes areas seldom featured in many of the collections of world myth, namely Southeast Asia, Tibet, Central and Eastern Europe, the Arctic Regions and the Caribbean. The several parts of each section are self-contained neighbours that provide an essential glimpse of each cultural area.

The most important primary sources are identified within specific cultural areas, distinguishing, for instance, between the early Indian hymns of the *Vedas* and the secondary *Brahmanas* (including the *Upanishads*) and the even later *Puranas* and *Tantras*, as well as the great epics, the *Maha'bharata* and the *Ramayana*. Others include the *Sibylline* Books of Rome, the Classics of China, the *Kojiki* and *Nihon-shoki* of Japan, the Maya *Popol Vuh*, the Greek *Iliad* and *Odyssey*, Hesiod's *Theogony* and the Finnish *Kalevala*.

The types of mythical materials include those of origin and cosmogony: see, for example, the section on China where Pan Gu is born from a primal egg that splits into heaven and earth, his body parts becoming elements of the natural world.

We also have myths of the family and mythological inventors. There are discussions of Hitler and mythology, gods of the Sacred Calendar, death and sex and even (in the

Oceania section) post-Christian mythology.

Some of the important mythological items treated include the following: larger-than-life heroines/heroes or saviours – the Egyptian

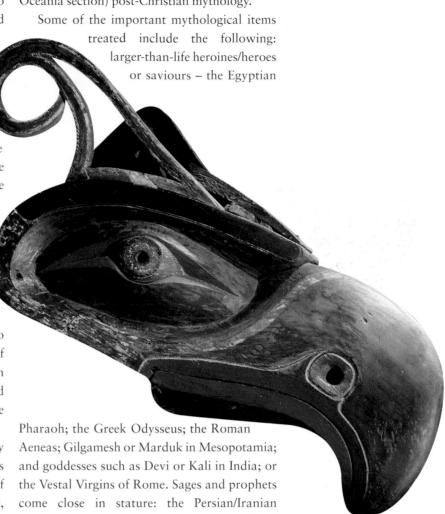

Pharaoh; the Greek Odysseus; the Roman Aeneas; Gilgamesh or Marduk in Mesopotamia; and goddesses such as Devi or Kali in India; or the Vestal Virgins of Rome. Sages and prophets come close in stature: the Persian/Iranian Zoroaster/Zarathustra, or Nigeria's god of wisdom, Ifa.

Trickster figures are well represented by the Korean Sokka, the Northern European Loki and the Greek Hermes. Tricksters are emphasized especially in the North American section. Other divine or semi-divine figures (for instance the dying and resurrected Osiris of Egypt) are portrayed, as are various religious systems: mystery religions in Rome; burials in Egypt; cleansing from pollution in Japan (where it leads to shaping the contours of the world); Vodun/Voodo in the Caribbean; Kami-no-michi/Shinto in Japan; Tantric religion in India; and cargo cults in Oceania.

Natural places and occurrences are treated ritually and mythologically in many places: sacred mountains such as Helgafell in Iceland; mandalic stupas in Buddhist cultures; the two great temples at the capital city of the Aztecs, Tenochtitlán; and of course catastrophes such as the Flood in Chinese and Israelite mythology, or the Northern European end of time fantasy of Ragnarok. In South America the very forest is the sacred world of spiritual beings. Myths and legends may explain natural events such as the aurora borealis in the Arctic; and compare both

A wooden head-dress in the form of the thunderbird, a creature associated with the deities of the northwest coast of North America. Identified by its downturned beak and feathered horns, the thunderbird was believed to cause thunder when it flapped its wings and lightning when it flashed its eyes.

This painting by Giandomenico Tiepolo (1727-1804) depicts the Trojans unwittingly giving the best Greek warriors, who are hiding inside the wooden horse, access to their city. During the night the Greeks let themselves out of the horse and opened the city gates to their army, who burned Troy to the ground.

the Arctic and South American divinization of solar and sky gods. The structure of the universe may be considered to result from a marriage of Heaven and Earth, as in Sumer and Northern Europe.

Fortunately, it is rare today to come across persons who consider mythological materials as belonging only to a 'primitive' level of cultural development. Instead, it is widely regarded as representing crucial aspects of any culture's self-understanding, a resource that mythopoetic reappropriations can use to revitalize culture.

Often foundational myths explain cultural origins (North America, Rome) or show how support of the State is embedded in mythic authorization (Korea, Japan). Myths of the origin of kingship are not uncommon, as seen especially clearly in Papua New Guinea. Myths have ideological and political implications: consider the impact of European myth, worldview and religion when Christopher Columbus impacted the Taino or Arawak, and the Caribbean, and that of Christianity upon Central and Eastern European areas.

Mythological accounts often contain instruction about geography and landscape, and may convey, as in Greek myths, information about a people's earliest history that is known only in archaeological findings and prehistoric vase paintings. Our authors share historical contexts for many of the cultural areas: see, for instance, in the box in the Sumer section, and notice how in both Japan and Egypt very early cultural conflict was replaced with uniformity,

within historical experience – perhaps best summarized by the intertwining of papyrus and lotus flowers on early Egyptian bas reliefs (see also the sections on China, and the Olmec, Maya and Aztec succession in the Mesoamerican section).

Isaac Asimov's *Words from the Myths*, an astute study of mythological traces to be found in everyday language, provides a reminder of just how many words in common usage derive from mythological terms. The days of the week, for instance, or phrases such as narcissism, apollonian wisdom, hermetic silence, saturnine personality, jovial humour (Jupiter) and many others.

Our arts are replete with mythically inspired masterpieces in music, dance and the graphic and plastic arts. Think only of the mythological themes and figures in the modern dances of Martha Graham, Stravinsky's *Le Sacre du Printemps*, Goya's monstrous painting of *Panic*, Picasso's erotic bull drawings that recall the Minotaur, or the plays of Edward Albee. In pop music recently the Paul Winter Consort has produced the album *Ikaros*, and David Byrne one entitled *The Forest*, with themes drawn from the Epic of Gilgamesh.

Did I mention the cinema? We have just had to exert herculean efforts to ignore the movie *Hercules*, and the Disney Studios and television studios crank out mythically-resonant films nearly every year. In 2001, a four-Oscar-winning film by Ang Lee, *Crouching Tiger, Hidden Dragon*, showed just how spectacularly hi-tech cinema animations can stage the mythical lore of Kung Fu (which recurs in many Hong Kong martial arts films). Science fiction has featured many mythical retellings, and there's even a series of fantasy novels by Jody Lynn Nye that begins with *Mythology 101*.

Sometimes seen as a product of New Age mentality, interest in mythologies is found now across the culture, particularly by those interested in matters mystical, Native American Indian or Australian Aborigine teachings, ancient cultures, Celtic symbolism, astrology, tarot and the like. The works of Sigmund Freud and Carl Jung are plumbed frequently for their mythic lore and perspectives. 'Learning to tell your own myth' or 'Realize the heroine within' pop psychology books are widespread, and many handbooks have been published.

Analytical and critical study of myth is currently flourishing. Myth sites on the World Wide Web are abundant, ranging from slick lists of mythical figures to scholarly resources (I recommend beginning with Kathleen Jenks's *Mything Links: An Annotated and Illustrated Collection of Worldwide Links to Mythologies, Fairy Tales, and Folklore)*.

From my perspective, the days of oversimplification of matters mythical and symbolic are over with. A few monomythic scholars (myths do only this or that) still speak of the origin/creation myth as any culture's single most important category. Mythological motifs are said to represent a number of a culture's aspects: its psychological infancy; secretly coded astrological subtexts; or violence at the core of human society, reflected obliquely in its myths, scriptures and rituals. My own preference is for an open-ended, cross-disciplinary approach that recognizes the plurality of ways mythological materials function within cultures, being especially effective at various times.

The authors of this volume speak from extensive experience in mythography, in a number of academic disciplines: linguistics, classics, international studies, social and cultural anthropology, archaeology, religious studies and theology. There is no single methodology enforced, but rather a variety of perspectives. I have noticed some common approaches – for instance the understanding that isolating an 'earliest' version of a story is less important than recognizing that transmission always means change.

Myths are not static, and may exist side by side with contrasting myths: witness the competition between the various origin myths of Egypt, each supported in antiquity by its own temple priests. There are many inter-borrowings,

so that the idea of a 'pure' myth is always questionable (see the North American section). Links and contrasts may occur within a very small geographical range: for instance between the Amaterasu cult associated with eastern central Japan and the Izumo Cycle with the coastal west.

Our universal storehouse of myths invites not worship of the past but responsibility for the future. It provides models of how things may have been and may be that are valuable to study. In *The Story of Lynx*, Claude Lévi-Strauss provides useful guidance: 'We should not think that myths, coming to us from very far away in time or in space, can only offer us already-played-out games. Myths do not consist in games finished once and for all. They are untiring; they begin a new game each time they are retold or read.'

Welcome to this treasure trove for the 'new game' in a new millennium.

William G. Doty
Tuscaloosa, 2002

Below: the two dragons on this fifth-century engraved stone is a depiction of the Sun, which was of great importance in Northern Europe. During the long, dark winters, the people held festivals to worship and celebrate the Sun, and to help it regain its strength in time for the spring.

First Divinities

The original inhabitants of the Nile valley were Palaeolithic peoples who settled there at least 7000 years ago, following the desertification of their previously fertile homeland in eastern Sahara. These were nomadic hunter-gatherer folk whose major creator-divinity was the cosmic serpent, itself a representation of the all-nurturing mother earth.

In the millennia following the original settlement of the Nile valley, the region was influenced by the early Neolithic cultures of the Mediterranean and Near East, whose prime divinity was a mother goddess with bird and snake attributes. In Egypt these motifs were differentially adopted and embodied in local fauna: Lower Egypt taking the cobra as its sacred emblem, while Upper Egypt (the region south of the first waterfall at Aswan) acknowledged the vulture. After the unification of all Egypt under one pharaoh in c.3100 BC, the kingship was associated with the sun.

CREATION STORIES

The opposition between the aboriginal cult of mother earth and the pharaonic identification with the sky is reflected in a conflict of ideas evident in the various accounts of Creation that appear in their mythology. Some of these stories, like the myths of the cosmic egg and the water bird, derive from the Palaeolithic culture of aboriginal Egypt. According to this cluster of myths, the world began when the first land emerged from the watery abyss called *Nun*. Some accounts say this primal land was called *Ma'at*, a feminine noun meaning 'truth', 'order' and 'justice', and associate it with the primordial mud of the Nile, from which all life grew. Another version says that a mystic lotus emerged from the primeval mud, opening to reveal an infant god who created the state of order called *Ma'at*. Other stories present the life-heralding waterbird, which in the earliest

Ma'at was the goddess who personified divine order who was begotten by air and first appeared as an egg, but later adopted a more conventional shape. Ma'at was responsible for ensuring that the world did not sink back into the chaos from which it first came. Ma'at also means harmony, truth and justice.

The original inhabitants of the Sahara
For much of the postglacial period the Sahara benefitted from more moist climatic conditions than at present and the area of full desert was significantly smaller than today. the pattern of lake levels shows that the wetter periods alternated with dry interludes, and after 4000 BC there was a rapid fall in level, indicating the onset of desertification. Finds of pottery, harpoons and rock art indicate that much of the area was inhabited before this time.

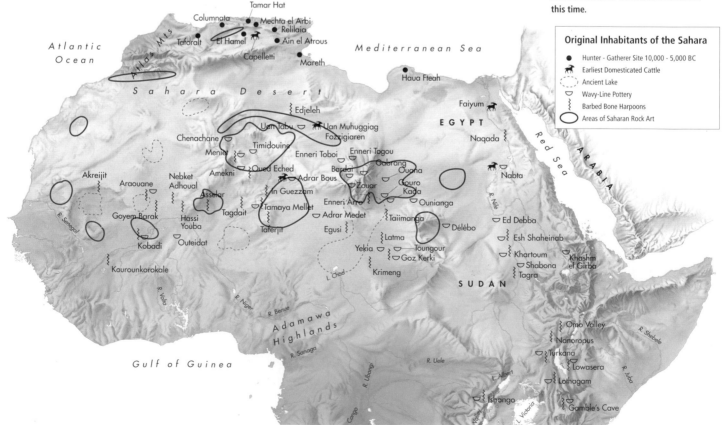

Original Inhabitants of the Sahara

- ● Hunter - Gatherer Site 10,000 - 5,000 BC
- Earliest Domesticated Cattle
- Ancient Lake
- Wavy-Line Pottery
- Barbed Bone Harpoons
- Areas of Saharan Rock Art

traditions is an aspect of the earth mother, as a manifestation of the sun god. A combination of earth goddess and sky god theologies appears in another creation myth. According to this, the forces of chaos issued four male-and-female couples, called the Ogdoad, from the watery abyss, who jointly formed the cosmic egg from which the sun god was hatched.

SEPARATION AND HIERARCHY

The clearest statement of intention to separate the antecedents of kingship and state from the all-mothering earth goddess appears in several

creation myths. In one of these, the first creator-deity was called Atum and emerged from the abyss in the form of a serpent, later taking human form. Feeling lonely, Atum took his phallus in his hand and produced semen, from which he formed the first divine couple, Shu and Tefenet, who were progenitors of a line of divinities.

A similar act of creative masturbation is told regarding the god Ptah, the master craftsman of the Egyptian pantheon. These stories appear to symbolize the em- ergence of a predominantly male ruling class which saw itself as intrinsically separate from, and superior to, the aboriginal population and its traditions of continuity with the primal earth. Nevertheless, the myth-makers of ancient Egypt ingeniously wove together creation myths expressing the interests of diverse groups and traditions so as to promote cohesion within a highly stratified and authoritarian social order.

At various times in Egypt's long history, economic collapse related to variations in the water level of the Nile, which led to political disintegration. There were three such periods, called 'intermediate' by historians.

The Heliopolitan cosmology, or Ennead, was the most important in Egyptian mythology. Atum was the original god of Heliopolis and the first creator-deity. He produced Tefenet, the goddess of moisture with the head of a lioness pictured here, and Shu, the god of air. From their union came Geb and Nut, god of earth and goddess of the sky respectively.

Above: Ptah was the Memphis god of creation and resurrection and from him, it was claimed, came Atum who founded the Heliopolitan Ennead. This was the Memphites' way of establishing their deity as the most important, since he began the process of creation.

A CONFLICT OF MYTHS

In about 3000 BC, invaders from the north-east speaking a Semitic language, overran Egypt and imposed on the unstratified stateless aboriginal communities, with their matrilineal and mother-focused social organization and gender equality, a hierarchical social order based on patrilineal descent and male pre-eminence. The invaders unified the previously autonomous regions of Upper and Lower Egypt into a single state ruled by a king with the title of *per'aa*, or 'pharaoh', meaning 'great estate', 'house' or 'palace'.

The pharaoh was assisted by a priestly class of which he was the foremost member: a being who was both man and god, mortal and immortal. Over time the pharaonic priesthood developed and transformed the creation myths and relatively simple pantheon of the aboriginal culture to reflect the ideology and power structure of the new Egyptian state. However, the priests were unable to erase collective awareness of the original religion of the earth and the cosmic serpent, so the latter was transformed into the evil snake Apep or Apophis, a symbol of darkness, chaos and a perpetual antagonist of the solar order established by the pharaonic kingship. Other, originally sovereign feminine deities such as Ma'at, were redefined as subordinate to the ruling male sun god, Ra (or Re).

Solar Myths

With the union of Upper and Lower Egypt under the pharaonic kingship in about 3100 BC, myths focused on the king as a solar being began to circulate. The most complex and enduring of these myths concerned Osiris, supposedly first of the pharaohs and an incarnation of the sun god Amon-Ra.

The god Osiris depicted on a fresco in the Tomb of Horemheb 1319–1307 BC, New Kingdom. As god of death and rebirth, Osiris was one of the most revered in the Egyptian pantheon; before a dead soul could have a life in the other world it had to pass before Osiris and only he could grant it immortality.

Deities worshipped in Ancient Egypt
The map locates the places where deities were worshipped.

The principal centre of sun-god worship for Ra throughout Egypt's ancient history was at Annu, called Heliopolis ('city of the sun') by the Greeks, and now a suburb of modern Cairo. He was depicted with the body of a man and the head of a hawk, the latter symbolizing height in the sky. In his nocturnal post-mortem journey through the watery afterworld, the god-king, Ra-as-sun, was constantly menaced by the primordial serpent Apep, the emblem of chaos, who was most powerful at the darkest hour of night. It was then the special duty of the sun god's priests to recite a long liturgy of curses detailing Apep's dismemberment and destruction by fire.

CHILD OF THE SUN

From early in the dynastic period the pharaoh was held to be a child of the deified sun. From time to time this solar blood-line was renewed by the god assuming the form of the reigning pharaoh, visiting the queen in her bedchamber and fathering her son. After the child's birth it was ritually presented to Ra in his temple, when the god was supposed to accept and acknowledge his divine offspring.

The long-dominant priesthood of Ra, a name meaning 'sole creator', displayed great ingenuity and political acumen in preserving and incorporating the older cults of Egypt in their rituals, insisting only that their priests

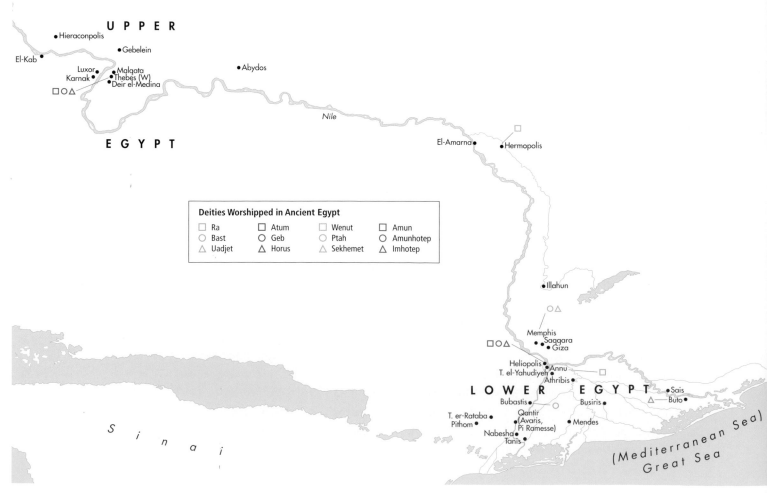

Deities Worshipped in Ancient Egypt

□ Ra	□ Atum	□ Wenut	□ Amun
○ Bast	○ Geb	○ Ptah	○ Amunhotep
△ Uadjet	△ Horus	△ Sekhemet	△ Imhotep

acknowledge the overall sovereignty of the sun god. Thus Osiris and Isis, the great goddess of the Nile, became absorbed into the pantheon of pharaonic Egypt. However, the more ancient myth of the dying and reborn Osiris proved eventually to exercise most appeal to the Egyptian imagination. This was because the powers of Osiris as king of the afterworld

included the ability to confer immortality on the souls of deceased humans. During the Later Dynastic Period the Osiris cult took on many of the attributes of the sun god. His perennial appeal could also relate to the fact that his myth reaches back to the prehistoric, pre-dynastic Egyptian Osirian myth-ritual of the divine king, whose sacrificial death and reincarnation in his young successor were held to guarantee the prosperity of the land and people.

THEOLOGICAL DEBATES

The many, often conflicting, ideas formulated by the priesthood of dynastic Egypt over the millennia are evidence of a lively tradition of theological debate. At various times the reigning theology was polytheism, henotheism (proposing a supreme god among many lesser divinities) and incipient monotheism. Egypt came closest to embracing monotheism during the reign of Pharaoh Akhenaton (1364–1347 BC), when the king tried to suppress the worship of all deities with the exception of Aton, a form of the sun god, with which he identified himself. A hymn in praise of Aton began, 'O thou beautiful being, who is ever renewed and made young again as Aton!'. However, after Akhenaton's death the country reverted to polytheism.

Even trinitarianism, familiar in Christian theology, found its advocates in a New Kingdom hymn to Amon, the original creator-deity, which proclaims his threefold nature as Amon the 'hidden' god, Ra (the sun) as his visible form and Ptah (one of the four creator-divinities) as his mystical body.

A colossal statue of Pharaoh Akhenaton from Tell Ell Amarna, 18th dynasty, New Kingdom. The pharaoh rejected most other cults, with the exception of the sun-god worship, and claimed that he was son of the sun-god.

Left: The supreme god of the Egyptian pantheon, Ra, was the creator sun-god of Heliopolis. During the later dynasties, Ra became linked with Osiris, god of death and rebirth, producing a single deity known as Amon-Ra.

GOD OF DEATH AND REBIRTH

Although Egyptians held that Osiris was the first to occupy the throne of the Pharaohs, his cult seems to have already existed in pre-dynastic times, particularly associated with the town of Abydos on the upper Nile. Later his identity became fused with that of the sun god Ra into a being known as Amon-Ra.

The many myths focused on the person of Osiris, the perpetually dying and reborn god-king, can be thought of as a collective meditation through five millennia of Egyptian history and prehistory on the theme of continuity through change and the pervasive patterns of cyclicity in human and cosmic existence. The most spectacular and most frequently recurrent of these cycles is the daily progress of the sun through the heavens, its dramatic disappearance at sunset and no less dramatic reappearance at dawn. Egyptian mythical thought saw this diurnal sequence of events as the ever-repeated birth, middle age (his highest point in the sky, at noon) and eventual death of the sun god. To achieve rebirth at the beginning of the next day, Ra travelled through the other world where Osiris had established himself as judge and king.

Myth and Magic

For Ancient Egyptians, as generally for peoples living in pre-modern, pre-industrial conditions, the world was experienced as a living environment in which every object, whether animate or inanimate in our terms, was inhabited by some form of consciousness or 'spirit', with which human beings could interact. In this situation, every priest was also a magician.

Depiction of Ra the sun-god's, voyage through the other world. During his journey, he would travel through heaven and the other world, encountering great dangers along the way. Ra would take many forms during this daily cycle, including a child and a scarab beetle.

The priests of Ra the sun god were passionately involved in the god's daily passage across heaven and through Tuat, the other world. It would be misleading to imagine that the priests thought of their elaborate rituals and liturgy as *causing* the regular movement of the solar body, its setting and rising; rather, they collectively participated in these recurrent events, as actors in a cosmic drama principally involving the opposed agents of order and chaos, led by Ra and the serpent Apep respectively.

RA'S VOYAGE

Egyptian cosmology supposed that the sky was a watery realm in some way mirroring the watery darkness of Tuat, the other world. So it was appropriate that the sun god progressed across the sky in a celestial boat accompanied by a number of gods, with Thoth and Ma'at acting as navigators and Horus, son of the great goddess Isis, as helmsman. When this boat reached the edge of the realm of darkness that is Tuat, they transferred, as 'dead' deities, to another boat. The other world was said to be a long, narrow valley, approached through a mountain pass. The valley contained a river on which the sun god's boat sailed, and it was divided into 12 sections corresponding to the hours of the night.

Every one of the 12 divisions saw distinctive episodes in the struggle between Ra and his companions and the forces of chaos; and throughout the journey the priests of Ra rehearsed the epic story in every detail. Near the end of the final hour the sun god entered the tail of a giant serpent, from which he emerged into the light of dawn as a young god-man, ready to begin another day's journey through the sky.

WORDS OF POWER

When the priests recited the story of Ra's journey through heaven and the other world, the most difficult part of their performance was not just the production of the words of the elaborate narrative, but their utterance in a certain manner that made them, as the Egyptians put it, 'words of power'. At a crucial stage in the struggle between Horus and Seth, the god of chaos, Isis (the mother of Horus) uses her 'words of power' to keep the monster at bay. All deities were thought to own such words, through which they accomplished miraculous deeds, and it was the ambition of mortal Egyptians to acquire them, so they could do likewise. According to some texts, these words lived in the hearts or livers of their divine owners.

SECRET NAMES

Related to the concept of 'words of power' is the idea, general in ancient Egypt, that every deity had a secret name through which he or she lived. One story about the god Osiris tells how he transformed himself from the essence of primeval matter into a god, merely by uttering his own secret name. A person clever enough to discover the hidden name of a deity could, it was believed, command the services of its divine possessor.

Isis, shown here holding her son Horus whom she saved from Seth, god of chaos, with her words of power, was a symbol of protection and success against adversity. This bronze statue dates from 600 BC.

Book of the Dead showing Thoth and the eye of Horus, 21st dynasty. Thoth was the moon god, and was often depicted as a baboon (as here), an ibis or a man with the head of an ibis, and it was believed that he had knowledge of magic.

THOTH THE INTELLECTUAL GOD

Among the cluster of divinities brought into being at the time of Creation, the god Thoth, together with his consort the goddess Ma'at, was particularly involved in the establishment and maintenance of order in heaven and earth. The duties of Thoth went much further than these matters, since he was responsible for the mathematical calculations behind the regulation of the cosmos. It was he who invented all the arts and sciences known to humankind; he was 'the scribe of the gods' and 'the lord of books'. Thoth measured and regulated the times and the seasons, in which role he was known as the moon god. He is also described as 'the tongue and the heart' of Ra the sun god himself. Some later Greek texts portray Thoth as the animator of human speech, giving him a nature similar to that of Plato's Logos. At its simplest, the term Logos means 'word', though in Greek philosophy logos encapsulated a general notion of reasoning or intellectual thought, expressed through reading and writing. In Greek philosophy reason was considered to be one of the guiding principles of the universe. Logos, therefore, embodies this principle as well as the expression of metaphysical knowledge. The ancient Greeks identified Thoth with their own Hermes, describing the Egyptian god as the inventor of astrology and astronomy, mathematics and geography, medicine and botany.

In hieroglyphic texts Thoth is sometimes portrayed as an ibis, sometimes as a kind of ape. The main centre of his cult was at Khemennu, or Hermopolis as the Greeks called it.

Mighty Goddesses

There were many powerful goddesses in the Egyptian pantheon, some of them fearsome, like Neith the goddess of hunting and war, and Sekhmet, the solar deity with the head of a lioness, who was associated with smallpox and other contagious diseases. The greatest of them all, however, was Isis, the consort of Osiris.

ISIS DISCOVERS RA'S SECRET NAME

One of the most interesting myths about Isis tells how she tricked the sun god Ra into revealing to her his secret name, and thus the source of his power. Apparently, the goddess was ambitious to become the equal of Ra in his mastery of heaven and earth. At this time Ra had become old, and dribbled on the ground. Isis collected some of his spittle and made a venomous serpent out of it, which she laid in Ra's path so that when the sun god passed that way, he was fatally bitten . She consented to use her healing words of power to expel the poison from Ra's body and allow him to live, but only after he had told Isis his secret name. The story implies that Isis did indeed realize her ambition to become the sun god's equal.

THE GREAT COSMIC MOTHER

Another goddess who shared many of the powers and attributes of Isis was Hathor, 'the Egyptian Venus', patroness of lovers. She also blessed singers, dancers and artists. Like Neith – mother of Isis, Horus and Osiris, and guardian goddess of men and gods – Hathor was already known in the pre-pharaonic period, when she was worshipped in the form of a cow. She was also identified with the sky and recognized as the principal female counterpart of Ra; as such, Hathor was the Great Cosmic Mother, a divinity with roots in the Palaeolithic era. Her most famous temple was at Dendara, south of Abydos.

The loving Hathor contrasted with the ferocious Sekhmet, who was sent by the gods to destroy humankind when they began to plot against the aged Ra. After many had died, the sun god decided to spare the rest. To distract Sekhmet from her orgy of slaughter, Ra ordered the high priest at Heliopolis to make a vast quantity of beer and to stain it red. When Sekhmet saw it she lapped it up,

This relief shows the face of Hathor, patroness of happiness, music and lovers, from the Temple of Hathor. Hathor, along with another goddess, Taweret, protected women and children and helped women conceive and give birth.

Isis, also known as the Great Mother or Queen of Heaven, was one of the most important of the Egyptian deities. She, as protector of the family and family values, represented everything human life stood for and her cult lived on after the fall of Egyptian civilization.

thinking it was blood, and became so drunk she forgot her murderous mission, and was transformed into the beautiful and pacific Hathor.

Eventually, however, it was the fame of Isis that became supreme. After Alexander's conquest of Egypt in 332 BC and its subsequent occupation by Rome, the cult of Isis and her infant son Horus spread through the Empire, including France, Britain and Germany. The image of the nurturing mother and the divine child was eventually mirrored in popular imagination with the image of the Virgin Mary and the infant Jesus.

FOREIGN INFLUENCES

Another powerful female deity in dynastic Egypt was Bastet, the goddess of love, sex and fertility, who was usually depicted with a cat's head and earlier in the pre-dynastic era, with the head of a lioness.

The influence of Near Eastern culture on Egyptian society and culture is evident in a myth that has Seth, the divine 'destroyer of boundaries' and embodiment of chaos, being given two foreign goddesses in compensation for ceding his right to the throne of Egypt to Horus, son of Isis and Osiris. The goddesses were Anat, sister and consort of the Canaanite deity Baal, and Astarte (Ishtar), the great Semitic goddess.

Limestone votive tablet showing the goddess Neith, second century BC. As well as being the fearsome goddess of war and hunting, Neith was also said to have been one of the creator-deities, emerging from *Nun* in order to create the world.

FEMALE POWER

Neith could well be the oldest of all the Egyptian deities, because images of this goddess of hunting and war, whose insignia was a bow, two arrows and a shield, have been found at the major site of pre-dynastic settlement at Abydos, suggesting that her cult was introduced by the aboriginal Palaeolithic immigrants from the Sahara. Later, Neith's main cultic centre was in the Delta city of Sais.

Archaeological work at the huge prehistoric burial ground near Abydos has also unearthed a remarkable and aesthetically powerful representation of a triumphant female figure who could also be Neith or perhaps a more generalized image of the Earth Mother. Examination of the graves has shown that the largest and most richly furnished were those of females, suggesting women had high status during this prehistoric period, contrasting with their political obscurity during the pharaonic era. Royal women were the exceptions to this rule in the pharaonic era, and included the historically famous Nefertiti, the fourteenth-century BC consort of Pharaoh Akhenaton, and Cleopatra (70–31 BC). Nevertheless, an Egyptian, married, commoner woman of the pharaonic era was substantially better off than, for example, her counterpart in nineteenth-century England, in so far as she could own property and initiate divorce.

Animals in Myth

For the Egyptians, animals obviously acted with intent, but in so far as their intelligence was non-human it appeared to be beyond human understanding and, therefore, divine. This explains the number and variety of zoomorphic divinities in the pantheon of ancient Egypt, from lioness-headed Sekhmet to the bovine horns of Hathor and images of Thoth with the head and tail of a baboon.

The most ancient of all divinities in Egypt appears to have been the serpent as emblem of the Earth Mother; in dynastic cosmology this originally beneficent deity was transformed into Apep, the embodiment of chaos. In the Late Pre-Dynastic Period the pre-eminent focus of worship in Lower Egypt was the cobra, whose principal shrine was at Per-Uatchet in the Delta. At this time the vulture was the prime deity of Upper Egypt, with its cult centre at Nekhebet (Eileithyiaspolis in Greek). After political unification the first pharaohs gave themselves the title 'Lord of the Cobra and the Vulture'.

SACRED BEASTS

Other wild beasts with the status of divinities in this early period were the lion, lynx, crocodile, turtle and hippopotamus, the latter worshipped in female form as Ta-Urt, goddess of women. Both the bull and the cow were divinized during the pre-dynastic era, the former as a symbol of courage and sexual potency, the latter as embodiment of maternal and nurturing powers. The goddess Hathor is customarily portrayed wearing cow's horns with the solar disc between them, and sometimes as having a cow's head.

A granite statue of Sekhmet, the lion-headed goddess from the 18th–19th dynasties, in the temple complex of Mut, Karnak. Possessing the power of the midday sun, Sekhmet was believed to be the personification of evil and had the power to kill men.

RAM OF MENDES

Another sacred animal that became famous in Egypt and beyond was the Ram of Mendes, whose cult was already known in 3500 BC, and was worshipped as a divine source of fatherhood and fecundity. When the animal died, its soul was held to unite with the souls of Osiris, Ra and Khnemu (the ram-headed creator-god of the Upper Nile), while its mummified remains were interred at Mendes with elaborate ceremony. A countrywide search was then undertaken for a successor beast, which could be identified by certain marks known only to the priests. Once located, the animal was duly enthroned at Mendes in its turn.

BULL OF APIS

Another celebrated sacred beast was the Bull of Apis, whose shrine was at Memphis. According to the Greek historian Herodotus, the peculiar characteristics of this divinized animal were that it was black, had a square white spot on its forehead, double hairs in its tail, the outline of an eagle on its back and a beetle image – probably a scarab – on its tongue. Such animals were regularly given hot baths and their bodies rubbed with precious ointments. During the reign of Ptolemy I Soter (305–284 BC) the cults of the Apis bull and Osiris were fused with the worship of the Greek divinities Hades and Asklepios in a composite deity called Sarapis (or Serapis). This divinity's cult centre in Alexandria was famous throughout the Middle East until its fourth-century demolition by the Christian patriarch Theophilus.

HUMAN HYBRIDS

Particularly characteristic of ancient Egyptian religion was the fusion of human form and animal head in images of a single divinity. The many examples of this hybrid include Tefnut, goddess of water, portrayed with a woman's body and the head of a lioness; Menthu, the lord of Thebes (Luxor), as a hawk-headed man; jackal-headed Anubis, guide of the dead; and ram-headed Khnemu.

Statuette of Apis, the Egyptian bull-god, whose cult centre was at Memphis. As a sacred animal, bulls enjoyed special treatment in Egypt, including being bathed and covered with ointment.

The scarab beetle was sacred to the Egyptians, and in later dynasties became associated with immortality. Dating from c.1259 BC, 19th dynasty, this is a heart scarab amulet that was placed on a mummy's breast with an exhortation stating not to be hostile to the deceased in Judgement.

THE BEETLE OF REBIRTH

The special reverence accorded in ancient Egypt to the sacred scarab or dung-beetle (*Scarabaeus sacer*) has intrigued and puzzled modern commentators. There is evidence that the cult of this insect originated in the early dynastic period. In the later kingdoms its importance grew to extraordinary proportions, with representations of the creature being inscribed on government seals and worn as amulets by the general population.

The insect's habit of forming pieces of cow dung into a sphere and rolling it towards its burrow in the sand suggested to the Egyptians a parallel with the work of the sun god in steering the celestial orb across the sky. Because the Egyptians believed the beetle laid its eggs in the ball of dung, the insect's life-cycle became a microcosm of the daily rebirth of the sun.

Later, the scarab became a symbol of the immortal human soul, its image appearing frequently in funerary art. Most importantly, however, the behaviour and life-cycle of this tiny creature proved to the Egyptians that the same principles of order – embodied in the Osirian myth of birth, death and rebirth – held throughout the cosmos, from the grandest solar scale to the humble level of the insect.

Burial Rites and Practices

No society in history has raised the burial of kings and other royals to such a level of magnificence as did the ancient Egyptians. The mode of construction of the vast pyramids designed to house pharaohs' tombs is still not properly understood and their dimensions are thought to encode arcane mathematical knowledge.

The Kingdom of the Pharaohs
Egypt was divided into two lands: Lower Egypt, the area of the Nile Delta, with its capital at Memphis; and Upper Egypt, with its capital at Thebes. The map shows the temples and pyramids of Pharaonic Egypt.

B elief in the survival of the dead in an afterlife is evident from early in Egyptian prehistory. The huge burial site at pre-dynastic Nagada (modern-day Naqada) contains numerous remains of corpses in the foetal position, suggesting readiness for rebirth. The graves are orientated towards the west, traditionally the domain of the dead. Gradually during the Old Kingdom (2686–2181 BC) the practice of royal mummification developed, reaching its apogee during the first millennium BC, after which it declined.

PREPARATION FOR THE AFTERLIFE

The art of mummification was a secret known only to the priesthood. Its intention was not just to preserve the body from decay, but to enable its reanimation in a new life. The whole complex process was motivated by a belief that because the body of the murdered Osiris had been saved from decomposition and restored to life by the gods, magical assimilation to Osiris and re-enactment of what the gods had done would guarantee a similar resurrection for the mortal dead.

In the Late Dynastic Period the pharaohs lost their monopoly on post-mortem mummification as the practice became general among rich commoners, and it remained popular until the ascendancy of Christian doctrine in the fourth century AD.

MYTHICAL OPERATION

The actual process of preparing the body for embalming – by removing the brain and internal organs, treating what remained with natron soda to dry it and then washing, anointing and covering it with bandages – had to occupy exactly the same 70-day period as in the exemplary case of Osiris. The washing was done with water from the Nile, in conscious

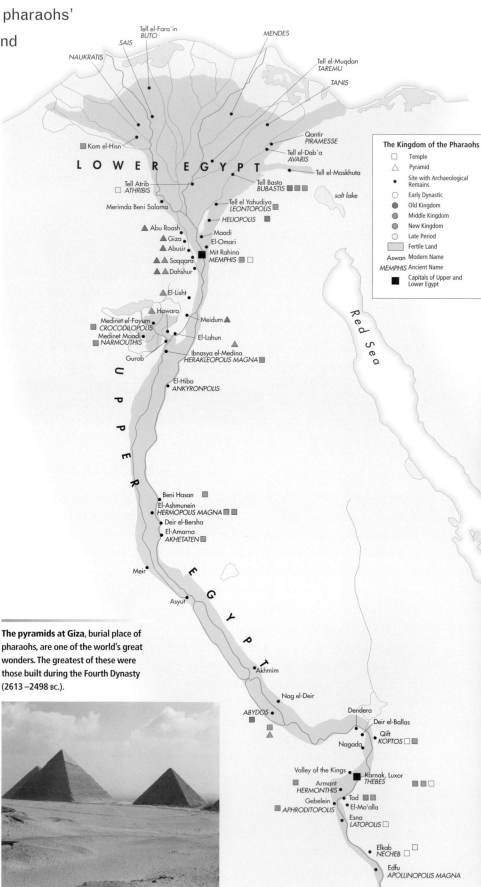

The pyramids at Giza, burial place of pharaohs, are one of the world's great wonders. The greatest of these were those built during the Fourth Dynasty (2613 –2498 BC.).

The Kingdom of the Pharaohs
☐ Temple
△ Pyramid
• Site with Archaeological Remains
○ Early Dynastic
● Old Kingdom
● Middle Kingdom
● New Kingdom
○ Late Period
☐ Fertile Land
Aswan Modern Name
MEMPHIS Ancient Name
■ Capitals of Upper and Lower Egypt

reference to the solar myth of the sun's daily rebirth, freshly bathed in the waters of the great life-bringing river. Cedar oil, myrrh, cinnamon and other sweet-smelling substances were rubbed into the dehydrated skin of the deceased person, while the priests simultaneously intoned the mysterious Osirian formulae guaranteed to rejuvenate the body and restore it to life. This treatment is said to have begun on the sixteenth day (the day of reanimation), in a special location called 'the place of making perfect'.

Afterwards, when laid in its tomb, the mummified, yet also mystically live, body was given food, drink and all the necessary furnishings; some tombs were even provided with a toilet. A prayer inscribed in the interior of one says, 'May you have enjoyment of all your limbs, may you count your members, now complete and whole, no evil staying with you, your real heart with you, and youthful strength restored.'

For the Egyptians, there could be no continued life for god or man without a body, hence the historically unparalleled battery of physical and magical techniques devoted to its preservation and reanimation. For good measure, the Egyptians frequently installed statues faithfully replicating the physical forms of the dead in the tombs alongside the mummies. After being properly inscribed and magically animated, these artefacts could also serve as 'bodies', in case the mummy was damaged.

The tombs of the wealthy were also provided with artwork depicting economic production, so the dead could still enjoy their former lifestyle.

Reverse of pharaoh Tutankhamun's gold and lapiz lazuli throne, featuring four snakes to protect the king's back, that was found when his tomb at Thebes was discovered in 1922. The child-king Tutankhamun reigned 1361–1352 BC during the 18th dynasty, and was buried along with treasures for him to have during the afterlife.

LIFE, DEATH AND RESURRECTION

According to the myth, Osiris was tricked by his brother Seth into lying down in a chest, which Seth and his followers then locked and threw into the Nile, where it was carried down to the sea. The grief-stricken Isis searched everywhere for her brother and consort Osiris, eventually discovering his body washed ashore at Byblos in Lebanon. Not content with killing his brother, Seth then cut the body of Osiris into 14 pieces and scattered them round the country. Isis and other divinities, including Anubis, then performed a supreme ritual of conjuration which reconstituted the slain and dismembered Osiris, and brought him triumphantly back to life. Immediately he began to eat and drink, put on clean linen and jewellery and soon afterwards begot his son Horus on the body of Isis. He then assumed his place as lord of the afterworld.

Subsequently, the mummification of the corpses of dead kings and royals, and later of wealthy commoners, was supposed to be accompanied by a ritual in which the priests faithfully re-enacted the secret, life-restoring ritual of Isis and Anubis.

Anubis was the jackal-headed god of the dead and of embalming. During the ceremony before a mummy was placed in its tomb, a priest would wear a jackal-headed mask to represent Anubis who, it was believed, led the souls of the dead into the Hall of Judgement.

Afterworld Beliefs

Ancient Egyptians entertained several concepts of the afterlife, of varying degrees of sophistication. The simplest envisaged a paradisical land rich in grain, figs and grapes, where no one had to work. More abstract theories situated the afterworld in the sky, or in some location nearer the world of the living, and the most sublime supposed that the souls of humans became stars.

Over time the Egyptian priesthood elaborated their picture of the world where the souls of the dead lived. Originally this place, held to be the same as that traversed by the dead sun god every night (see p.15–16), was believed to have an iron floor and to be so relatively close to earth that it could be reached by ascending the mountains of distant Sinai. Later it was thought that ladders were needed to reach it and Osiris himself is said to have used one to attain his domain. Model ladders were placed in tombs for the use of lesser beings.

THE AFTERWORLD

Once the souls of the dead had reached the afterworld, they faced the crucial ordeal of judgement in the Hall of Osiris by the great god Thoth. If the heart of the dead person weighed less than a feather (see Box), Thoth reported to Osiris that the deceased was 'holy and righteous' and deserving of a place in the Fields of Peace, the Osirian paradise. There the worthy soul was said to enjoy a life of ease, clad in white linen and white sandals, with his own home and estate.

TRANSFIGURED SPIRITS

Mummification and the elaborately furnished tombs reflected a perceived need amongst the ancient Egyptians to preserve and reanimate the body after physical death. On feast days the dead joined the living in celebration around the tomb. The dead person, now called a Ba, could take the form of a bird, such as a heron, falcon or swallow, which could be observed fluttering around on these occasions.

There was also a belief of wider scope, that the dead had become Akhu, or transfigured spirits, and assumed the form of the northern circumpolar stars. These heavenly bodies never set, hence appearing immortal. In this way, the once-human dead came to participate in the cosmic order of things. Even so, Osiris was felt to live in the recurrent cycles of the cosmos: in the annual rise and fall of the Nile, in the phases of the moon and in the alternation of day and night. The grandest transfiguration, then, was to become one of the stars circling the pole.

Painted on papyrus, the *Book of the Dead* was a series of chapters that were supposed to assist the deceased on the journey from this life to the next. As well as containing scenes from many of the major myths, they gave instructions to the deceased relating to the Hall of Judgement, for example.

MEANING OF DEATH

In its journey to its ultimate destination the soul was believed to cross a primeval ocean evoking, and even identical to, the watery darkness from which the land first emerged at the beginning of time; and descending into the tomb, the dead participated in the nocturnal voyage of the sun god. People were buried with a papyrus inscribed with a declaration of their innocence, combined with a spell to prevent their hearts rising up and bearing witness against them before Osiris.

In this dialogue between Osiris and Atum (one of the four creator-divinities) recorded in the *Book of the Dead*, a collection of spells that the wealthy had inscribed on their coffins, the creator-god explains the meaning of death, saying that 'in place of beer, bread and love, I have put transfiguration and a life without care'.

EGYPTIAN DYNASTIES

5000–3100 BC	Pre-dynastic Period
3100–2686 BC	Early Dynastic Period
2686–2181 BC	Old Kingdom
2181–2040 BC	First Intermediate Period
2040–1730 BC	Middle Kingdom
1730–1552 BC	Second Intermediate Period
1552–1069 BC	New Kingdom
1069–664 BC	Third Intermediate Period
664–30 BC	Late Period

Anubis, jackal-headed god of the dead, pictured weighing the heart of a deceased soul against the feather of truth in the Judgement Hall, presided over by Osiris. This scene is from the Papyrus of Hunefer and dates from the 19th dynasty, 1294–79 BC.

Below: A scene from the Papyrus of Ani in which Ani (kneeling) is presented to Osiris by Horus after his heart has been weighed and he has been pronounced innocent.

THE FATE OF THE DEAD

A key document called the *Papyrus of Ani* has graphically described the process whereby, as ancient Egyptians believed, the fate of the dead was decided in the Hall of Osiris. Here the gods sat in judgement while the dead person's heart, the seat of human conscience, was weighed against a feather. Upholding the fateful Balance (a contrivance used to weigh commodities in commercial transactions) was the dog-headed ape who was also a manifestation of Thoth, the divine scribe, while jackal-headed Anubis made sure that everything about the Balance was in its correct setting. If the heart proved heavier than a feather, the soul owning it was destroyed by the monster Amemet, the 'eater of the dead', described as standing behind Thoth.

Other texts describe the predicament of the souls of those who escaped destruction but lacked the 'words of power' needed to convey them to the paradisical Fields of Peace. These souls waited in their assigned portion of Tuat, the other world, for the nightly passage of the boat conveying the dead sun god Ra and his companions on their way to rebirth. For a moment they knew joy in the presence of Ra. Their bliss, though temporary, was renewed every night with the god's passage through their domain.

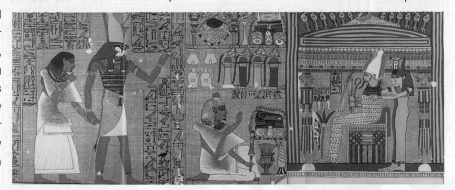

Sumerian and Babylonian Mythology

The myths of Sumer and Babylon contain themes from the cosmologies of different epochs and reflect the competing interests of the various cities of Mesopotamia, each with its own patron divinity, comprising the world's oldest urban civilization. This civilization reached its apogee in the great city of Babylon under Nebuchadnezzar (605–562 BC).

Through most of its history until the Babylonian ascendancy during 1795–1750 BC, Mesopotamia, a land of 25,900 square kilometres (10,000 square miles) between the rivers Tigris and Euphrates, was a scene of rivalry between a cluster of city states, among them Ur, Eridu, Lagash and Kish. The Sumerians arrived in southern Mesopotamia about 3300 BC and spoke a tongue related to the Turkic group of South-Central Asia. Its literature, written in the wedge-shaped or cuneiform script invented by the temple priests, includes 20 myths, nine epic tales and numerous hymns.

In about 1890 BC Semitic invaders from the north gained control of the country from their capital, Babylon. Later the country fell under the domination of Assyria (c.1225 BC), before the new Babylonian empire was established by Nebuchadnezzar in 605 BC. In 539 BC Babylonia was conquered by the Persian emperor, Cyrus.

THE MARRIAGE OF HEAVEN AND EARTH

With the initial unification of the country under Babylon, conscious attempts were made by the priesthood to consolidate the mythical traditions associated with the various city-states into a coherent cosmology. In this schema there were four major divinities: a sky god called An, an earth goddess called Ki (later renamed Ninhursag, Queen of the Mountain), an air god called Enlil (later recognized as Supreme Being) and a water god called Enki. There were many other divinities, including the moon god Nanna, his son the sun god Utu and his

The stone of Tak-Kersa bearing cuneiform inscriptions. Cuneiform, the script developed by the Sumerians, was a complicated series of wedge-shaped characters that represented words, vowels and syllables. It is from cuneiform tablets such as this one that most Sumerian myths are known.

The City of Babylon
The city of Babylon was at its greatest around 600 BC. Under the rule of king Nebuchadnezzar the city was considered the mightiest and most beautiful in the known world. Its culture was highly refined, having changed little in years, and scientifically and technically Babylon was the most advanced city in the world.

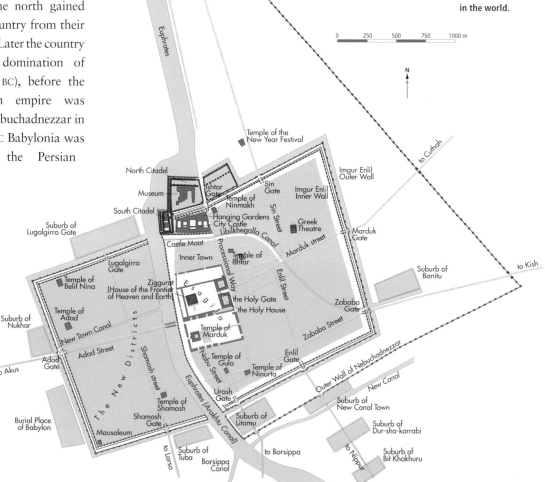

daughter Inanna, but it was the four major deities who invented an unalterable set of rules and limits which governed the whole cosmos; this was called the *me*. Outside these immutable laws, the life of humankind was held to be fundamentally insecure and uncertain. The gods had made humans out of clay, their purpose being to provide their divine makers with food, drink and shelter. No one could know his or her fate, which had been decided in advance by the gods. After death a human led a murky existence in the underworld. However, each person was supposed to have a special god or angel who might, with luck, be persuaded to intervene on his client's behalf with the distant divinities.

The population nonetheless retained a spiritual connection with the prehistoric Neolithic epoch before unification in the annual ritual known to posterity by its Greek name of *hieros gamos*, 'the sacred marriage of heaven and earth'. At the Sumerian New Year, the autumn equinox, when rain and fertility returned to a land parched by the hot dry summer, the people celebrated the return to light and life of the divine king Dumuzi, identified with earth, and his union with Inanna, goddess of love and queen of heaven (see Box).

In the *hieros gamos* this myth of rebirth from death was acted out by the reigning monarch and the chief of the temple prostitutes, an incarnation of the great goddess herself, and their ritual union was held to guarantee the fertility and prosperity of land and people.

Remains of Nebuchadnezzar's palace in Babylon, Iraq. Under Nebuchadnezzar's rule in the sixth century BC, in particular, Babylonia became one of Mesopotamia's greatest centres of power.

Terracotta relief of the winged goddess Inanna-Ishtar, wearing a crown of lunar horns and rainbow necklace with lions and owls, dating from c. 2000 BC.

THE CYCLE OF THE NATURAL WORLD

What seems to be the oldest motif in the mythical traditions of Sumer and Babylon is that of descent into the darkness of the underworld, death and rebirth into the light. A story only recently pieced together by scholars from cuneiform inscriptions on thousands of clay fragments (first discovered at Nineveh in 1852), tells of the cosmic ordeal of the great goddess Inanna, known to the Semites as Ishtar. Created Queen of Heaven, Inanna voluntarily leaves her high place and descends into the darkness of the world beneath the ground. Passing through each of its seven gates in turn, at each one she abandons part of her finery until at last she appears naked before Erishkigal, queen of the underworld, and is sentenced to death. She is eventually reborn and ascends to the sky to reign for ever as goddess of love and war, 'the lady of battles', but only on condition that she sacrifice her husband Dumuzi, the shepherd-king who mystically is also her son, to remain in the underworld in her place. In the end the sun god Utu decrees that Dumuzi will spend only half the year in the realm of darkness and death, this alternation symbolizing the annual cycle of nature in semi-desert Mesopotamia between fertility and growth, and aridity and decay.

Myths of Creation

In the beginning, according to Sumerian mythology, there was only water, an immense sea of infinite extent. This ocean engendered the universe, a flat earth with heaven above; between was the airy atmosphere from which the celestial sun, moon and stars were born. Then the animals and humankind appeared.

THE CREATION OF THE WORLD

The primeval ocean was personified as a goddess called Nammu. After the emergence of the world from her dark and formless depths the four creator-divinities of sky, earth, air and water brought everything else into being just by uttering its name.

YAMM, THE COSMIC SERPENT

The mythology of the Canaanite people of ancient Ugarit (now in modern Syria) tells of a similar mortal struggle as in the Sumerian story of Marduk and Tiamat (see Box). In the Canaanite version, the storm god Baal (He Who Rides on the Clouds), engaged in battle with the cosmic serpent, or dragon, called Yamm, said to have come from the sea. With the help of magical weapons supplied by divine craftsmen, Baal succeeded in killing Yamm and scattering his remains. Baal then became locked in mortal combat with Mot, the god of death and sterility, who is identified with earth. Initially, Mot was successful in forcing Baal to descend to the underworld for half a year, thus creating the annual summer drought. However, the supreme god El ruled that the conflict between Baal and Mot would be everlasting. If Baal won, a seven-year cycle of abundance would ensue, but if Mot was victorious, the result would be seven years of drought and famine.

ZOROASTRIAN MYTHS

In the cosmology expounded by the Persian prophet Zoroaster in around 600 BC, the origin of evil is traced to an act of free will at the time of creation. Spenta Mainyu (bounteous spirit) chose good, along with truth, justice and life, but his brother, Angra Mainyu or Ahriman (destructive spirit), chose evil, destruction and death, thus beginning an eternal battle between the forces of light and

darkness for the soul of humankind. Between these two opposed deities was Vayu, god of air and wind.

Another Zoroastrian myth tells how Tishtrya, the rain god, goes down to the primeval ocean in the form of a white horse, there meeting Apaosha, the god of drought, as a black horse. A three-day battle ensues, Apaosha wins and the land dries up. Tishtrya appeals to Ahura Mazda, the supreme deity, who helps him to defeat Apaosha and the life-giving rains return.

GREENING OF THE EARTH

The mythology of the Hittite people of Anatolia is concerned with the origin of the cyclical birth, death and rebirth of the vegetation on which human and animal life depends. In a story that symbolically explains this mystery, the god of fertility, Telepinu, stormed off sulking, for unexplained reasons, taking all the vegetation with him and became lost. For a long time, the gods searched in vain for their missing colleague, but finally they found him. Still he refused to allow the vegetation to return. Then the sun god Istanu persuaded a mortal man to purify Telepinu of his anger. The god of fertility flew home on the back of an eagle, bearing greenery, and earth was once again peaceful and prosperous, and the Hittite king and his consort assured of long life.

Ugarit mythology features Baal, the storm god, who was associated with renewal of life and fertility. Rainfall was important to the Canaanite people, indicating why their main deities were associated with the weather. In this sandstone stele from c. 1350–1250 BC, Baal is about to hurl a thunderbolt.

MARDUK SLAYS THE SERPENT OF CHAOS

The undifferentiated chaos of the primeval ocean was embodied in the cosmic serpent Tiamat, who played the same ambiguous role in Sumerian cosmology as the serpent Apep did in that of ancient Egypt (see pp. 14–17, 20). The most ancient traditions of Sumer represent Tiamat as a mother goddess who emerged from the sea and taught humankind the arts of civilization. Later, with the emergence of centralized kingship during the third millenium BC, the originally beneficent and nurturing Tiamat was presented as the chaotic enemy of order. The gods chose Marduk, whose name is also that of an early king of Sumeria, to fight Tiamat. After a gargantuan battle, Marduk slew the great serpent. It was said that Tiamat's blood flowed for three years, three months and a day. Marduk then split the remains lengthwise into halves, the upper half becoming the sky and the lower, earth, thus establishing the first great cosmic distinction.

Marduk's victory over the serpent of chaos was also presented as the triumph of hierarchy and socio-political order over anarchy and disorder, and was celebrated by the priests every New Year. Berossus, a Babylonian historian, wrote in the third century BC that 'where Tiamat prevails, the slaves become masters and rank is abolished'.

According to mythology proposed by Zoroastrianism in the sixth and seventh centuries BC, the supreme god, Ahura Mazda, created the entire universe, while his evil adversary provided demons and diseases. In this relief sculpture from Persepolis, Ahura Mazda is depicted as symbolically spreading his wings over the image of Darius I (550–486 BC) King of Persia and founder of the Persian Achaemenid dynasty.

The Flood

Stories of a catastrophic flood which threatened to destroy the whole human race are extremely ancient in Mesopotamia, and probably reflect folk memories of recurrent disasters connected with the overflowing of the great rivers Tigris and Euphrates. Archaeological evidence shows there were numerous inundations over the millennia, rather than one single catastrophic event. One of the oldest and relatively complete written versions of the story was composed around 2200 BC.

In another version of the Flood story dated to 2000 BC, the creator-god Enki and his wife and sister Nintur lived in a paradisical land somewhere south of Mesopotamia. Enki became irritated with humans and decided to drown the whole race. The enormous flood lasted nine months and everyone perished with the exception of a man called Ut-napishti in the Semitic language of Babylon, and Tagtug in Sumerian. After the floods subsided, Ut-napishti became a gardener and Enki taught him how to grow crops.

BEFORE AND AFTER THE FLOOD

The Great Flood constitutes the major landmark in historical time, according to the written traditions of Sumer and Babylon. Before the Flood, kingly reigns were measured in mythic thousands of years; afterwards, in more credible, human-scale spans of time. At the time of the Flood, according to the inscriptions, a king called Ziusudra reigned in the city of Shuruppak (roughly halfway between modern Baghdad and Basra), where the great deluge is said to have begun.

In another surviving text forming part of the *Epic of Gilgamesh* (see p. 32–33), Ut-napishti, the lone survivor of the Flood, is asked by Gilgamesh to reveal the secret of his immortality. Ut-napishti said he was in Shuruppak when the gods decided to send the Flood and wipe out

Much of our knowledge of Mesopotamian mythology, including the flood stories, comes from tablet inscriptions such as the one shown above.

The Flood
The Great Flood had a profound effect on the Mesopotamian people and marked the change from mythical reigns of kings, measured in thousands of years, to a human scale. Ut-napishti was said to be the sole survivor of the Flood. The city of Sippar was one of the few places that survived the flood and ancient texts were later found there.

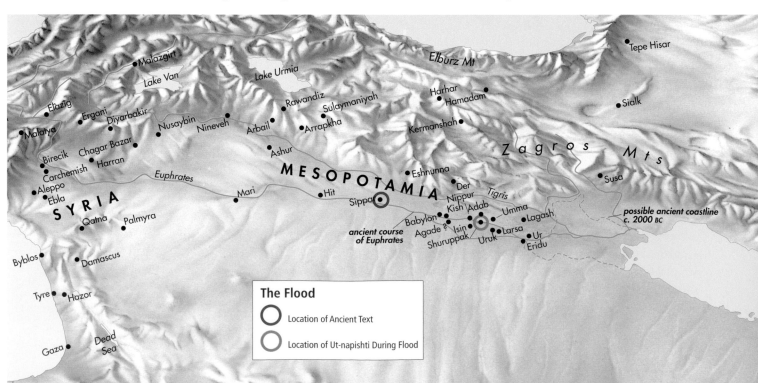

The Flood

○ Location of Ancient Text

○ Location of Ut-napishti During Flood

humanity. Before the floods came, the god Ea (god of wisdom and civilization) advised Ut-napishti to build an ark, in which he was able to save himself, his family and animals. The ark came to rest on the summit of a mountain. While the ark remained held there for days, Ut-napishti released first a dove, then a swallow, both of which came back being unable to find anywhere to perch. Then he sent a crow, which finding dry land, stayed there. Ut-napishti was encouraged to venture out and also discovered dry land. As a sign of his gratitude at being alive, he made abundant sacrifices to the gods. Then the deities, particularly Inanna (queen of heaven), began to voice regret for the catastrophe they had caused, seeing that without humankind they would have no one to labour for them and provide them with the necessities of life.

Inanna accused Enlil (god of air) of causing the Flood, while Enlil, for his part, reproached his colleagues for allowing even a single

human to escape. Ea joined in the accusations against Enlil. Finally Enlil, perhaps in repentant mood, conferred the gift of immortality on Ut-napishti.

The terror of the Flood is captured in these lines, translated from inscribed tablets dated from before the third millennium BC:

All the wild winds blew together,
  and the Flood knew no limits,
  in seven days and seven nights
  the waters covered the land.

Then Shamash the sun god reappeared,
  Ut-napishti prostrated himself before the god,
  and sacrificed a bull and a sheep.
  And Ut-napishti receives from Enlil
  the gift of life eternal.

Although the story of Atrahasis (see Box) portrays the Flood as a general catastrophe, Babylonian texts record that at least the city of Sippar survived, and ancient writings were buried there and later recovered.

The Epic of Gilgamesh is one of the best-known flood stories. In the myth, the hero Ut-napishti is instructed by the gods to build a boat onto which he should take every kind of living thing to escape the all-destroying deluge planned by the gods to punish the wicked city of Shurrupak.

Left: Running through the flood stories of Mesopotamia are common themes, including that of the ark and the sole survivor of the human race. In the Epic of Gilgamesh, their hero is Ut-napishti, whose ark is depicted here; in another myth the survivor is called Atrahasis.

ATRAHASIS AND THE ARK

According to the myth, the gods became angry because human beings were too numerous and their incessant noise prevented the gods from sleeping. First they sent diseases, but still human numbers increased. Then they sent famine, which resulted in starvation so extreme that people ate their own children. Still angry at the noisy humans, the gods decided to exterminate the human race, together with their animals. However, Enki, the god of wisdom and the waters, disagreed with this plan and resolved secretly to help a certain wise man escape destruction. This man was Atrahasis (the super-wise), and Enki instructed him to dismantle his house and build a boat with two decks, using bitumen to seal gaps between the timbers. Atrahasis gathered his whole family and both domestic and wild animals inside. Then the sun disappeared and there was total darkness. The wind howled and flood waters engulfed human habitations. Atrahasis cast off and, with his family and animal cargo, drifted for seven days and nights before striking dry land and gaining salvation. In the version of the Flood story included in the *Epic of Gilgamesh*, the surviving man is called Ut-napishti, and while adrift he sent a dove, a swallow and a crow to look for land.

The Epic of Gilgamesh

The *Epic of Gilgamesh* features a human hero and is considered to be the first major work of literature. Discovered in 1845 during excavation of the library of the Assyrian king Ashurbanipal in Nineveh, the first written versions of the story are thought to date from 2100 BC.

Gilgamesh is believed to have been a real king of Uruk in southern Mesopotamia, who reigned between 2700 and 2500 BC. A priest called Sin-leqi-unninni is credited with bringing together the various folk tales about this king some time between 1600 and 1000 BC. In the epic so created, Gilgamesh begins by angering his people through his arrogance. To teach him a lesson, the gods create a wild being called Enkidu, who is half-human, half-animal, and who is covered with hair, and send him to fight Gilgamesh. On the way to the royal palace, Enkidu is waylaid by a sacred prostitute who persuades him to make love to her and, in so doing, domesticates the wild man and introduces him to the arts of civilization. He cuts his hair, oils his body and dresses like other men in the city. The woman then takes Enkidu to meet Gilgamesh. The two men have a wrestling match which Enkidu wins, after which they become the best of friends.

THE GODDESS SPURNED

Gilgamesh convinces himself that it is his destiny to go to the sacred Cedar Forest of Lebanon, there to fight and kill the giant Humbaba, blamed for causing many evils that afflict Uruk. Enkidu persuades the king to take him as his escort, but before leaving on this perilous expedition the two friends seek the blessing of Ninsun, the queen, who is Gilgamesh's mother and also priestess of the sun god Shamash. Ninsun duly blesses the pair, and adopts Enkidu as her second son. Though fearful, Gilgamesh and Enkidu penetrate the great cedar forest and confront Humbaba. They kill him, fell his cedar trees and return home.

Gilgamesh is wooed by Inanna (called in the epic by her Semitic name, Ishtar), but the king refuses to have anything to do with the goddess, recounting how badly she has treated former lovers. Furious at being spurned,

King Ashurbanipal, pictured here on a frieze at Nineveh fighting a lion, ruled from c. 669–627 BC. The myth of Gilgamesh that dates from this time was written by the king's scribes, who constructed it from earlier Sumerian texts, reinterpreting them to create a continuous narrative.

Inanna begs her father Anu, god of the sky, to give her the Bull of Heaven so it can punish Gilgamesh. The Bull appears in Uruk, but Gilgamesh and Enkidu attack and kill it.

THE VAIN QUEST

Enkidu falls ill and dies. Distraught at the loss of his dearest friend, Gilgamesh goes on a long journey through a dark tunnel beneath Mount Mashu in search of Ut-napishti, the survivor of the Flood, hoping to learn the secret of this man's immortality. Eventually he reaches Ut-napishti, who takes Gilgamesh home by sea and shows him the plant of everlasting life on the ocean floor. Gilgamesh dives down and brings it back up. However, on his way home by land a serpent emerges from a river and steals the precious plant.

Escorted by Urshanabi, the boatman of Ut-napishti, Gilgamesh returns to Uruk. He points out to the boatman the majesty of the city. Then he inscribes the story of his travels on stone tablets and sets them in the strong walls of Uruk, so that people will remember him after his death.

Left: Assyrian stone relief of Gilgamesh with a lion, Khorsabad, eighth century BC. Gilgamesh was a legendary figure who, as claimed in the official records of rulers, ruled for 126 years. At the beginning of the epic he is described as two-thirds god, one-third human.

A modern depiction of Gilgamesh mourning the death of his friend, Enkidu, whose death resulted from the part he played in the killing of the Bull of Heaven.

ADVENTURER IN SEARCH OF IMMORTALITY

A number of commentators have remarked on the profound social and psychological symbolism informing the *Epic of Gilgamesh*. It represents the first coherent narrative in human history, where the central actor pits himself against nature and the world in a conscious bid for knowledge and mastery. As such, it became the inspiration, albeit for ages unconscious and unacknowledged, of a millennial literary tradition in Western civilization, a tradition of which the Greek tale of Odysseus and the *Odyssey* is a classic example.

Some have also seen in the Gilgamesh story a coded account of the struggle between ancient society's inheritance from the earth-centred religion of the early Neolithic and Palaeolithic epochs, and an insurgent and finally triumphant 'patriarchal' ideology. Feminist historians point to Gilgamesh's despoliation of the sacred cedar forest, his killing of the Bull of Heaven (symbolic in archaic religion of the moon and fertility) and his rejection of the great goddess Inanna-Ishtar as embodiments of a radical change in human consciousness. This change, signalling an epochal break with humankind's earlier sense of oneness with nature and its cyclic rhythms, heralds the emergence of masculine individuality and thrust for dominance. The reverse, however, is Gilgamesh's fear of death and futile quest for immortality.

Persian Myths

Persian traditional cosmology is profoundly dualistic, and its myths reflect the fundamental opposition of good and evil, light and dark. The two opposed deities are Ahura Mazda (wise lord), god of the sky, and Ahriman, who dwells in the darkness far below. The ultimate triumph of good is predestined.

AVENGING MANKIND

According to Persian mythology, Ahura Mazda decided to raise Mithra from his status as the god in charge of humankind, the guardian of contractual relations, to a place with him in the heavenly world of spirit. Mithra loses no time in using his new position to complain to the Wise Lord about man's lack of respect for him. Accompanied by Verethraghna, his avenging angel, Mithra is licensed to return to the earth, riding in a chariot drawn by four white horses reared in heaven, their fore-hooves shod with gold, their rear-hooves with silver. Mithra immediately launches a campaign of violent retribution against the followers of untruth, and of rewarding the virtuous. Thus those who honour their contracts are rewarded with riches, health and noble offspring, while liars receive sickness, death, poverty, misery and the loss of their children.

Meanwhile it is said that Ahura Mazda remained on high unsullied by the fray, while Mithra contended with the forces of evil in this world, where they still exerted great power.

TRIUMPH OF EVIL

This power became momentarily total on the earth when Ahriman, the Spirit of Destruction, who lived in the darkness below, invaded the material universe created by Ahura Mazda. One-by-one he conquered the sky, sea, land and vegetation, the cosmic bull, symbol of the spirit of light on earth, and Gayomart, the first created man.

Persian Myths
The Persian nation was made up of many tribes. The principal ones being the Pasargadae, the Maraphians, and the Maspians, of whom the Pasargadae were the noblest. The Achaemenidae, from which sprang all the Persian kings, were one of their clans.

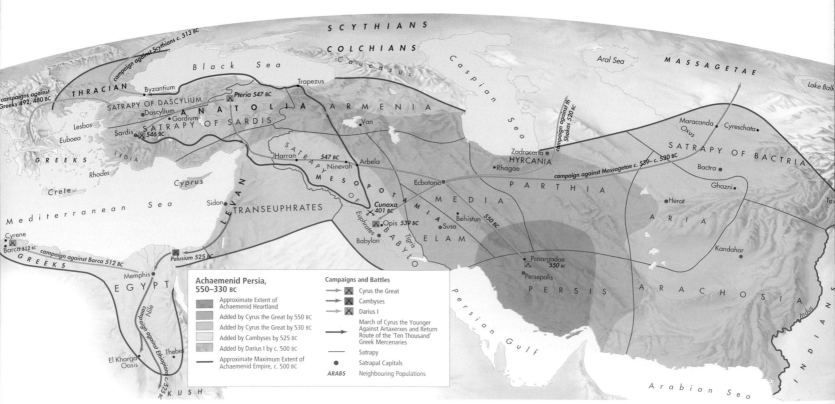

Achaemenid Persia, 550–330 BC

Approximate Extent of Achaemenid Heartland
Added by Cyrus the Great by 550 BC
Added by Cyrus the Great by 530 BC
Added by Cambyses by 525 BC
Added by Darius I by c. 500 BC
Approximate Maximum Extent of Achaemenid Empire, c. 500 BC

Campaigns and Battles

Cyrus the Great
Cambyses
Darius I
March of Cyrus the Younger Against Artaxerxes and Return Route of the 'Ten Thousand' Greek Mercenaries
Satrapy
Satrapal Capitals
ARABS   Neighbouring Populations

The death of the cosmic bull, which Ahriman had expected to signal the end of life on earth, had the opposite effect, however. Its brain and other organs fertilized the ground, causing grains and medicinal plants to germinate and flourish, while vines arose from its blood. Its seed engendered cattle and all kinds of animals with the exception of wolves and felines, which were held to be the creations of Ahriman. The apparent triumph of the forces of darkness was illusory.

THE GOLDEN AGE

A pre-Zoroastrian myth names the first man on earth as Yima. He was the first king. During his reign Yima deprived the *daevas*, the demonic servants of the evil Ahriman, of wealth, herds and reputation. Good men, on the other hand, enjoyed every comfort, and neither became sick nor grew old. Father and son walked together, each looking but 15 years of age. Yima extended the domain of the earth three times, making room for the increase in the human and animal population that had been made possible by his beneficent rule.

This golden age could not be permanent, however, and Ahura Mazda warned Yima that the wicked human race was going to suffer the affliction of winter, and that Yima must carve out a great dwelling place beneath the earth. There he had to shelter the finest men, women and cattle, the sweetest-smelling plants and most delectable foods. There they would all remain until the last days, which would be foreshadowed by a terrible winter lasting three years. Afterwards Yima and his noble race would emerge and repopulate the devastated earth.

Left: Gayomard, the first man who was created by Ahura Mazda according to Zoroastrian legend, reclines on a tiger skin. His seed fell to earth and turned into the first human couple. From a 15th century Persian manuscript.

Opposite: A rock relief at Naqshi, Iran. The figure on the right is Ahura Mazda, the Persian deity of truth and light, riding on horseback and trampling on Ahriman's snake-covered head. Their mythical struggle is mirrored on the left by a Persian king trampling on a political enemy.

Relief showing Ahura Mazda, the Persian god who endured permanent conflict with Ahriman, the god of darkness and evil. The prophet Zoroaster denounced the dualism of this faith, making Ahura Mazda the supreme god.

THUS SPRACH ZARATHUSTRA

The most famous human figure in Persian religious philosophy was the prophet Zoroaster (or Zarathustra), who lived between *c.* 628 BC and *c.* 551 BC. The scriptures he wrote, known as the *Avesta*, contain all that is known of traditional Persian religion, of which he is thought to have been a priest. The core of Zoroaster's highly original teachings is contained in a myth, according to which there were in the beginning just two twin spirits. One of them, who was wise, chose goodness and truth, but the other chose evil and illusion.

What is peculiar in this myth is its insistence that the material world is the concrete expression of the spiritual. Happiness and pleasure are the natural state of humankind and suffering is restrictive and evil. Material prosperity and spiritual progress go together and a sick body is a sign of a sick soul in Zoroaster's account.

Zoroaster denounced the polytheism of traditional Persian religion, extolling Ahura Mazda as the one true god. He particularly denounced the cult of Mithra and its sacrifice of a bull, which was thought to become the moon. This cult spread through the later Roman Empire and for a long period rivalled Christianity.

Biblical Mythologies

The Hebrew Old Testament abounds in mythical motifs current in the Near East about 3000 years ago, when the oral traditions of the Israelites were first written down. The central episode of the New Testament, the sacrificial death of Jesus, parallels the ancient myth-ritual of the dying and reborn king.

Painting by Diego Velázquez (1599–1660) of Jesus Christ on the cross. The theme of a king being killed so that his people might be saved is a common one in Near-Eastern mythology, reinterpreted in the New Testament story of Christ's crucifixion.

IN THE BEGINNING

The beginning of things, as described in the biblical Book of Genesis, resembles the creation stories of Sumer and Egypt in its description of the emergence of dry land and all life from an original state of formless, watery chaos. As in Mesopotamian mythology, the continuing, dominant theme of the Old Testament story is the conflict between order, associated with Yahweh, and the destructive chaos associated with his enemies. The Hebrew prophets used this common symbolic currency to describe Yahweh's war against all earthly powers seen as hostile to his divine purposes. In the Book of Isaiah, Canaanite and Mesopotamian images of the waters of chaos are fused as the prophet addresses Yahweh as the 'piercer' of the dragon Rahab, and the one who dried up the waters. These deeds, it is said, were done 'in primordial days', evoking parallels with the cosmic exploits of Baal and Marduk.

CONTROL OF NATURE

Psalm 74 goes further, asserting that Yahweh has not only destroyed the serpent of chaos, but has also established dominion over the cycles of nature; the succession of day and night and the seasons of the year. In the words of Psalm 29, 'Yahweh sits enthroned on the primeval sea, Yahweh sits enthroned as king for ever'.

Some of the Hebrew prophets also used the images of the deity's triumph over the forces of chaos to describe historical events such as the Israelites' exodus from bondage in Egypt and Babylon, or Israel's victory over the Pharaoh's army. In the story of the parting of the waters of

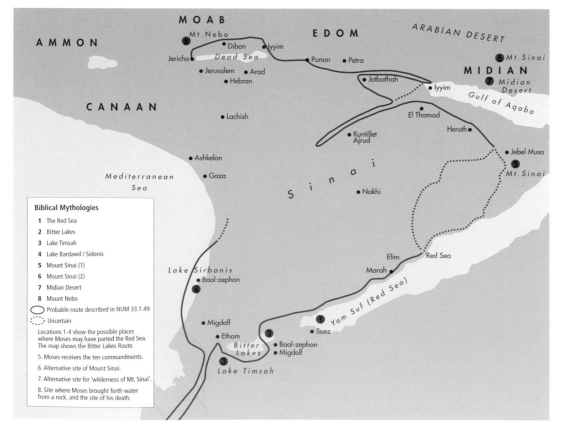

Biblical Mythologies
Moses was the subject of a number of biblical myths, which had many themes in common with those of Mesopotamian mythology. The map shows Moses's possible route of Exodus from Egypt and the probable sites of some of the biblical tales.

Biblical Mythologies
1 The Red Sea
2 Bitter Lakes
3 Lake Timsah
4 Lake Bardawil / Sidonis
5 Mount Sinai (1)
6 Mount Sinai (2)
7 Midian Desert
8 Mount Nebo
◯ Probable route described in NUM 33.1.49
⋯ Uncertain
Locations 1-4 show the possible places where Moses may have parted the Red Sea. The map shows the Bitter Lakes Route.
5. Moses receives the ten commandments.
6. Alternative site of Mount Sinai.
7. Alternative site for 'wilderness of Mt. Sinai'.
8. Site where Moses brought forth water from a rock, and the site of his death.

the Red Sea, Yahweh empowers Moses to stretch out his hand over the sea and control its movements; in the Book of Nahum the downfall of the great enemy of Israel, Assyria, and the conquest of Nineveh in 612 BC by the Medes and Persians, are celebrated in mythological terms by the prophet: 'In whirlwind and in storm is his way, he rebukes Yamm [the sea] and makes it dry, and all the rivers he dries up'.

SUBDUING THE WATERS

The central figure of the Biblical New Testament, Jesus of Nazareth, echoes the epochal exploits of the Mesopotamian and Canaanite culture heroes when he subdues the raging winds and waters of

PREHISTORY IN THE NEAR EAST

6700–3000 BC	Pre-dynastic Period
3000–2500 BC	Sumerian kingship
2500–2000 BC	Babylonian (Akkadian) supremacy
c. 1225 BC	First Assyrian conquest of Babylon
612 BC	Nineveh falls to Medes
539 BC	Babylon falls to Persians under Cyrus
331 BC	Alexander conquers Babylon

the Sea of Galilee (Lake Tiberius) and asserts his complete control of nature by walking on the sea. The story of the crucifixion of Jesus, his descent into the underworld of Hell (as told by the *Apostles' Creed*) and his final resurrection, evoke the immemorially ancient Near-Eastern theme of the divine king whose sacrificial death assures the salvation of his land and his people, and who also, like the Mesopotamian Dumuzi, descends into a dark underworld, to be reborn into the light in the person of his successor. The disciple and close companion of Jesus, the prostitute Mary of Magdala (Mary Magdalene), resembles Inanna/Ishtar, the incarnate goddess who served as consort of the divine king in the Mesopotamian 'sacred marriage' ritual (see p. 27).

Left: Moses, the Old Testament figure who leads his people out of oppression, represents the will of the divine over chaos as he, using God's power, is able to part the Red Sea. Taken from a sixth century AD mosaic.

THE SERPENT AS A SYMBOL OF CHAOS

The meaning of the serpent, in Palaeolithic and early High Neolithic religion symbolic of the great Earth Goddess herself, was transformed in the hierarchically organized kingdoms of the ancient Near East and Egypt into an embodiment of cosmic chaos and destruction. In Sumer and Babylon, the originally benign and maternal serpent Tiamat became the monster of darkness and evil, slain by the solar hero Marduk, while in Canaan, the storm god Baal similarly vanquished the serpentine monster Yamm. In the Old Testament the Hebrew supreme deity called Yahweh is celebrated as the victor over the sea monster Yamm, also called Rahab. In several other passages the prophet Isaiah refers to the cosmic monster as Leviathan (Lotan in the Canaanite myth) and calls its habitat, the sea, by the Canaanite name of Yamm. In the Book of Job it is said that Yahweh fatally 'pierced' the evil serpent.

Throughout the Old Testament there is a consistent association between the sea as a force of chaos and its personification in the form of a monstrous snake or dragon. As Yahweh says to Job: 'Who shut Yamm with doors... And said, "Thus far you may come and no more, and here shall the arrogance of your waters be halted?"'

Indian Creation Myths

The age and diversity of Indian culture and religion has resulted in one of the most complex and rich mythologies in the world. The enduring power of these myths whose origins are hidden in the mists of time is demonstrated by the vital role they continue to play in modern Indian society.

Details of the prehistoric and early historic period of Indian civilization are open to speculation. As no records survive, very little is known of India's ancient history. What is known is that an urban civilization which had far-flung links with Mesopotamia, flourished in north-western India in the Indus Valley region until its apparent demise around 1750 BC. A new social order began at this time, but whether it was a further development of the Indus Valley culture or was founded by incoming Indo-European nomads who brought with them iron-working, war chariots and cattle-herding is open to debate. Though many elements of Indian mythology must have their roots among the various other ethnic groups who lived in

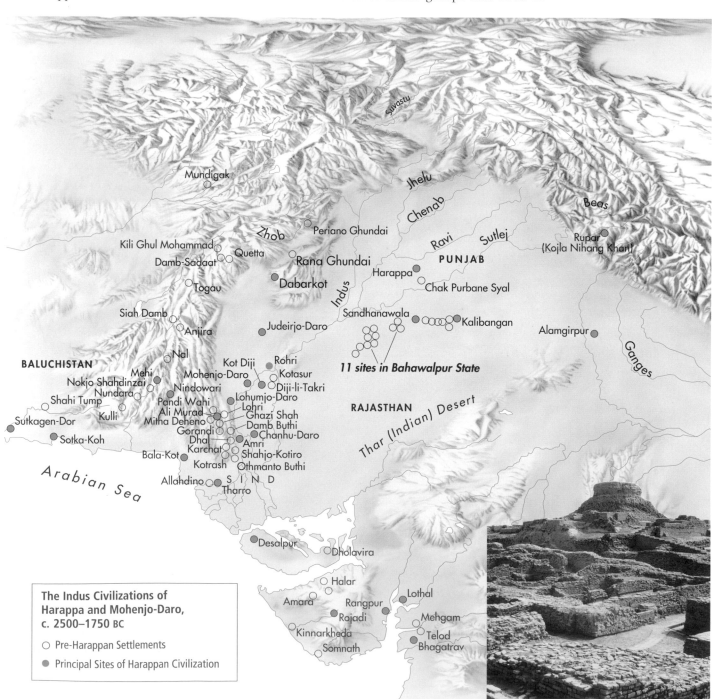

The Indus Civilizations of
Harappa and Mohenjo-Daro,
c. 2500–1750 BC

○ Pre-Harappan Settlements
● Principal Sites of Harappan Civilization

India, a large portion of the mainstream pantheon and its associated myths seem to derive from the Vedic culture attributed to the Indo-Europeans.

CREATION MYTHS

The *Vedas*, ancient Sanskrit hymns, and their secondary literature describe a number of creation myths. One typical concept is that of the universe coming into existence as a result of divine incest in which an unnamed father begets a daughter – perhaps symbolic of the sky and the earth – and then proceeds to join with her and produce other gods and the various features of the natural world. Often the major gods, headed by Prajapati, are considered to be primordially existent. Thus, a variant of the previous myth attributes creation to an incestuous act between Prajapati and his daughter. After his seed flowed forth and formed a lake, the other gods blew upon it and formed the domesticated animals of the world. In an alternative version, Prajapati creates the god of fire, Agni, when he desires to create some offspring. Prajapati then made sacrificial offerings to Agni, a key feature of classical Indian religion, and as a result Prajapati successfully generated his own progeny. A similar combination of sacrificial offerings and incest is found in accounts of creation involving Brahma, who split himself into a male and female being, who proceeded to generate living beings from their union. Brahma then made offerings, using parts of his own body in the ritual, and produced fire, water and food.

Other forms of creation are mentioned in early Indian sacred texts, such as the primeval sacrifice of Purusha (man) who is dismembered and his parts distributed to form the gods, the universe and all the living creatures it contains. Equally well known is the myth of the Golden Egg (*hiranya-garbha*) which floated upon the waters of chaos at the beginning of time. From this egg were born the other gods and then the rest of creation. Still another version is recounted in connection with the god Indra who slays the demon of chaos and releases the wholesome elements of creation.

Another key feature of Indian creation mythology, thought by some scholars to derive from the Indus Valley culture, is the concept of cyclical creation. The cycle involves the universe evolving from its creation and enduring for billions of years before being destroyed by fire or water; this whole process is then repeated. Living creatures also participate in this cycle as they are repeatedly reborn until they extricate themselves by attaining spiritual liberation.

A symbolic depiction of the Hindu (Brahman) creation myth. Common to all the various Indian stories of creation is the idea that the beginning of the world did not result from a single moment of creation, rather that order was made out of chaos.

Watercolour showing the saint Krakutsansa teaching Brahmin monks from the *Svayumbhu Purana*. Together with the *Ramayana* and *Mahabharata*, the *Puranas* are one of the main sources of Indian mythological and religious history.

THE SOURCES

Indian mythology is found throughout an enormous range of religious literature, much of which was intentionally transmitted orally for thousands of years. The oldest parts of the Hindu canon are the four *Vedas*, large compilations of hymns for worship and sacrifice. The oldest of these is the *Rig Veda* which is generally thought to have been composed between 1200 and 900 BC, but which already contains many of the key myths and accounts of the great gods who form a large part of the present-day Hindu pantheon. Over time, secondary literature of a commentorial and philosophical nature, known as the *Brahmanas* and which include the *Upanishads*, was appended to the *Vedas* and expanded many of the basic mythic themes of the *Vedas*. Later compositions include the numerous mythico-legendary histories, the eighteen *Puranas*, which were composed over the centuries from early medieval times onward, as well as the great epics: the *Mahabharata* and the *Ramayana*. Other Indian mythology must derive from ancient tribal and folk beliefs and probably only found its way into the mainstream of society by chance. Another category of scripture, the *Tantras*, are also important sources of mythology – especially for the myths which concern the various fierce goddesses such as Kala and Durga.

Vishnu

Though only mentioned occasionally in the *Rig Veda*, Vishnu (all-pervasive) soon became one of the most important deities in the Indian pantheon. While Brahma is often considered as the creator of the universe and Shiva as its destroyer, Vishnu is responsible for sustaining the world and all its living creatures, as is the sun (with which he is sometimes identified).

A shrine to Vishnu in Kathmandu, Nepal. Emerging from early mythology, Vishnu's role in maintaining the equilibrium of the universe has gained the deity many ardent devotees who honour him as a supreme god.

As the sustainer of the universe, Vishnu is generally portrayed in mythology as a benevolent, bountiful and all-pervading deity who intervenes on occasion to restore cosmic harmony when negative forces threaten the stability of the established order. Often when he does this, at the request of the other gods, he assumes a different form appropriate to the task. By early medieval times, 10 of these manifestations, known as *avataras*, were recognized, with groups of interconnected myths associated with each of them.

VISHNU AS SAVIOUR OF THE WORLD

One very ancient myth also known in India is that of a cataclysmic flood which threatened to destroy the entire world including Manu, the archetypal human. In one version, Manu protects a small fish which warns him of the impending flood and promises to save him. Manu builds a boat for himself and takes on board samples of all living creatures and plants. When the flood comes, the fish, which by now has grown to an enormous size, pulls the boat to safety while all else perishes. After this event, Manu realizes that the fish (Matsya) was none other than Vishnu. The manifestation of Vishnu as a boar (Varaha) seems to be a variant of this flood myth: at the beginning of time, the earth was hidden beneath the surface of a great ocean but Vishnu changed himself into a giant boar and lifted up the earth from below the waves and spread it out level.

GODS AND DEMONS

On another occasion, the gods and the *asuras* – the Indian equivalent of demons – wanted to obtain the elixir of immortality. Vishnu instructed them to throw various kinds of medicinal plants into the great ocean of milk and to churn it. In order to do this successfully using the golden mountain, Mandara, as a churner and the serpent king, Vasuki, as a rope,

Vishnu transformed himself into a giant turtle (Karma) as a pivot for the mountain. At first the ocean produced poison which was drunk by Shiva before the elixir began to be formed. Both the gods and the demons wanted the nectar for themselves but Vishnu intervened on behalf of the gods in order to prevent the demons from attaining immortality.

Two other manifestations of Vishnu are connected with demons who threatened to upset the order of the world. A demon, Hiranyaka-shipu, obtains immortality from Brahma as a result of great religious austerities he undertook. However, as his behaviour later becomes tyrannical, Vishnu becomes a half-man and half-lion being (Narasimha), to circumvent Hiranyaka-shipu's gift that protects him from destruction by gods, men or beasts. Hiranyaka-shipu's grandson, Bali, was also a virtuous demon – a curious Indian concept frequently encountered – who ousted the gods through his righteous rule of the world. Deprived of their rightful sacrifices, the gods ask Vishnu to help and he transforms himself into an innocuous dwarf (Vamana) who appears before Bali just as he is about to perform a great ritual that will seal his dominion of the world. The dwarf asks for a gift of ground – three paces in size – so that he may also offer sacrifices and the unsuspecting Bali consents. At this juncture, the dwarf reverts to his cosmic proportions and covers the earth, sky and heavens with three giant steps.

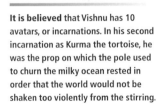

It is believed that Vishnu has 10 avatars, or incarnations. In his second incarnation as Kurma the tortoise, he was the prop on which the pole used to churn the milky ocean rested in order that the world would not be shaken too violently from the stirring.

Left: Vishnu depicted as half lion, half man, or Narasimha, on a 17th-century wooden panel. In this form Vishnu was able to defeat the evil demon Hiranyaka Shipu who had wished to be killed by someone who was neither human nor beast.

INDIAN REGIONAL MYTHOLOGIES

An enormous volume of mythological stories can be found in classical Indian literature but this may only represent one portion of the total riches the country has produced. Many elements of the 'official' mythology clearly have their origins in local cults associated with less prominent deities who were eventually assimilated into the mainstream of pan-Indian religious life. But it must not be forgotten that what is available in literature is only what the establishment has chosen to recognize and incorporate. Much mythology in India, even in the present day, exists only at a rural village level and is still to be recorded and understood properly. Some of these oral mythologies are very ancient and represent alternative religious traditions linked to other, non-Indo-European ethnic groups in India, such as the southern Dravidians or the remnants of the ancient Austro-Asiatic people in eastern and parts of central India. One of the best known of these folk mythologies is preserved by the Kondhs of Orissa in eastern India which tells of a rivalry between a male and female primordial deity. Some Kondhs regarded the male deity as the victor and another group claimed the female deity had won, with the curious result that the god's followers practise female infanticide while, until recently, the followers of the goddess practised human sacrifice.

Manifestations of Vishnu

While Vishnu acts as a world-saviour or as one who restores the balance between the gods and demons in the first five of his *avataras*, his role is somewhat different in the subsequent ones. Although still concerned with maintaining or restoring harmony, he now generally appears in human forms described in later myths that many Hindus believe have a quasi-historical basis.

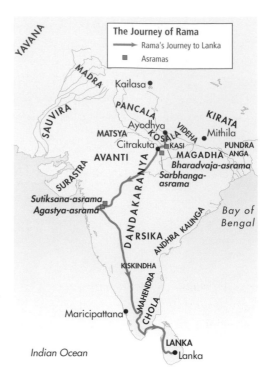

Indian Ocean

Though viewed as a mortal king throughout most of the epic poem that tells his story, Rama is 'revealed' as a manifestation of Vishnu in chapters that were appended to the core text of the *Ramayana*.

The central story of this epic concerns the life of Rama and his wife Sita, who is abducted by the demon Ravana. After Rama has battled with Ravana, defeated him and rescued Sita, his treatment of his long-suffering wife is cruel and

The Journey of Rama
The route that the banished king Rama took to rescue his beloved wife Sita from her confinement in Lanka by the demon Ravana. While partly mythical, this story inspired many medieval kings, who believed themselves to be infused with Vishnu's divine presence and descended from the family of Rama.

Vishnu's eighth *avatar* is Krishna, here pictured with a lotus flower, dancing in the rain, in a 17th-century Rajasthan school miniature. Krishna is one of the most popular Hindu deities and his followers offer him unconditional devotion as the One Supreme God.

selfish. Not willing to suffer his false accusations and rejection, the virtuous Sita tries to have herself burnt in a pyre but is finally saved and restored to Rama when the gods reveal to him his true divine nature, explaining to him that he took on a human form in order to defeat the demon Ravana.

VISHNU IN THE HUMAN WORLD

A vast range of popular myths are associated with Vishnu's manifestation in the world as Krishna. He is mentioned in passing in the great epic, the *Mahabharata*, where he seems largely to be merely a human hero, although he does reveal himself as a god in the course of the *Bhagavad-gita*, the famous dialogue with his friend Arjuna on the day of a great battle that is included in the epic. Nevertheless, Krishna really comes into his own as a god in the early medieval *Bhagavata-purana*, which recounts many episodes of his childhood, his love affair with Radha and his occasional battles with demons. As a form of Vishnu with many endearing human traits, Krishna has become one of the most revered gods in India and inspired the highly devotional *bhakti* form of Hinduism.

OTHER MANIFESTATIONS

A less well-known manifestation of Vishnu is his appearance as the genocidal warrior Parasurama who is mentioned both in the *Mahabharata* and the *Ramayana*. His main function seems to be that of a warrior who massacres all the kshatriyas, the Indian warrior-king caste, and liberates the world from their dominion so that the brahmans can assume their rightful place. A similarly unsavoury *avatara* myth claims that the Buddha was actually a form assumed by Vishnu in order to destroy demons. Since Indian demons are often virtuous, the best way to weaken them is by corrupting them with an evil doctrine. Hence, according to this myth, Vishnu became the Buddha to convert them to the false teachings of Buddhism and to turn them away from the *Vedas*, thus enabling the other gods to defeat the demons. No doubt this myth reflects the keen rivalry that existed between Hindus and Buddhists in India at one time – needless to say, the Buddhists also have their own myths about Hindu gods being tricked and vanquished by the Buddha and his divine assistants.

Although there are accounts of the final incarnation of Vishnu as Kalkin, this has yet to happen; Kalkin is a terrible messianic figure who will appear at the end of the current world age. There are many aspects of this myth that resemble Judeo-Christian concepts of the last days, which lead one to suspect that the idea of Kalkin was not ultimately of Indian origin. When the world has become corrupt and good people live short lives of poverty and oppression, Kalkin will ride forth on a white steed to destroy all the wicked rulers and their supporters. When this has been accomplished, Vishnu will restore the world to the state it enjoyed in the primal golden age.

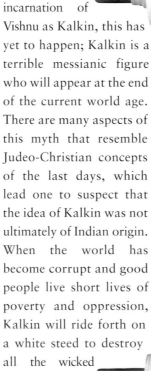

Although mentioned in the *Mahabharata*, Krishna comes into his own in the *Bhagavata purana*. It is these tales of Krishna in which his pranks and miracles, as well his human traits, are described that have endeared him to centuries of followers.

THE *RAMAYANA* AND THE *MAHABHARATA*

By the fourth century AD, the standard versions of India's two great epics had been compiled. Both of these works are rich sources of mythology and they incorporate much earlier material, almost at random. The *Ramayana* is both the shorter and the older of the two epics and tells the story of the life of Rama and his wife Sita, who is kidnapped by Ravana, a demon based in Sri Lanka. Rama eventually does battle with the demon and overcomes him with the aid of the monkey king Hanuman and his army. After his victory, Rama returns to his capital at Ayodhya where, after certain tribulations, the couple eventually die and ascend to heaven. The main theme of the vast *Mahabharata* is the war between two related families, the Kauravas and the Pandavas, who represent evil and virtue respectively. The central story may thus be understood on several levels, as a quasi-historical epic or as a spiritual battle of cosmic dimensions between good and evil, for example. Many subsidiary elements are woven into this encyclopedic work including portions that have achieved fame as independent scriptures, such as the *Bhagavad-gita*, a spiritual discourse on the nature of duty.

Shiva and his Family

While Brahma is identified as the god of creation and Vishnu the god who sustains the world, the dark god Shiva is the god of destruction and dissolution. Although the cult of Shiva became increasingly popular in the early medieval period in India, his status often eclipsed that of Brahma and Vishnu and gave rise to a complex mythology.

Shiva (the Kind One) is not mentioned by name in the *Vedas*, although a fierce deity known as Rudra is often identified with him. Indeed, it is very possible that Shiva's origins lie far back in the mists of time in the Indus Valley culture, which produced seals depicting a deity with attributes reminiscent of Shiva in his role of Pasupati, the lord of the beasts. In his myths, Shiva is depicted as the archetypal ascetic sage, sometimes generous and merciful, but often harsh and irascible, living alone in the mountains; he also reveals a highly charged, erotic side to his personality on occasion. A very large body of myths has developed that describe the many facets of this dark outsider god and in which he is also depicted quelling demons.

SHIVA AND HIS CONSORTS

Unlike the other gods, Shiva was often thought to be androgynous, and is sometimes shown iconographically as half man and half woman. His female side is said to comprise his dynamic powers (sakti) and is often represented in a female embodiment who becomes his consort – a view of Shiva which led to the rise of Tantrism and Saktism from the sixth century AD in India. At an early stage in Shiva's life, he was married to Sati, the daughter of Daksha, a son of Brahma and devotee of Vishnu. Because he considered the outsider Shiva's presence to be inauspicious, Daksha did not invite Shiva to an important sacrifice he was to hold. Angered, Shiva disrupts the sacrifice and beheads Daksha – though later Daksha is restored to life, albeit with the head of a goat, and the sacrifice is completed. In the meantime, Sati burns herself to death in her anger at this quarrel between Shiva and her father; in some versions of the story Sati is dismembered and the various parts of her body come to rest at locations that later became important pilgrimage sites.

KAMA

Sati was reborn as Parvati and desired to marry Shiva against the wishes of her parents; Shiva was living in splendid isolation, intensely engaged in ascetic austerities. In order to arouse Shiva, the god Indra sent Kama, the god of love, to tempt him, but angered at the disturbance, Shiva sent a shaft of fire forth from his third eye which reduced Kama to ashes. After many setbacks, Parvati eventually succeeds in her aim and marries Shiva and, at the wedding, asks Shiva to restore Kama to life as a favour.

Shiva is the god of darkness and destruction, and can be a frightening figure, surrounded by ghosts and goblins. However, the benevolent side to him shows mercy to his devotees and to the wayward elements of the universe, or *asuras*.

A detailed examination of the Shiva myths reveals an ambivalence in the identity of Shiva and Kama – it seems that Kama is actually Shiva's erotic alter ego whom he does not wish to acknowledge. Other myths deal with Shiva's adultery, his estrangement from Parvati and their eventual reconciliation.

A number of divine offspring were born from the union of Shiva and Parvati, including the god of war, Skanda or Karttikeya as he is also known. Better known is the much-loved, elephant-headed god Ganesha, who acts as a kind of male counterpart to Lakshmi or Sarasvati (see Box p. 47) since he is considered to be the god of wisdom and plenty. He acquired his elephant-head from Brahma when Parvati boastfully showed off her son to the god of the planets whose terrible gaze turned Ganesha's original head to ashes.

Every Hindu deity is associated with his female half, and as all gods are aspects of the One Supreme Divinity the female side is in turn an aspect of the Supreme Goddess. The goddess Parvati, Shiva's female aspect, is pictured enthroned with their child, the elephant-headed Ganesha.

Shiva is worshipped in the form of a stone *linga*, or sacred phallus; he is also god of the phallus. Various myths mention the *linga*, and are believed to be the source of the cult of *linga* worship.

TANTRISM AND SAKTISM

Certain innovative forms of religious practice were incorporated into the mainstream of Hinduism in association with the cult of Shiva, especially in conjunction with his female consort counterparts. The aim of Tantra is to elevate all humans to the level of divine perfection by awakening the cosmic forces that lie dormant within them through the use of various special meditational techniques and, in some cases, with sexual yoga. Tantra is also associated with Buddhism but its roots, if not its practices, seem to derive their inspirations from an entirely different source. Saktism shares many features with Tantrism but focuses more upon the female energy aspect of Shiva, worshipping a personification of his power (Sakti) as a mother goddess. The simple aniconic representation of Shiva is the stone *linga* pillar or phallus, while that of Sakti is a triangular *yoni* or vulva. These two symbols, either singly or combined as one, are still found in many Indian temples and worshipped by many, to whom the overtly sexual nature of the *linga* and *yoni* is less important than it would seem to the eyes of outsiders.

Goddesses

Known simply as Devi, the Goddess, the archetypal female deity, has been worshipped in India and adjacent areas to the east from prehistoric times. The basic concept of Devi was soon diversified, first as the need arose to provide wives for the male gods of the *Vedas* and later with the spread of Tantric and Saktic beliefs.

Apart from goddesses such as Sati, Parvati or Radha, who were closely connected with their male consorts, there are also an important group of goddesses who act largely in their own right. Some of the earlier of such goddesses seem to be personifications of natural phenomena or abstract qualities, such as Prthivi the earth goddesses, Ratri the night goddess or Ushas the dawn goddess. But since little developed mythology is associated with them, they are somewhat less interesting than goddesses such as Devi, Durga and Kali.

THE FEROCIOUS GODDESS

Devi, or Great Devi (Maha-Devi) as she is often named, was viewed as the ultimate creative force in the universe who is the mother of all things, and it was she who directed the male gods to act. Obviously this concept runs counter to the patriarchal view which ascribes creation to a male god, but both positions have been popular throughout Indian religious history. As a kind of matriarchal counterpart to Vishnu, Devi also may appear in ten different embodiments and is also often involved in the destruction of evil demons.

Shiva (left) and Parvati (right), from a frieze at Temples, Khajrato. Parvati, Shiva's gentle female aspect, is credited with domesticating this unruly ascetic, and in most mythology their life together is depicted as being extremely harmonious.

However, in this role she takes on various ferocious forms, including that of Durga. On one occasion, when the gods and demons were battling, all the demon sons of Diti were slain, so she had her daughter undergo great ascetic ordeals to gain an avenging son. Her efforts were rewarded with the birth of a great buffalo-headed being called Mahisha. Due to his great power, the demons began to gain the upper hand in their struggle with the gods and none could defeat Mahisha. When they met to complain of their misfortune, the anger of the gods became so great that its energy coalesced into the terrible form of the warrior-goddess Durga. After a dramatic battle in which Mahisha changes shape several times, Durga eventually slays him by cutting off his head – an image perhaps reminiscent of buffalo sacrifices, which are still commonly associated in India with worship of the mother goddess in her various forms.

KALI

Another important goddess is Kali, the goddess of death, whose cult and mythology seem to have originated among the tribal people of Assam and eastern Bengal, where her worship is widely associated with animal – and formerly human – sacrifice. On one occasion, when Durga and her seven assistant goddesses were trying to destroy the demon Raktabaja (Blood Seed), they were unable to make much headway since every time they wounded Raktabaja, copies of him sprang up from the drops of his blood as they splashed onto the ground – somewhat like the dragon's teeth of Greek mythology. Durga then summons the horrific Kali, who gleefully catches all the drops of blood on her long tongue, devours all the secondary Raktabaja demons and then goes

on to suck him dry. Though often functioning independently, Kali is also linked with the great ascetic god Shiva as his consort and depicted as a wrathful goddess, symbolizing primal energy, standing on the body of Shiva who lies corpse-like on the ground.

Other Indian goddesses are also rather unpleasant in nature, such as Sitala, originally a north Indian local village goddess who plagues people with smallpox – by way of a reminder that life has a dark side of pain and death. The role of Hariti is rather similar, though her speciality is to prey on new-born children as food for herself and her sons. Interestingly, Hariti is mentioned in several Buddhist sources where she is confronted by the Buddha who transforms her into a benign goddess who protects children.

This painting of Kali (the dark one) holding a head is one sold to pilgrims at her shrine in Khalighat. Kali's role in mythology is to destroy demons who threaten to upset the cosmic order.

THE CULTURAL FOUNDATIONS OF INDIA

4000 BC	Settlements in Indus Valley
2300–1700 BC	Indus Valley Culture flourishing
c. 1750 BC	Disappearance of Indus Valley Culture
c. 1650 BC	Entry into NW India of Indo-European migrants
c. 1000 BC	Compilation of *Rig Veda*
c. 700 BC	Early Indian states founded in North India
c. 600 BC	Composition of earliest *Upanishads*
c. 486–400 BC	Lifetime of the Buddha Shakyamuni
c. AD 400	Final versions of *Ramayana* and *Mahabharata*
c. AD 600	Final versions of early *Puranas*

BENIGN GODDESSES

Not all independent Indian goddesses are ferocious in nature. One ancient goddess is the beautiful and gracious Lakshmi (Good Fortune), also known simply as Sri (Glorious), who is widely worshipped as the goddess of surplus and happiness. When the gods and demons were churning the great ocean of milk, she is said to have arisen from the froth – somewhat like Aphrodite – perfect in her beauty. At times she is also considered to be the consort of Vishnu and was also the mother of the Indian god of love, Kama. Her association with moisture, fertile mud and abundance points to her origin as a fertility goddess associated with the potency of the earth. Another benign goddess is Sarasvati, a very ancient river goddess linked to the now-disappeared river of the same name in northwestern India. In that role, she is credited with bringing wealth, fertility and nourishment to humanity. After Vedic times, Sarasvati's role was expanded to include her role as the goddess of eloquence and learning, the inspirer of sacred songs. She eventually became so popular that her cult was also adopted by Buddhists, who in turn transmitted her worship as far afield as Japan, where she is still an object of veneration.

Humans, Gods and Spirits

The region of Southeast Asia is highly complex both geographically and ethnically, and this complexity is reflected in the rich cultural diversity of its people. The study of the prehistory of the region is at an exciting stage, but much research is still needed before a full picture of the distant origins of today's population can be established.

Geographically, Southeast Asia is divided into two: the mainland and the island arc. The mainland comprises Burma, Thailand, Laos, Cambodia, Vietnam and Malaysia. The island arc is made up of the more than 13,000 islands of the Indonesian archipelago and the Philippine islands; Indonesia lies across one of the world's most active volcanic regions. The tectonic Indo-Australian and Pacific plates are divided by the Makassar Strait, which separates the western islands of Kalimantan (Borneo) and Bali from Sulawesi (Celebes) and Lombok. The climate gradually becomes drier to the east, and there is also a transition from the Asian to the Australasian species of flora and fauna. The people of the eastern islands change in appearance too, with many more displaying Melanesian or Papuan heritage.

View of the paddy fields in an area called the Golden Triangle, near Muang Sing, northwest Laos. The large number of myths concerning rice is largely due to the fact that most of the population of Southeast Asia are village-dwellers who rely on wet-rice cultivation.

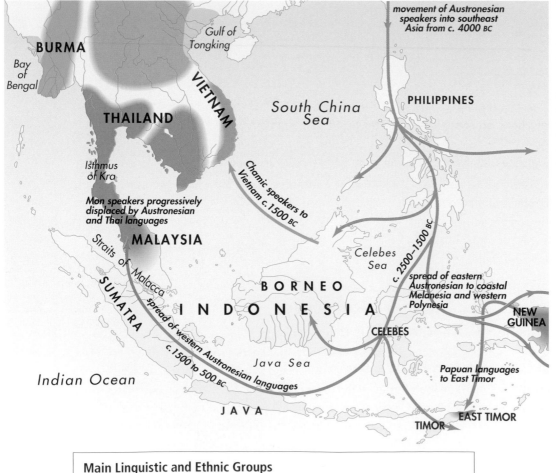

Main Linguistic and Ethnic Groups
Southeast Asia is divided into two main language groups: Austro-Asiatic and Austronesian. Most of the languages of the Philippines and Indonesia belong to the Austronesian family, which is thought to have expanded from a homeland in south China 6000 years ago. The map shows the route of this expansion as well as the other linguistic and ethnic groups of the area.

Main Linguistic and Ethnic Groups

Arakan	Thai-Lao-Shan	Khmer	Papuan
Burman	Mon	Chamic	Dai-Viet

→ Spread of Austronesian Languages   MALAYSIA   Modern State Names

CULTURAL ORIGINS

Remains of the earliest known human inhabitant of this region, Java Man, dates from the second millennium BC, but his origin is unknown. At the time when *Homo sapiens* first appeared here some 10,000 years ago, the mainland and the western islands were joined by a land bridge which facilitated the southward movement of the earliest inhabitants. A rise in sea levels flooded many low-lying regions and created thousands of islands.

The majority of today's population is of Mongoloid extraction, and the many different languages spoken belong to two major groups: the Austro-Asiatic and the Austronesian. Between *c*.5000 and 1000 BC there was a continuous movement of peoples from the north, possibly from southern China, into mainland Southeast Asia and the islands of Indonesia and the Philippines. It seems likely that members of the Austro-Asiatic linguistic group settled the valleys and hills of the mainland whilst the Austronesian peoples continued south, possibly via Taiwan and the Philippines, into Malaysia, the Indonesian archipelago and east into the Pacific.

Southeast Asia is a mixture of a multitude of cultures and its mythology reflects this diversity. From hill-tribe village dwellers in Laos, as pictured here, to hunter-gatherers in Malaysia and city dwellers in the Philippines, different population groups all have their traditional beliefs.

THE ROLE OF INDIA

The influence of India has been a major factor in the cultural development of the region. Southeast Asians have always been great seafarers, and trade led to interaction with Indian courts and religious centres. From about the beginning of the Christian era, Buddhist and Hindu religions and cosmologies were introduced to the larger cities and the concept of the king as intermediary between the celestial and terrestrial worlds became important. The king, his throne, palace and realm were believed to represent the universe in microcosm, and earthly order was seen to be a reflection of cosmic harmony. Often the king's name would incorporate the name of the god or *bodhisattva*, indicating his semi-divine nature. An unstable rule could result in chaos in nature: floods, drought and earthquakes were all believed to be the result of disharmony in the human world.

Indian religions played a major role in Southeast Asian culture and retain an influential role today, even in those regions which are now Muslim. Buddhism is still the principal faith on the mainland and Hinduism remains the religion of Bali, but Islam, brought by Arab traders in the fourteenth century, is practised throughout Indonesia and Malaysia. Christianity, brought by the Spanish in the sixteenth century, is practised in the Philippines, as it is among some of the hill-dwelling groups of the mainland. In Vietnam, a mixture of Buddhism, Confucianism, Taoism and Cao Daiism reflects a long connection with China. With the arrival of the colonial era, Portugal, Spain, France, Holland, Great Britain, the United States and Japan all came to play a part in the history of the region.

Novice monks in Mahamuni Pagoda, Mandalay in Burma. Although a large number of faiths are practised in the region, the dominant religion in mainland Southeast Asia is Buddhism.

Creation Myths: Boats and Serpents

The complex origins of the Southeast Asian peoples are reflected in many of their myths, some of which show affinities with those of India or China; Southeast Asia, however, has always maintained its own distinctive culture and belief system, despite centuries of external influence.

Southeast Asian tradition, which perhaps pre-dates the major influences of India, focuses on belief in powerful nature spirits which must be respected and placated if life is to unfold without mishap. These spirits may inhabit rocks, rivers or trees; they may be the spirits of humans who died unnatural deaths, or they may have no human connection. The Rice Spirit, usually in female form, is important throughout the region and is usually the focus of ritual and dance at rice sowing and harvest times. In many cases a household spirit is propitiated. This spirit maintains the well-being of the household and can be malevolent if not treated respectfully. A special post or place in the compound is dedicated to the house spirit. In practice there is little apparent conflict between these beliefs and the faith in Islam or

The *naga* (meaning 'serpent' in Sanskrit) is a fantastic creature found throughout the various mythologies of Southeast Asia. It has its origins in Hindu mythology, which tells of a race of snakes that were the ancestors of Indian princely dynasties. Pictured is a seven-headed *naga* from Angkor, Cambodia; the Angkor dynasty believed they were descendants of a *naga* princess.

A *palepai*, (ship's cloth) from Lampang, Sumatra. These cloths are woven from cotton on a linen warp, and the figures, ships, animals and geometric designs incorporated into the textiles are linked to a family's genealogy, revealing the whole course of the people's particular history. This cloth features a ship carrying two elephants who in turn are carrying ancestors on their backs.

Buddhism, and the two usually co-exist comfortably. When offerings are made to the Buddha shrine, for example, they must also be made to the house spirit if misfortune is not to befall the household.

ORIGIN MYTHS

The island peoples in particular speak of an original ancestor who came to their shores by boat, sailing from the north. Ancestral carvings sometimes incorporate a boat with a figure of the supreme ancestor. The people of Lampang, Sumatra, weave fine ritual hangings that include depictions of a ship bearing humans and animals.

Animal and bird ancestors are common. Many mainland groups trace their origins to a serpent or *naga*, a creature depicted symbolically throughout the Pacific regions. The Angkor dynasty of Cambodia (ninth to fourteenth centuries AD) is one of several to have claimed descent from the union of a *naga* princess and a brahmin; their iconography features multiple-headed serpents. The well-being and continuity of the Angkor kingdom was said to depend on the king passing part of each night with the *naga* princess, presumably in human form. The serpent imagery was adopted in Thailand after the growth of Thai hegemony from about the fifteenth century. In Thai iconography the serpent is often shown doing battle with a great bird; this is a theme found in Hinduism, where the bird is Garuda, mount of Vishnu, but it also occurs in remote regions little affected by Indian influence, such as Papua New Guinea. Presumably it represents the battle – or union – of the elements of earth and sky in the quest for fertility. The Ngaju people of Kalimantan, Borneo, speak of their descent from the hornbill Tambarinang, who also created the serpent, which it later destroyed when battling with the female hornbill.

The myth of Mother Earth and Father Sky is told in Flores, eastern Indonesia. The two were united in marriage and conjoined by a vine. When a dog severed the vine, earth and sky flew apart, ending in their present positions; one can still see the love of sky for earth when the bamboos are pressed down towards earth as the two embrace.

This beautiful puppet-head-dress from Bali, Indonesia, depicts the Hindu god Vishnu astride Garuda, the giant eagle. Puppets such as this feature in the dramatizations of myths which are widespread in Bali and Java.

THE MYTH OF HAINUWELE

From Ceram in the Moluccas comes the myth of Hainuwele. It relates how Ameta, one of the nine original families born from clusters of bananas, found a wild pig which he chased into a lake. The pig drowned and Ameta found a coconut hooked onto its tusk. He had not seen a coconut before, and that night he placed the nut in his house, covered with a cloth bearing a serpent motif. During the night he heard a voice telling him to plant the nut. He did so and within three days the nut had grown into a tree. A young girl emerged from the tree, and Ameta named her Hainuwele, literally 'frond of the cocopalm'. Hainuwele possessed an extraordinary gift: she excreted wonderful riches whenever she defecated. Being generous, she offered valuable gifts to the members of the nine families, gifts such as coral, knives, porcelain dishes and gold. The lucky recipients of the gifts, far from being grateful, were violently jealous of the girl. At the ritual Maro Dance they resolved to kill her. They began to dance around her in a circle marked on the ground, forcing her to fall into a deep hole at its centre. Having covered her with earth they continued to stamp out their dance on the ground above her body. When Ameta learned of Hainuwele's death, he cursed the people and dug up her body, cutting it into segments which he buried around the dance ground. From her limbs sprang many wonders such as yams and other foodstuffs unknown before, which became staples of the people's diet. The mother goddess was angry with the people's violent behaviour and resolved to leave them for ever. She ordered the people to walk through a gate after her to determine their future; those that managed to pass through the gate would see her again in the afterlife. Some failed to pass the threshold and turned into beasts; others walked through the gate in one direction and some in another direction. They became the ancestors of the two tribes found in western Ceram today.

Heads, Ancestors and Death

In many Southeast Asian communities, head-hunting was practised well into the twentieth century. The practice seems to have been more common among the Austronesian language groups of Indonesia, Malaysia and the Philippines, although the Naga peoples of western Burma were also fierce head-hunters.

The antiquity of head-hunting is unknown, but in Southeast Asia the head is widely believed to be the seat of man's life-force; in many countries the head is considered to be the most sacred part of the body. In head-hunting communities, the taking of a head brought renewed vigour and life-force to the victor's village and household, and thus added to the well-being and fertility of the community. Heads would be stored with the family heirlooms in the roof-space of a house – the part of the house nearest to the heavens – or above the doorway for protection. Head-hunting raids were usually accompanied by ritual feasting and dance, often of a sexual nature, highlighting the connection between the life-force of the head and the fertility of men and the soil. The heads of great warriors were the most highly prized.

MOTIF AND RITUAL

Weapons used in head-hunting raids were usually carved by the hunter with images of his immediate ancestors. These accompanied him on raids and imbued him with strength and courage. Sacred textiles were woven by the women to receive the heads, which the men bore back in triumph after a raid. Many stories concerning the brave capture of heads were recounted in these communities, and head-hunting motifs appear frequently in their wood-carvings and textiles. On the island of Sumba, eastern Indonesia, certain textiles bear the skull-tree motif in which a stylized tree bears not fruits but human heads. This relates to the once-common practice of placing heads on the branches of a tree at the village entrance, both as a warning to intruders and as protection for the villagers.

Rituals of bloodletting and sacrifice were traditionally thought to restore fertility to the earth and the community. As late as the nineteenth century, live victims were buried beneath the gateposts of palaces or other important buildings. In Burma, for example, young girls were buried underneath the gates of the palace at Mandalay. At Buwumatalao, victims were buried below the great staircase leading up the hillside to the village. It was believed that their spirit would act as protection for that building. The legacy of human sacrifice is a common one in Southeast Asia. According to oral tradition, children were once sacrificed to the spirit of the volcano as an act of propitiation.

A figurative post, sometimes known as a *hampatong*, from Borneo. Posts such as these were erected either to commemorate a successful head-hunt or as a memorial to a dead villager. The example shown here may depict a priestess and the plant forms the tree of life.

Amongst other images on this nobleman's mantle, or *hinggi*, from Sumba, Indonesia, are skull-trees displaying heads taken during war. Textiles such as this demonstrate the important role head-hunting played; warriors' spirits were believed to be enriched by the taking of an enemy's head in battle.

Effigies of ancestors in cliffs at Lemo, Torajaland, Sulawesi, Indonesia. Ancestor worship is widespread in Southeast Asia. Alongside the veneration of original ancestors is the importance placed on more recent ancestors who watch over their progeny, guiding and empowering them, particularly in battle.

ROLE OF THE ANCESTORS

The part played by the ancestors in head-hunting forays reflects the importance of the ancestors generally in many parts of Southeast Asia, particularly in the south and in those areas which most strongly reflect Chinese influence, such as Vietnam and Singapore. The ancestors are often considered to be a part of the community, to the extent that their graves stand at the centre of the village, as in Sumba, or overlooking the village, as in Torajaland, Sulawesi. Ancestors are propitiated at rituals and they take part in dance in the form of masked dancers. By treating the ancestors as being present in daily life, their descendants demonstrate a sense of continuity with the past, reinforcing their feeling of community.

RITUAL OF DEATH

Accompanying the cult of the ancestors in many island groups is a preoccupation with the paraphernalia of death. The Batak of Sumatra undertake elaborate funerary rites which involve, in some cases, the use of a *tao tao* or jointed wooden effigy representing the chief mourner of the deceased (if a man dies without leaving a son to mourn his death). The *tao tao* takes the place of his son and dances the ritual dance of mourning at his funeral. The Batak carved stone tombs in the shape of a rider on horseback, but the meaning of this imagery is unknown.

Among the Toraja people of Sulawesi, the dead are represented by clothed wooden effigies, which are placed in niches carved into the cliff overlooking the village where they lived. One has only to look upwards to see the silent ancestors gazing down at their descendants. The sense created is that the dead never leave their village, but continue to watch over their offsprings' welfare.

KELI MUTU

On the island of Flores, eastern Indonesia, the sacred volcano Keli Mutu plays a central part in the belief system surrounding the afterlife. The volcano has three craters, separated by a narrow ridge. Each crater contains a lake. The three lakes have water of three dramatically different colours, which gradually change over time but which always differ from each other. At the moment one is black, one is white and one is aquamarine. According to Flores's mythology, the lakes contain the souls of the dead: the black lake holds the souls of sinners, the white lake carries the souls of young men, virgins and the pure of heart, whilst the souls of those who die a natural death in old age dwell in the aquamarine lake. This fits well with the ancient belief, widespread in Southeast Asia, in the sacred nature of mountains, and of volcanoes in particular.

Myths of the Great Religions

Hindu myths, especially stories from the great epics *Mahabharata* and *Ramayana* are extremely popular, even though very few Southeast Asians are Hindu. Temple reliefs often take their themes from such tales.

The tale of the Churning of the Milky Ocean is related in the *Mahabharata*, and is famously depicted in relief on the walls of the great Angkor Wat in Cambodia. The story tells how the gods and demons decided to churn the Sea of Milk in order to bring various wonders to the surface. They took Mount Mandara as the churning rod and they pulled in turn on the great serpent (Ananta), who wrapped his body around the mountain and acted as the rope. Gradually wonders began to emerge, including the *Apsaras*, or heavenly maidens, and *amritsa*, or the elixir of immortality. The demons tried to grab the *amritsa* and drink it, but it was snatched from their grasp by Vishnu who had been warned just in time.

From Bali, this cloth painting which was probably used as curtains beside a temple couch, depicts the Hindu myth of the Churning of the Milky Ocean by the gods and demons at the dawn of creation, as described in the *Mahabharata*.

Southeast Asia, AD 300-1511
The map shows the location of important religious sites and temples in Southeast Asia between AD 300 and 1511.

Southeast Asia, AD 300–1511
- Towns with Inscriptions and Monumental Religious Buildings
- Temples with Inscriptions

THE MYTH OF THE HEROIC PRINCE

There are many tales of a noble prince who is courageous and pure of heart. The prince usually overcomes evil, manifested in the form of some powerful demon, and rescues a gentle and beautiful princess. Most popular of these heroes is Rama, of the Hindu myth *Ramayana*. This story is frequently retold in the form of dance and puppet theatre, and is also depicted on silver and lacquerware and on the walls of ancient temples such as Prambanan in Java.

SACRED ELEPHANTS

The white elephant is sacred in the Buddhist countries of Southeast Asia. It was a white elephant which, in a dream, entered the side of Queen Maya as she slept, resulting in the conception of her son, the Prince Sidhartha, who became the Buddha. Hindu myth refers to a white elephant as the mount of Indra, god of rain. Many temples in Burma and Thailand were built in the place where a white elephant rested on its journey, carrying religious texts or relics.

BUDDHIST MYTHS

The future Buddha, Sidhartha, was seated in deep meditation beneath the Bodhi tree. He was on the verge of Enlightenment when Mara, the Evil One, saw him and determined to prevent him from making that giant step. He sent his two scantily clad daughters to parade before the sage, but Sidhartha remained unmoved by their presence.

Enraged, Mara gathered an army of demons and vile creatures which rushed at the Holy One, brandishing horrible weapons. Again, Sidhartha sat unmoved. At this, Mara shouted at the prince, 'Who do you think you are, that *you* should attain Enlightenment?' Then Sidhartha pointed down to the earth and called upon it to bear witness that in this and in countless previous lives he had attained sufficient merit to warrant his becoming a Buddha. The earth quaked and the heavens brought forth torrential rain, as Mara and his forces fled in terror. The Holy One returned to his meditation, and that night he went on to attain supreme Enlightenment. In mainland Southeast Asia this is one of the best-loved Buddhist tales, and the depiction of the Buddha pointing to the earth is the most commonly seen representation. In some depictions one can see the earth goddess beneath the central figure, wringing out her wet hair, drenched by the rain. This scene reflects the blending of indigenous spirit cults with Buddhism.

On another occasion, the Buddha was seated in meditation when there was a storm, and the rain fell so hard that it threatened to flood the area where he sat. Seeing this, the serpent Mucalinda approached the Buddha. He lifted the Holy One up onto his coils and raised his many heads over the meditating figure to protect him from the rains. This act is also celebrated in many sculptures in which the Buddha is depicted seated in meditation beneath the cobra hoods.

Some Buddhist mythology has been absorbed into the folklore of other countries; a good example of this are the *Jataka* stories. There are 547 *Jatakas*, which recount the previous lives of Buddha, and each tale carries a clear moral message. The last 10 *Jatakas* are particularly popular, appearing on temple walls and on lacquer, silverware and woodcarvings.

The elephant is a highly regarded beast in Buddhist countries and the rare white elephant is considered to be sacred. These fabulous elephants are taken from a Burmese book of Buddhist cosmology, late 19th century.

Left: Prambanan Plain in Java, upon which stands the Loro Jonggrang complex, has the largest concentration of ancient sites in Indonesia. The Loro Jonggrang complex has three temples dedicated to the Hindu trinity, Shiva, Brahma and Vishnu. The Shiva temple is the most impressive of the three, standing at 46 m (152 ft) tall.

PRINCESS LORO JONGGRANG

This is a local story which has been attached to Prambanan, the great Javanese temple. The story is well known to the Javanese. A devout princess, Loro Jonggrang, was courted by a local prince, but as she did not wish to marry him she set him an impossible task: to build 1,000 temples in one night. The prince undertook the task, helped by a band of trolls, who could work only by night. The prince was so determined to win the princess's hand that he almost succeeded but Loro Jonggrang, seeing the danger, decided to trick him. She ordered her maids to begin pounding the rice. Since this was always done at dawn it confused the roosters, which started to crow. This frightened the trolls, who feared that they would turn to stone in the sunlight. They all fled and the prince failed in his task. Furious at the deception, he cursed the princess and she was turned into stone. Her petrified body still stands in the northern temple of Prambanan, where it is also known as a statue of the goddess Durga, fierce consort of the god Shiva.

Sacred Places

Southeast Asia's many different cultural strands find expression in a huge variety of sacred places, both ancient and modern. Hindu temples and Buddhist *stupas* are found mainly in the north but also in the Muslim south, where mosques are more usual. Chinese temples – focused on Confucianism and ancestral cults – are found in many large cities, and in Vietnam the composite Cao Dai religion has several large temples dedicated to the founders of the world's great religions: Confucius, Lao Tze, the Buddha, Moses, Jesus and Muhammad. There are Christian churches in many of the hill-tribe areas of the north and also in the Philippines, whilst shrines to the nature spirits are found throughout the region.

Balinese life is centred on the great volcano Gunung Agung. Directions are given in relation to the volcano, and Besakih, Bali's national temple, stands on its slopes; in 1963 Gunung Agung erupted at the start of Eka Desa Rudra – celebrated every 100 years on the mountain slopes. Before the start of the festival some people had questioned the accuracy of calculations which had determined the date, but the ceremony went ahead as the volcano rumbled. A few days later it erupted violently, killing over 1,000 people. Understandably, the Balinese took this eruption as a sign of the anger of the gods.

BOROBUDUR

The great *stupa* of Borobudur, in central Java, is the largest Buddhist monument in the world. Built in the eighth to ninth centuries AD, it is a square-based, round-terraced structure orientated towards the four cardinal points. It is solid, in that it has no interior, but is in fact built around a natural hill, and is made up of ten stone terraces, with a staircase in the middle of each face. The six lower levels are square in plan and the four upper terraces are round. The walls are adorned with relief carvings which relate stories from the earthly life of the Buddha and previous incarnations, particularly that of the pilgrim Sudhana. There are seated Buddha images made from stone on each level, 432 in total, which gaze impassively over the surrounding plain. The summit is marked by a circular *stupa* surrounded by smaller perforated *stupas*, each housing a Buddha image.

The monument combines the square and the circle, which both feature in Tantric meditation. The lengthy upward climb from level to level symbolizes the process of Enlightenment through initiation. It has been described as a great three-dimensional stone *mandala* or *yantra* – diagramatic meditational aids incorporating squares, circles and triangles. Some see Borobudur as a story in stone, relating the great tales of Buddhism in a highly symbolic form; it can also be seen as the ancient sacred mountain in a highly complex Buddhist context.

ANGKOR WAT

Angkor Wat, the magnificent Visnaivite temple built in Angkor, Cambodia, in the twelfth century, stands as a testament to the might and ritual status of the king. Covering an area of 1500 m x 1300 m (4922 ft x 4265 ft), it is the largest religious monument in the world. Laid out with great precision, it is aligned towards the west, the direction of the setting sun, of death and also of the god Vishnu. The central complex is made up of five towers linked by galleries. The central tower stands, mountain-like, high above the others. The towers stand on a series of terraces, each surrounded by roofed galleries decorated with relief sculpture. The reliefs around the outer gallery alone cover over 800 m (2,625 ft),

The vast Buddhist temple of Borobudur, Indonesia, resembles a mountain. According to Buddhist thought, mountain peaks are where contact with the divine truth may be had. Pilgrims to Borobudur would climb each of the eight concentric terraces that form the temple, drawing them closer to the top and to Nirvana.

MIGRATION AND SETTLEMENT IN SOUTHEAST ASIA

*c.*60,000 BC	*Homo sapiens* spreads through southeast Asia
1500–500 BC	Bronze age in northeast Thailand and Vietnam
*c.*500 BC	Trade with India begins
AD 780–850	Construction of Borobudur, Java
AD 1287	Mongol attacks on Pagan (Burma)
AD 1511	Portuguese gain control of Malacca (Malaya)
*c.*AD 1560	Spanish settle in Philippines
AD 1954	Geneva Conference: Laos, Cambodia and Vietnam granted independence
AD 1975	Whole of Vietnam united under communist rule

the longest continuous expanse of reliefs anywhere in the world. The reliefs depict historical and mythological scenes, the most famous being the Churning of the Milky Ocean (see p. 54). In this depiction, Vishnu is seated upon Mount Mandara, the churning rod at the centre of the relief, overseeing the miraculous event. The outer walls of the temple enclose a 200 m (565 ft) wide moat and ponds, corresponding to the Indian concept of the cosmos.

PAGAN

The old Burmese capital, Pagan (1044–1287), stands on a dry plain on the banks of the Irrawaddy river. Although it is now largely uninhabited, to the Burmese Pagan remains a symbol of Buddhist life and culture. Thousands of temples and pagodas, or *stupas*, still stand on the site, many crumbling and unused. All were decorated with stucco and many temple interiors were painted. Many wall-paintings depict scenes from the life of the Buddha or from the Tusita heaven, where he preached to his mother after her death. The Hindu gods Indra and Brahma often appear in this Buddhist setting, as they welcomed the Buddha's teaching into the world. The goddess Sri, who represents abundance, is also commonly found; she seems to have become fused with the indigenous goddess of rice and is invoked at rice harvests. Creatures such as the *naga*, or serpent, and the *kirtimukha*, or face of

glory, also appear in friezes around the *stupa* bodies. Guarding the city are the *Mahagiri Nats*, the brother and sister *nats* or spirits, in this case, of people who died unnatural deaths as a result of the jealousy of a king. The pair have assumed the role of guardians of a nation and as such are very powerful.

Left: Thien Mu pagoda in Vietnam is one of the country's most important cultural centres, and was the intellectual and political hub of Buddhist activity during the American engagement. Legend has it that the pagoda once contained a solid-gold Buddha on each of its seven layers, which were stolen in mysterious circumstances.

Dedicated to Vishnu, the temple of Angkor Wat, Cambodia took 30 years to complete. The five towers of which the complex consists are presently shown on the Cambodian national flag and are believed to represent the five peaks of Mount Meru, the home of the gods and the centre of the Hindu universe.

THIEN MU PAGODA

The Thien Mu pagoda in Hue, central Vietnam, is testament to the country's thousand-year contact with China. Originally founded on the banks of the Perfume River in 1601, its most famous structure is the seven-tiered pagoda, each tier of which is said to represent one of the Buddha's incarnations on earth. The pagoda was built by Lord Nguyen Hoang, who had come from Hanoi to govern the southern territories. On reaching the river he met an old woman who told him to walk eastward along the riverbank holding a lighted stick of incense. Wherever the incense stopped burning, he was told, was where he should build his new city. This he did, and founded the great city of Hue. In his gratitude he erected the Thein Mu Pagoda.

Origins

Chinese myths are as ancient as the culture itself: thousands of years in age and as varied as the people who contributed to the development of Chinese society. By the time they were put down in writing, many of them were already fragmentary and their significance half forgotten.

The origins of the Chinese civilization are to be found in the ancient cultures that arose along the fertile banks of the Yellow River in northern China where millet, hemp and mulberry trees were grown, and on the temperate flood plains of the Yangtze River in southern China that were conducive to fishing and the cultivation of rice and beans. These two societies which developed in Neolithic times were not the only ones to emerge in China but perhaps many of the enduring myths were first conceived there. Though writing was developed by the Shang Dynasty (1520–1030 BC) in North China and further refined by the later Zhou Dynasty

(1030–771 BC), myths were never used by the Chinese as the basis for great literary works, unlike in Indian or Mediterranean cultures. Although Chinese myths were passed down orally for many generations, there are only enigmatic allusions to them in a few philosophical works, and by the time any serious attempt was made to record the myths, it is clear that many writers no longer believed in them or even understood them in full.

MANY PEOPLE, MANY ORIGINS

There are numerous creation myths, but several of these are worthy of note, each perhaps

Early Chinese Agriculture
Chinese civilization was based around the fertile banks of the Yellow River in the north and the temperate flood plains of the Yangtze River further south. From around 6000 BC numerous sites in northern China reveal evidence of well-established agriculture based on the cultivation of millet. In the south, rice was the principal crop. Rice grows wild in southern China, and was soon being cultivated further to the north by the Yangtze valley farmers. In the lower Yangtze area evidence of wet-rice cultivation exists from around 5000 BC.

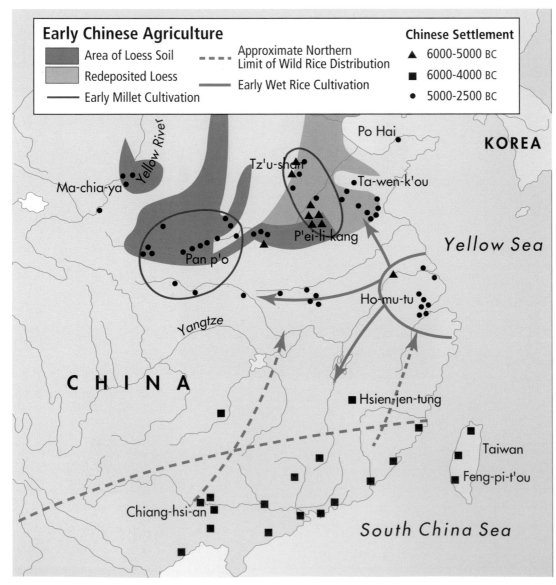

originating with one of the many different ethnic groups within ancient China. One of the best known concerns Nü Gua (Woman Gua), a strange snail-like or reptilian goddess who came to earth after it had been separated from the heavens. Some myths say that she created all things, including living beings, by going through 70 transformations. Others relate that although the natural world existed at that time, there were no humans in it. Feeling lonely, she saw a reflection of herself and took some mud and made a small copy of herself. When it came to life, she was delighted and began to create many thousands more, who populated the world while she remained as their teacher and protector.

Another well-known creation myth concerns Pan Gu (Coiled Antiquity), who was viewed as a primal deity or semi-divine human being. He was born from a primordial egg and when the egg split, the hard, opaque parts sank to become the earth while the soft, transparent parts became the heavens. Like Atlas, Pan Gu stood

up and held the heaven and earth apart until they solidified in their present state. Exhausted by his labour, Pan Gu lay down and died. Each part of his body then became something in the natural world: his breath the wind and clouds; his eyes the sun and moon; his hair the stars; his bones and teeth the rocks and minerals; and so on. The very insects crawling on his dead body became human beings.

The Yellow River in China's North Belt contributed to the founding of the first human civilizations in the area. Its fertile plains and rich alluvial soil supported a wide variety of plant and animal life, which in turn enabled people to establish thriving settlements.

YIN AND YANG

Other myths tell of the origin of the universe out of chaos, such as that of Hundun (Dense Chaos), who produced the world after he died after a misguided act of kindness, in which some fellow gods tried to carve him a face in return for his hospitality. The interplay of impersonal forces, such as the cosmic forces of the passive, dark, heavy feminine Yin and the active, sunny, light and masculine Yang, are also believed to have given rise to various elements in creation associated with their respective qualities.

Left: A seventeenth-century painting in which the yin and yang symbols are studied. The concept of yin and yang is important in Chinese philosophy: singly, yin and yang represent opposing cosmic forces such as water and fire, and male and female, but combined they form the harmonious universe.

THE SOURCES OF CHINESE MYTHOLOGY

For many centuries after the introduction of writing, the Chinese took surprisingly little interest in their heritage of myths. The first work that includes any myths, and then only in passing, is the Zhou Dynasty *Classic of Poetry,* dating from around the sixth century BC. Two later works are far more important compilations of myths, the *Classic of Mountains and Seas* (third century BC) with its numerous accounts of over 200 mythical characters, and a chapter in the *Songs of Zhu* (fourth century BC) which records the sacred history of the Zhu polity in central China. Mention should be made of a few works written with philosophical intentions, the Daoist Zhuangzi text from 340 BC and the *Confucian Classic of History,* which was composed around the same time but restricts itself to myths concerning the origins of government and kingship. Apart from what can be gleaned from the tantalizing information given by these works, it was not until the compilation of the great medieval Imperial encyclopedias that any serious attempts were made to record the wealth of Chinese myths but by then many must have been lost forever.

The Gods of the Cosmos

Unlike the mythologies of Mesopotamia, the Mediterranean and elsewhere, there is no structured pantheon of Chinese gods: literally hundreds are mentioned by name with brief myths associated with them in texts like the *Classic of Mountains and Seas*. Moreover, unlike other cultures, there are very few goddesses, perhaps reflecting the privileged status accorded to men in orthodox Chinese society.

The sun, moon and other heavenly bodies were of great significance to the ancient Chinese and their descendants and there are thus many gods associated with them. One of the best known cycles of myths concerns the divine archer, Yi – originally a stellar god. At one time there were ten suns in the sky above the earth and they all dwelt in a giant tree, Fu Sang, growing in a hot spring to the east. All of these suns were gods, the offspring of the Lord of Heaven, Di Jun, and the goddess Xi He (Breath Blend). It had been ordained by their parents that each of these suns should only shine in rotation, but the ten suns began to resent this arrangement, so they plotted how they could change things to their advantage. They decided to appear all at once on the Fu Sang tree and stay there indefinitely. This soon brought drought and misery to the inhabitants of the world and prompted Yao, the modest human ruler of earth, to entreat Di Jun to remedy the situation. Di Jun ordered his rebellious offspring to resume the old order of appearing one at a time but, now enjoying their freedom, they refused. Di Jun sent the great celestial archer Yi to frighten them and bring them back into line. However, Yi became angry with the suns and shot down nine of them from the Fu Sang tree.

Tein-Mou, the mother of lightning. There are very few goddesses in the Chinese pantheon; between them they represent aspects of the cosmos such as calendrical systems, paradisical bliss, nurture and wreakers of sacred violence in the form of plague and punishment.

MOON GODDESSES

Two goddesses are associated with the moon: Chang Xi (Constant Breath) and Chang E (Constant Sublime). Perhaps corresponding to the ten suns, Chang Xi gave birth to 12 moons, one for each month, while she dwelt in the wilderness of the west. It is said that she cared for her progeny by bathing them each night after their journey across the sky. Chang E, on the other hand, was the wife of the celestial archer Yi. While exiled in earth, Yi had been given an elixir of immortality – an amount sufficient for two people but which would cause a single person to depart for the heavens if they drank it. Chang E stole the

Left: The name of the supreme ruler of heaven varied according to the particular dynasty that was in power at the time. Yu Huang, or the Jade Emperor, as pictured here, was established as the supreme deity after an emperor of the Song dynasty (C. AD 960–1279) claimed that his instructions came directly from Yu Huang.

elixir from her husband and drank all of it herself, rising up to the moon immediately. Though her wish of immortality had been granted, she was turned into a toad with only a hare pounding a mortar and an old man chopping at a cassia tree for company – images no doubt inspired by the crater patterns on the moon's surface, not unlike the Western 'man in the moon'.

STELLAR DEITIES

Finally, one well-loved myth may be introduced here, the unhappy love of Zhi Nü, the Weaver Maid, and Oxherd, both of whom are stellar deities. Zhi Nü was the daughter of a sky god and dwelt in the Milky Way, weaving robes of cloud. Lonely, she fell in love with Oxherd and married him but, as she began to neglect her appointed task of weaving, she was punished. The sky god separated her from her husband, placing them at opposite ends of the Milky Way, only allowing them to meet once a year on the seventh day of the seventh month – a myth based on observations of the movement of the two stars, Vega and Aquila, associated with each of the lovers.

The goddess of spring is shown here with a number of her companions. The existence of a nurturing, creative goddess such as this may hark back to a time in when women played the central role in early Chinese society.

GENDER IN CHINESE MYTHS

Many scholars believe that the earliest human societies worldwide were matriarchal in organization, but with the advent of the Bronze and Iron Ages, if not earlier, a shift seems to have occurred in many cultures to a patriarchal system that down-graded the female status. There are a few goddesses mentioned in Chinese mythology that hint at the former importance of women in society, such as Nü Gua, Chang Xi and Chang E, but the later male writers who compiled collections of myths seem to have done their best to undervalue the significance of the female in tune with the orthodox Confucian views of society. Nevertheless, apart from those mentioned above, other goddesses were important in ancient times as founders of early dynasties. Jian Di (Bamboo-slip Maiden) is mentioned as the progenitor of the first person of the Shang Dynasty, while Jiang the Originator was said to have been the mother of the first of the Zhou people. Like Hariti and other goddesses in India, disease and disaster is sometimes attributed to a female source in Chinese myth in the form of the Queen Mother of the West, a fierce and cruel being with tangled hair, tiger's fangs and a panther's tail, who was accompanied by other ferocious felines.

Catastrophe Myths

It is inevitable that a vast country like China should repeatedly witness natural disaster – droughts in the north and floods in the south. As with many other mythologies throughout the world, the Chinese have a range of catastrophe myths that tell of these events, perhaps distant memories of particularly devastating occasions when human survival itself may have seemed in doubt.

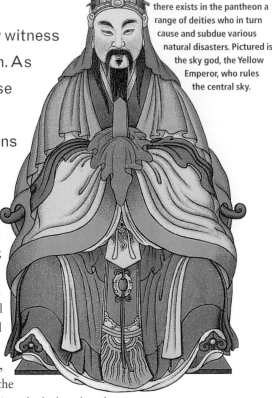

China is frequently at the mercy of the elements, and so there exists in the pantheon a range of deities who in turn cause and subdue various natural disasters. Pictured is the sky god, the Yellow Emperor, who rules the central sky.

Four important flood myths, sometimes interlinked, have been preserved in Chinese mythology, perhaps concerning different floods in various parts of the country or else the same event recorded by different people. One brief account relates how the world was saved from a combination of overwhelming floods and raging fires by the goddess Nü Gua. One of her mythological roles is that of the divine smith and as such she forged a cosmic, five-coloured jewel and restored the sky; she then cut the legs off a giant turtle and placed them at the four corners of the earth to prop up the sky; and finally she dammed the waters of the deluge with burnt reeds.

FIRE AND WATER

A second story tells of an ugly, misshapen god, Gong Gong (Work), sometimes seen as the water god. Dissatisfied with his lesser status in the natural order of things, he challenged the fire god, the benevolent and wise ruler of the universe, and churned up the waters of the earth so that they crashed against the bulwarks of the sky. This resulted in catastrophic floods throughout the world until he was subdued by the sky god. In some versions of this myth, this was the flood that Nü Gua averted.

This wall painting is from the inside of Shuimou Lou, or Water Goddess House, built in 1563, in the Junci Temple, Shanxi province.

A third myth speaks of a time when there was a world-threatening deluge. In order to deal with the situation, the gods nominated Gun (Giant Fish) to control the water. Two assistants were appointed to help him in this task: a divine owl which knew the secrets of the sky and a divine turtle which knew the secrets of the waters, but their help is insufficient. Gun has to steal a magical 'breathing-earth' (a special type of earth of divine origin that had vitality) from the supreme god – probably the sky god – to control the flood waters and repair the world. Gun is punished for his theft and condemned to die on a mountain from exposure, but once dead his body does not rot and his son, Yu, is born from it. Gun did not stay dead, for he was later miraculously revived and transformed into a yellow bear, perhaps the totem of the people from whom this myth originated.

Another important myth is known from two variants, involving the semi-divine Yu (Reptile Footprint), the son of Gun. In one version, Yu – unlike his father – was allowed to use the 'breathing earth' to repair the world and quell the floods; another version relates how Yu was commanded to deal with a devastating flood that had left everybody throughout China homeless by digging drainage channels.

The range of myths with water and floods as their central theme reflects the central role that rivers have played in people's lives throughout the history of Chinese civilization. Here, a Guilin peasant fishes on the placid Li River in the Guangxi province in southwest China.

DROUGHT

Myths which deal with droughts are perhaps linked to the North China environment. One myth relates that when a drought afflicted the Shang lands for seven years, one of the mythical Shang kings, Tang, volunteered himself instead of the human sacrifices his people wanted to offer to the gods. Just as he was about to be burnt alive, a great downpour of rain fell in response to his selflessness. Other myths involve various female deities. Nü Ba causes a drought at the behest of her father, Great God Yellow, when he is fighting the war god, Jest Much; the corpse goddess Nü Chou sacrifices herself in expiation for human wrong-doing and causes the rain to fall.

STRANGE LANDS

The myth of Yu and the flood, already mentioned, also involves his journey through a mythological world called the Nine Provinces. As he travelled, controlling the flood, Yu listed the names and customs of the various people he encountered. These perhaps are distant echoes of actual tribes living in the regions surrounding the heartland of central China. Though there were some great Chinese travellers, in many ways the Chinese have been very insular throughout their history, regarding foreigners with deep suspicion, but at the same time enjoying fantastic traveller's tales. To be sure, the information brought back by Chinese officials and pilgrims journeying abroad was accurate and a useful source of information to the state, but descriptions of many imaginary lands and people are also found throughout popular Chinese literature. Invariably, these strange tribes have some kind of peculiarity – some have only one arm or one leg, while others have two heads or holes in their chests. Still others are feathered and hatched from eggs like birds. Some of these accounts probably refer to garbled or misunderstood descriptions of the tribal people who still live in China today, such as the Miao-Yao, the Tai, the Tibeto-Burman Qiang or else the ancestors of the Huns, the Xiong-nu.

Cultural Gods and Heroes

In contrast to many other mythologies, Chinese mythology is quite rich in accounts of beings who introduced cultural innovations into the world. These beings are often ambivalent in nature, either being semi-divine humans or gods. This ambivalence between the divine and the mortal realms was to become characteristic of later Chinese concepts of sages and emperors. Whether they were deified humans or gods demoted to human status, the mythical ancestors of various dynasties and tribes in China are said to have played a key role in introducing cultural innovations into the world.

A series of ten divine or semi-divine kings are associated with the earliest phase of the Zhou people, according to their accounts. The first of these was Fu Xi, sometimes associated with the goddess Nü Gua, who appears in a number of myths but who is particularly associated with the invention of writing. According to this myth, Fu Xi was the ruler of the universe and observed the markings and patterns found on various creatures. Based on his observations, he devised the Eight Trigrams that form the basis of the divinatory manual, the *Yi-jing* (this is also known as *I Ching*, and means *Book of Changes*). He is credited with the invention of music and also, after watching spiders at work, made fishing nets for humans. His successor, Shen Nung, was the farmer god who invented the plough and taught humans the art of agriculture. He also discovered the medicinal qualities of plants by pounding them with his whip and evaluating them by their smell and taste.

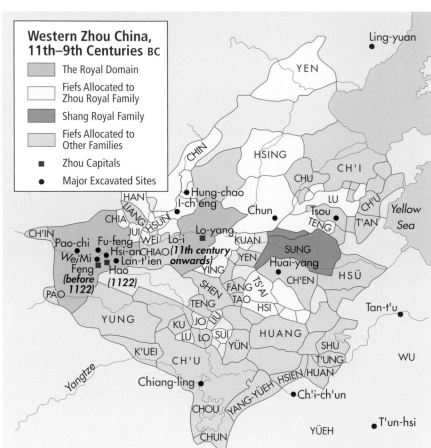

Western Zhou China, 11th–9th Centuries BC

- The Royal Domain
- Fiefs Allocated to Zhou Royal Family
- Shang Royal Family
- Fiefs Allocated to Other Families
- ■ Zhou Capitals
- ● Major Excavated Sites

MEDICINE AND CULTIVATION

A later divine king was the famous Yellow Emperor, Huang Di, who had over 20 sons, each of whom went on to sire important families of the Zhou dynasty. To him goes the credit for many innovations, such as the invention of the fire drill, by means of which he was able to clear forests and drive away wild animals using fire. Though he sometimes was viewed as a warrior god – during his contentions with Gong Gong, for example – he was generally seen as peace-loving and had an ancient connection with healing; the *Yellow Emperor's Classic of Medicine*, which still forms the basis of traditional Chinese medical treatment, was attributed to him. One of

Western Zhou China
In the early 11th century BC the Shang dynasty was supplanted by the Zhou. The early Zhou dominions comprised of a large number of domains. Some remained under court control, others were granted as fiefs to supporters and servants of the Zhou in a sort of feudal tenure. Much of the area shown on the map was still occupied by peoples of different ethnic origins who were gradually assimilated by the Zhou and their beliefs.

Here, women pray at the tomb of Fu Xi, Henan Province. The creator-god Fu Xi is believed to be the first sovereign, as well as being a cultural hero responsible for teaching humans how to rear domesticated animals and to play musical instruments. He also invented the first Chinese script.

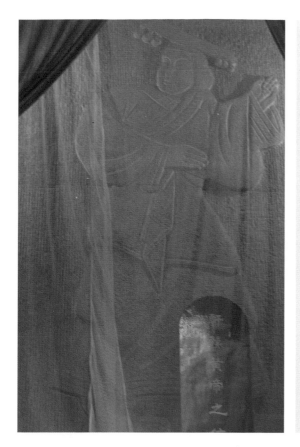

c. 5000–4500 BC	Hemudu Culture in south-east China
c. 4800–2500 BC	Yangshao Culture on Yellow River
c. 3800–2700 BC	Hongshan Culture in north-east China
c. 2000–1600 BC	Xia Dynasty; introduction of bronze working
c. 1600–1050 BC	Shang Dynasty; shaft graves at Anyang & earliest Chinese script
c. 1050–771 BC	Western Zhou Dynasty
770–221 BC	Eastern Zhou
551 BC	Birth of Confucius
c. 400 BC	Lifetime of Zhuang Zi
221–207 BC	Qin Dynasty; Shi Huang Di unifies China & constructs the Great Wall
206 BC–AD 220	Han Dynasty

Huang Di's successors was Ku, who was married to the goddess Jiang Yuan. She became pregnant after accidentally treading on Ku's footprint and gave birth to Hou Ji, the millet lord. Thinking the child was unlucky, she tried on three occasions to rid herself of him by having him exposed to the elements, but each time he was saved. When the child grew up he imparted to humans the knowledge of millet and bean cultivation and of how to use these in thanksgiving sacrifices.

YAO

Hou Ji was followed by the celebrated Yao, who was to be adopted in later times by the Confucianists as the archetypal model of the sage – intelligent, accomplished, courteous and reverent. It was during his reign that the world was devastated by the catastrophic series of floods which required the intervention of Gun, as already mentioned. Yao wanted to appoint his chief minister as his successor but the latter refused so Yao turned his attention to Shun (Hibiscus), the low-class son of Gu Sou (Blind Man). Shun had come to the attention of Yao because Gu Sou was an obstinate reprobate who tried to kill Shun on three occasions. Shun had miraculously escaped each time. Through his filial piety, a virtue always esteemed by the Chinese, Shun eventually reforms his father's behaviour. After having put Shun through various tests, Yao retired and passed the throne to Shun. Shun, in his turn, was eventually replaced by Yu, the son of Gun.

Left: An image of the Yellow Emperor, Huang Di, at his shrine in Shanxi. Huang Di is one of the mythical divine kings who are believed to have ruled in ancient times. As a warlike figure, he is also thought to have introduced the chariot wheel, armour, compass and ships to the people.

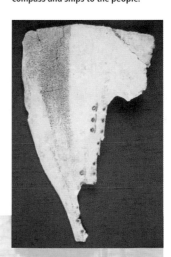

DIVINATION

The Chinese have always been fascinated by divination and in ancient times several techniques were of central importance to the rulers of the early dynasties. The Shang people made use of turtle shells and the shoulder blades of sheep and oxen in their divination. The question being put to the gods was written on the bone and heat was then applied with a heated rod to form cracks. It was from the pattern of these cracks that the will of the gods and the outcome of the question were known. The tens of thousands of these inscribed pieces of bone and shell which have been found date from the middle of the second millennium BC, providing the earliest examples of Chinese writing. Apart from these scratched questions, little else has survived from that period and scholars believe that writing was restricted to a handful of imperial diviners. An entirely different form of divination is associated with the agrarian Zhou dynasty, the use of the *Book of Changes (Yi-jing)* based on the 64 combinations that may be derived from the basic set of eight trigrams – patterns formed from three solid and broken lines. Though the Shang method of divination fell into disuse with the Shang people's demise, the *Yi-jing* is still widely consulted for divinatory purposes by many people.

Cosmogonies and Genealogies

Tibet's mythology stems from ancient pre-Buddhist beliefs, Indo-Tibetan Buddhism and Bon religion. Some myths are exclusive to one of these traditions but others are shared, although they are interpreted differently. Although many things, such as rituals or marriage, are regarded as having mythical origins, here the focus is on cosmogonies and genealogies.

Cosmogonic myths (myths of creation) are of three major types: cosmic egg, primordial being and conflict of forces. In variant accounts the cosmic egg constitutes the intermediary agency in the cosmogonic process, which starts with a void or with light; the egg then generates the master of the universe, the world, or a demiurgic being. One myth has six tortoise eggs giving rise to social classes and animals, and another eulogizes the world tree with six birds with eggs.

In the mythology concerning the primordial beings, the first being is a female serpent deity (*klu-mo*); in another it is a deity called Luminous God ('Od-gsal-lha).

One myth about the conflicting principles sees non-existence yielding a man as the master

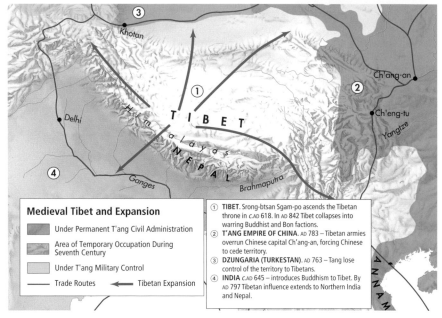

Medieval Tibet and Expansion

- Under Permanent T'ang Civil Administration
- Area of Temporary Occupation During Seventh Century
- Under T'ang Military Control
- Trade Routes ← Tibetan Expansion

① **TIBET**. Srong-btsan Sgam-po ascends the Tibetan throne in C.AD 618. In AD 842 Tibet collapses into warring Buddhist and Bon factions.
② **T'ANG EMPIRE OF CHINA**. AD 783 – Tibetan armies overrun Chinese capital Ch'ang-an, forcing Chinese to cede territory.
③ **DZUNGARIA (TURKESTAN)**. AD 763 – Tang lose control of the territory to Tibetans.
④ **INDIA** C.AD 645 – introduces Buddhism to Tibet. By AD 797 Tibetan influence extends to Northern India and Nepal.

of existence (*srid-pa'i bdag-po*). Then, amidst an absence of seasons, or day and night, white and black dots of light beget a black man (Black Misery, *Myal ba nag po*) who controls non-existence and dispenses calamities, and a white man (Radiance,'*Od zer ldan*) who controls the seasons and teaches noble things.

GENEALOGIES

The prevailing genealogy of the Tibetan people focuses on a monkey. In all Tibetan accounts a pre-Buddhist theme, possibly derived from China's borderlands, is clad in Buddhist guises. A monkey and an ogress (*sring-mo*) beget six monkeys. The father abandons the offspring in a forest but returns three years later to find 500 starving monkeys living there. He procures and seeds five kinds of grain, and the monkeys gradually metamorphose into humans.

In some variants of this myth, the union between the monkey and the ogress begets only

Medieval Tibet and Expansion
Many myths relating to the origin of the world and the Tibetan people feature the Yarlung Valley as the source of civilization. By the sixth century AD the Yarlung Kings had unified central Tibet, and the country emerged as a regional power. The Tibetan state collapsed in 842AD after the country disintegrated into warring principalities, divided between the Buddhist and Bon faiths.

Above: A form of Avalokiteshvara, the Merciful Lord, holding a rosary in one of his many arms. Avalokiteshvara is a *bodhisattva*, a Buddhist concept, who taught the way of wisdom and compassion. He is also venerated as the patron of Tibet.

Left: gNya-khri btsan-po is the legendary first king of Tibet, here depicted on a wall *tanak* (temple-hanging) in Tibet, dating from the eighteenth-century.

one son, who copulates with forest monkeys and produces 400 offspring. In others, the son is called Ye-smon rgyal-po, or is described as having a red flat face and as consuming flesh and blood. In Buddhist sources the first monkey is either guided by Avalokiteshvara to procreate, so that eventually Tibet may become a Buddhist land, or the monkey and the ogress actually embody Avalokiteshvara and Tara, two Buddhist deities.

There is one genealogy that stems from a succession of demoniac beings dominating Tibet, and another from the primordial man, Ye-smon rgyal-po, and a series of divine beings. The first humans in Tibet are also traced to King Riapati, who escaped from India during the war between the five Pandavas and the Kauravas, narrated in the Indian epic, the *Mahabharata*.

THE ANCIENT KINGS

The ancient kings of Tibet were seen as divine scions. Accounts about them are complex but the core theme is clear. The first king, gNya'-khri btsan-po, descended from the heavenly heights onto the sacred mountain of Yar-lha-sham-po and was greeted by men identified as chieftains or shepherds.

At the end of their earthly rule, the first seven kings returned to heaven by means of a sky-cord (*dmu*) or as rainbows. The eighth king, Dri-gum, challenged his chief groom to a duel and was killed after agreeing to fight without his magic spear and sword. Dri-gum and his successors were entombed at 'Phyong-rgyas near Yar-lung.

In one story, the royal dynasty is traced to the youngest of nine brothers called *the'u-brang*, originally divine beings but later perceived as

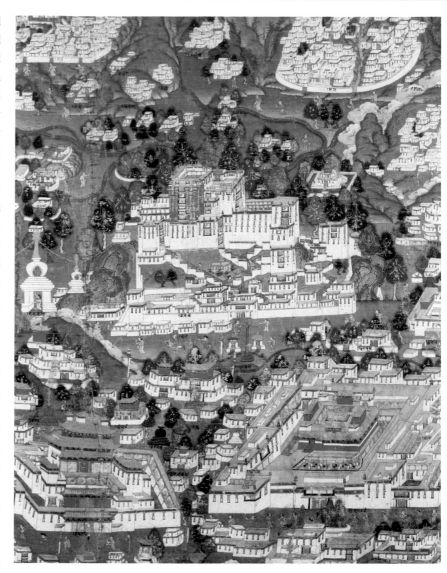

demons. Some Buddhist accounts trace the royal lineage to the descendants of the Indian kings Prasenajit or Bimbisara, who were the Buddha's contemporaries. One Bon-po account traces the first Tibetan king to the son of Pandu of the *Mahabharata*, which pre-dates the Buddha.

The Potala (shown here on a nineteenth-century temple hanging) is the monastery-palace residence of the Dalai Lama, Tibet's spiritual leader. Each successive Dalai Lama is believed to be a reincarnation of the *bodhisattva* Avalokiteshvara.

HISTORICAL OVERVIEW

The ancient Yarlung (Yar-klungs) Dynasty of 42 kings is divided into 32 prehistoric kings headed by gNya-khri btsan-po ('Od-lde spu-rgyal), and 10 historic kings from Srong-btsan sgam-po (died AD 649) to gLang dar-ma (murdered in AD 842). Thereafter the dynasty collapsed, the empire declined and the political stability fluctuated until the seventeenth century when the rule was taken over by the fifth Dalai Lama. The fourteenth Dalai Lama is Tibet's current spiritual leader.

Prior to the introduction of Buddhism during Srong-btsan sgam-po's time, the ancient beliefs focused on the sacral character of the kings, the cult of sacred mountains and local gods, and the ritualized guidance of the departed to the land of bliss; the ritual experts were called Bon-pos. As Buddhism gained power over the years, protagonists of the ancient beliefs counteracted and an open conflict developed. Buddhism triumphed but its opponents reasserted their distinctive identity as Bon-pos and their religion as Bon. While teaching higher doctrines and practices, Buddhism compromisingly absorbed many ancient gods and myths. The Bon-pos overtly affirmed their links with pre-Buddhist beliefs but at the same time recast their doctrines and practices through interaction with Buddhism.

The Land of Demons, Gods and Buddhas

In antiquity, numerous demons (*bdud*) and gods (*lha*) held sway over Tibet, the Land of Snows, and the religious imagination of its people. With the spread of Buddhism, their power was restrained, but they still survive and to this day function in folk beliefs or as guardian deities assimilated into both Buddhist and Bon-po pantheons.

A depiction of Buddhas with numerous wrathful guardian deities and spirits. Many of Tibet's countless indigenous gods and demons were assimilated into the Buddhist pantheon after the religion was established in the country.

Indigenous demons and gods embodied mysterious powers which they frequently discharged to inflict harm on the land and its people whenever their dispositions or habitats were disturbed by unsuitable human activities, such as digging or pollution. Whether demons or gods, they all were prone to do harm, although the gods were more benign. There were countless numbers of them, but since many among them had certain common features, they were eventually classified into generic groups as recorded in Buddhist and Bon-po sources. The bTsan (powerful ones) and gNyan (fierce ones) dwelled in the space above, the Sa-bdag (soil lords) in the soil of different places and the Klu (half-human and half-snake bodies) in lakes and underground waters. There were mountain deities that actually were mountains or deities within them; some mountains were worshipped as ancestral mountains or as the sacred spots where it was believed that ancestral deities descended to earth.

Minor spirits, such as 'Dre (evil goblins), were mostly harmful and caused all kinds of diseases and afflictions. Other deities, as their names indicate, controlled specific places or activities: rock god (*brag-lha*); path god (*lam-lha*); house god (*khyim-lha*); hearth god (*thab-*

lha); and trade god (*tshong-lha*). According to ancient beliefs, each Tibetan has a soul (*bla*), his double, and five guardian deities located in different parts of the body.

THE BUDDHIST PANTHEON

The pantheon includes a large group of transcendent Buddhas and *bodhisattvas* of the Mahayana tradition; wrathful and peaceful Buddha manifestations derived from the Buddhist tantras, such as Hevajra and Kalacakra embraced by their consorts; various grades of protective deities; and minor deities adopted from the mythology of ancient India, such as the world guardians (Lokapala), the eight planets (Graha) and the eight serpent deities (Naga). Numerous temples and monasteries house images and paintings of their favoured deities, who are worshipped with offerings and through simple or elaborate rituals.

Avalokiteshvara is venerated by all Tibetans as Tibet's patron deity, and the apotheosized Indian master Padmasambhava is venerated as

the subduer of pre-Buddhist deities into guardianship of Buddhism. The bodily remains of great teachers and important incarnate lamas (*sprul-sku*) are often enshrined in images or reliquaries (*stupa*) kept in temples.

THE BON RELIGION

Allegedly, the Bon faith originated in sTag-gzigs (in Central Asia). Its founder, gShen-rab, enlightened from birth but living as a prince with many wives, children and disciples, travelled magically to many regions, including Tibet, to spread the Bon teachings and ritualized forms of exorcism and propitiation. Late in his life he retired to a hermitage. gShen-rab is the central personality and mythic authority for the Bon scriptures and teachings. Long before the advent of Buddhism, and before it spread into Tibet, Bon flourished in Zhang-zhung (west Tibet around Kailasa), which remained its stronghold until becoming absorbed into the Tibetan empire in the seventh century. The Bon-pos have their own pantheon similar to the Buddhist pantheon, but deities are portrayed in distinctive iconic forms and veiled in different mythic guises.

Placating the local divinities on a Tibetan house-top. The act of honouring the spirits goes back to the earliest times in Tibet when people would seek the spirits' help before the start of a journey, for instance, as it was believed that they dwelt everywhere on earth, in places such as the mountains.

Left: Before Buddhism came to Tibet, a shamanistic culture dominated the country. In the eighth century AD the Indian mystic, Padmasambhava, brought Buddhism to Tibet, and subdued the local gods and spirits, formerly feared and venerated by the shamanic tradition, with his magical powers.

HIGH RELIGION AND ANCIENT BELIEFS

Although Buddhist and Bon religions teach higher doctrines and practices for gaining wisdom and enlightenment, they also have extensive mythologies about their higher deities that are relevant to religious practices, and about indigenous deities of folk beliefs. Legends and myths are recorded in religious texts, chronicles, histories and guides to pilgrimage destinations. Most mythic literature is religious in character but Tibet also has a voluminous epic about the adventures of the legendary king Ge-sar, ballads, tales and ghost stories. Biographies, predominantly of renowned teachers and sages, are also permeated with wondrous events and feats. There are colourful festivals linked with mythic stories and events. Every year temples and monasteries hold ritual dances performed by people dressed as various deities. Since ancient times the Tibetans have practised divination, and used spirit mediums and astrology derived from India and China. They also use charm boxes and amulets, hang prayer flags on trees and houses and burn juniper branches to gratify local deities. The awesome and mysterious powers are placated with propitiations and ransoms, or with special rites devised to appease or, if necessary, destroy them. Ancient folklore and beliefs coexist harmoniously with the lofty teachings of Buddhist and Bon religions.

The Origins of the Korean People

Around 1000 BC, Bronze-Age warriors of the Tungusic racial group invaded Manchuria and the Korean peninsula, mixing with its original inhabitants, and forming the basis for the modern Korean people. The Tungus are one of the three major ethnic groups in northern and central Asia, today inhabiting most of contemporary Manchuria and south-eastern Siberia. As a result of the invasion, the Korean people are racially and culturally distinct from the Chinese people, although they have also absorbed considerable elements from the Chinese Confucian élite culture, and use substantial amounts of Chinese vocabulary in their language.

Korean mythology, however, reflects the country's primordial, non-Chinese culture in the structure of its tales, and the characters and motifs which appear in them. Moreover, these tales bear strong similarities to the mythology of the modern Tungusic peoples of Northeast Asia. Korean myths are of two types: foundation myths about the origin of the people and state, and creation myths about the origin of the world. Because the foundation myths are so ancient, most of them are known only from older Korean or Chinese records and not from narration by contemporary storytellers. Creation myths, however, are known as vocal narratives which are sung by modern shamans as part of their ritual repertoire.

KOREAN MYTHOLOGY

The earliest record of a Korean myth, the Myth of Chumong, is found in the first-century Chinese miscellany the *Lun-hêng*. The most important extant early compilation of Korean myths and legends is the *Samguk yusa* (Memorabilia of the Three Kingdoms), compiled by the Buddhist monk Iryon (1206–89), who is arguably the first Korean folklorist. The *Samguk yusa* contains the classic version of the Myth of Tan'gun (see p. 72) and is the fullest record of the myths that describe the origin of the Korean people, their states and their clans. Other sources include the *sillok* ('veritable records') of the reigns of the kings of the Choson Dynasty (1392–1910). None of these records, however, contain examples of creation myths, myths which recount the origin of the world and its features. Creation myths are found only in the *muga*, songs of the shaman or *mudang*. Creation myths were not recorded until the early part of

the twentieth century when the *muga* were collected by folklorists, most notably Son Chint'ae (*c.* 1900–50), one of a number of influential intellectuals abducted and presumably executed by the North Koreans when they invaded South Korea in 1950.

Early States
In around 1000 BC Bronze Age Tungusic warriors invaded Manchuria and the Korean peninsula and formed the basis of the Korean civilization. By AD 300 the states of Koguryo, Paekche and Shilla had been established.

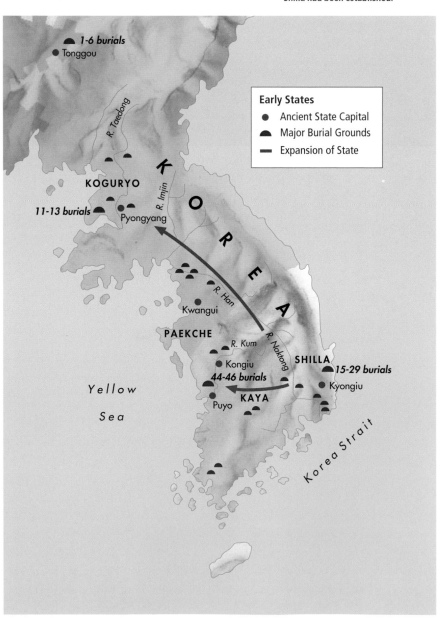

Early States
● Ancient State Capital
▲ Major Burial Grounds
— Expansion of State

MYTH AND RITUAL

Because most foundation myths now exist only as textual records, there are no longer any traditional rituals associated with them. One exception, however, is the Myth of the Three Clan Ancestors of Cheju Island, where separate rituals are addressed to them both as clan ancestors and as the ancestors of the island (see Box, p. 75). With the growth of twentieth-century Korean nationalism, foundation myths have inspired the creation of new religions, most notably Tan'gun-gyo and Taejong-gyo, which worship Tan'gun as the founder of the Korean nation. For the followers of these religions, *Kaech'on-jol* (Heavenly Foundation Day) held on 3 October is the most important day in the calendar as it is believed that this was either the day on which Tan'gun was born or on which he ascended to the Korean throne.

Heavenly Foundation Day also has been celebrated as a national holiday without any religious rituals. As creation myths are an integral part of the songs performed by a shaman, they are not heard separately but only during the performance of a *kut* or shamanistic rite. For example, the rite devoted to the guardian spirit of the home begins with the singing of the story of the creation of Heaven and Earth before proceeding to a description of earthly history.

Artefacts such as these lacquered baskets found in a tomb in the Chinese colony of Lelang (*c.* 330 BC– AD 300) in North Korea point to a period in Korea's history when there was some Chinese influence. Although Korea's mythology and cultural origins are different to China's, the languages of the two countries retain many similarities.

A festival is held in Seoul in 1995 to celebrate 50 years of liberation from Japanese imperialist colonial rule. Under Japanese rule, Korea was subjected to social oppression, which included banning the use of the Korean language and the study of Korean history.

CREATION MYTHS

The narrative of one *muga* creation myth is composed of five scenes which describe in turn the creation of the world, the origin of fire and water, the origin of human beings, the origin of time and the origin of the social and physical ills of the world. Miruk, who is the protagonist of the narrative, in the first three scenes creates the world and its inhabitants. However, he is not all-powerful as he must address questions in turn to Grasshopper, Frog and Mouse. The trickster Sokka then appears and challenges Miruk to a series of trials. Even though Miruk wins each trial, he finally gives charge of the world to Sokka with the result that not only is time created, but all the ills and woes of life begin. Although Miruk (Maitreya) and Sokka (Sakyamuni) are names for figures in Buddhism, they have undoubtedly been substituted for the original names which are now impossible to reconstruct. The creation narrative in the *muga* uses a structural pattern and narrative characters similar to the bird tales told by Palaeo-Siberian (the original inhabitants of Siberia) and North American peoples.

The Myth of Tan'gun

The Myth of Tan'gun is the foundation myth of the state of Ancient Choson, the first Korean kingdom, which occupied substantial areas of southern Manchuria and northern Korea, and which was the principal non-Chinese state on China's northern boundary during the last half of the first millennium BC. The kingdom of Wiman Choson, a successor state, was destroyed by the Han dynasty (206 BC–AD 220) in 108 BC and the territory of the state was absorbed into its empire. The earliest text of the Myth of Tan'gun is contained in the *Samguk yusa* from the thirteenth century AD. As it exists, the text of the myth shows redactions to explain the transfer of dynastic power from the Tan'gun dynasty to the Kija Dynasty, and to explain the origin of the cult of the Mountain God, San-shin, in which Tan'gun is identified as the mountain god.

The Myth of Tan'gun is composed of four dramatic scenes. In the first scene, Hwanung, the secondary son of the Ruler of Heaven, discusses with his father Hwanin, his desire to descend to earth to rule over mankind. The father then selects from amongst three mountains an appropriate place for his son to descend to earth, chooses the retinue which is to accompany his son and bestows on him the three *Ch'on puin*, or heavenly seals, which symbolize his authority to rule. The second scene describes how Hwanung then descends to earth on top of a mountain by a great tree, how he creates a sacred city as the centre from which he will rule mankind and how he brings civilization and culture to mankind. The third scene narrates the story of a bear and a tiger which desire to become human and are subjected by Hwanung to a trial which must be successfully completed before their wish can be granted. The bear succeeds, and is transformed into a woman; the tiger fails the test and is not transformed into a human form. In the final scene, the transformed Bear Woman pleads with the son of the Ruler of Heaven to marry her. He does so, thus symbolically uniting Heaven and Earth. Their offspring is Tan'gun, lord of the sandalwood tree, who then establishes the royal family and creates the first Korean state. After ruling for 1,500 years, Tan'gun transforms himself into the mountain god.

Ch'amsong-dan altar, said to have been erected by Tan'gun, mythical founder of the Korean nation. Foundation myths, in particular that of Tan'gun, have inspired new religions and rituals to be created in Korea, for example Tan'gun-gyo and Taejong-gyo in which Tan'gun is venerated as Korea's founder.

FUNCTION OF THE MYTH

Assuming the pre-existence of humanity and the world, the Myth of Tan'gun has three functions – to describe how civilization was brought to this world, to narrate how the first Korean royal house was established and to describe how the first Korean kingdom was created. Hwanung, the hero of the tale, is a culture-bearer who brings agriculture, medicine, law and moral knowledge to mankind. He is also a secondary son, with no right to succeed to his father's kingship, so he has no alternative but to leave his natal place and fulfil his destiny by founding a new nation. This is done with his father's blessing.

The Myth of Tan'gun, however, not only describes the gift of civilization but also explains social change – how a tribal confederation became transformed into a kingdom. The contest between the tiger and the bear symbolizes the change from a society in which the headship rotated amongst the heads of various clans (Heaven, bear and tiger) to one in which the rulership became fixed in one family, symbolizing the union of Heaven and Earth. Kingship is depicted as a divine gift. Finally, the myth describes the origin of the cult of San-shin, the mountain god, ruler of all the mountains of Korea and everything which lives on them and which is buried under them.

A typical image of the mountain god, seated upon a tiger under a tree. Images of the mountain god are very common and found in shrines all over Korea. The mountain god is said to rule all the mountains of Korea, and is often identified with Tan'gun who is believed to have transformed into the mountain god after his death.

THEMES

The Myth of Tan'gun is unusual in having two motifs portraying a cosmic axis – the sacred tree and the sacred mountain – through which mankind communicates with the heavenly realm. The ruler is thus depicted as a shaman linking his people to the celestial world. A key motif in the Myth of Tan'gun is the descent of the god (Hwanung) as the founding ancestor. In this myth, the founding ancestor is also portrayed as the culture hero who brings to the people their distinctive culture.

The ancestral descent motif is found in other Korean foundation myths, such as the Myth of Suro, which describes the first paramount ruler of a group of city-states called the Kaya Federation. As with the Myth of Tan'gun, the Myth of Suro depicts a pre-existing human society into which the god descends. In this case, the first paramount ruler, Suro, and the first rulers of the other city-states descend to earth in a box on a purple cord. This golden box contains six eggs from which each of the boy rulers is born. Once born, these boy rulers then set about establishing a state and founding a royal house. Divine descent of an ancestral spirit is the most common motif for the ancestors of royal and non-royal clans in south-eastern Korea. As in the Myth of Suro, this motif is often combined with the oviparous birth motif. In one case, the ancestor of the royal Sok clan of the kingdom of Silla is found in a box (which has the same function as a container of the eggs) which is brought to the shores of Korea in a boat.

The Myth of Chumong

The Myth of Chumong relates the story of the founder of the Kingdom of Koguryo. Following the collapse of Chinese rule in southern Manchuria in the third century AD, the Koguryo, whose royal house claimed descent from the Puyo royal house of central Manchuria and who appear to have migrated to the south-eastern mountains of Manchuria, created a powerful state in northeast Asia which was in turn responsible for the collapse of the Sui Dynasty (581–618 AD) and nearly toppled the T'ang Dynasty (618–907 AD). Koguryo was finally vanquished by the combined forces of T'ang China and the southeastern Korean kingdom of Silla around 670 AD, but re-emerged at the end of the century as Parhae (Bohai); this dynasty survived until it was destroyed by the Khitan in 926 AD. The territory of Koguryo and Parhae included most of Manchuria, the northern half of Korea and large swathes of land north of modern Vladivostok.

The narrative of the Myth of Chumong as recorded in the *Samguk yusa* is composed of four scenes. The first describes how a local ruler discovers that the daughter of Habaek, the river spirit, has been raped by a sky spirit. In the second scene, after Habaek has given birth to a giant egg, the king tries to destroy the egg by putting it in front of various animals but they refuse to step on it or break it. In his first act of heroism, Chumong, the hero, breaks out of the egg and rapidly learns the art of warfare. In the third scene, after having been warned by his mother of the jealousy of his half-brothers, the king's natural sons, Chumong tricks the king and flees. When he and his friends reach a river, he cries out to the river animals that he is a son of the sky and a grandson of the river. Instantly, terrapin and fish form a bridge for him to cross

The Myth of Chumong
The story of the foundation of the state of Koryugo forms the basis of the Myth of Chumong. The map shows the areas where the state of Koryugo emerged, its unification with Paekche and Silla, under the Silla State, and the re-emergence of of the Koguryan ruling clan in the state of the Parhae.

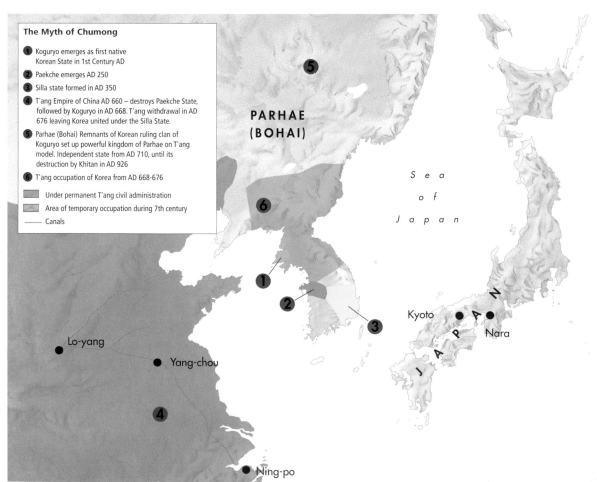

The Myth of Chumong

① Koguryo emerges as first native Korean State in 1st Century AD

② Paekche emerges AD 250

③ Silla state formed in AD 350

④ T'ang Empire of China AD 660 – destroys Paekche State, followed by Koguryo in AD 668. T'ang withdrawal in AD 676 leaving Korea united under the Silla State.

⑤ Parhae (Bohai) Remnants of Korean ruling clan of Koguryo set up powerful kingdom of Parhae on T'ang model. Independent state from AD 710, until its destruction by Khitan in AD 926

⑥ T'ang occupation of Korea from AD 668-676

▨ Under permanent T'ang civil administration

▨ Area of temporary occupation during 7th century

— Canals

PARHAE
(BOHAI)

Sea
of
Japan

Lo-yang

Yang-chou

Kyoto

Nara

JAPAN

Ning-po

over. In the final scene, once he is over the river, he establishes a royal residence, creates a royal surname and founds a new nation.

NARRATIVE STRUCTURE

The four-fold narrative structure of the Myth of Chumong is the basic pattern for the majority of foundation myths told by the Tungusic peoples of northeast Asia, whether they had achieved state-level societies, such as the Manchus, or lived in tribal communities. Unlike the Tan'gun myth, the Myth of Chumong is concerned only with the establishment of the state and not with the origin of the people's culture, and Chumong, as the founding ancestor, is not simultaneously depicted as a culture hero. In the Myth of Chumong, although the oviparous birth motif is used, as in the Myth of Suro (see box p.73), no motifs depicting the divine descent of a ruler or a clan ancestor are used. Instead it introduces the motif of the acclamation of the ruler by nature, symbolized by the respect of the animals for the giant egg, and the animals' response to Chumong's cry for help. The acclamation of nature motif is found commonly in many Korean foundation myths.

The Myth of Chumong differs from heroic tales told in Europe and the lands surrounding the Mediterranean, which use the motif of the flight of a hero from his place of birth. In those western Eurasian myths, although the hero flees, he eventually returns home to claim his patrimony, while in the myths of the Chumong type, the hero flees, creates his own new kingdom and never returns home.

THE MYTH OF THE THREE CLAN ANCESTORS

Unique amongst the myths of Korea, the Myth of the Three Clan Ancestors of Cheju Island differs from peninsular foundation myths both in terms of its narrative structure and motifs. It is first recorded in the fifteenth-century AD work the *Koryo-sa* (*History of Koryo*). The mythic narrative is composed of five scenes which recount how the primal ancestors of the three clans of Yang, Ko and Pu emerged simultaneously, but in ranked order, from holes in the ground. The ancestors then established a hunting and gathering society, and one day while hunting on the shore, the three ancestors discovered a floating box which contained three princesses, the primordial Five Grains, calves and ponies. The ancestors married the three princesses, and then the male and female ancestors went on to establish an agricultural society. The narrative of this complex myth

describes the origin of the three principal clans of Cheju, the origin of the island's primal culture and the change from a hunting and gathering society to an agrarian society. Although there are no parallels to this myth in Korea, the narrative structure parallels the foundation myths of tribes in Melanesia, Micronesia and Taiwan. In those cases, the myth describes the emergence of the primal ancestors from the ground or from a rock, the marriage of the male and female ancestors, and the establishment of society, paralleling scenes from the Cheju myth. Two interesting aspects of the Myth of the Three Clan Ancestors are the description of joint rather than single clan origins and the high status accorded to the princesses who, as culture-bearers, make a new type of society together with their husbands.

Above: Stone monument giving the history of Won'gak temple. The stele rests on a granite tortoise.

Japanese Origins

Modern Japan exhibits a high degree of cultural homogeneity which derives from the centralization of power throughout most of the past 1500 years. However, the picture that is now emerging through recent archaeological and genetic research tells a different story. It now seems that Japanese society in prehistoric times was characterized by a surprising diversity that has contributed silently to the later culture.

Although Japanese history has only been documented since the sixth century AD, with the introduction of a writing system from China, the hundreds of islands that make up Japan have been inhabited for thousands of years. Traces of the earliest population date back at least 50,000 years; these migrants must have made their way there overland, as Japan was linked to mainland Sakahalia in the north and to Korea in the south until about 12,000 years ago.

THE PREHISTORIC ORIGINS OF JAPANESE SOCIETY

Around 12,000 years ago, a very long-lived, late-Palaeolithic and Neolithic culture emerged in Japan, known as the Jomon ('cord-marked') Culture, after its characteristic pottery. To the Jomon people goes the credit of having made the oldest pottery known to archaeologists; later samples of their work dating from 6000 BC have been discovered as far afield as Fiji. Though formerly dismissed as primitive hunter-gatherers, it is now known from archaeological sites such as Sannai Maruyama that the Jomon people developed a highly sophisticated society with large sedentary populations supported by marine products and some agriculture. The Jomon also engaged in long-distance trade both within Japan and overseas. Especially noteworthy are the high-quality ceramic figurines, known as *haniwa*, that provide valuable data concerning the appearance, dress and accoutrements of the Jomon people.

THE YAYOI

The vibrant Jomon culture was transformed rapidly with the arrival of newcomers from the Asian mainland around 300 BC; they established the so-called Yayoi Culture by introducing innovations, such as iron-working, advanced rice cultivation and a more complex social organization. Although their numbers were probably small initially, it was these people who

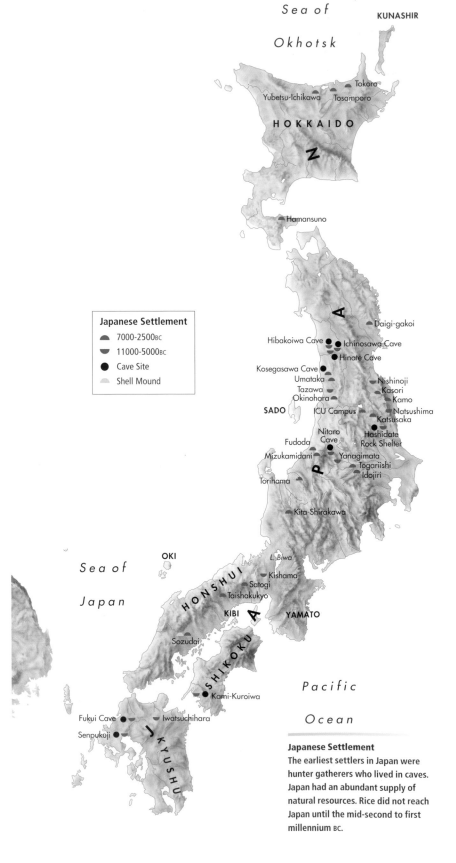

Japanese Settlement
The earliest settlers in Japan were hunter gatherers who lived in caves. Japan had an abundant supply of natural resources. Rice did not reach Japan until the mid-second to first millennium BC.

were to form the basis of much of the present-day Japanese population. At first they occupied the southern area of Japan, encroaching from the island of Kyushu and making their way northwards over the ensuing centuries until the emergence of the first large unified state of Yamato, which governed all of southern and central Japan (AD 300–710). This ancestry was corroborated in the 1990s by DNA studies of the Japanese population which indicate the presence of two main racial groups in Japan: the predominant one which has links to the Koreans and, surprisingly, the Tibetans, and which radiates out from south and central Japan; and the other, more ancient group, whose traces are strongest among the inhabitants of northern Japan and other outlying regions, including

various small islands dotted all around the coast of the Japanese main islands, both to the north and to the south (including Okinawa).

Whether the Jomon people themselves had discovered rice cultivation independently, as now seems likely, it was the Yayoi people who introduced other new techniques and materials – such as the use of bronze and iron – which revolutionized life in Japan. It was during the Yayoi period that a gradual consolidation of tribes took place, leading to the establishment of ever-larger political units that culminated in the Yamato state, which is believed to have been centred on central western Honshu. The power of its rulers, who claimed descent from the sun goddess Amaterasu, is demonstrated by the series of great *kofun* or tumuli that were constructed as graves for their dead, such as the enormous keyhole-shaped tomb on the Osaka plain dating from the early fifth century AD. Large portions of surviving Japanese mythology are intimately connected with the Yamato state, as the state derived its legitimacy from a belief that its rulers descended from the dominant gods and goddesses of mythology.

Ceramic figures, such as this *haniwa* of a warrior, provide an invaluable source of information about the Jomon Culture which produced them. The large number of such figures, as well as other Jomon artefacts that have been found, point towards an advanced culture.

Left: Rice planting as depicted on woodblock print. Rice cultivation was introduced to Japan by the Yayoi Culture, and since has become central to the Japanese way of life. Today cultivation of rice continues much as it has done over the centuries, with farmers working on their own paddies.

SANNAI MARUYAMA

Though little known outside of Japan, the extraordinary archaeological find of a large Neolithic Jomon coastal settlement at Sannai Maruyama in northern Japan in 1992 has revolutionized our understanding of Jomon culture. Covering over 35 hectares, the site contains the remains of over 500 wooden buildings that functioned as dwellings, storage facilities and religious structures, forming a complex, planned settlement that was inhabited continuously between 3500 BC and 2000 BC. Based on the evidence of these buildings, it is believed that the average population of the settlement was in the region of 600; their culture represents a sedentary transitional phase between a purely hunter-gatherer society and an agrarian one. In addition, an enormous amount of pottery, ceramic figurines, stoneware, bone tools and wooden artefacts bear witness to the unexpectedly high level of sophistication of life here. Other materials found on the site, such as obsidian, asphalt and jade, suggest that the Sannai Maruyama inhabitants engaged in long-distance trade over hundreds of kilometres. Though largely marine-based, there is also clear evidence that the villagers' diet included the products of early agriculture, such as walnuts; and there is unprecedented evidence for rice cultivation, as well as indirect traces of alcohol production from fermented elderberries.

The Creation

Overall, Japanese mythology is rather monolithic in nature, lacking the richness of Mediterranean mythology, since it largely represents the ideology of the early centralized state of Yamato, although traces of rival or earlier beliefs may still be discerned. Therefore, the account of the creation of Japan and the events that immediately ensued seem to be unconnected with later sun goddess beliefs.

The Japanese creation myth as recounted in the *Kojiki* and *Nihon-shoki* does not tell of a creation *ex nihilo* but speaks of an unbounded, amorphous, chaotic mass. This existed for many aeons until an area of light and transparency arose within it – Takama-gahara, the High Plains of Heaven. Three primordial gods materialized there, followed by a further two lesser gods who in turn engendered five generations of gods culminating in the primal couple, Izanagi and Izanami. Little is related about the divine beings who existed before Izanagi and Izanami beyond their names; these may just be remembered remnants of earlier, lost mythologies.

IZANAGI AND IZANAMI

Izanagi and Izanami were charged by the other divinities with bringing creation to completion and to this end they stood on the Floating Bridge of Heaven and together stirred the oily brine below with a jewelled spear. Drops falling from this spear fell to produce the first island where they took up residence. There they were joined together as the first couple, but their offspring was the deformed Hiruko (Leach Child), whom they abandoned in a reed boat. In consultation with the other gods, it was found that this child had been deformed since, during their courtship ritual, the goddess Izanami had spoken first to Izanagi. When they re-enacted their marriage in the correct manner with precedence being given to the god Izanagi, Izanami was able to give birth successfully to a large number of offspring. This episode, it is believed by scholars, was included through Chinese patriarchal influences.

The Wedded Rocks at Futami in Ise Bay, which are believed to have sheltered Japan's primal couple, Izanagi and Izanami. The rock on the left of the picture has a Shinto *torii* or gateway on top of it, indicating that it is a shrine, and the rocks are connected by ropes which are symbolic of the unity between male and female.

Among Izanami's children were the other islands that make up the Japanese archipelago, as well as the gods of the mountains, the plains, wind, trees and so on. While giving birth to her last child, Kagutsuchi, the god of fire, Izanami was so badly burnt that she died. As she lay dying, she gave birth to more divine beings, such as the god and goddess of metals and of earth, and finally Mizuhame-no-mikoto, the goddess of death. However, like the Greek Orpheus, Izanagi decided to seek out Izanami in the underworld of Yomi, the abode of darkness, and bring her back with him. Izanami said she would discuss this with the gods of the underworld, but as she disappeared into the gloom, she warned him not to look at her. Wanting to see her again, Izanagi broke off a tooth from his hair-comb and lit it as a torch. He was horrified to see that Izanami was now a maggot-infested, rotting corpse and tried to flee from her. Angered by his act, Izanami sent a horde of demon hags and warriors to pursue him. When he reached the entrance back into the realm of the living, Izanagi found three peaches which he threw at his pursuers and managed to turn them back. At this point, Izanami, now transformed into a demon, gave chase herself. Before she could reach him, Izanagi barred her way with a great boulder with which he sealed the entrance to the underworld. Here they confronted each other a final time and dissolved their marriage vows.

An example of Chinese script. It was not until the introduction of writing by the Chinese in c. 600 AD that any Japanese mythology was written down. The two sources of myths, the Kojiki and the Nihon-shoki, were written in order to establish the divine descent of Japan's imperial family; the myths included in these records are likely to have been clan myths, as myths from rival claimants would have been excluded, explaining why there are few recurring figures or themes in the mythology.

EARLY LITERARY SOURCES

The first historical mention of Japan is found in AD 57 in the annals of the Chinese Han Dynasty in which Japan is described as a land divided into about a hundred tribal communities, lacking any central government. Later Chinese sources indicate that there was a degree of consolidation into larger political units in the following centuries, but the details are sparse. The Japanese themselves did not begin to keep accounts of their society until around AD 600 when a writing system was introduced, along with many other cultural innovations from China. The two main sources for Japanese mythology and early history are the *Kojiki* and the *Nihon-shoki*. The *Kojiki* or *Record of Ancient Matters* was compiled in Chinese in AD 712, but was based on earlier oral traditions. It relates various myths, legends and historical events concerning the imperial court from the age of the gods down to the time of the Empress Suiko (AD 593–628). The slightly later but longer *Nihon-shoki* or *Chronicles of Japan*, written in AD 720 betrays a greater influence of Chinese cultural attitudes, but covers broadly similar ground to the *Kojiki* although it relates events until AD 697. The theology of Shinto developed mainly through an interpretation of the mythology recorded in both the *Kojiki* and the *Nihon-shoki*.

Amaterasu

The sun goddess Amaterasu is of central significance to Japanese mythology, since the imperial family claimed descent from her until Japan's defeat in the Second World War. She is also unusual as a paramount female deity in a land where male pre-eminence has always been the norm, although there are stories connected with her that hint at male dissatisfaction with this state of affairs.

After his return from the underworld, Yomi (see p. 79), Izanagi bathed to purify himself ritually from the pollution (*imi*) of contact with the dead. He then gave birth to a further sequence of gods and goddesses, culminating in the sun goddess Amaterasu, the moon god Tsuki-yomi and the storm god Susa-no-o. Before withdrawing from the world, Izanagi entrusted Amaterasu with rulership of the High Plains of Heaven, Tsuki-yomi with the realm of the night and Susa-no-o with the ocean. Susa-no-o was dissatisfied with his assignment and jealous of the ascendancy of his sister Amaterasu and so was banished by Izanagi.

A nineteenth-century Japanese woodblock print of the sun goddess Amaterasu emerging from the earth. Ameterasu is regarded as Japan's protector, as are the emperors' ancestors. She is worshipped at Ise, the most important shrine in Japan.

DIVINE CONFLICT

Before he was due to leave, Susa-no-o arranged to meet with Amaterasu to say farewell but suspecting that he was plotting to overthrow her, Amaterasu armed herself and confronted her brother. He then challenged her to a contest which would prove who was really the mightiest – whoever could give birth to male gods would be the winner. Amaterasu took Susa-no-o's sword and broke it into three pieces from which she produced three goddesses, while Susa-no-o took her sacred *magatama* beads and produced five male gods. Amaterasu claimed she had won since his gods had come from *her* beads but Susa-no-o refused to accept defeat.

Susa-no-o then embarked on a series of foul outrages against Amaterasu, such as destroying the heavenly rice fields, defecating in the ritual hall of offerings and casting a skinned pony through the roof of the sacred weaving hall. This last act resulted in the death of one of Amaterasu's maidens after a shuttle pierced her genitals (according to some accounts it was Amaterasu herself who was injured). Either way, she was so terrified that she hid and sealed herself inside a cave. The entire human world and the heavens were cast into darkness and misery ensued. In vain the gods tried to entice her out with various stratagems but they all failed. Then the beautiful goddess of the dawn, Ama-no-uzume, who was the archetypal *miko* or shamaness, stood on an upturned rice barrel and began a sacred erotic dance baring her body. Hearing the excitement of the gods and their praises for Ama-no-uzume, Amaterasu peeped out of a crack and asked what was happening. She was told that the gods were rejoicing at the sight of a goddess more beautiful than herself. In disbelief, she opened the crack wider and as she gazed out, one of the gods held up a sacred mirror and Amaterasu saw her own reflection in it.

While Amaterasu was entranced with her own reflection, one of the other gods seized her by the hand and pulled her out of the cave while others barred the cave with a magic rope. Upon this Amaterasu returned to the heavens where all the deities agreed to punish Susa-no-o with banishment from the heavens, fined him and cut off his beard and nails.

This account of divine rivalry may preserve distant memories of ancient power struggles in Japanese society between rival patriarchal and matriarchal systems of rule, although the outcome is uncharacteristic in world mythology inasmuch as it was the female, the goddess Amaterasu, who eventually emerged the winner rather than the male.

The importance of goddesses in Japanese mythology indicates that a matriarchal society may have characterized early Japanese civilization. Pictured is an incarnation of Seiyro gorgen from the thirteenth-century Kamakura period.

MATRIARCHY IN JAPAN

Various aspects of Japanese mythology and legendary records hint at a matriarchal system in early Japanese society. From the first to the third centuries AD, the Chinese noted that a number of the tribal groups were ruled by women. Whether this was a feature of Yayoi society or a vestige of the Jomon culture is uncertain, but it seems that women during this period sometimes combined leadership with religious duties of a shamanic nature. Queen Himiko is the first named ruler in Japan, of a state called Yamatai, known from Chinese historical records; she lived probably in the third century AD. Her name has intriguing implications for the myth of Amaterasu as it means 'sun daughter'. She is said to have been unmarried and some legends say she had a younger brother who brutally murdered her by thrusting a loom shuttle thrust into her vagina. Traces of the ancient shamanic role of women in Japan still persist in the shape of the *miko* priestess attendants found attached to Shinto shrines and the *itako* women who act as mediums between the living and the dead at various cultic centres, such as that at Mount Osorezan in northeastern Japan.

The Izumo Cycle

A small but important group of myths known as the Izumo Cycle, concerning the activities of Susa-no-o and of his descendants, seems to preserve traditions from another tribal group unconnected with those who transmitted the main Amaterasu myths. In contrast to the Amaterasu cult associated with eastern central Japan, the Izumo Cycle is intimately linked with the coastal regions of western central Japan.

Izumo was the place where the god Susa-no-o lived after he was exiled from heaven. After he had killed an eight-headed monster, Susa-no-o married the princess Kusanada-hime and settled in Izumo. Myths tell of his expanding the territory and developing the region for human habitation.

SUSA-NO-O AND OKUNINUSHI

One of Susa-no-o's descendants, possibly his grandson, the god Okuninushi, also features in many of these myths as a bringer of civilization and culture. Okuninushi had numerous older brothers who wanted to marry Ya-gami-hime of neighbouring Inaba. Going to visit her, they meet a furless rabbit which they torment. Okuninushi kindly helps the rabbit regain its fur and in return is told that he will be the successful suitor of the princess while his brothers will become his retainers. This all comes true but his brothers soon become dissatisfied and quarrelsome. Though they manage to kill him twice, each time he comes back to life and he eventually decides to visit Yomi, the underworld, for advice about ridding himself of his troublesome brothers.

SUSERI-HIME

In the underworld, Okuninushi meets Suseri-hime, the daughter of Susa-no-o, and marries her without Susa-no-o's consent. Angered by this, Susa-no-o tries to kill Okuninushi three times but on each occasion Okuninushi is saved by a magic scarf given to him by Suseri-hime. Eventually the pair decide to escape to the land of the living while stealing a bow, sword and *koto* that belongs to Susa-no-o. Although Susa-no-o eventually catches up with him, he forgives Okuninushi out of admiration for his cunning and bravery. It is at this point that Okuninushi – Great Ruler of the Land – is given his name, foretelling his conquest of the whole country.

Japanese Shrines

○ Shrines

— Provincial Borders

▨ Provincial Governerships (*Shugo*), Held by the Hojo Family in 1330

Japanese Shrines
Virtually any feature in the Japanese landscape can act as a cultic centre. These centres are often marked by a small shrine that acts as a gateway between the sacred and profane. Two of the most important shrines are at Izumo and Ise. Ise in central Japan is connected with the sun goddess Amaterasu and Toyouke-no-okami, the god of rice and harvests. Izumo in western Japan is associated with Amaterasu's rival brother Susa-no-o and his grandson, Okuninushi. The map marks both shrines and the old provinces.

After his return from Yomi, the underworld, Okuninushi followed Susa-no-o's advice and hunted down his older brothers, eventually killing them all and becoming sole ruler of Izumo. Abandoning Ya-gami-hime, his earlier wife, he then went to live with Suseri-hime in a palace he built at Uga-no-yama in Izumo. After his return to Izumo, Okuninushi takes on many of the characteristics of a cultural hero, which perhaps reflects the early colonization and cultivation of that area. Much of the country was still wild and unformed at that time, and there was nothing but dense forests, swamps, ferocious animals and evil spirits. Mindful of Susa-no-o's prediction, Okuninushi began to clear the regions near Izumo with a magical weapon called Yachihoko, 'Eight Thousand Spears'. With it he walked tirelessly around the land and killed many demons, making places safe for people to live in.

A number of lesser myths are associated with Okuninushi, such as his encounter with the tiny, lame god Ku-e-hiko. Okuninushi adopts Ku-e-hiko as his brother and they become inseparable companions, continuing the work of clearing the land of evil and opening it up for habitation. Together they introduced silk worms and weaving, new crops and many medicinal herbs.

The trouble-maker, Susa-no-o. Susa-no-o was the son of Izanagi, one of Japan's primal figures. It is believed he was born from his father's nose while Izanagi was bathing to rid himself of the pollution of the underworld.

The Shinto ceremonial gate, or *torii*, at Ise, leading the way to the shrine. Shrines are usually dedicated to one particular *kami*, although it may host smaller shrines dedicated to other *kami* that local people should worship. The shrine at Ise is dedicated to Amaterasu, the sun goddess and Toyuke-no-okami, goddess of cereals.

CULTIC CENTRES

The divine forces of nature or *kami* are thought to reside in rivers, rocks, mountains and trees, meaning that almost any feature in the Japanese landscape may act as a cultic centre. These may be marked by a small shrine for offerings or else just a *torii*, a stylized gateway demarking the boundary between the profane and the sacred. Other places in Japan are home to much larger shrines which act as national cultic centres though their importance has waned since the political demotion of Shinto in the wake of the Second World War. Most notable are the ancient great shrines at Ise and Izumo, both of which have their origins in prehistoric times. Ise in central Japan is connected with the sun goddess, Amaterasu, and Toyouke-no-okami, the god of rice and harvests. Until the fifteenth century the Ise shrine was considered to be so sacred that only members of the imperial family were allowed to visit it. The shrine at Izumo in western Japan is associated with Amaterasu's rival brother, Susa-no-o and his grandson, Okuninushi. A characteristic feature of all Shinto shrines is the complete absence of any form of iconographic depiction of the divinities enshrined in them. Instead, certain sacred objects are displayed on a simple altar such as a mirror, a sword or the comma-shaped *magatama* beads.

The Foundation of the Yamato State

Until very recently, the imperial family of Japan claimed an unbroken line of succession dating back to the mythical age when gods and goddesses roamed the earth. The myths relating the transition between the age of gods and humans hint at prehistoric events involving various rival tribes.

A fter Okuninushi and his descendants had made the land prosperous, their rule grew lax and evil gods once again made life unpleasant for the people. Amaterasu, who had wanted to extend her rule to that region for her descendants, decided to take advantage of the situation. After several failed attempts, she sent two trusted and brave gods, Futsunushi-no-mikoto and Takemikazuchi-no-mikoto, to tell Okuninushi to surrender the land to her. They sat on the tips of their upturned swords embedded in the crest of a wave in the sea off Inasa in Izumo and then delivered their ultimatum to him. Okuninushi was most impressed by this and after consulting with his son, he eventually conceded – on condition that a place should be reserved for him among the gods worshipped in Izumo.

THE ORIGINS OF THE JAPANESE STATE

After this, Okuninushi's clan was supplanted by Amaterasu's descendants. Her grandson Ninigi-no-mikoto came to earth carrying the three symbols of sovereignty: the mirror, the *magatama* beads and a sword. He had two sons – Ho-teri (Fireshine) and Ho-ori (Fireshade). Ho-teri, the eldest, fished using a hook, while Ho-ori was a hunter. Ho-ori was dissatisfied and suggested changing their occupations, which they did but Ho-ori was unsuccessful, even losing the fishing hook. When Ho-teri asked him to return it, he offered several substitutes but Ho-teri insisted on having the original. Ho-ori drifted far out to sea in shame and eventually reached the palace of the sea god, Watatsumi-no-kami, who not only

Yamato State

The Yamato state was founded in the early centuries AD and quickly expanded. Large tombs or mound cemeteries were built for its leaders, and over 100,000 can be found throughout Japan. The Yamato state eventually united the Islands although there was considerable resistance in Hokkaido in the north, as evidenced by the hillforts that were built by the Ainu who lived there.

The Yamato State
- ◖ Major Burial Grounds
- ▬ Mound Cemetery
- ■ Early Yamato Palace (AD600-650)
- ⊞ Ainu Hillfort (Chashi)
- ▬ Expansion of State

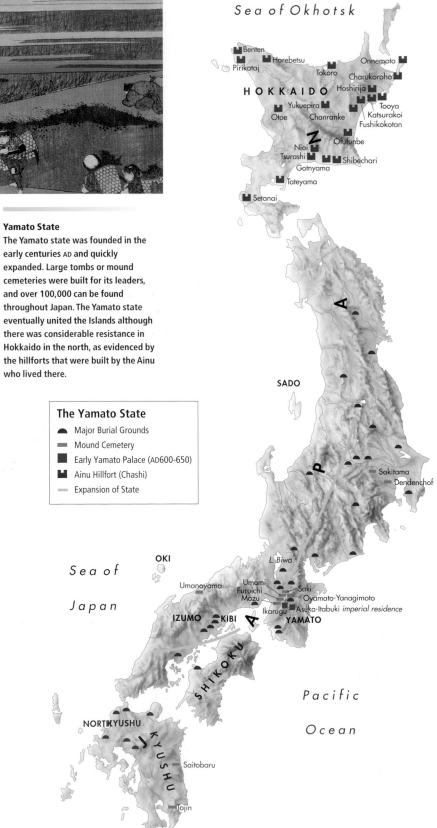

JAPANESE CULTURE AND STATE

50,000 BC	Earliest human occupation of Japan
12,000 BC	Proto-Jomon period
c.9,000 BC	Jomon Culture manufactures first pottery known worldwide
c.3000 BC	Jomon pottery finds in Vanuatu
c.3500–2000 BC	Occupation of Sannai Maruyama settlement
c.300 BC–AD 300	Yayoi Culture in Kyushu and southern Honshu
AD 57	King Nu mentioned in Chinese annals
AD 239	Queen Himiko sends embassy to China
c.AD 300	Construction of the great tumuli in central Japan
AD 552–710	Late Yamato period
AD 712	Compilation of *Kojiki*
AD 720	Compilation of *Nihon-shoki*

A musical performance at the Shinto shrine at Ise. Festivals are held at Shinto shrines each year; at a *matsuri* or festival, the resident *kami* is carried through the streets of the town; other festivals are dedicated to fertility and purification, long-standing elements of ancient Shinto. All festivals serve to bring a community together.

retrieved the fish hook but also gave Ho-ori his daughter in marriage. When the time came for Ho-ori to return home, Watatsumi-no-kami gave him two jewels, one to make the sea rise and one to make it fall. When Ho-ori got home, he returned the hook to Ho-teri who, nevertheless, continued to complain, so Ho-ori then threw one jewel in the sea causing a flood. In terror, Ho-teri begged for forgiveness so Ho-ori threw the other jewel into the sea and it receded. In gratitude, Ho-teri swore that he would serve his younger brother in perpetuity.

The grandson of Ho-ori was Jimmu, the legendary first emperor of Japan. Jimmu seems to have set out from the island of Kyushu in the south in search of new lands to rule. When he and his followers reached the Kumano area, near present-day Osaka, a local deity put them in a deep sleep. However, Amaterasu appeared in a dream to one of Jimmu's retainers and revealed to him the existence of a magical sword. Awakening, the retainer found the sword and roused Jimmu. They then continued their march of conquest led by a giant crow. When Jimmu finally reached east central Japan, he married a local princess and founded the Yamato state. This state formed the precursor of the historic ruling hegemony.

SHINTO

Shinto is the indigenous religion which flourished in Japan before the introduction of Buddhism in the sixth century AD and has remained a vital force in all aspects of Japanese culture up to the present day. Shinto means 'the way of the gods' and as its name suggests, its central concern is the *kami*, a term that includes both the gods of myth and also the numinous powers inherent in all natural things. Though lacking a sophisticated metaphysical theology or philosophy, the aim of Shinto is to regulate human activities within the natural world in a harmonious manner. Unlike in Buddhism, the concept of ritual pollution (*imi*) – anything that disturbed the intrinsic harmony of nature – played an important role in Shinto in the past, and various methods of ritual cleansing were prescribed. Though early Shinto sacred places are natural features such as waterfalls, tall trees or imposing rocks, shrines were also built and maintained by families of ritual specialists who emerged by the sixth century AD; to a certain extent these places are still recognized as being sacred today. Although every town and village has its own Shinto shrine, those at Ise and Izumo are of national importance. Also associated with these shrines are colourful annual festivals (*matsuri*) in which the resident *kami* is paraded in a portable shrine.

Foundation of Greek Mythology

The stories of Greek mythology forged the common Greek identity and have been a key influence in the development of Western European art, music and literature since their debut in the eighth century BC, via the epic poems of Homer. These poems mark the introduction of the Olympians; divinities with human flaws, who presided over the fortunes of mortal men.

In about 1900 BC, Greek-speaking peoples from the Caucasus migrated to the southern European peninsula known today as Greece (or Hellas). There they found a land of valleys and mountains, one of which, Mount Olympus, was so high (2917 m/9750 ft) it seemed to touch the heavens – it therefore had to be the home of the gods. Since this peninsula was bounded on three sides by seas (the Ionian, Aegean and Mediterranean), the newcomers naturally looked for trade to neighbouring maritime peoples, as far afield as Asia Minor (eastern Turkey) and North Africa. From these ancient cultures, the Greeks took music, poetry and names of exotic deities, like Hera and Athena; they also took their alphabet, probably from the Phoenicians (southern Syria).

ORIGINS OF GREEK CULTURE

As city-states, like Athens and Sparta, grew and colonization developed, by the fifth century BC hundreds of Greek communities had arisen, lying round the shores of the Mediterranean ('like frogs about a pond', as Plato put it), the Black Sea, southern Italy and North Africa. Small wonder that the Greek imagination

Ruben's (1577–1640) famous depiction of Diana and her nymphs, surprised by satyrs. The rich mythology of Ancient Greece has inspired countless generations from Roman times to the present day: dramatists, philosophers and artists have all been influenced in some way by this fabulous heritage.

Sites of Oracles
In ancient Greece the oracles were priests or priestesses who acted as mediums, conveying divine advice or prophecy to those seeking advice. Apollo, the primary oracular divinity among the Greeks, had oracles at Delphi, Claros and Didyma. Zeus had oracles at Dodona, Olympia, and the Oasis of Siwa in Libya. The healing god at Asklepios had them at Epidaurus and Rome.

peopled the seas with monsters, giants and sirens whom heroes such as Jason, Odysseus, Theseus and Heracles had to overcome.

LASTING MYTHS

In 338 BC Greece fell to Philip II of Macedonia and soon became part of Alexander the Great's empire. But less than two centuries later, in 146 BC, the expanding power of Rome saw Greece reduced to a Roman province. That was not the end of Greek culture however, for many of its gods and heroes were adapted by the Romans under different names (Zeus became Jupiter, Aphrodite – Venus, and Heracles – Hercules).

Greek belief in gods reached its peak between 800 BC and 330 BC. Every city of the ancient Greek world possessed its own myths, heroes and festivals. Despite the diversity, there were rites and festivals, such as the Olympic Games, in which all freeborn Greeks could take part. In addition, the great epic poems of Homer, Hesiod and other bards were known throughout the Greek world. Universal themes – of the Argonauts journeying in search of the Golden Fleece, of the 12 tests of Heracles, of Odysseus's adventures on his return from the Trojan War – helped form a sense of nationhood.

ORAL CULTURE

The myths were passed on and adapted by the storytelling tradition, from mouth to mouth. So the pantheon of gods was well established by the time the myths were written down in about 750 BC. When Athens became the centre of Greek intellectual life in the fifth century BC, well over half the adult male population of the city could read and write. The level of literacy in all Greek cities of this period was higher than at any period of Western culture before the twentieth century. It is also important to bear in mind two factors. First, for many purposes Greek culture remained an oral culture. Second, literacy did not extend to slaves (who in Athens accounted for a third of the population) or women. Ancient Greece was *not* a true democracy and the *polis* was essentially a male association. True, the most powerful figures seen in Greek tragedy are women, and several goddesses (Hera, Athene, Demeter) show more independence than their sisters in other pantheons, but only men were supposedly endowed with reason (*logos*) and were therefore the decision-makers in the real society.

The Parthenon on the Acropolis at Athens was completed between 447 and 438 BC. In Greek culture, temples served as a public site for the expression of mythological and real events, such as battles, in friezes and sculpture. The Parthenon was dedicated to Athens' patron goddess, Athene.

The symposion, or 'drinking together', was an important social event for Greek men. At the symposion, and as well as drinking and socializing, the men would enjoy the recital of poetry with mythological themes. The cups used on these occasions frequently depicted mythical or Dionysiac scenes. This vessel shows athletes drinking and playing the flute.

FESTIVAL AND SYMPOSION

Ancient Greeks listened to myths on two major occasions, one private – the symposion – and the other public – the festival. Much of what we know about myths comes from inscriptions and decorations on pottery used in the male drinking group or symposion. Early on, poetry, music and pottery had been specially created for this group, which met in a private men's room or andron. The men would lie on couches beside low tables with snacks and jugs of wine poured by young male or female slaves, who might also provide music, dancing and sex. The only women permitted in the symposion were the *hetairai* or 'call girls'.

The festivals were great public spectacles where as many as 16,000 men could enjoy a mixture of public feasting, religious sacrifice and theatre. Poetry recitals based on myths were given by professional performers called *rhapsodes*.

Myth in Society

For many centuries, Western civilization looked upon mythology as Greek mythology. Only when collections of myths were made from other cultures was it clear how unique Greek myths were and what an important role they played. Over the centuries, faith in the absolute veracity of the old tales gradually faded. But Greeks had never wholly believed in their own interpretations of nature and history, so there is no standard version of a myth or epic.

In the traditional early versions of Jason and the Golden Fleece (of which only fragments remain), Jason's ill-fortune is put down to the wiles of his wife Medea. Yet, later, Apollonius of Rhodes gives us a different version in which Medea is described as a victim of Jason's infidelity and madness. Again, Homer has the beautiful Helen as prize for Paris of Troy; he elopes with her, so causing the Trojan War. Later poets (Stesichorus, Euripides), however, deny that Helen ever went to Troy at all. The historian Herodotus sums it up when he says that, 'Homer knew the story, but it was not such an attractive subject for verse'. In his *Republic*, the philosopher Plato rejects virtually all the old myths, calling them immoral, and suggests new ones.

A nineteenth-century depiction of the story of Jason and the Argonauts. Jason is one of Greek myth's great heroes and undertakes a great journey to find the Golden Fleece, accompanied by 50 warriors known as the Argonauts. Various accounts tell of his adventures, and of his tragic death upon returning home, having recovered the Golden Fleece through completing many seemingly impossible tasks.

Each new bard, therefore, had the right to interpret historical tradition in his own way and the audience did not feel obliged to accept any one as received truth. In fact, the very dynamic nature of myth was intended to stimulate discussion of such virtues as truth, morality and ethics.

UNIQUENESS OF THE MYTHS

Greek myth is unusual in other ways. It very rarely involves talking animals, unlike myths from other parts of the world. Mostly the incidents described are no more than an embellishment of everyday life rather than fantasy adventures. The great bulk of Greek tales also features heroes: men and women from a particular time and place. True, they have greater powers than ordinary mortals, but they are not all-powerful. In Homer's *Iliad*, when Diomedes and Patroclus attack the gods, Apollo reminds

Pictured is the Athenian hero Theseus slaying the Minotaur. Theseus was revered for unifying the state of Attica in which Athens was the supreme city, and the myths in which he figured served a dual purpose. Firstly they established Theseus as a hero whose actions should be emulated, and they also described through him the ideal democratic state.

them: 'Remember who you are! Gods and men can never be equal.' By contrast, for example, Norse and Egyptian mythologies are far more concerned with gods than heroes.

Another quality of the myths is the educational role they played in society. In fifth-century BC Athens, aristocratic boys had as many as 12 years of schooling, divided into literature, music and physical education. The literature element mainly meant learning verse-myth by heart, taking in its moral content and debating issues raised. From Homer to the late tragedies, it is through myths that poets develop their deepest thoughts. The myths also provide a history of the Greek people, as well as contributing rich material for philosophical debates. In addition, they give ample subject matter for all the visual arts, from the great sculptures and statues adorning temples to mosaics and pottery paintings.

Left: A marble bust of Homer, whose epic works the *Iliad* and the *Odyssey* are two of the main sources of Greek mythology and were key in the teaching of literacy. The Greeks did not regard mythology merely as a collection of stories: it was dynamic and as such was subject to constant reinterpretation.

MYTHS AND HISTORY

Myths are all that later Greeks knew about their early history, apart from a few remarkable remains, such as the citadel of Mycenae and the Cyclopean walls of Tiryns. There was a time, especially in the nineteenth century, when some people were sceptical about any truth in the myths. But archaeological evidence at Mycenae, Troy and Crete shows, for example, that Mycenae really had been 'rich in gold', as Homer claimed (before its fall in about 1150 BC); that the city of Troy had been destroyed by war in about 1190 BC, perhaps as described in Homer's *Iliad*; that Knossos in Crete had possessed a great palace and Labyrinth, as well as a sporting ritual involving bulls. Myths, then, preserved names, great events and historical places, even if they used poetic licence to embellish them.

Olympian Gods

Ancient Greece had its cosmogonies, myths of how the world began and other stories of the gods. Although the gods travel far and wide, they always return to their homes beyond the clouds on Mount Olympus. Hence they are known as the Olympic gods or Olympians. Each god has his or her own home, although they usually come together in the palace of Zeus, father of the gods. There they feast on ambrosia and nectar, served by the lovely goddess Hebe and entertained by Apollo on his lyre. It is an immortal world of feasting and discussion of the affairs of heaven and earth.

Zeus, though known as the father of the gods, has a beginning. His father and mother are Cronus and Rhea, of the race of Titans, themselves children of heaven/Uranus and earth/Gaia. They, in turn, sprang from Chaos ('the yawning abyss'). Zeus and his two brothers, Poseidon and Hades, shared out the world, with Zeus taking the heavens, Poseidon the seas and Hades the underworld.

BEGINNINGS AND MAJOR DEITIES

The lame god Hephaestus was architect, smith and artist for the gods; he even forged thunderbolts which Zeus hurled at his enemies. In gratitude, Zeus gave him Aphrodite, goddess of love and beauty, as his wife. Some myths say that she was born of sea foam and clothed by the seasons. Eros, god of love, is her son; armed with his bow and arrows, he fires his love darts into the

Sacred Sites and Settlements
The map shows the sacred sites and settlements in Attica in ancient Greece. Early settlements were open and undefended but during the eighth century, the population expanded dramatically and more settlements were fortified. There are many religious sites in Attica, such as the temple of Poseidon where Poseidon still reigns, overlooking the sea.

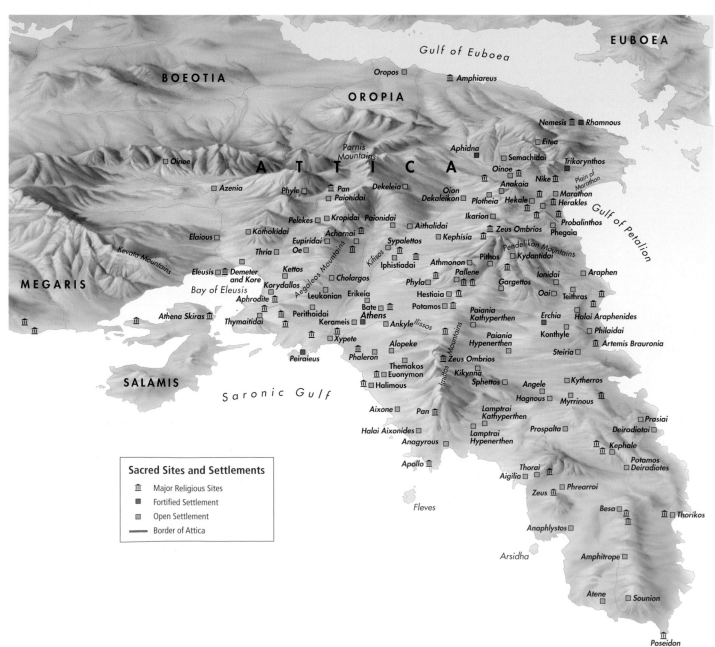

Sacred Sites and Settlements
- 🏛 Major Religious Sites
- ■ Fortified Settlement
- ▫ Open Settlement
- — Border of Attica

hearts of gods and humans. Athene, goddess of wisdom, sprang fully adult from the head of Zeus; it was she who gave her name to the city of Athens and to the most famous of all Greek temples, the Parthenon (built between 447 and 438 BC) or Athene Parthonos (Athene the Virgin).

OTHER GODS

Hermes, messenger of the gods, is usually seen wearing a winged cap and sandals. He is also the god of trade, wrestling and other sports, even thieving – whatever requires skill and dexterity. Dionysus, god of wine, presides over sacred festivals to mark the grape harvest, wine being sacred and its drinking ritualized. Dionysus is often portrayed with male and female satyrs (horned creatures, half human, half-

goat) and maenads (fauns). Since he is also the god of passion, many temples were named after him and festivals held in his name.

The nine Muses, who were daughters of Zeus and Mnemosyne (Memory), were originally goddesses of memory, but later each becomes identified with song, verse, dance, comedy, tragedy, astronomy, history, art and science. The three Graces (also Zeus's daughers) bestow beauty and charm on humans and preside over banquets, dancing and all elegant entertainment.

The three Fates control every person's birth, life and death. Also known as the Cruel Fates, they spend their time spinning the threads of human destiny and cutting them with shears whenever they wish. Finally, the three Furies punish all transgressors mercilessly, usually with a deadly sting. Greeks preferred to call them the Eumenides (Good-Tempered Ones), as it would have been bad luck to use their proper name.

As well as god of wine, Dionysus was god of disguise and illusion, and many festivals of drama were held in his honour. Satyr plays were a favourite at such events, bawdy comedies in which men would don satyr costumes, and were frequently performed following a tragedy.

The statue of Athene the Virgin, sculpted by Pheidias, outside the Parthenon in Athens. Athene was patron of Athens, where her cult was centred, and was honoured as the protector of cities. Having been born from her father Zeus's head, she was linked with wisdom and her wisdom was believed to rival even that of her father.

THE CREATION

In the bard Hesiod's great epic *Theogony*, he describes the creation of the world. 'In the beginning was Chaos...'. Chaos was evidently a gaping void out of which came Gaia (earth), Tartarus (underworld), Eros (desire), Erebus (gloom) and night. Gaia gave birth to Uranus (sky) and together they produced the first gods: 12 giant Titans, three Cyclops and three Hecatonchires (monsters with 100 arms and 50 heads each). When Uranus locked them in the underworld, Gaia had the youngest Titan, Cronus, castrate his father and seize power.

Cronus had five children but, afraid of being overthrown, swallowed them at birth. When his wife Rhea produced a sixth child, Zeus, she tricked Cronus into swallowing a stone and had nymphs raise the baby. Once Zeus had grown up he took revenge on his father and made him vomit up his brothers and sisters (Poseidon, Hades, Hera, Demeter and Hestia). The victorious Zeus became the supreme god.

Origins of Humanity

Early Greek mythology had no agreed account of the origin of humanity. Sometimes humans emerged from clay, stones or ash trees. Much later, Plato claimed that the first man was a round ball with eight limbs but Zeus cut him in half to form the first man and woman. The best-known origin tale is that concerning the Titan Prometheus, who one day made a man out of clay and water in the image of the gods. But he had to pay for his bold deed.

To help men, Prometheus (whose name means 'forethought') stole fire from the sun's chariot and took it to earth hidden in a fennel stalk. Zeus was furious. He ordered Hephaestus to make a woman out of clay and send her down to earth. Her name was Pandora and, being made in heaven, she possessed every possible gift – including curiosity. At the home of Prometheus's brother, the slow-witted Epimetheus (meaning 'afterthought'), was a sealed jar that Pandora was told never to open. Of course, she opened it, so releasing all the suffering and torment that beset human lives to this day. In fear, she replaced the lid, trapping just one thing inside: hope. The jar became known as Pandora's Box.

PROMETHEUS'S PUNISHMENT

Zeus then took revenge on Prometheus. He had him chained to a rock on Mount Caucasus where an eagle pecked out his liver. Being immortal, he could not die; the liver grew back in the night, and his torment started again with each new day.

In another myth, Zeus sent a flood to drown all humans. Deucalion, Prometheus's son, and his wife Pyrrha (daughter of Pandora and Epimetheus) built an ark in which they survived the flood, ending up on Mount Parnassus. They prayed at the Oracle of Delphi and were told to throw stones over their shoulders as they walked along. Those tossed by Deucalion turned into men, those by Pyrrha into women. Thus the human race was recreated on earth.

THE FIVE AGES

According to Hesiod, in his *Works and Days*, there were five ages of humanity. In the first, the golden age, people lived in peace and plenty. The earth gave its riches freely, wine flowed from the vine and milk came of its own accord from cows and sheep. Inasmuch as people never grew old, death was no more terrible than falling asleep. In the course of time, the golden age gave way to the silver age. For the first time the year was divided into seasons and people had to build houses to protect themselves from winter wind and autumn rain. Since all sons were subject to their mothers, there was no cause for war.

It was not until the bronze age that evil entered people's hearts and wars started. Fear, greed and hatred ruled the earth. Next came

Prometheus chained to Mount Caucasus after stealing fire for mankind. This myth was a way of explaining why humans suffered such hardships on earth and why, due to the actions of one man (Prometheus), the gods came to regard mankind as inferior to them, having been previously treated as equals.

PROMETHÉE DÉCHIRÉ PAR UN VAUTOUR.
Prometheus tortured by a Vultur.

Prometheus durch einen Geyer zerrissen.
Prometheus door een Gier verscheurt.

the heroic age, when Zeus restored some human virtues in order to see heroes through the Trojan War and other semi-mythical events of early Greek history. But the worst age of all was the iron age, when weapons of iron helped people destroy each other. Yet people always lived in hope that the ages would be repeated over time: one day Cronus would return and bring back the golden age, and nature would again produce her gifts freely, snake and weed would lose their poison, goat and sheep would come home without need of a shepherd and sheep would grow fleece in different colours.

Women had an inferior role to men in everyday Greek society and mythology only served to reinforce their lower status. In one myth, Zeus had a woman carved from clay, decorated with flowers and fine garments and given to mankind. However, she was given a deceitful nature that made her a curse to men: they could never be satisfied with her, neither could they be satisfied without her.

MYTHS AND WOMEN

Myths (composed by men) defined the nature and status of women in relation to men. Thus, as with the story of Adam and Eve, that of Pandora puts the blame for all evils squarely on women. Pandora was adorned with every type of beauty, but was also given deceit by Hermes. One version of the myth says that Pandora brought her box down to earth with her under strict instructions not to open it. That she did so is a measure of women's unconstrained curiosity and guilt in causing men such torment and the human race so many diseases. Her only saving grace is that she shut the box in time to retain hope.

The Trojan War

The heroic period of myth is not some remote and dateless past. It spanned only two or three generations, focusing on the Trojan War. This can be dated to the twelfth century BC: based on archaeological findings, scholars have calculated that Troy fell around 1190 BC. The reason that the myths of this period are so well known is thanks to the oral storytelling tradition, from which one man, Homer, stands out. Homer's epic poetry, especially his *Iliad* and *Odyssey*, is truly a jewel in the crown of Western literature.

The tales related by storytellers were important to Greeks because they told the story of their ancestors and glorious past. Homer's epics and other verses were widely performed and children learned them in school. They described a heroic age in which gods freely intervened in human affairs, though mortals had to know their limits. But heroes were brave and adventurous, unafraid of self-sacrifice. Thus, when the warrior-hero Achilles is offered a choice by the Fates of a long life of ease or a short one with immortal glory, he naturally chooses the latter.

TROY AND GREEK HISTORY

Troy (called Ilium in antiquity – hence the *Iliad*) was a city located near the coast in Asia Minor (eastern Turkey). Troy was strategically important because it guarded the Hellespont Straits. The story starts with Paris of Troy who is asked to judge a beauty contest between Hera, Athene and Aphrodite. Each promises him a reward: Hera – untold wealth, Athene – wisdom and fame; and Aphrodite – the most beautiful woman in the world. Paris opts for Aphrodite, so earning Paris the eternal enmity of Hera and Athene.

Mycenaean Greece
The mountainous topography of late Bronze Age Greece led to the rise of a number of small independent communities, each dominated by a fortified palace complex associated with massive beehive-shaped Tholos tombs in which the elite were buried. Tablets inscribed with Linear B, an early form of Greek, reveal details of the administrative and economic importance of the palaces.

Mycenaean Greece, c. 1700–1200 BC

- ■ Major Settlement
- ▱ Smaller Settlement with *Tholos* Tomb
- ◣ Other *Tholos* Tombs
- ⌂ Major Fortification
- ◪ Fortification
- ■ Major Palace
- ◍ Finds of Linear B Tablets
- — Trade Route
- ▨ Fertile Plains
- --- Ancient Coastline
- ······ Possible Ancient Coastline

Paris's prize is Helen, wife of Menelaus, King of Sparta. Enchanted by 'the face that launched a thousand ships and burned the topless towers of Ilium' (Christopher Marlowe), Paris elopes with Helen to Troy. Alone among the Trojans, Paris's sister, Cassandra, foretells the destruction of Troy brought by the abduction. With his brother Agamemnon, King of Argos, Menelaus organizes a great fleet to sail to Troy. The Greeks set up camp outside Troy and besiege it for nigh on ten years. It is at this point that Homer takes up the story.

ACHILLES AND ODYSSEUS

Two of the most famous Greek warriors, Achilles and Odysseus, at first refuse to join the expedition, but are finally tricked into going. Achilles is a typical Greek hero: strong and proud, but also brutal and headstrong, embodying the paradox of the hero, as seen especially in Heracles. Like many other heroes, he was brought up in the hills by the wise tutor Chiron, a centaur. His mother, hoping to make him invincible, dipped the young Achilles into the River Styx; the heel by which she held him remained the only vulnerable part of his body.

DEATH OF ACHILLES AND HECTOR

During the siege, Achilles falls out with Agamemnon over the king's acceptance of a Trojan priest's daughter, Chryseis, as war spoils. Achilles refuses to fight and lends his armour to his best friend Patroclus, who is killed in battle by the Trojan commander Hector, King Priam of Troy's eldest son. Achilles returns to the fray bent on revenge. He pursues Hector three times round the walls of Troy and finally kills him in a sword fight. Such is Achilles's fury that he mutilates Hector's corpse and refuses to return it to Priam for burial. However, the angry gods force him to hand over the body and, recklessly, he continues fighting, before being killed by an arrow shot in his heel by Paris. In turn, Paris is killed by a Greek archer. The *Iliad* ends with the games held for Hector's funeral.

In the legend of Troy, Agamemnon incurs the wrath of Achilles after claiming Achilles' prize, the lady Briseis, as his own. On his return from Troy, he also enrages his wife by bringing a new lover with him; his wife eventually stabs him to death. This golden mask is said to be Agamemnon's funerary mask.

Procession of the Trojan horse in Troy by Giandomenico Tiepolo (1727–1804). The sacking of Troy is the culmination of a chain of events begun some years before when Hecuba, Queen of Troy, predicted her son Paris would bring destruction to the city and abandoned him at birth. After the successful siege of the city by the Greeks, it appears that his mother's premonition turned out to be correct.

THE WOODEN HORSE

With Achilles dead, his armour and command pass to Odysseus. Odysseus conceives a plan that involves building a hollow wooden horse in which the best Greek warriors hide as their fleet apparently sails away. The horse is then left outside the city walls and, thinking the wooden horse is an offering to the gods, the Trojans drag it inside. That night, the Greeks let themselves out of the horse and open up the city gates to the army, which has come ashore along the coast. Under Odysseus the victorious Greeks set fire to the city and raze Troy to the ground, killing King Priam and his sons and taking Trojan women back to Greece as slaves.

Creatures and Monsters

Many are the horrifying monsters sent to test the strength and guile of Greek heroes – Jason, Heracles, Odysseus, Perseus, Theseus. They all have to journey to the very edge of known civilization and beyond into realms of fantasy where, time and again, they have to overcome giants, dragons, many-headed serpents, sirens, huge bulls and sea monsters of every sort. The creatures of Greek myth are the archetypal villains of the European consciousness, rich material for the fertile imagination of artists, poets and children.

Some monsters, notably the giants, differ from men mainly in their size and ugliness. The human giants, such as the Cyclops (with one eye in the middle of their forehead), King Amycus of Bebryces (covered in thick black hair and beaten by the Argonaut Polydeuces in a boxing match) or Antacus (who is defeated by Heracles at wrestling) resemble ordinary mortals in proportions, and join in love and war with them.

GIANTS

Superhuman giants, on the other hand, war even with the gods and are of vastly grander proportions: Typhon, with his 100 arms, makes war on Zeus who slays him with a thunderbolt. He is so huge that it takes Mount Etna to cover the corpse. His brother Enceladus provides the flames of Mount Etna's volcano with his breath. For his part in the war against Zeus, the Titan Atlas has to hold up the heavens on his shoulders. It is Atlas's three daughters, the Hesperides, who bring Heracles the magical golden apples.

FEMALE MONSTERS

It can hardly have been coincidence that many of the monsters who test heroes are female. Oedipus (who has further troubles with women, unwittingly marrying his own mother) has a trial with the Sphinx, which has a woman's head and breasts, a lion's body and a bird's wings. The Harpies, fierce winged creatures with sharp claws, possess women's faces. These filthy beasts snatch food from the blind Phineus during Jason's journey to Colchis. The three Gorgon sisters, led by Medusa, have writhing snakes for hair and can turn their victims to stone with a single glance. With divine aid, Perseus cuts off Medusa's head while looking at her reflection in a polished shield.

Not all female monsters are ugly brutes. Beautiful *femmes fatales* out to trap unwary

In one myth, the hero Odysseus entered the cave of Polyphemus the Cyclops while searching for food. Polyphemus blocked the entrance to the cave, and it was only after Odysseus had tricked him and then blinded him that he was able to escape, clinging to the underbelly of a ram.

heroes include the Sirens, half-women, half-birds, whose song so bewitches sailors that they throw themselves overboard and drown. The Argonauts escape by having Orpheus drown out their Siren song with his lyre, while Odysseus has himself bound to the mast while his sailors fill their ears with wax.

Dryope and her sister nereids (naiads), the 50 daughters of the sea god Nereus, are lovely nymphs who entice Hylas of the Argonauts down into their pool. The Amazon queen Hippolyte and Heracles's wife Deianeira both meet their end through witchcraft. The abundance of female monsters preying on men stem, it would seem, from the male fear of infidelity by wives and the belief that women are different from men in their predilection for the blacker, more orgiastic and less rational aspects of belief and ritual. Myth is a way of endorsing and defining women's natural role as loyal, obedient wives and mothers and legitimizing the male-dominated patriarchal society.

Relief showing Perseus killing the Gorgon Medusa. Medusa was one of three Gorgons who had writhing serpents instead of hair and anyone who looked directly at Medusa would be turned to stone. Perseus was sent on a quest to fetch Medusa's head. Through Perseus's cunning and magical equipment given to him he is able to kill Medusa and claim his prize.

Attic red figure vase showing Amazon fighting cavalry, from the fourth century BC. Amazon women lived in female-only societies, and were regarded as barbarians as they lived in the East, did not grow crops or live in cities. They wore men's clothes and fought in battles; however, as they always lost their battles the myths only served to reinforce male superiority.

THE CENTAUR

One strange monster in Greek myth is the centaur. These half-men, half-horse creatures are accepted into human companionship as the only monsters to which any virtues are assigned. But their bestial nature is always liable to show itself, especially after drinking wine. Some centaurs, however, are wise and kindly. The most celebrated was Chiron, who lived in a cave on the rocky slopes of Mount Pelion overlooking the port of Iolcos, and many a Greek family entrusted their son's education to him. He taught hunting and fighting skills, as well as music and poetry, mathematics and astronomy. He was also renowned as a teacher of healing the sick, being tutored by Asklepios, god of medicine. The sign of a serpent entwined round a staff became his attribute.

Human Heroes and Demigods

The distinction between heroes and demigods is unclear. While some heroes, like Jason and Oedipus, are sons of mortal parents, others, like Heracles, Perseus and Achilles, come from the union of gods or goddesses with mortals. Zeus and Alcmene produced Heracles (his name 'Glory to Hera' was meant to appease Zeus's wife, the goddess Hera); Zeus and Danae produced Perseus; Peleus and the sea-nymph Thetis were responsible for Achilles; while rumours of divine intervention surround both Theseus (Poseidon is his putative father) and Odysseus (the putative bastard son of Sisyphus, offspring of Aeolus, god of winds).

Many rival states claimed a hero as their founder and protector, no doubt embellishing their origins: Theseus of Athens, Jason of Iolcos, Ajax of Salamis. Noble families also asserted a hero as their ancestor. Alexander the Great, for example, claimed descent from both Achilles and the Egyptian god Amon (Ammon) and insisted that his own semi-divine status was recognized throughout Greece. The bards, including Homer and Hesiod, who sang for their living, often took care to extol the ancestors of their patrons and audiences. The catalogue of ships in Homer's *Iliad* leaves

The Journey of the Argo
The map shows the route taken by Jason and the Argonauts during his journey to obtain the Golden Fleece of Colchis at the behest of his uncle Peleus.

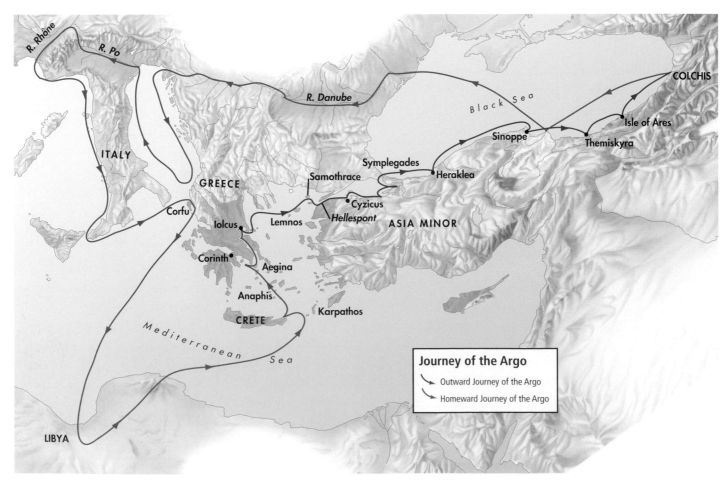

Journey of the Argo

- Outward Journey of the Argo
- Homeward Journey of the Argo

no Greek state off the roll of ancient glory; the 50 Argonauts are each attributed to a noble Greek family.

HERACLES – A NATIONAL HERO

The figure most akin to a national hero is Heracles. He never settled in any one city that could take full credit for his exploits, and his wanderings carried him beyond the bounds of Greece – far into Africa and Asia Minor. He was one of the earliest mythical heroes to be featured in Greek art (dating from the eighth century BC) and on the coins of city states (on which he is usually depicted strangling snakes while in his cradle). As a symbol of national patriotism he is the only hero to be revered throughout Greece; he is also the only hero to be granted immortality.

COMPLEX CHARACTERS

What makes Greek heroes particularly interesting is their depiction by bards as deeply complex characters. Typically, they follow a common pattern: unnatural birth, return home as prodigal sons after being separated at an early age, exploits against monsters to prove their manhood and subsequent kingship or glorious death. Super strong and courageous they may be, mostly noble and honourable, but all have to contend with a ruthless streak that often outweighs the good. Heracles, for example, hurls his wife and children into a fire in a fit of madness and his uncontrollable lust forces him on King Thespius's 50 daughters in a single night. Nor is he averse to homosexual affairs (with Hylas, for instance), though Greek pederasty is mostly excluded from the myths.

Despite recapturing the Golden Fleece for Greece, Jason never finds contentment; he deserts his wife Medea and dies when the *Argo*'s rotting prow falls on him. Theseus is also disloyal to his wife Ariadne, abandoning her on the island of Naxos; he kills his Amazon wife Antiope and causes the death both of his son Hippolytus and his father Aegeus. Even the noble and fearless Achilles, the Greek hero of the Trojan War, a man who cannot bear dishonourable conduct, violates the dead hero's code by desecrating Hector's corpse and refusing to hand it over to the Trojans.

Like the heroes, therefore, cities that turn their hero's burial places into shrines (and oracles) receive good fortune, but they also risk invoking the hero's unpredictable temper.

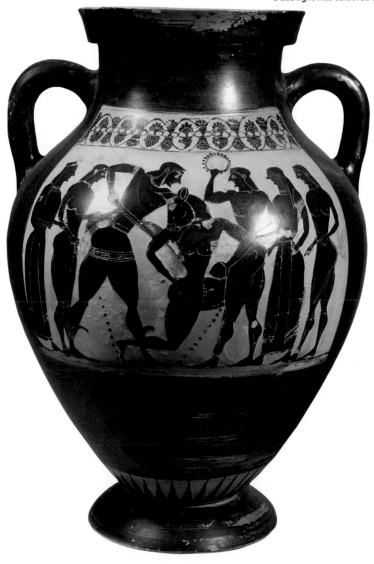

Left: Heracles was the greatest of the Greek heroes. There are countless tales about him, the most well-known being those that told of the 12 tasks set him by King Eurystheus, which included destroying the Hydra, killing the lion of Nemea, catching a wild bull and stealing Hippolyte's girdle.

Theseus and the Minotaur, as depicted on a black-figure Attic amphora, from the mid-sixth century BC. In the fifth century BC, the epic Theseus was composed, celebrating his heroic exploits, which sadly has been lost. Such was his importance in Athens that any poetry casting him in a bad light was censored or destroyed.

THESEUS

Theseus, the patron hero of Athens, was honoured at least since the sixth century BC for unifying the region of Attica into a single, strong state. It is not surprising that his adventures have to fit local pride. His first and most famous feat is to kill the half-man, half-bull monster, the Minotaur, which King Minos of Crete kept in an underground maze. Each year Athens had to pay a tribute of seven boys and seven girls for sacrifice to the Minotaur. Theseus not only slays the beast, but is able to retrace his steps through the maze by means of a ball of thread given him by Minos's daughter Ariadne.

Excavations and later historians, like Thucydides (fifth century BC), indicate that King Minos was 'the first man we hear of to have a fleet' and was ruler of much of the Aegean. It is likely that Athens had to pay him tribute until 'Theseus destroyed his power'.

Sources of Greek Myth

Greek myth has been passed down principally from song recitals and plays. In ancient Greece, myth dominated the subject matter of both. From generation to generation, professional bards known as *rhapsodes* committed to memory whole epics which they then passed on. The earliest of these epic poems known to us are the *Iliad* and the *Odyssey*, though both refer to earlier epics now lost. It was not until about 750 BC that the epics were written down for the first time.

HOMER

In the middle of the eighth century BC, about the same time as the first written epics were made, a wandering minstrel by the name of Homer became the first of his profession to benefit from the new written records. His *Iliad* and *Odyssey* are narrative poems, both many hundreds of pages long, which tell the tale of Greek gods and heroes.

The *Iliad* centres on the Trojan War and, besides the warrior heroes like Achilles, Ajax, Hector and Odysseus, it describes the many gods on Mount Olympus and their various responsibilities, habits and foibles. The *Odyssey* is concerned with the hero Odysseus's ten-year journey home from the Trojan War, though the

Most of the tragedies written by Sophocles drew their subjects exclusively from Greek myth. In his day, he was the most popular of the three great Attic tragedians (the other two being Euripides and Aeschylus). Although his plays may not have shown epic grandeur, he was a master at characterization and evoking pathos.

Greek Colonization in the Mediterranean World
Homer was a professional bard whose poems were originally passed on through song. In 750 BC they were written down for the first time. At this time Greece was colonizing much of the Mediterranean world and this process of discovery had a strong effect on the imagination of the bards, whose stories often described long journeys and distant lands.

Greek Colonization in the Mediterranean World 750-550 BC

- ▨ Greek Heartland in 750 BC
- ■ Greek Parent Community
- ● 8th-Century Greek Colony
- ● 7th-Century Greek Colony
- ● 6th-century Greek Colony
- ● Phoenician or Punic Settlement
- ● Etruscan City
- ● Philistine City

verses concentrate only on the last 40 days. It is a poem of the sea as well as land, and reaches into the realms of fable, even the underworld, introducing us to the lotus-eaters, Cyclops, Sirens, Scylla and Charybdis.

Both the *Iliad* and the *Odyssey* constitute truly great literature and encapsulate virtually all we know of Greek mythology. Ironically, our knowledge of their author is extremely sketchy. The many ancient accounts of the life of 'The Poet', as he was simply known, have him as a blind bard from Chios, born about 750 BC (Herodotus), but there is absolutely no evidence to verify this. We do not even know if he could read or write. All we can say is that, then as now, the epics ascribed to Homer emanate from a unique interaction between tradition and individual talent.

HESIOD

The other great rhapsodist was Hesiod, who was composing poems and winning singing competitions about 50 years after Homer, in 700 BC. Not only was he evidently the first to write his songs down, in his main epics *Theogony* and *Works and Days*, he was the first author of a systematic mythology. It is from Hesiod that we learn of the creation, the beginning of the gods and the world. Although Hesiod gives no account of the creation of humanity, he does tell us of Prometheus and Pandora.

Both Homer and Hesiod were born in Asia Minor, and their interpretations of mythology show many similarities with ancient Sumerian and other Near Eastern civilizations (the Phoenicians, Hurrians and Hittites). Nowhere else, however, have myths attained such a peak of written excellence as in the Greek epics.

PLATO

Philosophers later challenged a literal belief in mythology. The great philosopher Plato (427–347 BC), an aristocratic Athenian, especially criticizes many of the myths immortalized by Homer and Hesiod for presenting gods and heroes as morally flawed and vengeful characters. Such characters would have had no place in his ideal society, which he describes in the *Republic*. In his work the *Timaeus*, he provides his own cosmology.

What all the epic bards, dramatists and philosophers show is that Greek mythology was ever changing, giving rise to yet more exciting artistic productions in every area of creativity.

A Roman mosaic portraying Plato's School of Philosophy. Plato's attitude towards mythology was ambivalent and his two major works, *Republic* and *The Laws*, describe in detail his thoughts on the subject. His ideas have had a long-lasting appeal and have influenced philosophers, artists and writers ever since.

THE TRAGEDIES

Some 200 years after Homer and Hesiod, the theatre became the main stage for the performance of myths, particularly in Athens. Many thousands of people packed into amphitheatres to see the great tragedies of Aeschylus, Sophocles and Euripides.

Aeschylus, the father of Greek tragedy, was born in 525 BC near Athens. Like other bards and dramatists, to be successful he had to work his way up through competitions (in poetry, songs and plays), until he was eventually defeated in 468 BC by Sophocles. His most famous play, the *Agamemnon*, deals with the tragic King Agamemnon, leader of the Greek army in the Trojan War, who was subsequently murdered by his wife Clytemnestra and her lover Aegisthus. His play *Prometheus* consists of speeches and choruses that describe the pathos of the god's fate.

Sophocles was born 30 years after Aeschylus, at Colonus. A great singer, he wrote about 100 plays, the most remarkable of which tell the tragic story of Oedipus (*Oedipus Tyrannus* and *Oedipus at Colonus*) and of Ajax, hero of the Trojan War.

Euripides was born 16 years after Sophocles. An outstanding athlete and painter, he excelled in writing plays about women. In *Medea*, he draws a moving picture of a loving wife and mother driven mad by her husband Jason's infidelity. In *The Trojan Woman*, he shows the horrors of the *Trojan War* from a woman's perspective.

The Underworld

The afterlife was of great importance to the ancient Greeks. Beyond the grave or funeral pyre lay a land of shadows, the underworld. It was ruled by Hades, brother of Zeus and Poseidon, who also gave his name to his dark realm. Because the gloomy underworld was opposed to bright heavenly Olympus, Hades was not accepted as an Olympian god, and his servants were never invited to sup in Zeus's palace.

Dead souls are taken by Hermes, messenger of the gods, down through gloomy caves and long, winding, underground paths until they come to five rivers. First they must be ferried by Charon across the black River Styx (hate) to the Gates of Hades, which are guarded by the three-headed hound Cerberus. Once inside they must then cross four more rivers: black Acheron (woe), Phlegethon (fire), salt-teared Cocytus (wailing) and Lethe (oblivion). Unless the soul has money (put in the corpse's mouth) to pay the ferryman, the ghost will be left to wander for 100 years on the far side of the Styx.

JUDGES

Once across the five infernal rivers, the dead go before three stern judges: Minos, Rhadamanthus and Aeacus, who help Hades assess people's lives and determine their fate. Exceptional heroes might find themselves assigned to the blissful Elysian Fields, also known as the Isles of the Blessed, far off in the western seas where they can relive the joys of life without memory of their sins. For those whose crimes are bad enough to warrant a sentence to eternal punishment, there are special torments in the darkest regions of Erebus and Tartarus, where they are deprived of oblivion, being eternally reminded of their sins. This is true of King Tantalus who stole nectar and ambrosia from the gods: his punishment was to find that food and drink are always just beyond his grasp (hence our word 'tantalise'). Those who have done evil are also handed over to the three merciless Furies (Erinyes) before being led off to their appointed torment.

It was one of Heracles's 12 tasks to seize Cerberus, the fearsome three-headed dog (pictured) that guarded the underworld and drag him back to earth. After wrestling with the hound, Heracles managed to bring him back to the surface and present him to Eurystheus, who had set him the task, before sending him back to where he had come from.

For the common dead, neither very good or very bad, their sad fate is to dwell forever in shadowy gloom. On occasion they may gain a glimpse of the strange garden of Persephone, queen of the underworld, with its bloomless poppies, pale beds of rushes and green grapes, which she crushes into deadly wine.

JOURNEYS INTO HADES

Few heroes or gods manage to venture down into Hades and return. Those that do often meet a sad fate. The three best-known figures to achieve this are Heracles, Orpheus and Persephone. Heracles's last test is to bring up the hound Cerberus. He is led by Hermes to a cave near Sparta from where he descends into Hades, passing the Fates and Furies, eventually coming to the gloomy palace of King Hades and Queen Persephone. Hades gives him the hound to see if he can overcome it with his bare hands. He does so, but returns it to Hades having accomplished his mission.

Orpheus, the greatest of all singers, is grief-stricken when his beloved wife Eurydice dies. So he goes with his lyre into the underworld and persuades Hades to let Eurydice return to earth. Hades agrees but there is one condition: Orpheus must not look back as he leads his wife out. Sadly, at the exit, he looks round at her and she has to return to Hades forever. In his grief he pledges never to remarry and a band of women suitors angrily cut him to pieces. Yet even after his death his head and lyre continue to sing and play.

The legend of Orpheus and Euridyce as depicted by Enrico Scuri (1805–1884). After Orpheus, the tragic hero of this myth, was killed and his body cut into pieces, a temple was constructed over his head, from which prophecies were supposedly delivered.

THE SHAPING OF GREEK CULTURE

1900 BC	Migrations of Hellenes into Greece
800–330 BC	Peak of myth recitals and Greek cultural influence
750 BC	First written records of myths
338 BC	Greece becomes part of Macedonian empire
146 BC	Greece reduced to a Roman province

PERSEPHONE

Persephone, daughter of Demeter, goddess of grain and harvest, is one day kidnapped by Hades and taken in his chariot to the underworld. When Demeter finds out, she is so angry she refuses to let grain grow, so starving the world. Hades has to agree to return the girl, but before she leaves he gives her some pomegranate seeds to eat. She is not to know that this act will condemn her to stay in the underworld forever. But Zeus comes up with a compromise: Persephone can spend two-thirds of each year at Olympus with her mother (spring and summer) and one-third (winter) with Hades. This explains the Greek mythological explanation of fertility: the seed is sown, it vanishes into the darkness, and yet it lives and rises again.

The Birth of Roman Mythology

From around 1500 BC, the Italic peoples began to settle the fertile Italian peninsula. Though mostly farmers, they were forced into almost constant conflict with marauders from the north. Rome had yet to be founded, but the idealized figure of the farmer-soldier – determined, disciplined and dutiful – had its origins here and was to inspire the Romans and the approach they took to their religion throughout their history.

I n the eighth century BC, two new groups of people began to settle the Italian peninsula. The Greeks formed colonies (known collectively as Magna Grecia) along the southern coasts, while in central Italy a people of uncertain origin, the Etruscans, emerged. At around the same time, the Italic Latins and Sabines were living south of the Tiber in the Alban Hills around the site of what was to become the city of Rome. The family and household were the centre of religious activity for these small agricultural communities and unwittingly functioned as the crucible for what was to become the religion of Rome. They clearly, however, did not live in isolation, either from neighbouring Italic tribes or from the more advanced Etruscan and Greek civilizations to their north and south.

SPIRITS AND DEITIES

Scholars have argued that Roman religion was akin to an early form of animism which in time was overlaid with the more sophisticated beliefs and deities of foreign cultures. Certainly, a vast multitude of deities and spirits pervaded every aspect of life for the nascent citizens of Rome: a Numen, a manifestation of sacred power, was considered to be a part of all phenomena, activities and processes. These manifestations were often faceless, formless and sexless, and most were too vague to receive a name. However, they still required the correct performance of rituals, so that their energies might be renewed and the home and community thrive.

The distinctly Roman ethic of *pietas* (duty) permeated religious life.

What mattered was whether or not a worshipper performed the appropriate ritual correctly; beliefs and morals were inconsequential. This emphasis on orthopraxy (correct practice) rather than orthodoxy (correct belief) persisted in later Roman religion.

The Peoples of Italy
By 500BC, Italy was inhabited by a mixture of peoples. In the south and in Sicily the coastal plains had been settled by colonists from Greece in the seventh and eighth centuries, while the city-states of Etruria had long had cultural and economic links with the eastern Mediterranean. Around the same time the Italic Latins were living south of the Tiber near what would become Rome and the Carthaginians from North America were in Corsica, Sardinia and the south of Italy. All these peoples brought their own beliefs and mythology to Roman culture.

The Peoples of Italy, c. 500 BC

Carthaginian		Greek
Etruscan		Italic

HOUSEHOLD DEITIES AND HIGH GODS

Family rituals were supervised by the father of the family: the *paterfamilias* or household priest. The *paterfamilias* embodied the Genius (guardian spirit) of the family. He ensured that family members worshipped the gods and tended the household shrine known as the Lararium after the household Lar. Among the most ancient Italic divinities, these Lares seem originally to have been either field deities or divine ancestors. The Penates, with whom the Lares were closely associated, were primarily guardians of the storeroom, who ensured families had enough to eat. Offerings were made to the Penates before each meal. Sometimes these consisted of special cakes, wine or honey and, occasionally, a blood sacrifice.

As Rome emerged as the dominant power in Italy, so Roman religion evolved to serve the political needs of the state. Mars and Jupiter, originally local agricultural deities, became the great god of war and the mighty protector of the state respectively; Venus, the goddess of vegetables and the garden, became the goddess of love and the mother of Rome's founding heroes. But, while some spirits and deities eventually acquired individual, more complex, characteristics, the Romans continued to hold dear the traditions of their farmer-soldier ancestors, and the concept of Numen, of a world suffused with sacred powers, persisted alongside.

Most Roman households had small shrines to the Lares or household gods. This Altar of the Lares from the House of the Vettii in Pompeii dates from the first century BC. It shows members of the household making offerings to the gods.

The goddess Vesta (seated) is shown here with four of her priestesses in a relief dating from the first century AD. Each Vestal virgin served for 30 years. In the first decade she learned her duties; in the second she performed them and in the third she passed on the teaching to new priestesses.

VESTA AND THE VESTAL VIRGINS

Like many Roman deities, Vesta, goddess of the hearth, was originally worshipped privately in homes but later took on a public role. The circular Temple of Vesta, founded in 715 BC, was the oldest and most sacred shrine of the Forum (Rome's civic centre containing the city's main temples and public buildings) and served as the hearth of the Roman community. The fire of Vesta symbolized nourishment of the state. A prestigious priesthood of six specially chosen women (all virgins and daughters of Roman patricians) supervised worship of Vesta and the flame of her hearth.

Chosen at puberty, each Vestal served for 30 years. If she let the fire go out she was severely punished; if she lost her virginity, she risked being buried alive. Nonetheless, the Vestals enjoyed many privileges. Like men, they were not required to have a guardian and could testify in court, dispose of property or make wills. They also wielded a degree of political power. After 30 years, a Vestal could choose to take a generous dowry provided for her by the state, retire and marry. Most, however, chose to remain priestesses.

The Foundation of Rome

From at least the third century BC the Romans worshipped Aeneas under the name Jupiter Indiges. However, it was not until the reign of the great Emperor Augustus (31BC–AD14) that the Roman poet Virgil transformed the story of Aeneas, and his role in founding the settlement from which Rome was to spring, into a great epic.

According to the Greeks, Aeneas fought against them in the Trojan War of the twelfth century BC. Virgil's *Aeneid* tells how, as Troy burns about him, Aeneas is commanded in a vision to flee and to found a great city overseas. Carrying his father Anchises on his back and clutching the household gods of Troy, Aeneas makes his escape with his son Ascanius Iulus at his side. However, in the confusion of leaving the burning city, his wife disappears. Though Aeneas scours the streets for her, he encounters only her ghost, a piteous phantom, who informs him that he is to go to a land where the Tiber River flows and where a kingdom and a royal bride await him.

Aeneas embarks on his long voyage, stopping at, among other places, Thrace, Delos, Crete, Carthage and Sicily before finally reaching the mouth of the River Tiber. Latinus, the king of the region, welcomes him, but others resent the Trojans and war breaks out. The Trojans are victorious. Aeneas marries Lavinia, the daughter of Latinus, and founds Lavinium, the parent town of Alba Longa (which Ascanius comes to rule) and of Rome. Though some traditions say that Aeneas founded Rome itself, Virgil succeeds in marrying the story of Aeneas with the account, already well known, of Rome's foundation in 753 BC by Romulus, who is said to be descended from the royal line of Alba Longa.

Frederico Baroccio (1528–1612) here depicts the flight of Aeneas from the city of Troy. According to one account, it was Aeneas's piety which moved the Greeks to allow the hero, together with his son Ascanius and father Anchises, to leave the city.

CULTURE WARS

Homer's great epics the *Iliad* and *Odyssey* date back to the eighth century BC – the same century in which the Greeks founded colonies in Italy, claiming descent from the Homeric heroes of the Trojan War. The Roman story of Aeneas developed, at least in part, as a way of opposing Greek cultural superiority and endowing Roman land and lineage with ancient tradition. 'The house of Aeneas shall rule the whole world: and their sons' sons and those who shall be born of them,' says the great god Apollo in the opening pages of the *Aeneid*.

Virgil had, during his early years, witnessed the end of the Roman Republic, a period that was riven with civil war and conflict. The *Aeneid* celebrated the arrival of peace under the Emperor Augustus and encouraged a renewed pride in Rome: 'Rule the people with your sway, spare the conquered, and wear down the proud,' says the ghost of Aeneas's father. Rome, hopes Virgil, will bring to the world the gifts of peace, justice, order and law.

THE ROMAN PROTOTYPE

The Augustan Age (31 BC–AD 14) was one in which the emperor sought to rekindle the traditional Roman values of duty, self-denial, obedience to the gods, responsibility and family devotion. Pious, heroic, true hearted, dutiful and persevering, Virgil's Aeneas was the perfect hero to emulate, a prototype of the ideal Roman.

Many great Roman families, including the Julii to which the emperor Augustus as well as Julius Caesar belonged, claimed direct descent from Aeneas. The magnificent Forum of Augustus housed statues not only of Aeneas but also of his son Ascanius and the succeeding kings of Alba Longa.

A dish from Faenza, 1497, which shows detail of the arrival of Aeneas at Delos.

DIDO AND AENEAS

Since Virgil's time, the story of Dido, Queen of Carthage, has inspired countless writers and artists. Ovid's *Heroides*, St Augustine's *Confessions*, Chaucer's *Legend of Good Women* and Henry Purcell's opera *Dido and Aeneas* have all sought to interpret Dido's struggle to cope with ill-fated love. In the Renaissance alone she inspired more than 20 tragedies.

In Virgil's account, Dido flees her homeland Tyre in Phoenicia to North Africa after her husband is murdered. She resolves never to marry again and begins to build up a thriving city, Carthage. Independent and strong minded, she proves to be an effective ruler. On his voyage to Italy from Troy, Aeneas is shipwrecked on the coast of North Africa. The queen receives him at her palace and the two fall in love. As Dido yields to her desire for Aeneas, her city ceases to prosper. Aeneas likewise succumbs to love until Mercury, the Roman messenger of the gods, reminds him of his duties. When Aeneas abandons Dido to resume his voyage, the queen kills herself after vowing revenge on Rome. Her words serve to justify Rome's war against the Carthaginian general Hannibal, which lasted from 218–201 BC. The tale of Dido and Aeneas sets personal fulfillment against public duty. Though the latter wins, it is clearly at a cost.

Romulus and the Kings

Many historians think that the Etruscans, from north of the Tiber, conquered the area around Rome in the sixth century BC and that they may have provided the impetus for the development of the early city. However, tradition has it that Rome was founded in 753 BC by a man named Romulus.

The story tells how Numitor, King of Alba Longa (a town south-east of Rome), is overthrown by his younger brother Amulius. Rhea Silvia, Numitor's only child, is forced by Amulius to become a Vestal Virgin but is seduced by the great god Mars and gives birth to twin boys. Amulius immediately orders that they be drowned in the Tiber, but the basket in which they are abandoned floats away, coming to rest at the future site of Rome. A wolf suckles the children until they are found by the shepherd Faustulus.

Romulus and Remus grow up to lead a gang of bandits. When Remus is taken prisoner and dragged before the king, Romulus hastens to his rescue, kills Amulius and restores Numitor to his throne. The young men decide to start a city of their own, at the place where they had been found by the shepherd. Through *auspicium*, they seek the advice of the gods as to which of them should be the founder. (*Auspicium* was a means of determining the will of the gods by observing the flight – and sometimes the eating habits – of birds. It was usually overseen by Augurs, men who learned secret rules which were said to enable them to discern the meaning behind the birds' behaviour.) Remus is the first to see an omen (six vultures); Romulus sees 12 vultures. A dispute breaks out as to which of them has won. Romulus kills Remus and gives his name to the new city.

THE RAPE OF THE SABINE WOMEN

One of Romulus's first deeds on founding the city is to offer asylum to people in trouble in other communities. Though Rome initially flourishes, a lack of women means that it is likely to die out after a single generation. At his wits' end, Romulus invites the neighbouring Sabines to a magnificent festival. In the famous Rape of the Sabine Women, his bandits seize the Sabines' womenfolk (the most beautiful reserved for the senators) and drive off the men. Romulus

promises the young girls that they will have the status of wives and the men cajole them with protestations of love.

War breaks out between the Romans and the Sabines, led by their king Titus Tatius. Eventually, the women rush into the fray to stop the fighting and a treaty is drawn up whereby Tatius becomes joint king with Romulus. A few years later, Tatius is killed by a mob, leaving Romulus sole king again. After a long rule he mysteriously disappears in a storm. He later came to be identified with the god Quirinus.

This statue of a she-wolf dates from around 500 BC; the suckling Romulus and Remus are Renaissance additions. In Graeco-Roman mythology, the wolf is sacred to Ares, Apollo and Silvanus.

The Origins of Rome
Rome developed in several stages. It began life around the ninth century BC as a cluster of small huts on the Palatine Hill, with a cemetery in the marshland below. During the late seventh century Rome began its evolution into an urban centre, when a public square was created in the former marsh. Most of the major buildings were constructed between the fifth and the second centuries BC.

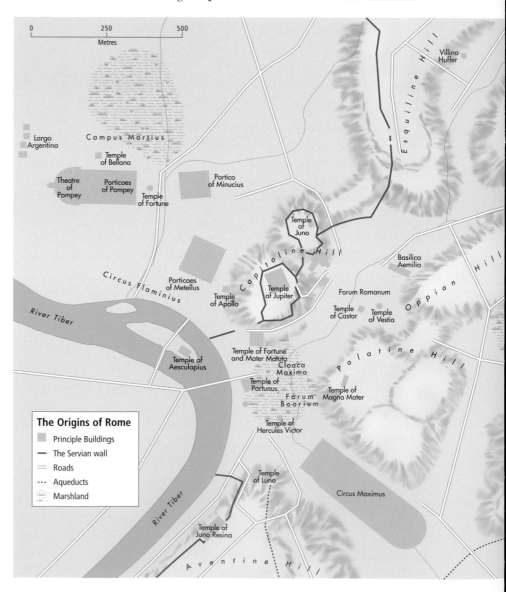

THE RAPE OF LUCRETIA AND THE FOUNDING OF THE REPUBLIC

According to tradition there were only seven kings between the founding of Rome and the establishment of the Roman Republic. The sixth king was Servius Tullius, originally, by tradition, a slave. Servius Tullius succeeds Tarquinius Priscus, an Etruscan. The story tells of how Servius's daughter persuades her husband, the son of Tarquinius Priscus, to murder her father whereupon the young man assumes the throne, becoming known as Tarquinius Superbus (the arrogant). While the king is away at war, his son Sextus rapes the beautiful and virtuous Lucretia, the wife of a relative. After exacting an oath of vengeance against the Tarquins from her father and her husband, Lucretia plunges a dagger into her heart and dies. Her family then leads a revolt against the king, driving the Etruscan Tarquins from Rome and founding a republic. The event is traditionally dated 509 BC.

THE SEVEN KINGS OF ROME

1. Romulus
2. Numa Pompilius
3. Tullus Hostilius
4. Ancus Marcius
5. Tarquinius Priscus
6. Servius Tullius
7. Tarquinius Superbus

Romulus allegedly promised the Sabine women who had been seized by the men of Rome that their husbands would treat them with extra kindness to compensate for the parents and the country they so missed. The scene here is by Giovanni Sodoma (1477–1549).

This altar, dating from the first century AD, shows a relief sculpture of Romulus, Remus and the she-wolf. It comes from the port city of Ostia which, according to legend, was built by Ancus Marcius, the fourth king of Rome.

THE LUPERCALIA

The Lupercalia (feast of the she-wolf) was a hugely popular purification and fertility ritual celebrated annually on 15 February. It was supervised by two colleges of priests: the Luperci Quintilii (traditionally founded by Romulus) and the Luperci Fabii (traditionally founded by Remus). On the 15th, the two colleges of priests met at the Lupercal, a cave at the foot of the Palatine Hill where, according to tradition, the wolf suckled Romulus and Remus.

The priests sacrificed goats and a dog and offered up cakes prepared by the Vestal Virgins. Two high-born youths were smeared with the blood of the victims, then wiped clean by the priests with wool soaked in milk. The youths then had to burst into laughter, gird their loins with goatskin and participate in a feast. Afterwards, they and the priests ran through the city striking bystanders with strips of goatskin. Women believed that if they were struck by the goatskin they would be granted fertility and ease in childbirth.

Pope Gelasius I finally suppressed the feast in AD 494 and announced that it would henceforth be the Feast of the Purification of the Virgin Mary. Some people believe that the celebration of St Valentine's Day is a survival of the Lupercalia.

A Multitude of Gods

Augustine of Hippo described the Romans as 'men who loved a multitude of gods'. While the sheer number of Roman deities can indeed be overwhelming, early myths associated with them were remarkably undeveloped. In time, however, a more emotionally engaging mythology was to arise, due largely to the influence of the Greeks.

Etruscan Italy
From the beginning Roman mythology and religion was influenced by Etruscan deities. The map shows the evidence of Etruscan culture in Italy.

The Greek god Pan was often identified with the Roman Faunus. Both deities were associated with nature and fertility as well as dance and music. This Roman sculpture shows a celebratory procession in honour of the god.

From their earliest days, the gods of Rome were influenced by Greek, Etruscan and Italic deities. The Romans also imported many deities wholesale, in accordance with their policy of tolerance towards other peoples' gods. Considering, also, that many deities had numerous aspects and names, it is not surprising that the Roman priests kept lengthy catalogues of their gods.

at the very beginning of the fifth century BC. According to legend they had helped Rome to victory in a battle against the Latins. Another early direct import from Greece was Apollo, officially admitted in 431 BC.

INFLUENCES AND IMPORTATIONS

Janus, the god of entrances, is the only deity to appear solely in Roman mythology. Another early god, Saturn, was possibly of Latin origin, while Quirinus (with whom Romulus was later identified), was worshipped by the Sabines. Jupiter, who had his origins in Etruria, formed a very early triad with Quirinus and the Italic god Mars. However, by the start of the Republic in 509 BC, he had become Jupiter Optimus Maximus, chief god of the Roman state and head of the Capitoline Triad, flanked by Juno and Minerva, also from Etruria. Another triad was composed of the grain goddess Ceres together with Liber and Libera. The temple of this group, set on the Aventine Hill, was dedicated in 494/3 BC. Ceres came from southern Italy, though she had been influenced by the Greek Demeter before becoming established in Rome.

The twins Castor and Pollux were the earliest Greek gods officially introduced to Rome,

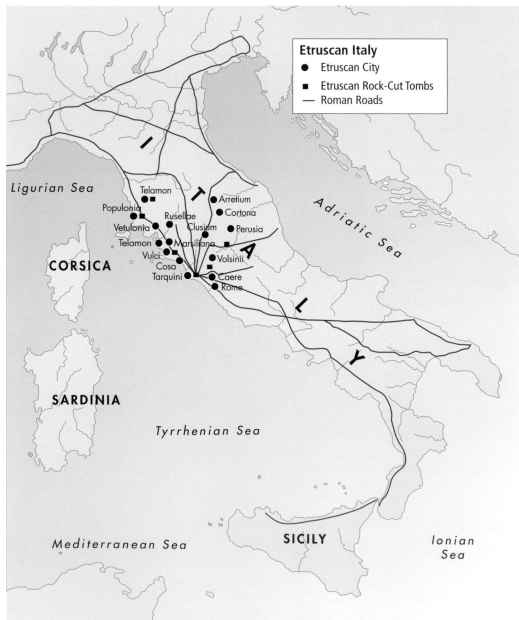

Etruscan Italy
● Etruscan City
■ Etruscan Rock-Cut Tombs
— Roman Roads

Ligurian Sea

Telamon
Populonia
Rusellae
Vetulonia
Clusium
Telamon
Marsiliana
Vulci
Cosa
Volsinii
Tarquini
Caere
Rome

Arretium
Cortona
Perusia

ITALY

Adriatic Sea

CORSICA

SARDINIA

Tyrrhenian Sea

Mediterranean Sea

SICILY

Ionian Sea

THE DII CONSENTES

As Greek culture strengthened its grip, the Roman deities increasingly came to resemble the Greek gods. The Dii Consentes, corresponding to the 12 Greek Olympians, were especially honoured. Listed by the poet Ennius in the third century BC, they numbered Jupiter, Juno, Neptune, Vesta, Mars, Minerva, Venus, Mercury, Diana, Vulcan, Ceres and Apollo.

It is widely assumed that the Dii Consentes were the 12 gods present at a famous *lectisternium* (banquet of the gods) held in 217 BC. Determined to find favour with the gods following early defeats by the Carthaginian general Hannibal, the Romans celebrated the Greek rite by setting images of their gods around a table laden with food. Although this was not the first *lectisternium* to be held, the Romans had, until now, insisted that the attendant gods should be invisible. The new development is seen as a huge cultural leap, indicating that the Roman gods now shared fully in the full-blooded mythology of the Greeks.

Twelve years after the *lectisternium*, in 205 BC, the Romans officially introduced the mysteries of the goddess Cybele from Asia Minor. The mystery religions, with their appeal to individualism, threatened official Roman religion as never before. A tolerant, all-embracing approach to foreign deities proved to be at once the strength of Roman religion and its fatal flaw. The golden age of the emperor Augustus, who did much to restore the ancient deities, was yet to come, but the seeds of the downfall of the Roman gods were sown.

Flora, the Roman goddess of spring and flowers, is shown here crowned and garlanded with flowers and foliage in the famous painting *Primavera* by Sandro Botticelli (1445–1510). The painting draws on Roman mythology to represent the arrival of spring.

THE SIBYLLINE BOOKS

The worship of Rome's foreign gods was overseen by the Quindecemviri Sacris Faciundis. These fifteen priests (originally two) also guarded the Sibylline Books. The Sibyls were priestesses of Apollo, traditionally associated with prophecy. One story tells how a Greek Sibyl living at Cumae, southern Italy, during the reign of Tarquinius Priscus offered to sell him nine books which contained the destiny of Rome. Tarquinius refused to pay the price, whereupon the Sibyl burned six of the books. Eventually, Tarquinius was prompted to pay the original price for the remaining three books and they were installed in Rome's chief temple. The Sibylline Books were consulted at times of public crisis such as military defeat or the outbreak of illness. Their prophecies would frequently direct the Romans to introduce a foreign god to the city.

According to the historian Livy, the senate consulted the Sibylline Books when an epidemic broke out in 431 BC and was instructed to bring the Greek god Apollo to Rome. During a similar crisis in 293 BC the senators were directed to introduce the Greek god of medicine (Asklepios). Aesculapius, as he was known in Rome, arrived in the form of a sacred snake and took up residence in a temple which the Romans visited in times of illness.

Public Religion

The religion of the Roman state was in many ways an extension of family religion and ritual. Just as the paterfamilias was the family priest, so the king (or, from the time of the Republic, the religious leader) was chief priest to the people and responsible for public religious activities.

Tradition credits Numa Pompilius, the second king of Rome, with establishing Roman religious rites. The idea of a contract between the gods and the state, the *pax deorum* (peace of the gods), was developed whereby the gods would ensure the preservation and prosperity of Rome if Rome, through the public performance of rituals, helped to sustain the gods in return.

When the last king, Tarquinius Superbus, was ousted and the Republic instated (509 BC), a new office of Rex Sacrorum (king of rites) was created in order that the former monarch's religious duties might continue to be fulfilled. The Rex Sacrorum was a priest appointed for life from amongst the Roman patricians (the powerful, wealthy class). He was prohibited from holding any other office in order to prevent him gaining undue power. Nonetheless, Roman religion and politics were inextricably entwined: priests were quite often politicians or generals. Julius Caesar was, for example, the Pontifex Maximus or chief priest, though he himself was agnostic.

PRIESTS AND COLLEGES

Priests and other religious professionals were usually elected in a general assembly by male citizens of Rome, then organized into colleges. The most prestigious of these were the College of Pontifices and the College of Augures, both of which had 16 members by the time of Julius Caesar. Priests of the former (which was led by the Pontifex Maximus) were said to have 'authority over the most

The Forum was for centuries the centre of Rome. Situated at a crossroads, it was the site of social, political and religious functions and housed several temples including those of Vesta, Castor and Pollux, Saturn and, later, Faustina and Romulus.

important matters in the Roman state' and were responsible for sacrifices to the gods. Members of the College of Augures were responsible for establishing the will of the gods by, for example, studying the flight of birds and marking out the sacred space within which sacrifices and important meetings were held and omens taken.

The Flamines were individual priests devoted to individual gods. The three major Flamines participated in rituals for Jupiter, Mars and Quirinus, and were distinguished by the apex, a leather hat which they had to wear in public. The Haruspices were Etruscans rather than élite Romans; their duty was to read the entrails of animals to determine the favour or disfavour of the gods. Many other priesthoods arose, to some extent as occasion demanded. They included the Salii, the Luperci, the Fetiales and the Fratres Arvales, to name but a few.

FESTIVALS

With the rise of the state, festivals which had originally been a part of family and farming life were adopted and magnified into public spectacles, organized and paid for by the state. The Compitalia (held in December) was, for example, transformed from a private agricultural ritual into a public urban event. Among the more notable festivals were the Aedes Vestae (March) – the lighting of the Vestal fires, the Cerialia (March) – an offering to Ceres, the Lemuria (May) – to chase evil spirits from the home, the Saturnalia (December) – a carnival in honour of Saturn, and the October Horse – in honour of Mars.

While the priesthoods were dominated by the Roman élites – and often used to their advantage – the festivals could be enjoyed by the plebeians (common people). Nonetheless, state religion catered mainly to the upper classes, giving them influence, standing and most important of all, power.

Diana, the Roman goddess of nature and fertility is depicted here by Francois Boucher (1703–1770). Originally a moon goddess worshipped in sacred groves, she became particularly important to plebians and slaves. Women worshipped her as the giver of easy births.

WOMEN, PLEBEIANS AND SLAVES

Roman public religion was largely the preserve of the patricians. However, there were a number of deities whose cults existed at the fringes of official religion and civic life. Several goddesses, including Diana, Bona Dea and Ceres, appealed particularly to women and the oppressed, often being seen as their protectors. In the early Republic, the grain goddess Ceres came to be associated with the plebeians when her temple on the Aventine Hill became the centre of a political movement directed against patricians. The Aventine Hill was also a centre for the worship of Diana, who appealed especially to plebeian women, and Bona Dea, 'the good goddess'. Bona Dea's rituals included animal sacrifice, singing and dancing and the avoidance of myrtle, a plant associated with female sexuality. Men were usually excluded from Bona Dea's rituals, although freed slaves were sometimes admitted to her priesthood. The Vestal Virgins were the only women who could belong to an official priesthood. However, a few women were allowed to be priestesses. The wife of the Flamen Dialis, the priest of Jupiter, was known as the Flaminica Dialis. Her husband lost his position if she died.

Heroes and Emperors

With the eastward expansion of her territory, Rome encountered many new customs. Among these, the practice of worshipping kings as gods proved to be particularly compelling. Though a useful political tool, the association was sufficiently innovatory for it to be left tentative both in Rome and throughout the West.

The idea that a great man could, on his death, become a god was rooted in the founding myths of Rome: Romulus was worshipped as the god Quirinus and Aeneas as Jupiter Indiges. Roman rituals gave divine attributes to dead ancestors and by the third century BC prominent Romans were claiming that their families were descended from deities. However, the notion of an actual living god did not sit easy with the Western frame of mind and for a long time the military honour of *Triumphator* was the closest a living Roman came to being honoured as divine.

THE TRIUMPH

The Triumph was a religious ceremony of Etruscan origin. In order to receive the honour, a Roman general had to triumph over a foreign enemy and return to Rome with at least a token army. The Senate then decided whether the general was worthy to be granted the accolade.

On the day of his Triumph, the hero, his face painted red and wearing a purple toga, rode in a golden chariot through the streets of Rome, from the Campus Martius to the temple of Jupiter on the Capitoline Hill. A slave would stand behind him, holding a golden crown over

Julius Caesar (shown here on a Roman coin crowned with laurels, a symbol of victory) became elevated virtually to the rank of a god during his own lifetime. His enemies, threatened by his power, assassinated him on the Ides of March 44 BC.

The Roman Empire
The map shows the the expansion of the Roman Empire from the accession of Augustus, the first emperor, to the Empire's maximum extent in the second century AD.

his head and whispering in his ear, 'Remember, you are mortal'. The day ended with feasting throughout the city. The troops of Julius Caesar would march ahead of their great Triumphator, carrying placards bearing the words *Veni, Vidi, Vici* (I came, I saw, I conquered) or displaying maps of the territories he had conquered.

EMPEROR WORSHIP

It was with Julius Caesar (100–44 BC) that the Romans began the regular practice of deifying their dead leaders. Remarkably, whilst still alive, Caesar was granted the distinction of receiving divine honours in the city of Rome itself: his image was carried next to that of Quirinus in processions and he was allocated his own priest. Such honours set Julius Caesar above all other Romans. On his death, the appearance of a comet in the sky was interpreted as a sign of his ascent to heaven and two years later he became Divus Iulius (the deified Julius), an official god of the Roman state.

Augustus (63 BC–AD 14), the first Roman emperor, never outrightly claimed divine status, but he trod a fine line. At one stage he experimented with claiming Apollo as his father, but later thought better of it; he also promoted himself as a second Romulus and allowed worship of his Genius and Numen. Although every Roman had a Genius (something akin to his generative force), the Numen belonged to the realm of the sacred. In the eastern nations of the empire, however, Augustus allowed himself to be worshipped as a god, largely as a means of integrating the diverse peoples of the region, and usually in association with worship of Roma, the goddess of Rome. After Augustus died, a senator took an oath swearing that he had seen him ascend into Heaven. From then on, it became routine practice for Rome to deify her dead emperors.

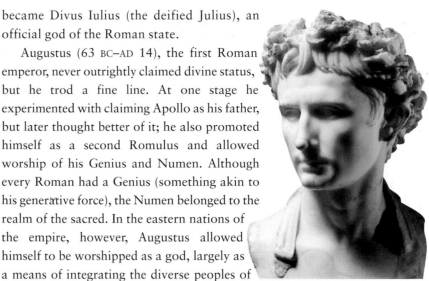

The first Roman emperor, Augustus (63 BC–AD 14) kept peace in Rome for many years. In an attempt to bring moral and social cohesion to the empire, he sought to revive traditional Roman religion and ordered many temples to be built.

The Temple of Hercules, shown left, is the oldest of a number of temples found in what has become known as the Valley of Temples in Sicily. Built in the late sixth century BC, it originally had 38 columns.

HERCULES

According to tradition, Hercules arrived at the future site of Rome while carrying out one of his seven labours. As he lay sleeping on the banks of the Tiber, he was tricked by the fearsome Cacus and, on waking and discovering his enemy, killed him with a single blow. The king of the region at this time was Evander, originally from Greece. Evander announced that his mother had prophesized that Hercules would become a god and suggested that a shrine, the Ara Maxima (great altar), be built on the site of his victory. One day, he added, the altar would belong to the most powerful nation in the world. Hercules built the altar and two local families, the Potitii and Pinarii, participated in the first sacrifice. This was said to be the one foreign rite adopted by Romulus, who was deeply impressed both by the courage of Hercules and by the fact that it had won him immortality. Situated in Rome's cattle market, the Ara Maxima was looked after by the Potitii and Pinarii families until the early fourth century BC, when it was taken over by the Roman state. Hercules is thought to have been introduced to Rome from Magna Graecia in southern Italy, where he was known as Herakles. The altar can, however, be traced back to the Phoenician god Melkart.

Mystery Religions

From the third century BC several so-called mystery religions began to arrive in Rome, mainly from the Middle and Near East. Their appeal seems to have been emotional and spiritual, while some also provided a moral code. They were not, however, always looked on kindly by Roman officials.

The mystery religions offered their followers the possibility of an afterlife and had as a central theme the death and resurrection of a deity. Their teachings were kept secret from all but initiates and, unlike the state religion, they encouraged worshippers to enter into a personal relationship with the deity. In an increasingly complex world, they were a source of identity formation and expression.

THE MAGNA MATER AND ISIS

The cult of Cybele, the Great Mother or Magna Mater, was introduced to Rome on the instruction of the Cumaean Sibyl, a priestess of Apollo from Cumae, a city founded by the Greeks on the coast of Italy in the eighth century BC. Under threat of invasion from Hannibal's army, the Romans consulted the oracle and were told that their enemy would be driven off if the goddess were brought to Rome from Phyrgia in Asia Minor. A deputation was sent to obtain the black stone, the symbol of the goddess, and on 4 April 204 BC it was placed in Rome's Temple of Victory.

Cybele's priests, the Galli, castrated themselves on entering the priesthood and during the annual celebration of the death and resurrection of her consort, Attis, they slashed themselves and led ecstatic dances. When the Roman officials learned of such activities, they kept the cult of Cybele under strict control and, until the reign of Claudius (AD 41–54), forbade any Roman to become her priest.

Cybele, the great mother goddess, was introduced to Rome from Asia Minor. She is shown here on a Roman shield dating from the fifth century AD with her consort Attis, whose annual death and resurrection was marked by a period of mourning followed by joyful celebration.

Mystery Religions
Mystery religions began to arrive in Rome from the third century BC. They filled a void created by a need for spirituality and offered the possibility of an afterlife and a personal relationship with a deity. These religions were practised in secret and often frowned upon by officials who saw them as subversive.

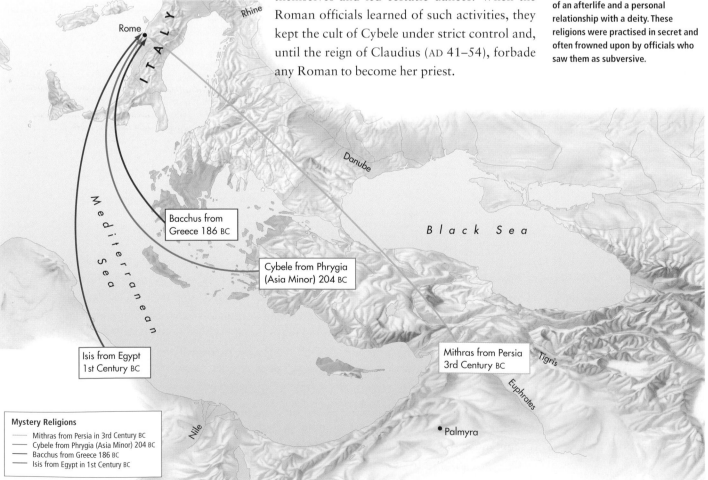

Rome
ITALY
Rhine

Bacchus from Greece 186 BC

Cybele from Phyrgia (Asia Minor) 204 BC

Mediterranean Sea

Danube

Black Sea

Isis from Egypt 1st Century BC

Mithras from Persia 3rd Century BC

Tigris

Euphrates

Nile

• Palmyra

Mystery Religions
— Mithras from Persia in 3rd Century BC
— Cybele from Phyrgia (Asia Minor) 204 BC
— Bacchus from Greece 186 BC
— Isis from Egypt in 1st Century BC

Like the cult of Cybele, the cult of Isis was especially popular with women devotees. Worship of the Egyptian mother goddess reached Rome early in the first century BC but was banned by the emperor Augustus who associated the goddess with his arch enemy Cleopatra. However, by the early first century AD the worship of Isis was again flourishing, though the satirist Juvenal (*c*.AD 60–130) said her priestesses were no more than bawds.

BACCHUS

About two decades after the Magna Mater's grand entry into Rome, the senate acted against another mystery cult, this time from Greece.

Bacchus (the Greek Dionysus) was a saviour god and god of the vine. His rites, the Bacchanalia, were notorious for their drunken licentiousness, supposedly an aid to ecstatic religious experience. In 186 BC the senate restricted the cult, believing not only that it gave free rein to untold depravities but that it also provided an opportunity for the lower classes to conspire against the authorities. All secret Bacchic rites were banned throughout Italy and Romans were forbidden to be priests. The punishment was death.

MITHRAS

Mithraism, which flourished from the second to fifth centuries AD, differed from the other mystery religions in that it allowed only men into its community. Meetings were held in small underground chapels, hundreds of which have since been found across the Roman Empire. Such was the secrecy surrounding the religion that much about it remains unclear. However, it seems to have been related both to sun worship and to astrology. The most important stage of initiation was the sacrifice of a bull and the application of its blood to the initiate as a symbol of the victory over death. For a long time, Christianity and Mithraism were fierce competitors. When Christianity finally won, it took over many of the underground chapels as Christian prayer rooms.

Mithras first appealed to slaves and freedmen but later became a god of soldiers and traders. This sculpture from the second century AD depicts the famous tauroctony or bull-slaying scene whereby the god was believed to have released the generative powers of nature.

Bacchus, the Roman god of wine, came to be identified with the Greek god Dionysus. Caravaggio's painting of the young god suggests the drunken licentiousness for which he was notorious. The Bacchanalia, celebrations in honour of Bacchus, were banned by the Roman Senate in 186 BC.

THE ARRIVAL OF CHRISTIANITY

Like the other mystery religions, Christianity was regarded with suspicion by Roman officials: it attracted the lower classes and encouraged them to assemble together in secret. Rumours about cannibalism and magic practices arose. More importantly, Christians worshipped only one god and refused to participate in the state cults; some even refused to join the army and to respect the emperor. Persecution of the Christians began with Nero's bloody repression of AD 64 and continued intermittently until, in AD 311, the emperor Galerius issued a death-bed edict of toleration. The following year, the emperor Constantine claimed to have had a dream or vision on the eve of battle in which the Christian god promised him victory. On the defeat of his enemy, Constantine embraced a pro-Christian policy. Like subsequent emperors, Constantine clearly made use of Christianity's unifying potential, though he remained Pontifex Maximus and continued to consult haruspices (priests who divined the will of the gods by examining the entrails of sacrificial animals) and appoint new priests to Roman priesthoods. In AD 380, Emperor Theodosius made Christianity the official religion of state and in AD 392 banned pagan ceremonies. In many cases, Christians took over the symbols, ceremonies and even identities of pre-Christian deities and made them their own. The crescent moon of Isis became a symbol for the Virgin Mary and Saints Walpurga and Brigid, for example, took the place of Ceres as grain protectresses.

The Mystery of the Celts

The Celts left a rich legacy of myths, legends, customs and folklore, which are among the oldest and most enduring in Europe, though they did not form an empire and their kingdoms comprised a wide variety of countries and cultures. Perhaps because of this their identity remains controversial, and our image of them is reworked by each new generation of Celtic scholars.

The mystery of the Celts arises from the fact that they left no written accounts of themselves. Consequently, our knowledge of them is based on indirect evidence provided by archaeology, linguistics and Classical commentaries.

Celtic material culture emerged in Central and Western Europe in the first millennium BC. It is first encountered in the artefacts of the Halstatt period (700–400 BC), so-named after an important archaeological site in upper Austria. The origins of the culture are much earlier, however, in the later Bronze Age settlements of non-Mediterranean Europe and probably even earlier still in the first Neolithic farming communities c. 4000 BC. The La Tène period (fifth century BC to the Roman occupation c. AD 45), which is named after a site on the shores of

Lake Neuchâtel in Switzerland, represents the full-flowering of the culture. Finds have been made over much of Europe from northern France to Romania and from Poland to the Po Valley. This evidence portrays a heroic and hierarchical society in which war, feasting and bodily adornment were important. In many respects this confirms the picture of the Celts painted by Classical writers from the sixth century BC onwards.

EARLY RECORDS OF THE CELTS

Hecataeus of Miletus and Herotodus, writing in the sixth and fifth centuries BC, recognized a group of peoples to the north of the Greek port of Massalia (Marseilles) as having sufficient cultural features in common to justify a collective name, 'Keltoi'. By the fourth century BC commentators

This bronze cover of a shield made of leather and wood found in the River Thames at Battersea, London, is a ceremonial object thought to date from the third century BC. The abstract, geometric designs in the metalwork are a good example of La Tène craftsmanship, which drew on the natural world – plants, animals, human faces – for its motifs.

Celtic Europe
Because the Celts left no written account of themselves their identity is disputed. However, by the fourth century BC the Celts had expanded into many parts of Europe and were accepted as one of the great Barbarian peoples of the world alongside the Scythians, and the Libyans.

had accepted the Celts as being among the great Barbarian peoples of the world, along with the Scythians, and Libyans; they were said to occupy a large swathe of Western Europe from Iberia to the Upper Danube. Later, Mediterranean writers such as Livy and Polybius report that in the fourth and third centuries BC Celtic tribes spread south into Italy and east to Greece and Asia Minor, where they settled as the Galatians. The same writers record heavy defeats for the Celts by the Romans towards the end of the third century BC and the subsequent occupation of their heartlands in Gaul by the mid-first century BC. Nowhere do the ancients refer to Britain as a Celtic land and debate continues over the precision with which the label 'Celt' was applied by Classical writers.

CELTS AND ETHNICITY

Without their own accounts it is impossible to say whether the Iron Age tribes of Europe, including Britain, saw themselves as collectively 'Celtic'. It is true to say, however, that Caesar recognized similarities between Britain and Gaul, and there is ample evidence of the La Tène culture in the British Isles. In the absence of archaeological evidence to show a migration of peoples from Gaul to Britain, it seems likely that it was the culture which spread; the indigenous peoples simply became Celtic through social contact and trade. Thus, when we refer to 'the Celts' we are not referring to an ethnic group but a culture adopted across non-Mediterranean Europe between the sixth century BC and the fifth century AD. It is ironic that the Irish and Welsh literature to which we owe so much of our understanding of Celtic mythology originated among peoples who may not have seen themselves as Celts.

The fearsome Galatians proved to be a useful mercenary force for the Hellenistic rulers of Asia Minor. In a punitive campaign, the Romans defeated Celtic forces at Magnesia in 190 BC and took 40,000 prisoners. This first-century BC Roman marble sculpture shows a Celtic warrior falling before a Roman onslaught.

The Expansion of the Celts

Celtic heartland by 200 BC

GALICIA

7th–6th century BC

Rome • 390 BC

BALKANS

Delphi • 279 BC

GALATIA

276 BC
ANATOLIA

LANGUAGE AND THE ORAL TRADITION

Celtic languages belong to the Indo-European family. The parent dialect of all Celtic tongues emerged around 2000 BC when ancestors of the Celts began to appear in present-day Switzerland and southwest Germany. Features in the area still retain their Celtic names. The Danube, for example, was named after the goddess, Danu (divine waters).

The earliest linguistic evidence for the Celts, dating from the last few centuries BC, comprises inscriptions, coin legends and names (people and places) recorded in Classical texts. They show that, by this time, Celtic languages were spoken in Central and Eastern Europe, Britain, Gaul, northern Italy and Spain.

There are no Celtic written texts from this period. Priests, known as druids, trained for twenty years to memorize Celtic law. Bards carried tribal history, legend and folklore in their heads. Written Welsh first appears in the eighth century AD as notes on Latin texts. Manuscripts written entirely in Irish appear in the twelfth century.

The eloquence and rhetoric of the bards were highly valued in Celtic societies. The power of poets and singers lay in their inspired performance – what the Welsh call *hwyl*. The earliest recorded bards include Aneirin and Taliesin (sixth century AD). The bardic tradition continues today, most notably in Welsh cultural festivals called *eisteddfodau*.

Gods and Heroes

The Celts were polytheistic. The names of over 200 gods have been recorded. It is likely that individual deities went under several titles, so there were probably fewer than this. The scene remains complex, however, and attempts to reduce the Celtic pantheon to a coherent system have met with varying degrees of success.

The Celts had gods for all of the important aspects of their lives: warfare, hunting, fertility, healing, good harvests and so on. Much of the difficulty in classifying them arises from the fact that very few were recognized universally. In much greater numbers were local, tribal and possibly family deities. Our knowledge of the Celtic pantheon is based on the interpretations of contemporary observers, later vernacular literature (mainly from Ireland and Wales) and archaeological finds.

Very little iconography in the form of wood or stone sculptures has survived from before the Roman conquests, although a vast amount of perishable material must have existed. The earliest archaeological evidence from this period is from Provence and Central Europe. At Roquepertuse and Holtzerlingen, Celtic deities were represented in human form as early as the sixth and fifth centuries BC. Roman influence witnessed the production of many more permanent representations of the gods; dedicatory inscriptions reveal a huge array of native god names.

ROMAN INTERPRETATIONS

Caesar identified Celtic gods with what he saw as their Roman equivalents, probably to render them more comprehensible to a Roman

Detail from the Gundestrup Cauldron showing Cerunnos, the horned god of fertility. He is sitting cross-legged and holds a torc (neck-ring) and a snake. Cerunnos is surrounded by animals who acknowledge them as their lord.

Celtic Religious Sites
As the Celtic influence spread so did the Celtic religion. The map shows evidence of Celtic religious sites in northern Europe from 800 BC.

Celtic Religious Sites from 800BC
✠ Celtic Religious Sites

North Sea

✠ Newstead
✠ Coventina's Wall
✠ Tara
BRITISH ISLES
✠ Emain Macha
✠ Llyn Cerrig Bach
✠ Long Wittenham
✠ Silchester
✠ Wilsford
✠ Heathrow

Atlantic Ocean
English Channel

✠ Msecke Zehrovice
✠ Libenice
GERMANY
✠ Tomerdingen
✠ Manching
✠ Holzhausen

✠ Le Bernard
✠ Source de la Siene
FRANCE

✠ Roquepertuse
✠ Entremont

Mediterranean Sea
ITALY

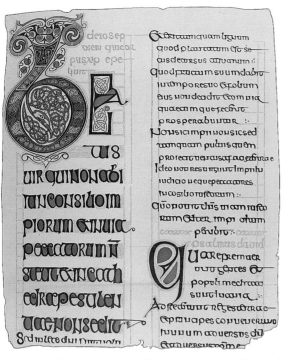

Left: page from a seventh-century AD **Irish psalter,** *Beatus Vir,* showing ornate celtic script.

Stone carvings of the Sheela-na-gig, from medieval Ireland and elsewhere, show a naked woman in a revealing pose. They are probably fertility figures used as a cure for barrenness and may be reminders of the Earth Mother, whose rule over life and death predated Christianity. Many examples are found in churches and serve as a warning against lust and sin.

deities. Very little was committed to paper before the monks began writing down Irish tales in the sixth century AD. The earliest written Welsh material dates from the twelfth century. Informative though they might be, however, the stories are influenced by Romano-Christian thinking and no doubt the monks censored the worst excesses of heathenism.

The stories are collected in sequences which follow the exploits of heroes, legendary kings and mythical characters from their unusual forms of conception and birth to their remarkable deaths. Along the way we learn of their expeditions to the otherworld, their loves and their battles. Many of the Irish legends are contained in three such collections. The first, known as the *Mythological Cycle,* records the imagined early history of Ireland. The second, the *Ulster Cycle,* tells of Cú Chulainn, a hero with superhuman strength and magical powers. The third is the story of another hero, Finn Mac Cumaill, his son Ossian and their warriors, the Fianna. This is known as the *Fenian Cycle.*

The pagan character of the mythology found in Irish literature is very clear. The Welsh tales, collected mainly in the *Mabinogion,* are much later (fourteenth century) and are contaminated more by time and changing literary fashions.

readership. He said of the Gauls that the god they revered the most was Mercury and, next to him, Apollo, Mars, Jupiter and Minerva. Lucan (AD 39–65), a famous Roman poet, named three Celtic deities: Teutates (god of the tribe), Taranis (thunder) and Esus (multi-skilled). Other commentators identify Teutates with Mercury, Esus with Mars and Taranis with Dispater (the all father). Inscriptions on altars and monuments found across the Roman Empire, however, identify Teutates with Mars, Esus with Mercury and Taranis with Jupiter. By Caesar's time, the Romans had lost touch with their own gods and this sort of confusion is not unexpected.

VERNACULAR SOURCES

It is to Christian monks that we owe the survival of the ancient oral traditions of the pagan Celts and a more lucid insight into the nature of their

DUALISM AND TRIPLICITY

In the vernacular literature there is a recurring dualism between the male tribal god and the female deity of the land. This structure is undoubtedly of pagan origin and is seen most clearly in the Irish tales in the relationship between the Dagda and his consort, the Morrigan. The Dagda is the all-competent protector of the tribe who controls warfare and the provision of wisdom. The demonic Morrigan is both fertile and destructive. She represents sovereignty, and her union with the Dagda on the night of the festival of Samain ensures the continued prosperity of the tribe, the fertility of the land and that of their livestock.

The number three had tremendous power for the Celts. It featured in their iconography and in the form of their (mainly female) deities. The Morrigan, for example, often appears in triple form with her 'sisters' Badb and Nemain. Brigit and Macha also occur as triads. Similarly, the Deae Matres or the Matronae are three mother goddesses who together form a unity representing strength, power and fertility.

The love triangle is a common theme in Celtic romances. Typical is the story of the handsome Diarmaid who absconded with Grainne, the beautiful young wife of the ageing Finn MacCumaill.

Rites and Rituals

Caesar wrote that the Gauls burnt men alive in huge, wicker effigies. Lucan speaks of 'cruel Teutates, horrible Esus and Taranis whose altar is as bloody as that of the Scythian Diana'. Medieval accounts tell of men hung from trees and torn to pieces in honour of Teutates, and of victims burnt in hollow trees as sacrifices to Taranis.

How reliable or typical these horrific tales may be is a matter of judgement. It is to be expected that Caesar and the sycophantic Lucan might emphasize the cruelty of Celtic cults to justify Roman massacres and the systematic extermination of the druids. Equally, Christian historians had an interest in discrediting paganism.

THE DRUIDS

Druids may be named after the oak, their sacred tree. They were highly esteemed in Celtic society not only as holy men but also as teachers, philosophers, judges, diviners and astronomers. There were no druidesses as such, although priestesses are reported to have stood alongside the druids as they tried to resist the Roman occupation of Anglesey (AD 60).

The male head adorned with two opposed, mistletoe-shaped leaves is a persistent motif in Celtic art found as early as the fifth century BC and as late as the first century AD. If the head-dresses are indeed mistletoe, then the heads might represent druids, for whom the plant was sacred.

It was forbidden for the druids' secrets to be written down lest they be profaned and lose their power. Consequently, laws, histories, traditions and magic formulae, which took many years to learn, were lost to posterity.

Without authentic written records Druidism is shrouded in mystery and obscured by romanticism, but the writings of Classical observers, such as Caesar, give us some idea of Druidic customs. We know, for example, that they were a well-organized, inter-tribal group who met annually to confer and to elect a leader. They held their ceremonies in forbidding, sacred groves which were allowed to grow thick and wild, and they presided at sacrifices, some of which might well have been human. Druids taught that the soul does not perish after death but that it transmigrates or moves into a new body. Perhaps some of the victims were willing participants who saw themselves as dying for the good of the tribe.

Mistletoe, a perennial plant, was considered sacred by the druids. They saw the relationship between the plant and the trees on which it grew as similar to that between the soul and the body. Like the soul, mistletoe was thought to proceed from the gods.

The tolerance shown by the Romans to the religions of the vanquished did not extend to the druids. The emperors Augustus, Tiberius and Claudius all sought to eradicate them. They painted a grim picture of them as unsavoury figures associated with disgusting ritual practices. This persecution was probably born of fear rather than moral scruple. The druids were a powerful group and a potential focus for rebellion.

GROVES, SPRINGS AND SHRINES

Certain Celtic deities were associated with particular places such as sacred groves, remote mountains and lakes. Springs were thought to be the homes of goddesses in the service of the Earth Mother, the source of all life. Sulis, for example, guarded the hot springs at Aquae Sulis (present-day Bath).

The Celts believed that their gods and goddesses had powers to heal and protect, and to influence the outcome of important and everyday events. Celts asking a favour of a particular deity would make a sacrifice. If they were appealing to a water goddess, they might throw valued possessions into the water. Archaeologists have made some of their most important discoveries of weapons and other Iron-Age objects in the mud at the bottom of lakes.

A Celtic stone head from southwestern England. The Celts regarded the head as the centre of the spiritual power and as such, attributed a protective function to representations of human heads in their art.

The fourth-century BC Lindow Man was found in Cheshire in 1984, and appears to have been a sacrificial victim. He was discovered in a well-preserved state in a peat bog and judging by his well-manicured nails, was well-born. He underwent a threefold killing by a blow to the head, a slit throat and strangulation, and an examination of his stomach revealed mistletoe pollen and burnt oatcakes.

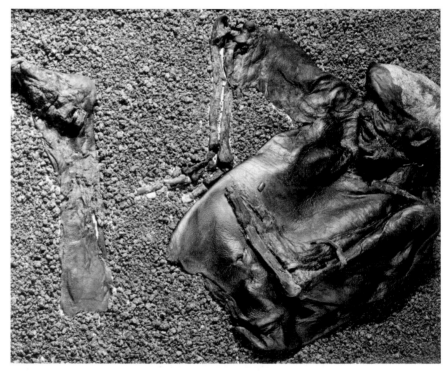

THE CULT OF THE HEAD

The Classical commentator, Diodorus Siculus, tells us that the Celts ritually decapitated their fallen enemies and kept the heads as trophies or offered them in shrines. There is archaeological evidence to support this. In the pre-Roman, clifftop shrine of Roquepertuse, near Marseilles, the portico was adorned with niches containing the nailed-in skulls of vanquished warriors. In Britain, there are signs that heads were mounted on poles to protect the entrances to strongholds such as Bredon Hill (in present-day Worcestershire).

As well as providing proof of prowess, head-hunting may well have had a religious purpose. It is said that the Celts believed the head to be the dwelling place of the immortal soul. By possessing the head of an enemy they may have believed they gained control over his spirit, too.

There are several accounts in the vernacular literature of severed heads talking and counselling the living. An example is the Welsh story of Bran the Blessed, whose head was eventually buried in London to deter invaders from the Continent. Another common aspect of the cult of the head in the myths is the beheading game in which heroes such as Cú Chulainn and Gawain prove their valour by literally putting their heads on the block.

Saints and Survivals

The religious practices of the Celts survived well into the Christian era. This is shown by resolutions passed at Church councils in the sixth century AD and by the edicts of Charlemagne (AD 789) against 'the worshippers of stones, trees and springs'. Powerless to supress the old beliefs, Christianity assimilated aspects of paganism.

This appropriation accounts for the large number of saints rooted in Celtic gods and heroes, the springs dedicated to saints or to the Virgin and the sanctuaries built on sacred mounds. Indeed, the Christian religion is a rich source for the study of Celtic spirituality.

THE CELTIC CHURCH

From AD 432, St Patrick established a form of Christianity in Ireland to suit a society that was still tribal. Rural monasteries, where monks followed the teachings of their founders, varied from the urban system of churches and Bishops, which was favoured by Rome. This was a much more familiar approach for the Celts, whose structures centred on the family, the clan and powerful local leaders. This form spread to other Celtic countries until the Celtic and Roman Churches met at the Synod of Whitby (AD 664) where the Roman approach prevailed. Thereafter, many of the teachings favoured in Ireland and Britain were forced underground.

The Celtic church was distinctive in many ways which betrayed its ancient roots: its affinity with nature in all its aspects, for example; its respect for the seasonal festivals; the equality it afforded women; and the active participation of the congregation during worship.

THE SAINTS

The Christian church adapted stories of Celtic divinities as miraculous events in the lives of the saints. Many reflect the Celtic sympathy with nature and the ability of the gods to assume the shape of animals. St Ciaran, for example, trained a fox to carry his psalter; St Kevin had his psalter returned by an otter when he dropped it in a lake; and St Columba subdued the Loch Ness Monster.

In the sixth and seventh centuries, masons in Irish monasteries were producing roughly hewn stone slabs bearing precisely carved cross symbols. By the eighth century these had evolved into 'High Crosses' such as this. The elaborate decoration was clearly inspired by the La Tène metal-working traditions.

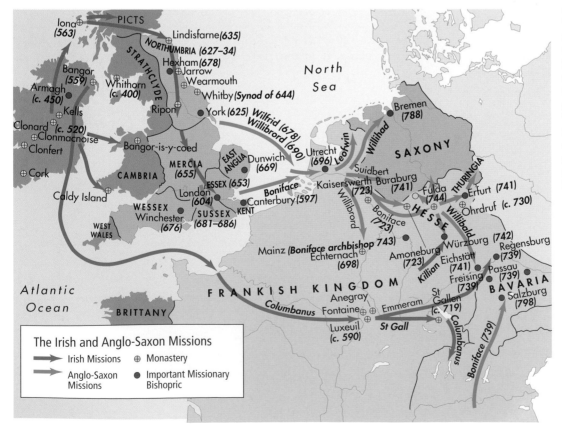

The Irish and Anglo-Saxon Missions
Irish missionaries such as Columba (AD 521-597) and Aidan (d.AD 615) were instrumental in converting Scotland and northern England to Christianity; Columbanus (d.AD 615) founded monastries in the Frankish kingdom. The Anglo-Saxon kingdoms also sent missionaries (with Roman and Frankish support) to western Germany. The most important were Willibrord (AD 658–739) and Boniface (AD 675–754), bishops Utrecht and Mainz.

The Gothic abbey of Mont St Michel in Brittany. This conical, granite island was sacred to the Celts as a solar sanctuary called Dinsul or Belen and dedicated to St Michael in AD 710. According to the twelfth-century writer, Geoffrey of Monmouth, Arthur killed a giant here, who had carried off the Duke of Brittany's daughter.

In its employment of knotwork and spiral devices, and its mimicking of enamel and glasswork, the decoration in the *Book of Durrow* bears a marked resemblance to metalwork and jewellery. While monks were illuminating the Christian gospels in monastery scruptoria, others were collecting and writing down the legends of the pagan Celts.

St Patrick was attributed the most miracles, many of which arise from his struggle with the druids; it was said he could take the form of a deer.

RELIGIOUS FESTIVALS

The four main religious festivals of the Celts that were absorbed into the Christian calendar were Samain, Imbolc, Beltaine and Lughnasa. Samain (1 November) marked the end of the agricultural year and the beginning of the next. It was a time for important communal rituals, meetings and sacrifices, as well as being a period when spirits from the otherworld became visible to men. Under Christianity this celebration became Harvest Festival and All Souls Day. The eve of the festival, known today as All Hallows Eve or Halloween, was particularly dangerous.

Imbolc (1 February) was sacred to the fertility goddess, Brigit, and it marked the coming into milk of the ewes and the time for moving them to upland pastures. It was subsequently taken over by the Christians as the feast of St Brigid.

At Beltaine (1 May), people lit bonfires in honour of Belenus, a god of life and death. The festival was seen as a purification or a fresh start. It is likely, too, that the fires were used to fumigate cattle before they were moved to the summer pastures. Under Christianity it became the feast of St John the Baptist.

Finally, there was the festival of Lughnasa (1 August), which the Christians renamed Lammas. It honoured the sun god, Lugh.

THE SACRED LANDSCAPE

In AD 601, following the example of saints such as Patrick and Columba, Pope Gregory ordered his missionaries not to destroy pagan places of worship, but to bless them and convert them to Christian shrines. Thus holy wells and springs dedicated to Christian saints survive throughout the Celtic lands.

To the Celts the power of the earth was represented by the dragon. The mythical, subterranean creature came to be reviled under Christianity as the embodiment of paganism. To the early Christians, lairs of the beast were evident everywhere: in Celtic burial mounds, strongholds and sacred enclosures. It is thought that such landmarks were favoured by the Christians as sites for their churches, thereby claiming the land for Christ and suppressing the evil lurking below. Distinctive mountains were associated with the sun and revered by the Celts as places of light and enlightenment. There are few more striking holy mountains than St Michael's Mount in Cornwall and Mont Saint Michel in Normandy (St Michael commonly supplanted the Celtic deities originally associated with such mountains). On the summit of Glastonbury Tor in Somerset, traditionally held to be a gateway to the otherworld, a church dedicated to St Michael was planted to prevent the demonic hoards of Gwynn ap Nudd, a king of the otherworld, from swarming through.

Recurring Themes

The myths of the Celts, found in Irish, Welsh and Continental vernacular literature, have inspired the imagination of poets and storytellers from the twelfth century to the present day. Their archetypal themes and imagery, though cloaked in novel forms by each new generation, never lose their potency.

No Celtic creation myth has survived, although Caesar, among other ancient commentators, testifies that they did have one. The nearest we have is a collection of stories in the *Book of Invasions* (twelfth century), which provide a mythical history of Ireland from the Flood to the coming of the Gaels (Celts).

DIVINE LOVE AND THE GIANT'S DAUGHTER

Love is a central theme in Celtic mythology; love between deities and between gods and humans. The love triangle is a recurring variation, often involving a young couple and an unwanted suitor or an older husband. The outcome is often tragic. Typical of this genre are the Welsh story of Pwll and Rhiannon and the Irish tales of Diarmaid and Grainne, and Deirdre and Naoise.

Sometimes the triangle involves the young woman's father, who is often represented as a giant. In these stories the hero is frequently set seemingly impossible tasks to complete before winning the daughter's hand. A primary example is the Welsh tale of Culhwch and Olwen. Here Culhwch seeks the help of Arthur and his band of warriors to complete a list of tasks which culminate in a hunt for the monstrous boar, Twrch Trwyth.

Another theme is that of sacral kingship and sovereignty, in which the coupling of the king and the goddess of fertility ensures prosperity in the land. The goddess sometimes appears as a hag who turns into a beautiful young woman following the ritual.

SHAPE-SHIFTING, MAGIC AND ENCHANTMENT

Magic is an essential feature of Celtic myths. It is commonly used as a means of escape, as in the case of Diarmaid and Grainne who evade Finn's huntsmen for years using a cloak of invisibility, borrowed from Óengus, a love god. A typical form of magic found in many of the myths is the

A second- or first- century BC sandstone carving of a boar-god from Euffigniex (Haute-Marne) in eastern Gaul. The carving may depict shape-shifting, the ability of Celtic gods and heroes to adopt the form of animals. Eye motifs found on the carving may equip the god with the ability to ward off the evil eye, another recurring theme in the Celtic myths.

FEASTING

Other common themes are the otherworld feast and the feast where dramatic events occur. Such a feast might include a seduction, as in the story of Diarmaid and Grainne, or a dispute, as in the tale of Briccriu's Feast. In the latter, an argument over who should receive the choicest cut of meat leads to the contenders taking part in a game to prove who is the most courageous. This involves their submitting without flinching to beheading. Because he is the only one brave enough to go through with it, the Ulster hero, Cúchulainn, is spared the ordeal and wins 'the champion's portion'.

The image of a slain bull on the base of the Gundestrup Cauldron is a reference to the widespread practice of bull sacrifice among the Celts. The strength, ferocity and virility of the untamed bull were admired, and the animal had close associations with the supernatural.

First century BC gold model boat from Broighter, County Derry. According to Irish myth, the earliest Celts sailed to Ireland from Spain. One of the first episodes in Bran's voyage to the otherworld is an encounter with the Irish sea god, Manannán Mac Lir, riding his chariot over the waves.

Celtic deities' ability to transform themselves or others into a variety of creatures. For example, Midir, the Irish lord of the otherworld, turns himself and the beautiful Etain into swans to escape from the palace of Óengus. The skill is also commonly used to deceive and punish. Cú Roi and Sir Bartilek are transformed into giants for the beheading game, to make them unrecognizable to Cúchulainn and Gawain. When Math returns home to discover that his foot-maid has been raped by his nephews, Gwydion and Gilfaethwy, he punishes them by turning them into a succession of animals, one male and one female, demanding they produce offspring every year.

Love and enchantment are intimately linked in Celtic tales: Oisin is enchanted by Naim's beauty; a love potion is the undoing of Tristan and Iseulte; Diarmaid is enchanted by Grainne; Naoise is enchanted by Deirdre.

THE OTHERWORLD

The Celtic otherworld is an invisible realm of gods, spirits, fairies and giants. Sometimes it is an enchanting place, sometimes it is hellish. When the Irish gods of light, the Tuatha Dé Danann, retired underground they became the *sidhe* folk living in comfortable burial mounds. The defeated Fomorians before them, however, had to suffer miserable conditions in damp chambers under lakes and seas.

The divide between the land of the living and the otherworld is indistinct in the myths. Enchanted groves, springs and pools are seen as thresholds between the two, over which seers and heroes freely pass. While hunting, Pwll wandered inadvertently into Annwn, the Welsh otherworld, and offended its lord, Arawn, a winter deity. His penance was to swap places with Arawn for one year and fight his enemy, Hafgan, the spirit of summer.

Imram, or voyages to the otherworld, are common in Irish mythology. Typical is the story of Bran, Son of Febal. Bran sailed to the Land of Women where there is no grieving, winter or want. He returned after an eventful journey to find that time had passed much quicker in the land of the living. His family and friends were long dead and he was barely remembered.

The Arthurian Legends

Tales of King Arthur and his Knights of the Round Table, which swept Europe in the Middle Ages and beyond, were designed to entertain. But, like the Irish and Welsh legends, they were echoes of the mythology which must have existed in Ireland, Britain and Gaul at the time of the Roman conquests.

The nineteenth-century revival of Arthurian legend inspired painters as well as poets and writers. Guinevere first appears in Geoffrey of Monmouth's 'History', where she is portrayed as a Roman noblewoman who betrays Arthur for Mordred, the most infamous of the Knights of the Round Table.

E arly references to Arthur appear in a Welsh poem by Aneirin (sixth century AD), the writings of the British monk, Gildas (sixth century AD) and of the Celtic historian, Nennius (eighth century AD). A tenth-century Latin history of Wales lists his victories and his defeat at the battle of Camlan. There is no proof that Arthur actually existed, but it is possible that he was a Romanized *dux bellorum* (battle leader) who lived in Britain in the late fifth century and was famed for resisting the Saxons. By the Middle Ages he and his band had become firmly imbedded in the popular imagination, sharing many of the attributes of Finn MacCumaill and the Fianna.

THE FACES OF ARTHUR

Arthur had many faces before emerging as a Christian king, the epitome of medieval chivalry and the once and future saviour of his people. In early stories he is given the epithet *Horribilis* and is called a tyrant. The eleventh-century Welsh story, *Culhwch and Olwen*, the earliest, fully fledged Arthurian tale in a Celtic language, portrays him as a Celtic king and benefactor touched with magic. In later romances he is shown as flawed, falling into slothful states from which it is difficult to arouse him.

ARTHURIAN LITERATURE

The popular image of King Arthur was begun by Geoffrey of Monmouth. His twelfth-century *History of the Kings of Britain* inspired the Norman poet, Wace, who wrote a more courtly version and introduced the Round Table. The French poet, Chrétien de Troyes, developed the story later in the twelfth century, adding novel elements from Continental sources and the songs of Breton minstrels. It was Chrétien who introduced the idea of courtly love and the earliest version of the Grail legend. In the thirteenth century, Layamon wrote a longer,

English version, replacing love and chivalry with earlier Celtic traditions and Dark Age brutality. German contributions followed and, in the fourteenth century, the greatest single Arthurian legend in Middle English, *Sir Gawain and the Green Knight*, appeared. In the fifteenth century Thomas Malory published the *Le Morte d'Arthur*, which was to become the best-known and most complete version of the story.

THE ONCE AND FUTURE KING

The pagan roots of Arthurian legend are clearly evident in typical devices such as the band of warriors (the knights), the love triangle (Arthur, Guinevere and Lancelot), the search for a magic cauldron (the Grail), the beheading game (Sir Gawain and the Green Knight) and the otherworld (Avalon, Arthur's final resting place). Medieval authors, from Geoffrey of Monmouth to Malory, found inspiration in these themes, and wove them with other elements into a form which spoke to their courtly contemporaries. So powerful and archetypal is the imagery that it continued to enthrall succeeding generations. In the nineteenth century, English poets such as Alfred, Lord Tennyson (1809–1892) and Algernon Charles Swinburne (1837–1909) revisited the themes. In the twentieth century, further Arthurian interpretations and adaptations appeared in literature (T.H.White's *Once and Future King* – 1958) and in new

THE DIFFUSION OF THE CELTS

*c.*750 BC	Start of Halstatt (Celtic) Iron Age
500–100 BC	La Tène art begins to appear throughout Europe
*c.*450 BC	Spread of Celtic culture
*c.*390 BC	Celts sack Rome
*c.*300 BC	Celtic fortified settlements (Oppida) begin to appear in France and Britain
279 BC	Celts attack Delphi
*c.*50 BC	Western Celtic world as far north as the English Channel comes under Roman control

media such as film and television. The latter range from the brutally realistic (John Boorman's *Excalibur* – 1981) to the ridiculous (*Monty Python and the Holy Grail* – 1974).

The most celebrated Celtic Grail-like vessel is the silver Gundestrup Cauldron, which was found in a peat bog in Denmark. It is one of the most famous examples of Celtic religious art and dates from the second to first centuries BC.

THE GRAIL

The quest for the Holy Grail is one of the central themes of Arthurian legend. The Grail is said by some to be the chalice used by Christ at the Last Supper, and by others to be the cup used to catch his blood at the Crucifixion. The Grail objectifies purity and perfection, and it became the purpose of many an unsuccessful quest among the Knights of the Round Table, including Gawain, Perceval and Lancelot. It was Galahad, the noblest of the knights, who achieved the Grail, thereby restoring life and fertility to a stricken land.

The origins of the Grail quest may be found in the recurring Celtic theme of the magic cauldron. The Dagda's cauldrons could never be emptied, except by cowards; Bran's could revive the dead; others contained *greals* or 'brews of wisdom'. In the tenth-century Welsh poem, *'The Spoils of Annwn'*, Arthur leads a band of warriors on a raid into the otherworld to steal the cauldron of its lord, Arawn.

The most archaic form of the Grail legend is found in the story of Peredur in the *Mabinogion*. This was adapted by Chrétien de Troyes (Percival) and Wolfran von Eschenbach (Parzival); the definitive version is found in Malory's *Le Morte d'Arthur*.

The Myths of The North

Evidence for the mythology of Northern Europe is fragmentary, relying heavily on a few sources, but there is no doubt that to the ancient peoples of the North, gods and myths were hugely important. What we do know reveals a colourful and lively mythology, and a pantheon of fascinating characters.

After the decline of the Roman Empire by the fifth century AD, Germanic tribes settled in Northern Europe in territories formerly claimed by the Romans. They brought with them their languages – the predecessors of English, German, Dutch, Flemish, Danish, Swedish, Norwegian and Icelandic – as well as their religion and mythology.

In mainland Europe and England, early conversion to Christianity means that little evidence for the ancient beliefs has survived, so we have to turn to Scandinavia and Iceland, where Christianity took hold much later, to discover the details. Nevertheless, the importance of their gods to the Northern peoples, and the far-reaching influence of this mythology as part of a European heritage, is witnessed by the fact that in English, and other languages descended from Germanic, we still recall the Northern deities in the days of the week: Tuesday is Tyr's day; Wednesday is Odin/Woden's day; Thursday is Thor's day and Friday is Frigg's day.

THE MYTHS AND THE PANTHEON

The best-known of the Northern European deities were Odin, Thor, Loki, Baldr, Njord, Freyr and Freyja. These had the most distinct and vivid personalities, though there were other,

A ninth-century AD picture stone from Gotland showing a Viking ship. The main sources of Northern mythology come from Iceland in the late Viking Age, AD 800-1100, and include both manuscripts produced in Christian monasteries and artefacts, such as the memorial stone pictured here, which depict scenes from this rich mythological heritage.

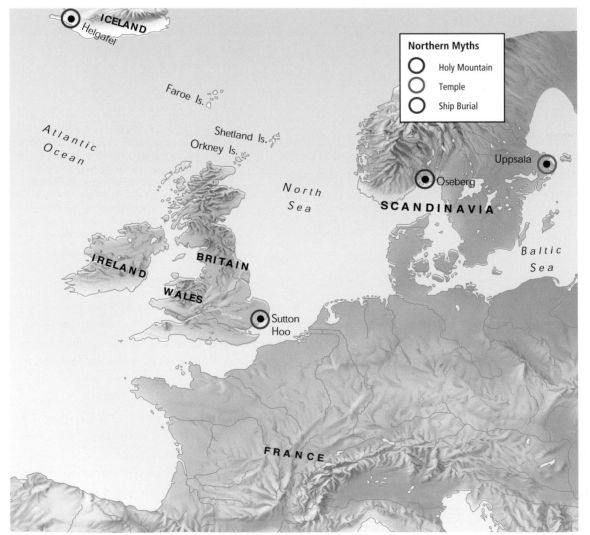

Northern Myths

Holy Mountain

Temple

Ship Burial

Northern Myths
Northern gods **were** often worshipped in temples like the one at Uppsala in Sweden. Sometimes natural features of the landscape were chosen for worship, such as, Helgafell (Holy mountain) in Iceland. Evidence of Northern mythology can also be found in the ship burials excavated at Sutton Hoo in East Anglia in England and Oseberg in Norway.

more shadowy figures such as Tyr, fearless god of war. Njord, Freyr and Freyja belonged to a sub-group of fertility gods known as the Vanir, while the others belonged to the main group of gods known as the Aesir.

The myths deal in conflict between the gods and giants, representing the constant struggle between chaos and order. An intense sense of fate also permeates Northern mythology: Odin chose those who would die in battle; and Ragnarok, the final great battle between the gods and the giants, was unavoidable. The people believed that their destiny was not within their own control and their myths helped them accept this, following the example of their gods. Mirroring the strong family ties of Northern society, the gods were a close-knit group that helped and supported each other, with very clear loyalties to their own kind.

Northern mythology takes us from the formation of life from the fusion of extremes – ice and fire – to the end of the world, when fire and water will again claim the life they have engendered. Yet existence does not finish there completely: the earth will reappear after Ragnarok has passed, washed clean and renewed, when the sons of the gods will pick up where their fathers left off and life will begin again.

RELIGION AND WORSHIP

Worship of Northern gods was conducted in many different ways, ranging from huge statues of Thor, Odin and Freyr in the magnificent temple at Uppsala in Sweden, where sacrifices included humans, to the simple sacrifices of foodstuffs brought to groves, rocks and stones in which patron gods were thought to reside. Altars of piled stones were also created in the open air for such sacrifices.

Natural features of the landscape might also be chosen for worship or veneration. An example is *Helgafell* (Holy mountain) in western Iceland. Thorolf Mostur-Beard, a devoted follower of Thor, held this mountain to be so sacred that no one could look at it unwashed, and no living creature could be harmed there. He was an early settler in Iceland whose story is related in the first chapters of the Icelandic saga *Erbyggja saga*. He lived in the late ninth century, the time of settlement of the newly discovered Iceland, and died in AD 918.

The sagas are important sources of evidence of the practices involved in worship and this one is particularly rich in evidence for the worship of Thor. However, the fact that the sagas were written down in the Middle Ages (twelfth or thirteenth centuries) – *Erbyggja saga* is thought to have been written in the mid-thirteenth century – and contain what was then still known, understood or had been passed down of religious practices three or more centuries earlier, shows how our picture of early Scandinavian worship is a delicate web constructed from piecing together disparate and fragmented clues.

The climate and landscapes of Northern Europe can be harsh and cold. These often extreme environments had a profound effect upon the mythology: one creation myth tells of life beginning at Ginnungagap, the point where the boundaries of flaming Muspell in the south met icy Niflheim in the north.

Left: A bronze image of Freyr, the god of fertility. Freyr, often depicted with an erect phallus, was one of the most popular gods in the Northern pantheon; his cult was particularly widespread in Viking-Age Sweden. Sagas from Iceland describe places devoted to the god, and families who worshipped him in the hope he would bring prosperity to their land.

THE EVIDENCE

The Germanic runic alphabet, which had mystical significance and figures in Northern mythology, was not designed for writing long passages, so we only have contemporary written evidence from outside observers such as from the Roman historian Tacitus. The crucial written sources for the Northern myths date from the thirteenth century and come from Iceland, where belief in the old gods lasted the longest. About AD1220, Snorri Sturluson, a brilliant Icelandic scholar, major landowner, important political figure and a Christian, wrote a book detailing all the information still available about the heathen gods and myths so that it would not be lost forever to poets of the future. Thanks to his foresight in preserving the material, we have our fullest view of Northern myth, from his book, the *Edda*. The other major source for mythological information was also from thirteenth-century Iceland, though presumably dates from earlier: a collection of mythological poems known as the *Poetic Edda*. Additionally, there is fragmentary evidence from Icelandic sagas and important evidence from archaeology, such as the finds from the magnificent ship burials excavated at Oseberg in Norway and Sutton Hoo in East Anglia in England. From all these we can piece together a picture of the mythology.

Creation

In answer to the question every culture asks – how did everything we see and experience come to be? Northern creation myths are complex and evocative. They cover the construction of the cosmos, the engendering of life, the establishment of the heavenly bodies and the population of the world.

In the beginning there was a gaping void: Ginnungagap. To its south was flaming Muspell; to the north lay freezing Niflheim, where a spring, Hvergelmir, gave rise to the eleven rivers of Elivagar. As the rivers flowed along, poisonous substances accompanying them hardened and turned to ice. Vapour from the poison froze into rime, and layer upon layer of rime increased until it had spread right across Ginnungagap. When the rime met hot gusts emanating from Muspell it began to melt and drip and there was a quickening from the drops – the first signs of life.

THE EARLIEST LIVING CREATURES

The drops formed the shape of a giant, Ymir. While Ymir slept he sweated, and from the sweat in his left armpit two beings were formed, a male and a female. Ymir's two legs mated with each other, producing a monstrous son. These beings began the race of frost-giants.

Next, a cow called Audhumla came into being from the dripping rime, who nourished Ymir with four rivers of milk from her udder. For her own sustenance Audhumla licked the salty rime stones. As she licked, by the evening of the first day, a man's hair was visible, on the second day a man's head, and by the end of the third day a complete man had emerged. This man was called Buri. He begot a son, Bor, who married Bestla, daughter of a giant called

A depiction of the myth in which Ymir suckles from the cow Audhumla as she licks salty stones, resulting in the creation of the first men, Buri and Bor (seen on the left of this picture).

Bolthorn. They produced three sons: the gods Odin, Vili and Ve, who killed the huge primeval giant Ymir. When he fell, the whole race of frost-giants was drowned in his blood (except one, Bergelmir, who became the progenitor of a new race of giants).

CREATION OF THE EARTH

Odin and his brothers then used Ymir to create the world. Carrying his enormous body out into Ginnungagap they formed the earth from his flesh and rocks from his bones. They made stones and gravel from his teeth and any bones that had been broken. They made his blood into the lakes and sea. Ymir's skull they formed into the sky and set it up over the earth, placing one of four dwarves, Nordri, Sudri, Austri and Vestri (North, South, East and West), at each corner to hold it up. They created plants and trees from Ymir's hair and threw his brains up into the sky to form the clouds.

The earth was circular, and the gods arranged the sea around it. Along the shore they gave land to the giants, while inland they made a fortification from Ymir's eyelashes within which they placed Midgard, the realm of men.

Then the gods created people to inhabit the world. They took two tree trunks and created a man and a woman. Odin gave the new beings breath and life, Vili gave consciousness and movement and Ve gave them faces, speech, hearing and sight. The man was called Ask (ash tree – a fitting name for a person made from a tree trunk) and the woman Embla (of more obscure meaning, possibly elm, vine or creeper). From these two the human race descended.

This stone from Gotland, fifth century AD, is engraved with dragons and the sun, which is here represented by the whorl. To people from the North, used to long, dark winters, the sun was of major importance. As well as various myths concerning the creation of the sun, midwinter festivals were held to ensure that the sun would regain its strength and bring its life-giving force back to the people by the spring.

THE HEAVENLY BODIES

While creating the universe Odin, Vili and Ve caught the sparks and glowing particles flying out of Muspell and set them in the firmament as the stars and planets, above and below the earth, to light the sky. They gave positions to all of them, and ordained their courses.

They also organized the cycle of night and day and thereby the passing of time – days, months, weeks and seasons – by enlisting a giantess called Night, black and dark in accordance with her race, and her son Day, who was bright and fair. Odin set Night and Day up in the sky with horses and chariots to ride around the earth every 24 hours. Night rode ahead on a horse called Hrimfaxi (Rime mane), who bedewed the earth with drips from his bit, while Day's horse, Skinfaxi (Shining mane), lit up the earth and sky with light shed from his mane.

The gods also fashioned the sun and the moon, giving them chariots of their own. The sun and moon raced across the sky because two wolves, sons of a giantess, were perpetually chasing them. Skoll chased the sun, while running ahead, trying to catch the moon, was Hati Hrodvitnisson. At Ragnarok, these two hungry wolves finally caught their prey.

Cosmology – the Structure of the Universe

The dramas of Northern myths were played out against the background of a complicated cosmology, peopled with diverse races of beings. In the course of the mythological narratives, the gods would travel from land to land over differing terrains and vast distances, and a rich and varied picture of the world emerges.

The Northern cosmic structure consisted of three different levels, one above the other like a series of plates. On the top level was Asgard, the stronghold of the gods, where the Aesir lived in their magnificent halls, as well as Vanaheim, home to the Vanir, and Alfheim, land of the elves.

On the level below lay Midgard, the world of men, and Jotunheim, mountainous realm of the giants. Svartalfheim, where dark elves lived, and Nidavellir, home of the dwarves, were also here. Asgard and Midgard were connected by a flaming bridge, Bifrost, which was very strong and built with more skill than any other structure. Humans knew Bifrost as the rainbow.

The lowest level was cold Niflheim, which included Hel, the dwelling place of those who died of sickness, old age or accident. Warriors who died in battle were received into Odin's hall, Valhalla, or Freyja's hall, Sessrumnir, on the top level in Asgard, where they became part of Odin's personal army. Those dying at sea

Bifrost, or the rainbow bridge, which led from Asgard, dwelling place of the Aesir, to Midgard, the land of men.

went to another place again: the hall of the sea gods Aegir and Ran, at the bottom of the sea.

The axis and supporting pillar of the universe was an enormous ash tree, Yggdrasill, also known as the World Tree. This gigantic tree formed a central column linking the worlds of gods, men, giants and the dead, and also protected and sheltered the world. Yggdrasill's fortunes mirrored those of the universe it sheltered; it suffered alongside the world at the same time as sustaining it under its protection.

GIANTS, DWARVES AND ELVES

Besides gods and men, the Northern cosmos was also inhabited by dwarves, elves and giants. There were two types of elf in Northern myth. Light elves, living in Alfheim, were thought to be more beautiful than the sun. Dark elves were blacker than pitch, and unlike their light counterparts in nature. The dark elves lived underground in Svartalfheim, and appear to have been similar to, and perhaps interchangeable with, dwarves.

Dwarves were not in fact thought to be particularly small, but were believed to be ugly. They were famous for their extraordinary craftsmanship, particularly in working precious metals, especially gold. They were able to fashion remarkable objects with magical powers. Most of the treasures belonging to the gods, including Mjollnir, Thor's hammer, were made by dwarves. Dwarves were thought to have been generated from the soil: they first took form as maggots in the flesh of Ymir, the primeval giant whose body became the earth, and the gods then gave them consciousness and intelligence.

Giants, certainly thought to be of great size, played a significant part in the mythology. They represented the forces of chaos and negativity, and were usually hostile. The gods continually strove to maintain the order of their universe against these unpredictable external forces. The relationship between gods and giants was not always straightforward, however. Giants were not invariably the enemy – many gods had affairs with or even married giantesses, or were descended from them – but more often than not dealing with them involved the crashing down of Thor's hammer, which could both punish and protect gods and ordinary mortals.

A representation of the ash tree Yggdrasill, or the World Tree. Its branches were believed to reach round the whole world and its three roots were responsible for joining the three levels of the universe together.

YGGDRASILL, THE WORLD TREE

The central support of the universe, Yggdrasill's branches extended over the whole earth, and its roots reached all three levels of the world: one root was embedded in Asgard, at the well of Urd (fate) where the gods held council every day; one delved into Jotunheim, at the well of Mimir where Odin had left one of his eyes in return for a drink; and the third reached the spring of Hvergelmir in Niflheim.

An all-knowing eagle sat in Yggdrasill's uppermost branches, with a hawk called Vedrfolnir between its eyes. Ratatosk, a squirrel, ran up and down the tree carrying insults between the eagle and a monstrous serpent, Nidhogg, who lay deep down in Niflheim. Four stags, Dain, Dvalin, Duneyr and Durathror, also lived amongst the branches. The tree nourished the creatures that lived in and under it, but as well as providing protection and succour for the world, symbolized by the animals living in it, the tree was said to suffer anguish and bitter hardships. The stags and squirrel bit it, its sides rotted away and Nidhogg, together with more serpents than could be counted, gnawed at it. In this way Yggdrasill bore the tribulations of the world.

Odin

Odin was the most complex of the Northern Gods. Although known as 'Allfather', he was not a benevolent father god, but a powerful and fickle character, as treacherous as he could be generous. He was respected and worshipped – particularly by kings and nobles – but was not entirely to be trusted.

Odin, head of the Northern pantheon, was a terrifying figure. The awesome god of magic, war and wisdom, he was invoked for victory in battle, but could be faithless and was often accused of awarding triumph unjustly. Bloody sacrifices would sometimes be necessary to appease him.

GOD OF MAGIC

Odin's mastery of magic was legendary. He could change his shape at will, or be transported instantly to distant lands while his body lay as if asleep. His magical abilities made him a formidable opponent; with mere words he could calm or stir up the sea, extinguish fires or change the winds.

Odin went to great lengths to acquire magical learning. He had only one eye, as he

had pledged the other as payment for a drink from the well of Mimir, which gave inspiration and knowledge of the future. Another story relates how Odin gained this wisdom and information from the decapitated head of Mimir, the wisest of the Aesir, which he kept after it was cut off by the Vanir, a group of fertility gods. Odin preserved the head with herbs and chanted incantations over it, making it able to speak to him.

GOD OF KINGS, POETRY AND THE DEAD

While he was particularly favoured by kings, Odin was also god of poetry, which perhaps explains the prominence the poetic sources accord

Statue of Odin, god of magic, wisdom, war and death, who ruled the Asgard, the realm of the gods. Although he was highly revered, he was a wily and ruthless god, renowned for bestowing great rewards on those he favoured, only to destroy them on another occasion.

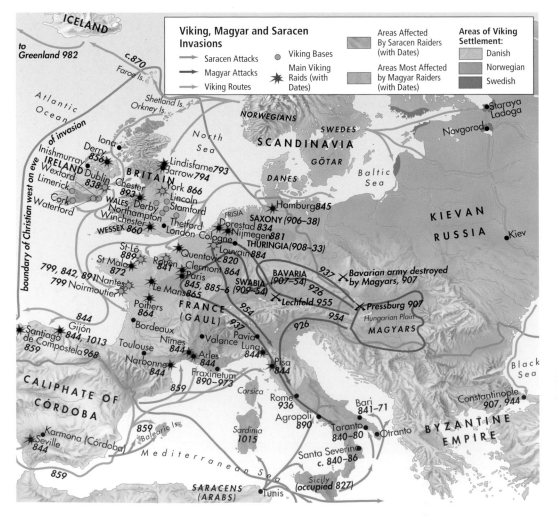

Viking, Magyar and Saracen Invasions

Viking, Magyar and Saracen Invasions		
→ Saracen Attacks	● Viking Bases	
→ Magyar Attacks	✷ Main Viking Raids (with Dates)	
→ Viking Routes		

Areas Affected By Saracen Raiders (with Dates)

Areas Most Affected by Magyar Raiders (with Dates)

Areas of Viking Settlement:
- Danish
- Norwegian
- Swedish

Viking, Magyar and Saracen Invasions
In the ninth and tenth centuries, large parts of maritime Europe were devastated by Viking, Magyar and Saracen raiders. The Vikings, perhaps inspired by the warrior religion of Odin and Thor, also established bases throughout the continent.

him. It was said that Odin himself spoke only in poetry and that poetic inspiration was his gift. Odin was also god of the dead, particularly of those who died in certain ways. Casualties of battle, especially those killed by the spear – a weapon sacred to Odin – were seen as an offering to him, and fallen enemies could also be dedicated to him. Hanged men were also sacred to Odin; he could bring them back to life. Hanging and gashing with a spear were sacrificial rites associated with Odin, and a mysterious and fascinating myth concerning the god tells of his own self-sacrifice, hanging on the World Tree for nine nights without food or water, slashed with a spear and 'given to Odin, myself to myself', to win the sacred runes, source of wisdom and magical lore.

ODIN'S TREASURES

Odin owned two particular treasures that had been forged by dwarves: his mighty, unstoppable spear, Gungnir, and a gold arm-ring, Draupnir, from which eight other rings of equal weight and value would drip every ninth night. Odin also possessed an extraordinary horse named Sleipnir, which had eight legs and was the fastest of horses, able to carry Odin on his errands through the sky and over the sea.

Odin was regularly portrayed walking amongst men as a sinister, one-eyed old man, cloaked and wearing a broad-brimmed hat or hood. He was married to Frigg, queen of the gods and goddesses, who shared with him the ability to foresee the future, although she did not make pronouncements. Frigg was beautiful, gracious, stately and possessed of deep wisdom. She was highly respected, both in Northern mythology and by the population, and as a maternal figure was invoked by women during childbirth and by those wishing to conceive.

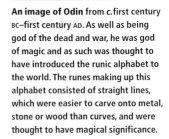

VALHALLA

Those who died in battle were thought to go to Odin's hall, Valhalla (Hall of the Slain), in Asgard, to join Odin's personal host, the Einherjar. Here they fought with each other during the day for sport and feasted together at night, waiting for Ragnarok when they would be called upon to fight for Odin in the last great battle.

Valhalla was an enormous building with many doors, and rafters and tiles made from spear shafts and shields. The Einherjar ate the meat of the boar Saehrimnir, cooked each day in a pot called Eldhrimnir by the cook Andhrimnir, and the boar was miraculously whole again each evening. The flesh of Saehrimnir would always be sufficient to feed all the Einherjar, regardless of their number. They drank a never-ending supply of mead from the udder of a goat named Heidrun who stood on top of Valhalla.

Those to fall in battle and join the ranks of the Einherjar were chosen by special envoys of Odin, the Valkyries. These female spirits waited on the Einherjar in Valhalla and went down to the battlefields at Odin's decree to lead the slain back to Valhalla. The name Valkyrie means 'chooser of the slain'.

Thor – the Thunder God

The best-loved of the Northern gods, the mighty figure of Thor, strode the cosmos, fighting the forces of evil: giants and trolls. He was the protector of Asgard and the gods could always call upon him if they were in trouble – as could mankind– and many relied on him.

Ordinary people put their trust in Thor, for Thor's concerns were with justice, order and the protection of gods and men. Ancient inscriptions on rune stones, such as 'may Thor bless these runes' or 'may Thor bless this memorial', or sometimes just 'may Thor bless' are common. Sometimes Thor's protection was invoked merely with a carving of a hammer. Thor's hammer as a symbol of protection is also seen in miniature version in the form of little hammers of silver or other metals which were placed in graves alongside

Thor, as god of the sky and of thunder, was a popular figure in Northern mythology. People loved to tell of his massive strength as he marched through the world, leaving slain giants in his wake, with thunder and lightning identifying his path. Here he is grasping Mjollnir with which he protected the gods.

Scandinavian Colonies in Britain and France
The first Viking colonists were Norwegians who settled in Ireland and Scotland and raided the coast of Britain. Other Norwegians settled in the Scottish Islands. The Danes settled in East Anglia, the Midlands and the north of the Humber from AD 876 onwards. In England control of the area of Viking settlement – the 'Danelaw'– was only finally secured by the kings of Wessex in the mid-tenth century. In Scotland the earldom of Orkney encompassed much of the highlands and was only returned to Scotland in the 15th century.

THOR AND THE GIANTS

Thor's main occupation was destroying giants, a constant threat to the worlds of gods and men. Thor actively sought them out, with the express intention of their annihilation, and seldom hesitated to raise his hammer when he encountered one. If any gods were threatened, Thor would instantly appear. Famous stories tell how Thor defeated the giant Hrungnir, strongest of all giants, in a duel; and how he destroyed the giant Geirrod, in spite of Geirrod's attempts to attack him. The situation was not always clear-cut, however. Giants were occasionally helpful – although Geirrod and his two daughters made many attempts to defeat Thor, another giantess, Grid, chose to forewarn Thor and lent him a staff and some iron gloves. Thor even had two sons, Modi and Magni, with a giantess, Jarnsaxa. Nevertheless, Giants were usually Thor's hostile adversaries.

Many tales of Thor are affectionately humorous, attesting to the fondness the populace had for him. When Thor's hammer was stolen by a giant demanding Freyja as his wife, Thor, to his horror, had to agree to be dressed up as the bride and delivered to the giant in order to destroy the giant and thus reclaim his hammer. Gentle humour is also evident in the tale of Thor's encounter with a magical giant king, Utgarda-Loki. Thor's brute strength is not enough when pitted against Utgarda-Loki's magical wiles, but even so the giants have to retain a healthy respect for Thor for trying.

Thor's ultimate adversary at Ragnarok – which according to the myths is yet to happen – will not be a giant, but the World Serpent, and one myth (see Box below) tells of an encounter before this final one.

the buried bodies.

Thor's mighty strength excelled that of all other gods. He was huge, with red hair and beard and red eyebrows that sank down over his face when he was angry. Thunder was thought to be the sound of Thor's chariot driving across the sky, and his fierce, red, flashing eyes befitted the god of thunder and lightning. Thor also had an enormous appetite, regularly devouring more than a whole ox at one sitting.

Thor's most important possession was his hammer, Mjollnir, which could never miss its mark, whether raised up or thrown, and would always return to Thor's hand. With this weapon Thor kept the forces of evil at bay, protecting the gods and mankind. Furthermore, Mjollnir held the power to sanctify and could be raised for the purpose of blessing. As well as Mjollnir, Thor owned a belt of strength which doubled his already formidable might when buckled on, and a pair of iron gloves, without which he could not wield Mjollnir.

Thor fishing for the Jormungand, the World Serpent. This popular myth tells of how Thor and the giant Hymir went in search of the serpent, Thor's old adversary. In Poetic Edda, Snorri Sturlsson, the Icelandic scholar, tells of how storytellers could not decide whether or not Thor actually hit Jormungand; they all agree that the serpent escaped.

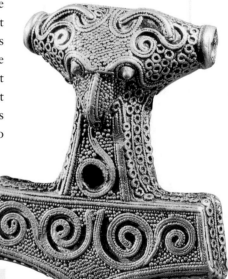

Mjollnir, Thor's hammer. Its name is associated with a thunderbolt; with this weapon Thor defended the Asgard against their enemies. When Christianity came to Northern Europe, the Christian symbol of the cross merged with that of the hammer, the representation of the cult of Thor. This silver amulet would have been worn as a lucky charm.

THOR FISHES FOR THE WORLD SERPENT

Disguised as a young boy, Thor went fishing with a giant, Hymir. Secretly, he took the head of a huge ox for bait – he had plans. Hymir thought Thor rowed exceptionally hard. At the usual fishing place, Thor wanted to row still further. Later, Hymir warned they were now so far out it would be dangerous because of Jormungand, the World Serpent. But Thor insisted on rowing further, making Hymir very anxious.

When Thor finally laid down the oars he threw the ox-head overboard on a line. Deep under the sea the serpent took the bait. A huge hook inside the ox-head pierced the roof of the serpent's mouth, and it jerked violently. Thor summoned all his strength, pushing down so hard that both his feet went through the bottom of the boat, bracing him against the sea-bed. But when he pulled up the terrible serpent Hymir panicked, and as Thor lifted his hammer to strike the monster its deathblow Hymir cut Thor's line. The serpent sank back into the sea and Thor threw his hammer after it. Thor was furious at Hymir, punching him so hard that he fell overboard. That was the end of Hymir, and Thor waded ashore.

Loki the Trickster

One of the most extraordinary characters in Northern mythology, the strange figure of Loki was not a god, yet he was ranked among the Aesir, and was the blood brother of their chief Odin. There is no evidence that Loki was worshipped as a god, but he appears to be an essential character within the mythological kinship. His presence is pivotal to many of the mythical events. He was both the constant companion and great friend of the gods, and at the same time an evil influence and a deadly enemy.

Loki was handsome, witty and charming, but was also malicious and sly. He was descended from giants – his father was the giant Farbauti – but his wife Sigyn was a goddess, and they had two sons, Narfi and Vali. Loki plays a crucial role in Northern myth, although he is not one of the gods. He takes part in most of the gods' escapades and it is his presence that causes many of the events in the myths to happen.

Loki was full of mischief, and often caused the gods great trouble with his tricks, but equally as often it was Loki's artfulness that saved them again. Loki caused the theft of Idunn's apples, yet also reversed the disaster. To keep from ageing, the gods had to eat golden apples guarded by the goddess Idunn. At the behest of a giant, Loki lured Idunn out of Asgard, where the giant abducted the goddess together with her apples. Without the apples the gods quickly grew old and grey, but Loki found Idunn and brought her home, and enabled the Aesir to kill the pursuing giant.

This forge stone shows the head of Loki having had his lips sewn together by the dwarves as punishment for his trickery. Loki is a contradictory figure, being in turns the friend and foe of the gods; his sex is sometimes in doubt and it is not clear whether he is a giant or a god.

LOKI THE SHAPE-SHIFTER

Loki could take on the shapes of animals, birds and, in particular, insects, reflecting his insidious nature. He became a fly when trying to distract dwarves from their work during the making of Thor's hammer and a flea in an attempt to steal the Necklace of the Brisings from Freyja. He used the form of a fly to enter Freyja's house and when he found Freyja asleep with the clasp of the necklace beneath her, Loki became a flea and bit the goddess. She turned over and Loki stole the necklace.

THE DARKER SIDE OF LOKI

The conflict between Loki and the gods was serious and far-reaching, however. When Loki brings about the death of Baldr, most beloved of the gods, his true malevolence shows through,and the gods no longer tolerate him. They shackle him until Ragnarok, when he will break free and is destined to show his true colours – fighting on the side of the giants.

LOKI'S CHILDREN

Loki also produced three monstrous children with a giantess, Angrboda: Jormungand, the World

Serpent; Hel, guardian of the realm of the dead, and a huge wolf, Fenrir. These three terrifying creatures all played significant roles in the myths and it was believed the wolf and World Serpent would ultimately destroy Odin and Thor at Ragnarok.

The gods were all afraid when they discovered Loki's three children were being brought up in Jotunheim (Giantland). Odin had to decide their fate and sent gods to bring the monsters before him. He threw the serpent into the ocean, where it grew until it encircled the world, biting on its tail. Hel, Loki's hideous half-dead, half-alive daughter, Odin cast into Niflheim, the land of the dead, charging her with giving food and lodgings to all those sent to her – those who died of sickness or old age. The wolf, Fenrir, the Aesir decided to restrain in Asgard, to keep an eye on it, though only the god Tyr was brave enough to tend it.

An illustration from a manuscript in the Royal Library in Copenhagen in which the blind god, Hod, is stabbing Baldr to death with a poison dart, given to him by Loki. The death of Baldr incurred the wrath of the gods and although Loki tried to escape from them by changing into a salmon, this time his cunning was not enough to evade capture.

Left: The 'bound devil'. Detail from a carving on a cross at Kirkby Stephen, Cumbria, showing Loki the trickster strapped to rocks after contriving Baldr's death. His punishment for killing Baldr is to be bound until Ragnarok, at which time he would be freed to fight with the giants against the gods. In Northern mythology, Loki is the embodiment of deceit.

BALDR'S DEATH

The death of Baldr is probably the most famous of all Northern myths. Baldr, son of Odin, was the wisest, most beautiful and most beloved amongst the gods. So loved was he that, to safeguard him, his mother, Frigg, extracted oaths from all substances not to harm him. After that, the Aesir – one branch of the family of the gods – would throw things at Baldr for fun, for nothing would hurt him. Loki discovered that the only thing that had not sworn to Frigg was mistletoe, and, out of malice, he fashioned a dart from mistletoe and gave it to Baldr's blind brother, Hod, to throw. When Baldr fell dead the gods were devastated. They made a deal with Hel, guardian of the underworld, that if everything in the world would weep for Baldr, then she would relinquish him. Everything did, but at the last minute a giantess called Thokk refused to weep, so Baldr was not released. That giantess was widely thought to be Loki in disguise. The distraught gods seized Loki and bound him with the ripped out entrails of his son Narfi to three stone slabs, where the hideous fetters turned into iron, and a poisonous snake constantly drips poison onto him. There he must lie until Ragnarok, the end of the world.

The Fertility Deities

In the constant struggle with difficult terrain and climate there was much cause in Northern mythology to rely heavily on fertility deities. A group of gods known as the Vanir were especially associated with fertility, peace and prosperity. The population looked to these gods for bountiful harvests, plentiful fish, wealth, increase and peace.

The most prominent of the Vanir were the sea god Njord and his twin children, Freyr and Freyja. These were the offspring of Njord's union with his sister. She is not named, but such unions were apparently permitted amongst the Vanir. When Njord and his children later came to live amongst the Aesir, Njord married a giantess, Skadi, in a myth that has been seen as the joining of a fertility deity with the cold and dark of winter represented by Skadi, who lived high up in the mountains, wore skis or snowshoes and was known as the ski goddess.

Njord was worshipped in his own right, but relatively little information about him has survived. Best known as god of the sea, he was invoked for sea travel and success in fishing as he controlled the bounty of the sea and the wind and waves. Like the other Vanir, Njord was closely associated with wealth. It was thought he could grant land and possessions to any who prayed to him for them, and a rich man was said to be 'as rich as Njord'.

FREYR, THE SUNSHINE GOD

Freyr, Njord's son, was the principal god of fertility and plenty. A radiant god of sunshine and increase, Freyr ruled the Sun and the rain, holding sway over the harvests. Marriages were also occasions to invoke Freyr, as he was not only responsible for increase in the produce of the earth, but for human increase too – an important aspect of fertility gods. Furthermore, Freyr was considered to be the bringer of peace. Weapons were banned in his temples and the shedding of blood or sheltering of

These tiny gold foils from Sweden date from the eighth to tenth centuries AD and are believed to be *euldgubbar*, which were probably used with fertility rites. Each foil depicts a couple, who have been identified as Freyr and Gerd, embracing. The marriage of the pair was seen as a symbol of the sun's warmth shining down on the earth, resulting in corn being produced.

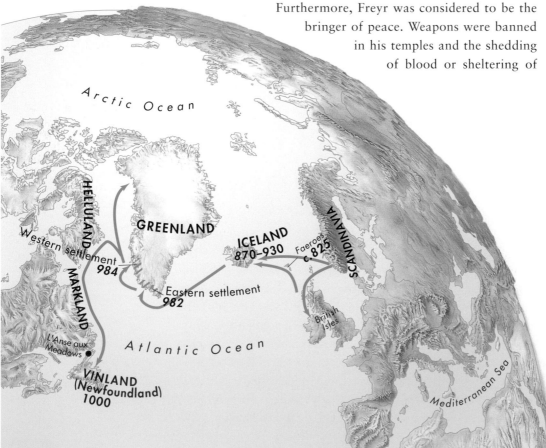

Viking Exploration
In their dangerous sea voyages and quests for new lands the Vikings relied heavily on Njord, the fertility deity responsible for sea travel. The settlement of Iceland began in AD 870 and was completed in two generations. The Vikings later reached Newfoundland but never properly settled there.

outlaws in his sacred places was taboo. Peace and fertility appear to have been closely linked in the Northern psyche: sacrifices were often made for fruitfulness and peace together, and the fertility gods had special responsibilities regarding peace.

Freyr owned two treasures made by dwarves. The first was Skidbladnir, a ship which was large enough to hold all the gods, yet could be folded up and kept in a pouch when not in use. It would always have a fair wind when launched and so could travel anywhere at will. The other was a golden boar, Gullinbursti (golden bristles), which travelled through the air and over the sea faster than any horse and would light up its surroundings, however dark, with the light shed from its bristles.

MARRIAGES OF THE FERTILITY GODS

Famous myths tell of both Freyr and Njord's marriages. Freyr's union is the productive relationship between a fertility god and the earth. Freyr saw the beautiful Gerd, who had giantess blood on her mother's side and whose name is related to 'gard' (field), from afar and fell hopelessly in love. Gerd was in the clutches of the giants, representing winter, but eventually Freyr's servant Skirnir, 'the shining one', personifying the Sun, brought them together. Njord's marriage was not so successful, demonstrating the incompatibility of a fertility god and the barren cold of winter. Njord and the giantess Skadi tried to live alternately for nine nights in her mountain home, and nine nights at Njord's home, Noatun, (enclosure of ships, harbour), but eventually had to admit irreconcilable differences, just as winter must give way to fertile spring.

Freyja was the principal goddess of the Vanir. She is shown here wearing the Necklace of the Brisings, which was fashioned in gold by the dwarves. The myth telling of her overwhelming desire for this beautiful object and the way in which she eventually obtained it reveal her to be lustful and passionate.

FREYJA: GREAT GODDESS OF THE NORTH

Freyja was more than just a fertility goddess. She was also goddess of sensuality and erotic love, and – like Odin – an expert in magic and a receiver of the slain. She was invoked in matters of love, and was a distinctive figure in the myths.

Beautiful, strong-willed, powerful and passionate, it was Freyja after whom the giants lusted: when a giant built a wall around Asgard the payment he craved was Freyja for his wife. Thrym, lord of the giants, stole Thor's hammer as hostage, demanding Freyja as his wife; the giant Hrungnir threatened to kill all the gods but keep Freyja for himself.

Freyja also had strong desires herself. She was accused of running about at night after men and taking all the gods and elves as lovers, including her own brother. She had lusts other than sexual, such as her craving to own the Necklace of the Brisings. Gold was particularly associated with Freyja and this necklace was the most famous of her many gold possessions. Her high passion was also evident in her wrath: when Loki and Thor tried to make her marry the giant Thrym, all the halls of the gods shook beneath her fury.

Ragnarok – The End of the World

The concept of inescapable fate informs all Northern mythology: destiny is preordained and unavoidable. It culminates in Ragnarok, the expected destruction of the world, of which all the details were known. This apocalypse must be faced, but will not be the end of everything; afterwards a new world will begin.

For the gods, and perhaps for the population as well, Ragnarok was both a cataclysmic event in the future and, because all the elements were understood and anticipated, something they lived with in the present.

The gods could not stop Ragnarok – it had to come to pass as prophesied – and their spirited bravery in the face of inevitable annihilation reflects the Northern sensibility concerning pre-destiny. Fate was a fact of life, something that could not be avoided or changed. Even one's death was already decreed and must be faced with calm and brave acceptance. To laugh in the face of death was one of the greatest achievements a Northern warrior could attain, and such a warrior would be long remembered by his peers.

THE EVENTS OF RAGNAROK

Ragnarok will be preceded by fierce battles raging throughout the world for three years. Brothers will kill each other and no ties of kinship will prevent slaughter. Next a bitter winter, Fimbul-winter, will last for another three years with no summer in between. The sky will darken and the sun will not shine. The wolf chasing the sun will finally swallow it and the other wolf will catch the moon. A terrible earthquake will uproot all trees and bring the mountains crashing to the ground. All fetters and bonds will break. Fenrir, the huge wolf, will become free, and so will Loki. The World Serpent, Jormungand, will fly into a giant rage and come up onto the shore, causing the ocean to surge over the land.

A ship made from dead men's fingernails, Naglfar, will ride the wild ocean, filled with giants, with Loki at the helm. Fenrir will advance with his mouth gaping, one jaw against the sky and the other against the earth, his eyes and nostrils spouting flames. Jormungand, spitting poison, will bespatter the sky and the sea. The sky will open and from it will ride Muspell's sons, led by Surt, the fire-flinging

guardian of Muspell, holding aloft his flaming sword, surrounded by burning fire. They will all advance to the plain, Vigrid, where the last battle will take place.

Sensing Ragnarok's approach, the watchman of the gods, Heimdall, will then stand up and blow mightily on Gjallarhorn, the horn used to awaken all the gods and alert them to danger, so that they can hold counsel together. The ash

The Andreas Stone showing Odin being eaten by the monstrous wolf Fenrir at Ragnarok, the Doomsday of the Gods. Ragnarok is the legendary destruction and re-creation of the world when the giants, led by Loki the trickster, will fight against the gods, and monsters, including the World Serpent, will be released.

whole. After a fierce fight, Freyr will succumb to Surt, and Loki and Heimdall will slay each other.

Then Surt will fling fire over the whole earth. Flames, smoke and steam will shoot up from the burning earth to the firmament. The sky will turn black and the stars will disappear. The earth will sink down into the engulfing sea.

Left: Fenrir, the giant wolf who consumes Odin at Ragnarok, with the god Tyr. The child of Loki, Fenrir was kept in Asgard so he could be watched over. After he grew to a huge size, the gods fettered him and played games with him. Fenrir dared one of them to put their hand in his mouth: Tyr was the only one brave enough to do this, but lost his hand after Fenrir bit it off.

Yggdrasill will shake – and all heaven and earth will be terrified. The gods will arm themselves and, with the Einherjar, will advance onto the plain. Odin will ride in front brandishing his spear, Gungnir, and attack Fenrir. Thor will be unable to help him for he must fight the World Serpent. He will vanquish it, but will step away only nine paces before succumbing to the poison it will spit at him. Fenrir will swallow Odin

RELIGIOUS DEVELOPMENTS IN SCANDINAVIA

AD 822	Archbishop Ebo of Rheims is sent to Denmark as a missionary
AD 856–862	The great Viking raids on England and France
c.AD 870	Settlement of Iceland by Norwegians
AD 885–886	Viking siege of Paris
AD 960	Denmark becomes Christian due to the baptism of Harald II 'Bluetooth' Gormsson
c.AD 1000	King Olaf Tryggvason is credited with converting Norway to Christianity
c.AD 995–1035	Cnut (Canute) the Great, ruler of England, Denmark and Norway

A depiction of Ragnarok. Ragnarok looms in Northern mythology as an unavoidable catastrophe which nothing or nobody can prevent. This fatalistic attitude reflects the view of the Germanic peoples who believed in a force greater than anything, against which the world and all individuals were helpless.

NEW BEGINNINGS

Terrible as it may seem, Ragnarok will not be the end of everything. Eventually the world will re-emerge, cleansed and purified, and a new golden age will begin. When at last the fires and raging ocean have subsided, the earth will shoot up out of the sea, green, fair and fertile. Odin's sons Vidar and Vali will still be alive, and so will Thor's sons Modi and Magni, with Thor's mighty hammer, Mjollnir. Baldr and Hod will arrive from Hel and they will all sit on the grass and discuss what happened in former times. These gods who will rule the new world will talk of their secrets and of the old gods, and will find in the grass the beautiful golden playing pieces that had once belonged to the Aesir.

The sun will have begotten a daughter, no less fair than herself, just before she was swallowed, who will follow her mother's path across the sky. The human world will be re-populated by two people, Lif and Lifthrasir, who will have hidden in the great ash Yggdrasill while the events of Ragnarok raged. Thus the cycle will begin again. The world may be destroyed, but life itself is indestructible.

Peoples of the Region

Central and Eastern Europe is a complex region, home to many peoples, principally the Slavs, the Balts and the Finno-Ugrians. To a large extent the Balts and the various groups of Slavs share mythological traditions. Although closely related, the Finno-Ugrians have different linguistic roots and their own tales to tell.

In the first and second centuries AD the ancestors of the Balts and the Slavs occupied north-eastern Europe and were known to Classical writers, such as Tacitus, as the *Vanedi* – 'the people living beyond the Vistula River'. Today these people are spread throughout Central and Eastern Europe, speaking Indo-European languages such as Russian, Slovak, Slovene and Lithuanian. The languages of the Finno-Ugric peoples, who include the Finns and the Lapps, belong to a different group, the Ural-Altaic family, which spread from the direction of the Ural Mountains, which is the traditional dividing line between Europe and Asia.

THE SLAVS AND THE BALTS

It was only in the sixth century AD that the Slavonic-speaking peoples emerged as a distinct group from the varied, mobile mass living in the Balkans and Central and Eastern Europe. Slavic tribes dispersed in various directions from the region of the Carpathian Mountains to form the three groups we recognize today: the Western Slavs (Poles, Czechs, Moravians and Slovaks), the Eastern Slavs (Russians, Ukranians and Belorussians) and the Southern Slavs (Bulgars, Serbs, Croats and Slovenes). The Balts, to the north, also formed three groups: the Lithuanians, the Latvians and the Prussians.

A typical nineteenth century peasant dwelling of the Onega area of Russia (Kizhi Island). By combining the living quarters and farm buildings under one roof, it enabled inhabitants to spend weeks indoors during the long and bitter northern winters.

Peoples of the Region
The settlement of Germanic and, later, Slav peoples within the Mediterranean world in relation to the rest of Europe. The Germanic kingdoms were in a real sense the heirs of Rome, and local populations accomodated in the barbarian groups, many of whom originally settled among them as Roman allies or 'federates'.

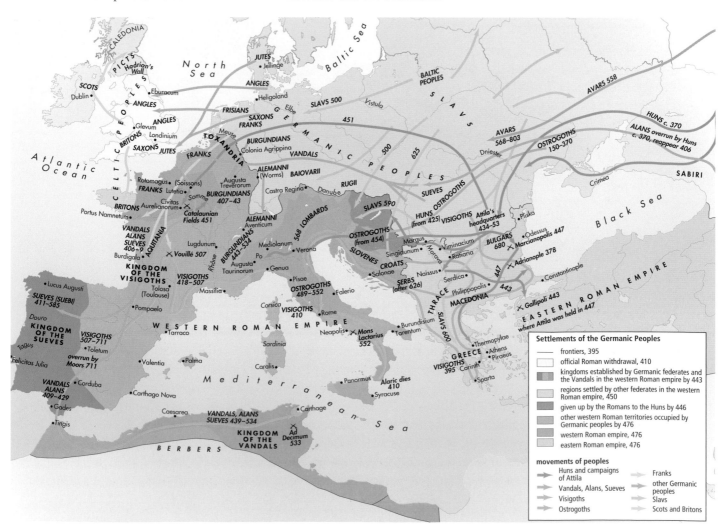

Settlements of the Germanic Peoples

- frontiers, 395
- official Roman withdrawal, 410
- kingdoms established by Germanic federates and the Vandals in the western Roman empire by 443
- regions settled by other federates in the western Roman empire, 450
- given up by the Romans to the Huns by 446
- other western Roman territories occupied by Germanic peoples by 476
- western Roman empire, 476
- eastern Roman empire, 476

movements of peoples
- Huns and campaigns of Attila
- Vandals, Alans, Sueves
- Visigoths
- Ostrogoths
- Franks
- other Germanic peoples
- Slavs
- Scots and Britons

THE FINNO-UGRIANS

The Finno-Ugric peoples comprise four main groups. The first includes the Finns, Lapps, Livonians and Karelians; the second, the peoples of the middle and upper Volga; the third, those inhabiting the Russian provinces of Perm and Vyatka; and the fourth, the Voguls and Ostyaks of western Siberia.

Although Estonia is generally regarded as being a Baltic country, the Estonians are usually included in the first group. The Hungarian Magyars, also, who originated in western Siberia and are normally considered a Turkic people, are usually included in the fourth group.

THE COMING OF CHRISTIANITY

Our knowledge of the non-Christian world of the pre-literate Slavs, Balts and Eastern Europeans is scant. Christianity began to spread through these regions at the end of the first millennium AD. In-fighting between tribes in what was to become Russia was settled when Rurik, a Viking chief, took power and based himself in Novgorod in AD 862. His successor, Oleg, chose Kiev as his capital and, in AD 987, Grand Prince Vladimir I, a descendent of Rurik, was converted to Orthodox Christianity. Paganism was banned at the end of the tenth century AD and Russia remained an Orthodox country for 1,000 years. From the beginning, however, it was only in the cities that this new religion was embraced with any conviction. People living in remote rural areas continued to believe in the old gods throughout the Middle Ages, while participating outwardly in Christian ritual. They sustained this dual faith until possibly as late as the fifteenth century and vestiges of the old religion survived well into the nineteenth century.

It is due to this persistence of pagan belief and practice, and a widespread rise of nationalism in the nineteenth century, that we have an insight into the mythology of the peoples of Central and Eastern Europe. Patriotic historical researchers, such as the Russian, Alexander Afanasiev (1826–1871), and the Finn, Elias Lönnrot (1802–1884), scoured the countryside collecting folklore, folktales and evidence of rustic traditions as part of a mission to establish the antiquity and the heritage of their respective countries. Afanasiev published 640 Russian myths, legends and folktales in eight volumes between 1855 and 1867. Lönnrot's master work is the *Kalevala* (see p. 149)

This gold shield boss in the form of a stag dates from the sixth century BC, typical of the Animal Style of the ancient Steppe nomads of southern and western Russia. These animal figures are believed to be totems, animal ancestors and kin of the tribes that venerated them. The totems would then develop into gods and spirits, rulers of the world in subsequent generations.

Doors decorated with icons of Christian saints (below) and the Annunciation of the Virgin Mary (above). Icons of the Virgin 'miraculously' appeared at pagan sites in Russia between the eleventh and fifteenth centuries. They were planted secretly by Christian clergy to convince the credulous that the pagan gods had submitted to the new religion.

MOIST MOTHER EARTH

The rich mythology which developed among the early Slavs was determined largely by the nature of the lands in which they settled. To the north there was flat, marshy country divided by broad rivers and cloaked in snow for much of the year. Central Europe was largely grassy steppe while to the south, towards the Adriatic, Aegean and the Black seas, the climate was drier and warmer. Those who ventured due east found themselves in dense forests broken by great lakes and teeming with wildlife.

People lived by fishing and hunting, by farming and by tending cattle in clearings and natural meadows. They relied on the elements for their livelihood and on the forest for shelter. They personified the land as Mati-Syra-Zemlya (Moist Mother Earth), whom they honoured in the good times and to whom they appealed in times of drought and bad weather. In the early morning, before starting work in the fields, they would invoke Moist Mother Earth, pouring oil on the ground and entreating her to subdue the powers of evil. They would also listen for her voice in the breeze, or in the sound of the sleigh gliding over snow, for enigmatic predictions of the future.

Origins and Development of the Myths

We know very little about the remote religious past of Central and Eastern Europe. There are few contemporary reports. Brief, often obscure references may be found in the writings of Greek chroniclers, Roman historians and Arab geographers. The observations of later, Christian monks are more informative though inevitably unreliable given their antipathy to paganism.

Long before Prince Vladimir established his capital in Kiev, storytelling was an art practised by all classes in Slavic society. By the beginning of the second millennium AD it was the main vehicle for preserving and transmitting traditions and it remained such until the nineteenth century. Storytellers were invariably illiterate, but their narrative skill lay in a prodigious ability to memorize tales and to recreate them afresh at each performance without changing their substance. It to these gifted narrators, and the evidence that has been obtained from folklore and folksongs, proverbs and persistent religious customs that we owe our knowledge of the ancient beliefs of the peoples of this region.

SLAVIC MYTH

An analysis of Slavic myth suggests that it evolved through three overlapping stages. Its most primitive form was a belief in the creative power of light (good) and the destructive power of darkness (evil). Human well-being was believed to depend on the ability of people to control these opposing forces.

Next came ancestor worship and the belief that every household was protected by the spirits of dead relations who determined the health of the living, their prosperity and their fertility. The interest in fertility was also associated with the cycle of the seasons, with death and rebirth, and with rituals involving contact with the souls of the dead in the otherworld.

Anthropomorphic gods appeared

in the third stage, personifying the sun, the moon, earth, sky, fire, thunder, war, trade, fertility and so on. It was at this stage that myths originated portraying, for example, the sun and the moon as lovers, marrying in spring and parting in winter. The stars were cast as their children and their quarrels produced earthquakes.

The Finno-Ugrians
Much of what we know about the Finno-Ugrians and their religion and mythology comes from the storytelling tradition in Slavic society. The storytellers were usually illiterate but memorized the tales to pass them to successive generations. The map shows the location of the Finno-Ugrians.

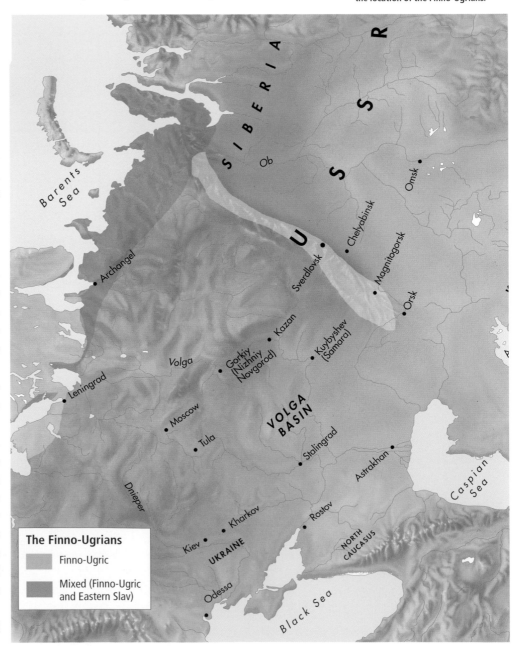

The Finno-Ugrians

Finno-Ugric

Mixed (Finno-Ugric and Eastern Slav)

look forward to the coming of mortal kings and the founding of an independent Finnish state.

On the whole, the *Kalevala* is the imaginative product of its compiler, who used classical models to transform and embellish his raw oral materials. As such, it illustrates the legacy of Europe's pagan folklore but it is not a reliable indication of the pre-Christian beliefs of the Finno-Ugrians. These centred on the ancient practice of Siberian shamanism and are only indirectly discernable in the symbolic world of the *Kalevala*.

Left: The Russian illustrator, Ivan Bilibin (1876–1942) brought Slavic folk tales vividly to life in his paintings. This example is from the stories of Queen Marya Morevna. The folklorist Alexander Afanasiev (1826–1871) saw the characters in these tales as latter-day personifications of the sun, moon and elements.

This process is thought to have unfolded across the region, resulting in a more or less common, rustic and diffuse mythology. Only around Kiev and in the Baltic are more sophisticated systems found with hierarchies of superior gods.

FINNISH MYTH

The chief source of Finnish myth is the *Kalevala*, a long, continuous epic poem that was compiled in the early nineteenth century by the Finnish scholar, Elias Lönnrot. Its second, definitive edition, published in 1849, is seen by many as the national epic of the Finns. It is compiled largely from authentic folklore collected among the peasants of eastern Finland and Russian Karelia.

The book tells of the struggle between Kalevala, the Land of Heroes, and the back country or the icy northern regions. It deals with the story of creation and the deeds of various heroes, such as Väinämöinen, finishing with a

In another of Bilibin's illustrations, Ivan, the hero of the tale *The Firebird*, is seen plucking a feather from the creature's tail. At that moment, Ivan discovers it is the Firebird that has been stealing his father's golden apples. The journey resulting from this discovery takes him on a journey in pursuit of the bird, during which he has many adventures.

THE WONDERTALES

Slavonic written sources date from the ninth and tenth centuries AD. Among the earliest are the *Wondertales* – the *volshebnye skazki*. Although these were written down in the ninth century AD, they date from much earlier. They are old Russian epic poems which relate the exploits of the Bogatyrs, heroes with magical powers. With the coming of Christianity, the Bogatyrs became champions of the new religion.

The *Wondertales* follow a fairly standard pattern. The hero leaves home on a mission occasioned by some villainy such as a theft, abduction or banishment. He encounters a friend who provides him with a magic agent to help him achieve the quest, and is then involved in combat with an adversary (the most important form is slaying a dragon) before returning home, sometimes pursued. Often this structure is more complicated; on his way home the hero might be captured and detained. Later he escapes, is subjected to trial by difficult tasks, marries and becomes king, either in his own kingdom or in that of his father-in-law. A typical example is the tale of the Firebird. Ivan Vyslavovich is sent to find the creature which is stealing the golden apples of the king, his father. The helper in this case is a shape-shifting grey wolf.

Gods and Demigods

Ancient Slavic religion was not a unified or structured system embraced across the region, but more a collection of different but closely related traditions. The northern, Baltic approach was different in many respects from that of the old capital of Russia, Kiev, not only in the rituals observed but also in the names and identities of the gods.

The god of thunder, lightning and war was known as Perun in Russia and by various other names in the north, including Perkunas and Peron. Widely venerated and greatly feared, it was Perun's role to fertilize the land with the spoils of battle and to inseminate Mother Earth with rain and lightning bolts. Perun rode in an iron chariot across the sky, pulled by an enormous billy goat. His sacred tree was the oak, which it was thought attracted lightning. His weapon, suggesting a thunderbolt, was the mace or the battle-axe, and was magic, returning to Perun when he cast it at evil people or spirits. Perun lived in high places with commanding views of his people. Wherever he chose to reside, on a mountain or on the uppermost branches of a giant oak, this was considered to be the centre of the earth.

Perun, god of thunder, lightening and war, controlled the elements of nature and so was widely worshipped at harvest time.

SLAVIC HIGH GODS

Svarog, equivalent to the Baltic deity Svantovit, was the 'shining one', the god of the sky, the all-father, the all-competent craftsman and smith of the gods. He was the father of Dazhbog (the sun) and Svarozhich (fire). These were the most important elemental gods as they provided light and warmth in a land which was cold for much of the year.

Mokosh, the mother goddess, was the only female deity in the earliest Kievan pantheon. Handmaiden of Moist Mother Earth, she was associated with sacred wells and springs as well as being the goddess of spinning, childbirth and animals. Mokosh was courted by Iarilo, the god of love and regeneration, who clothed her with oceans, seas, rivers, lakes and plant life. Together they populated earth and sky with every creature, including mankind.

MINOR DEITIES

A popular legend of the Slavs tells that when Satan and his followers were expelled from heaven, some of them fell into the underworld, where they became goblins. Others fell into the woods, streams and rivers, some remained in the air to affect the weather and others attached themselves to peoples' homes and farms.

Through tales such as this, Christian folk were able to sustain a belief in a host of lesser, ancient deities – the imps, nymphs, dryads, elves and goblins – who were thought to influence their daily lives. Spirits of the household were held to be more benevolent than those of the countryside. Among these friendlier spirits were the Domovoi, the chief of the ancestors, and the Bannik, the spirit of the bathhouse. In the countryside, troubled Rusalkas were said to haunt rivers and lakes while in the forest lurked the shadowless Leshy (see Box, p. 155).

GODS OF THE KALEVALA

Finno-Ugrian religion was essentially animistic, more authentically described as nature worship than a belief in a structured, hierarchical pantheon. However, in the act of recording shamanic lamentations and incantations, Lonnröt transformed them into a Finnish national epic with celestial deities, gods of earth and water, and spirits of the underworld. Among these the supreme sky god is Jumala; the earthy, moss-cloaked Tapio was invoked to ensure a successful hunt; and Ahto, the chief water god, lived in black slime in an undersea cave.

Plaques such as this one from Russia dating from the fourth century AD were sewn into clothing. This plaque is thought to represent the ritual marriage of a king with a female deity. Mystical marriage to a deity was considered a guarantee of the stability and well-being of the tribe. The king drinks an elixir of immortality while the goddess holds a mirror.

This sixth-century BC Scythian golden fish from southeastern Russia is though to be a shield ornament or the frontlet from a horse harness. The fish is a symbol for both creation and destruction. In Finno-Ugric and Siberian myth, the world emerges from the sea, while the Slavs believed that evil spirits lurked in lakes and dragged unwary travellers to their deaths.

THE CREATION OF THE WORLD

From Siberia comes the story of Erlik, the first man, who was created from a speck of mud by the sky god, Ulgan, to help build the universe. When Erlik was sent by Ulgan to fetch more mud from the ocean floor he hid some in his mouth, intending to create his own world from it. He was forced to spit it out, however, after Ulgan caused it to swell. This piece of mud, mixed with Erlik's saliva, was to become those parts of the world, marshes and swamps, which are damp and putrid. The story in the *Kalevala* involves Ilmater Luonnotar, the daughter of Ilma, god of the air. Feeling lonely and unfulfilled she dropped into the ocean where she was impregnated by the foamy waves. She floated in torment for 700 years, looking for a place to rest and to have her children. Eventually, a duck landed on her knee, looking for somewhere to nest. It laid seven eggs on which it sat for three days until Ilmater Luonnotar became uncomfortable and shifted her position. The eggs rolled off her lap and into the slimy depths of the ocean from which their broken pieces emerged as earth, the heavens, the sun, the moon and the stars.

Custom and Ritual

Unlike the Balts, eastern Slavs had no temples and no priesthood. All Slavs, however, practised a variety of rituals and customs well into the twentieth century to appease a host of minor domestic and rustic spirits. The Finno-Ugric peoples practised an animistic religion centred on the supreme power of the shaman.

Southern and eastern Slavs offered up their sacrifices under a tree (generally an oak) or beside running water. The sacred rituals were performed by elders or leaders who fulfilled the functions of priest, king and judge. The Russian prince, Vladimir I, celebrated the start of his reign in AD 980 by erecting a group of wooden idols on the hillside near his palace. These included Perun (god of thunder and war), with a silver head and golden moustache, and Mokosh (the mother goddess). Following the prince's conversion to Christianity in AD 987 the idols were destroyed.

TEMPLES AND SHRINES

The Balts had priests and built substantial temples to their gods, often fortified and usually in inaccessible places. Sventovit (the Baltic variant of Svantovit) was worshipped at the temple of Arcona, on the island of Rügen, a famous citadel built on a rocky promontory washed by the sea. At harvest festival, feasts were held there and people came from all over the island to sacrifice cattle and join in the chanting.

APPEASING THE SPIRITS

Slavs believed themselves surrounded by a multitude of genii, or spirits, whose goodwill had

The shaman's costume, impregnated with various spiritual forces and 'spirits', represents a religious microcosm, qualitatively different from the surrounding profane space. Merely by donning it, the shaman transcends normal space and prepares to enter into contact with the spiritual world.

Custom and Ritual.
Some of the Slavic and Baltic holy sites in Central and Eastern Europe. Many Slavic holy sites were not commemorated by temples, being located around oak groves and individual oak trees instead.

Custom and Ritual

1. Site of Temple of Ancona for the Worship of Sventont
2. Vladimir I commemorates the start of his reign by erecting wooden idols in Kiev
3. Novgorod Site of Eternal Fire of Oak Branches maintained in honour of Perun
4. Holy Oak Venerated at Czestochowa
5. Ancestral Centre in Oak Grove at Vilnius, established in 6th Century AD
6. Shrine at Romuva Dedicated to Lithuanian Gods
7. Holy Island of Khortisa Situated in River Dnieper
8. Temple of Triglar, at Szczecin
9. Temple of Gerovit, on Holy Island near Wolgast

to be won by prayers and offerings. Household spirits, or Domovi, were thought to be more benign, but it was customary to treat them with respect to enlist their help. Superstition prevented people from mentioning the Domovoi by name and it was customary to refer to him as 'grandfather' or 'himself'. To please the less benevolent Dvorovoi, the spirit of the yard, people put a little sheep's wool, bread or glittering objects in the stable.

Shamanic mountain people, to the south of the Siberian Plain, would attach bags made of birch bark to trees and fill them with gifts for the good spirits. They were still sacrificing horses and hanging up their skulls and hides on poles in the early twentieth century. In the *Kalevala*, Väinämöinen does the same with the remains of a bear, which he takes to the top of a mountain and hangs from a sacred tree.

THE SOUL DEPARTED

For the Slavs, the soul exists independently of the body and is able to wander freely during sleep. The Slavs imagine souls gathering on mountain tops and fighting battles. Victory brings prosperity for the sleeping owners but defeat means they will never wake. In Russia, souls are said to haunt houses in the form of the Kikimora, a female spirit who hinders incompetent housewives. The windows and doors of a peasant hut are left open after a death to allow the soul of the departed to flutter in and out like an invisible bird. The soul of an unbaptized or stillborn child is pictured among the Macedonians as a bird seeking its mother and attacking women in childbirth.

For the Finno-Ugrians, body and soul are indissolubly linked, and they die together. Ingrians stopped weeping over a grave after the body had had time to decompose. For the Voguls, the soul resided in the heart and lungs, and warriors ate these organs to absorb the life force of the vanquished. The Lapps preserved the skeleton of a sacrificed animal, believing that the gods would use it to make a new animal.

Shamanistic totems put up by Siberian Buryats as offerings to the Great Spirit and the local spirits of the place. Travellers traditionally make offerings of money or food at totems such as these. As believers in sympathetic magic, they also tie pieces of cloth to totems to attract good luck.

SHAMANISM

The role of shamans is central in the animistic religion of the Finno-Ugrians. As healers, sages and mystics, the shamans' potions, rituals and proverbs give them a unique authority.

The word shaman (feminine 'shamanka') comes through Russian from the Tungusic shaman and means 'one who is excited or raised up'. It refers to the trance-like states into which these magicians fall when their spirits are believed to be wandering in the otherworld. Sometimes their spiritual journeys are described as climbing a ladder or tree, sometimes as flying in the form of a bird or on the back of a winged horse.

Siberian shamans and shamankas wear caftans hung with iron disks and figures representing mythical animals. They are also blindfolded so that, undistracted, they enter the spirit world by their own inner light. The essential instrument of their trade is an oval drum with which they commune with the souls of trees, stones and sky. Thus prepared, they travel unseen to the otherworlds, above and below, and return with the wisdom of the Great Spirit.

Vestiges of Shamanism have survived into modern times in many remote parts of Siberia. It is not a feature of Central Europe, however, except perhaps in Hungary where it can be traced back to tenth-century AD Magyars.

Legacies

By the nineteenth century, the pagan beliefs and practices of Central and Eastern Europe had either passed into folklore or been transformed and assimilated by the Christian church. In these guises the myths of the ancient inhabitants of the region have survived, and continue to enrich the religious and cultural experiences of people today.

Among the old deities adopted and adapted by Christianity was Perun, the ancient god of thunder and lightning. His function and personality were assigned to the Old Testament prophet Elijah, who crossed the heavens in a fiery chariot. The character was further transformed in the *Wondertales* as the mighty hero, Murom, who rode the skies bringing bandits to justice. Similarly, the shepherd, priest and martyr, St Vlasii, absorbed the name and qualities of Volos, god of cattle, flocks and commerce. Female examples include Kupalnitsa, goddess of lakes and rivers, who became St Agrippina, and Mokosh, who was transformed into the saintly Paraskeva, patroness of spinning, health, marriage and fertility.

Today the Christian calendar sits comfortably over the old, annual cycle of seasonal festivals. The mid-winter celebrations have become Christmas, and the rites of spring, Easter. The bringing together of Iarilo's day and the feast of St John the Baptist, at the time of the summer solstice, is a typical example of a Christian saint supplanting a mythical, pagan deity. It is also an example of a pagan god surviving in the guise of a Christian saint.

FOLK ART

Images and symbols of pagan deities have endured in Slavonic folk art. Well into the twentieth century, the icon corner was the focal point of a Russian house as well as a reminder of the dual religious heritage of these peoples. Here could be found a collection of Christian icons and figurines, draped with towels embroidered with pagan symbols and interspersed with household objects similarly decorated.

Common decorative devices are the sacred tree, the sacrificial altar, deities, animals and Perun's axe. Abstract motifs are also found, based on natural forms with magical power. Examples are the zig-zag (lightning), the disk (sun) and the swastika (fire), all suggestive of sky deities.

Among the artists and designers who worked with Diaghilev, founder of the Russian Ballet, was the painter Léon Bakst (1886–1925). Bakst's colourful and intensely decorative style, owing much to the nineteenth-century interest in Persian designs, breathed new life into traditional Slavic tales. Shown here is a cover for his *Le Dieu Bleu*.

A magazine illustration depicting Baba Yaga. In the Christian era, Baba-Yaga was down-graded to a fearsome witch and was the personification of death. In her earlier form, she displayed an aspect of the Great Goddess, Mati-Syra-Zemlya, and as such was the patron goddess of women and childbirth; as a witch she was also occasionally benevolent.

FROM FOLK TALE TO HIGH ART

In the opening decades of the twentieth century, Russian folktales, and their interpretation in the music and visual arts of the time, were at the centre of a cultural revolution known as Modernism. The years 1910 and 1911 saw the world premieres of Igor Stravinsky's (1882–1971) ballets, *The Firebird* and *Petrushka*. *The Rites of Spring* by the same composer appeared in 1913. These works were staged by the inspirational founder of the Russian Ballet, Serge Diaghilev, who brought together innovative composers, musicians, dancers, costume designers and set designers to create an exciting and internationally renowned theatrical experience. A particularly remarkable element of the music was its innovative shamanic rhythms which, by all accounts, proved something of a challenge for the choreographer, Michel Fokine.

Stravinsky was influenced by Nikolai Rimsky-Korsakov (1844–1908) who, as can be seen in his *Sadko* and *The Snow Maiden*, also used the folk tale and old Russian epic stories as his inspiration. The Czech composer, Antonín Dvorak (1841–1904), was another who drew on his Slavonic heritage for material for the opera, *The Rusalka*.

WAR AND PEACE IN EASTERN EUROPE

AD 862	Vikings seize Kiev
AD 906	Moravia attacked and destroyed by the Magyars
1569	Union of Lublin between Poland and Lithuania
1684	Peace of Carlowitz between Venice, Austria and Poland-Lithuania to push the Ottomans back (Russia joined in 1686)
1703	Foundation of St Petersburg
1912–13	Balkan wars
1914	Heir to the Habsburg throne assassinated, leading to outbreak of First World War
1980	Solidarity campaign begins in Poland
1992–95	Civil war in former Yugoslavia

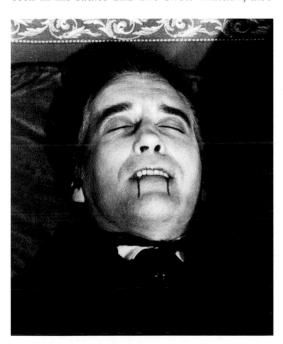

FROM ANCIENT BEGINNINGS

In the 1980s, gold and silver funerary objects – such as jewellery, combs, mirrors, vessels and figurines, many of which were decorated with animal motifs – were excavated from burial mounds in the region south of the Ural mountains. These objects date from the fifth century AD and were made by Steppe nomads, ancestors of the Eastern and Central Europeans. Their religious significance has yet to be understood, but the public response to the exhibition of these artefacts at the State Hermitage Museum in St Petersburg showed their enduring fascination and power.

Left: The vampire is a stock character of horror films. The word originates from the Serbian *vampir* or 'undead'. The myth may come from the Black Sea belief that ghosts could be persuaded to return from the underworld by supplying them with fresh blood. Modern belief in vampires is based largely on Bram Stoker's novel *Dracula*.

MALEVOLENT SPIRITS

While household spirits are often benevolent, those believed to dwell in the countryside are at best tricksters and at worst openly hostile. The Leshy, the spirit of the forest and guardian of the animals, led people astray and often to their deaths in treacherous conditions. Among the spirits of the water, the Rusalka, or souls of drowned infants and maidens, were believed to lure men happily to their deaths. They were not unpleasant, however, unlike the slimy and bloated Vodianoi who took pleasure in drowning his victims.

Amongst the most fearsome demons familiar to the Slavs and their neighbours are werewolves and vampires. Werewolves are people who change into wolves at night, usually involuntarily under the influence of the full moon. Lethal to mankind, they are believed to be invulnerable to all except silver weapons. The idea of the wolf-man might derive from Odin's frenzied warriors, the Berserkers, who wore bear- or wolf-skins into battle.

Vampires are corpses that return to life at night to feed on the blood of the living. They too can be shape-shifters, assuming the form of a wolf or a bat at will. They can be killed only by exposure to sunlight or a sharpened crucifix stabbed through the heart.

Inuit Myths

Inuit are the most geographically widespread of the Arctic's indigenous peoples. They are also one of the most culturally diverse and, while they have different names, they are now known collectively as Inuit.

Yup'ik live on the Siberian and south-west Alaskan coasts, Inupiaq inhabit north and northwest Alaska, while Alutiiq live on the south coasts. In Canada the Inuit are known as Inuvialuit in the north-west and Inuit in Nunavut Territory; while the three Inuit groups in Greenland are the Kalaallit on the west coast, Inughuit in the far north-west and Iit on the east coast.

RAVEN AND THE ORIGINS OF THE WORLD

Among the Inuit groups of Alaska, powerful varieties of myths exist concerning Raven. Many of them share the common motif that before the beginning of time, only darkness existed until a trickster figure called Raven emerged into the primordial night and created the world. The Inupiaq have stories and myths which tell of how Raven was created by a primal shaman. In these stories Raven harpoons a whale whose

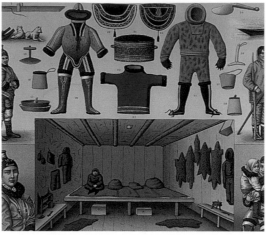

This illustration depicts a variety of Greenland Inuit clothing, hunting equipment (including harpoons), methods of travel (a kayak and a dogsledge) and living accommodation.

The Thule Inuit
Early Inuit culture became increasingly well adapted to the Arctic environment, culminating in the Thule tradition which survives to the modern age. The map shows the spread of Thule Inuit.

body becomes the land. Once he has done this, Raven reveals the daylight and creates the first people. Raven appears in several variants of a compelling myth which say something about the dual nature of both humans and animals. The usual theme of these variants is that Raven is set adrift on an ice floe in bad weather. After some time, he encounters a village of people, where he settles and marries a

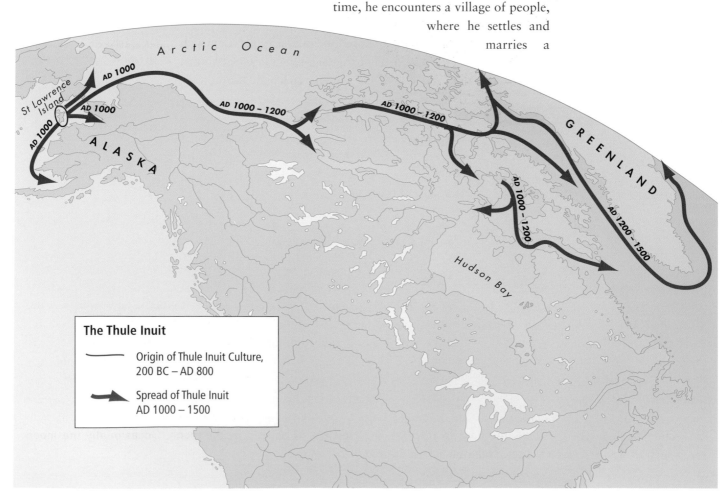

The Thule Inuit

—— Origin of Thule Inuit Culture, 200 BC – AD 800

➤ Spread of Thule Inuit AD 1000 – 1500

beautiful woman. Raven and his human wife have a number of children who travel back with their father to his own land. Once there, the children become ravens but retain the ability and power to change back into human form. Eventually, the descendants of Raven's children forget how to change into people and become ravens forever.

SILA

Sila is often translated as the Inuit word for the weather. Indeed, Inuit do talk of *sila* as weather, the elements, or air and refer to *sila* as a person – '*Sila* is angry', or '*Sila* is disappointed'. But *sila* is more than the weather – it is understood to be the fundamental principle, a universal mind, underlying the natural world and manifest in each and every individual. It is spoken about variously as an all-pervading, life-giving spirit, a universal consciousness and breath soul which connects each person with the rhythms of the universe, linking the individual self and the environment, the personal and the universal. A person's soul is an element of *sila* as an eternal unitary principle. *Sila* also refers to a person's consciousness and

awareness. A person who lacks *sila* is said to be separated from an essential relationship with the environment, which is necessary for social and psychological well-being.

THE SEA WOMAN

One of the most vivid and colourful myths of the Greenland and Canadian Inuit is about the Sea Woman. Known as Sedna in the eastern Canadian Arctic, the Sea Woman was a girl who refused to get married. Her father punished her by marrying her to a dog and banishing her from her village to a nearby island. One day she escaped from her dog-husband in a boat and was rescued by a handsome stranger and married him. After some time, she discovered that her new husband was a petrel who had assumed human form. Once more she escaped, taking her husband's kayak, and was spotted by her father and brothers who were out hunting. While she was climbing into their boat, the petrel appeared and caused a great storm with a ferocious flapping of his wings. Sedna clung to the side of her father's boat, but fearing they would all drown, he cut off her fingers and her thumbs with his hunting knife so that she slipped down into the lower world at the bottom of the sea and her fingers and thumbs became the marine mammals. Sedna now lives in a cave, where she is mistress of the seals, whales and walrus. Once she has been propitiated, she releases the mammals to be hunted by humans.

An Inuit carving of a polar bear, from marine ivory. According to Canadian Inuit myth, it was not until humans began to perform creative acts that the universe, which until then had lain dormant, was brought into being. Similarly, Inuit carvers believe that images of animals are concealed with ivory or soapstone, waiting to be discovered by the carver's knife.

Left: Coastal scenery in the Chugach Mountains region of southern Alaska. The climate in which the Inuit live is harsh, and life can be very hard in these regions. The mythology of the people reflects this daily struggle with the elements.

THE SUN, THE MOON AND THE HEAVENS

In Greenland, Inuit stories about the origin of the elements, the sun and the moon, and other celestial bodies, are related to myths about the balance between daylight and darkness, time and space, and between the human and natural worlds. One myth tells of how the sun and the moon were originally human siblings who had sexual relations. Under cover of darkness, a man crept into his sister's igloo over the course of several nights and made love to his sister who, desiring to know her lover's identity, smeared soot from her lamp onto his forehead. The following morning she identified him as her brother and confronted him with the evidence that he had seduced her. The girl ran away with her brother chasing after her and, as she ran faster, she climbed into the sky and became the sun. Her brother also ascended into the sky, where he became the moon. The myth relates how, to this day, the sun is still chased by the moon. Occasionally the moon overreaches the sun – when they embrace, an eclipse is produced.

Myths of Siberia

The peoples of Siberia are reindeer herders, hunters and fishers, living in forests, on tundra and the coast. They include the Chukchi, Even, Evenk, Nenets, Nivkhi, Itelmen and Yukaghir. The Saami also live in the Kola Peninsula in northwest Russia, and Yup'ik live along the far eastern coasts of Siberia.

Arctic peoples have a belief in a great guardian spirit which protects all animals, acting as a protector, owner, master or mistress. The figure embodies the essence of the animals in its care and presides over the correct ritual treatment after an animal has been killed by humans for food. The guardian also facilitates or prevents an animal being hunted – for example, the guardian releases the animals in its care to a respectful hunter, but keeps them away from people who do not follow the rituals and procedures to ensure the return of an animal's soul to the spirit world. In Siberian reindeer-herding societies such as the Chukchi and Nenets, the guardian, known as Reindeer Being, is protector of the reindeer herds and is often visualized as an old man. At times of great scarcity and bad weather, the shaman of the village journeys to visit the guardian of the herds to ask for his guidance and assistance in helping the people and the herds to survive and prosper.

For the Chukchi, pictured here in an illustration from 1822, as with other Siberian peoples, fire plays a central role in their lives. It was from a fire that the first reindeer emerged and when a reindeer is sacrificed, its blood is collected in a ladle and poured into the fire; it is also used to paint designs of the Reindeer Being onto people's faces.

Siberian People
Siberia is a land of hunters, reindeer herders and fishermen. The Chukchi, Even, Evenk, Nenets, Nivkhi, Itelmen and Yukaghir all believe in a great guardian spirit which protects all animals. The map shows the location of these people.

THE BEAR

Traditionally, Siberian peoples practised rites and held elaborate ceremonies both before and following the killing of an animal. Essentially, the purpose of these rites and ceremonies was for people to honour the animal, for the hunter to ask its forgiveness for having killed it and to ensure the safe return of its soul to the spirit world. Bears, in particular, were given funeral rites. In the worldviews of Siberian peoples, bears share the same spiritual essence as humans, but are more human-like and therefore more ambivalent than most other animals. Bears can stand on their hind legs and have an anatomical similarity to humans when skinned. The bear is also renowned and respected as a great hunter. As well as competing with humans for the same food, bears are also known to hunt humans as prey. At once feared and respected, the bear has special power and is believed to bring great prowess to any hunter who kills one, but danger to the entire community as well if its guardian does not wish to release the bear's spirit. Following a successful bear hunt and kill, a great and elaborate feast is held, in which the bear's head and shoulders are seated at the table, and in which the dead bear is the guest of honour.

THE SACRED FIREBOARD

Among Siberian reindeer-herding peoples such as the Evenki, Koryak and Chukchi, guardian spirits looked after the well-being and good fortune of families and households. The form of the guardian spirit was symbolized by, and often believed to be incarnated in, a sacred wooden fireboard. This was used to light the fire in the hearth which was the centre of each home. The fireboard was often carved in human form to represent the deity of the family fire. Because some peoples, such as the

Koryak and Chukchi, believed the fireboard to be an aspect or manifestation of the Reindeer Being, it was often carved in the shape of the master of the reindeer herds, who was sometimes visualized as a white-bearded man. It is not difficult to understand why fire was revered and deified by Siberian peoples: it made survival possible in sub-zero temperatures, especially in the depths of the long, dark Arctic winter. Even today, fire is essential for heating and cooking, and the fireboard is still a central feature of everyday life. For Siberian peoples who are dependent on reindeer herding, the fireboard protects the family; fire ceremonies also play a vital role in both the welfare and the ritual sacrifice of reindeer. Reindeer, say the Koryak and Chukchi, have their origins in fire – the supreme being pulled the first reindeer out of a sacred fire, and in Koryak tradition, the sacred fireboard is lit to celebrate the return of the reindeer from pasture.

The Reindeer Being ensures that only those who respect the reindeer and understand how to kill it so that its soul returns to the spirit world are allowed to hunt these animals. If the correct rituals and practices are not carried out after a reindeer is killed, the community risks the wrath of malevolent spirits.

A Siberian shaman from the Lower Amur, with some of his ritual equipment. If the delicate balance of the natural world is disrupted, such as an animal being killed incorrectly, the shaman will visit the spirit world to right the wrong that has been done.

MASKS AND THE SPIRIT WORLD

Like other Inuit, the Siberian Yup'ik of Chukotka and St Lawrence Island carved masks from wood or made them from animal skins. Masks were central to ceremonial and ritual life and depicted spirits, animals and mythical beings. Mask rituals and ceremonies did not always have a religious purpose, but masks were commonly worn when people from neighbouring villages met for feasts and dancing or for trade and to exchange gifts. Both shamans and persons without spiritual powers could wear masks, but shamans wore them during their healing rites and visions. Shamans often instructed mask-carvers to shape elaborate masks in the form of the spirits and mythical figures they encountered on their spirit journeys. In a sense, to wear a mask was to incarnate and attempt to gain influence over a spirit. Shamans wore masks which represented their helping spirits in an attempt to ensure success in hunting and fishing.

Animals in Myth

Marine mammals, reindeer, caribou and other animals remain the basis for the cultural and economic life of the Arctic's indigenous peoples. Hunted or herded, animals make life in the Arctic possible. They provide meat for food and furs for clothing, whether for consumption by the household or wider community and region. In the past, whalebone and reindeer antlers provided materials for hunting implements, tools and other equipment. Myths and stories emphasize the spiritual relationship between humans and animals.

Animals are conceptualized by the indigenous peoples of the Arctic as non-human persons, endowed with their own consciousness and intelligence. Some species of animal are said to live in communities similar in social organization and structure to human communities. For example, the Yup'ik of Alaska and Siberia say that seals live according to the same kinds of social rules that humans are subject to. Yup'ik stories describe how young seals learn appropriate social and moral rules from their elders. Such rules may be guidelines for negotiating the dangers present in the everyday life of the seal. A fate more dangerous to a seal than being hunted would be to approach a hunter who appears to be a careless and disrespectful person, who would not honour the soul of the seal.

In Athapaskan mythology and stories from the Distant Time (a remote ancient time), animals and humans are similar to one another in many ways, notably in the way in which animals have distinct and unique personalities just as humans do. In the myths and oral histories of many Arctic peoples it is common to find stories describing how humans and animals were not as clearly distinguished from each other as they are today. Stories tell of a time when they lived together in the same communities, often sharing the same household, and of how humans had the power and ability to transform themselves into animals and vice-versa.

The Arctic peoples rely on animals for everything they need in their lives as agriculture is impossible in this harsh environment. Their importance is reflected in the mythology of the region: animals feature as tricksters and as helpers in many tales, and are believed to have their own souls which must be respected for the good of the whole community.

HELPING SPIRITS

In the traditional religious life of Arctic peoples, the shaman was a central figure in the maintenance of good relations between humans and animals. Shamans acted as intermediaries in the transactions between humans, the souls of animals and the guardian of the animals. Inuit myths, for example, relate how a shaman would acquire his or her powers by undergoing a long, solitary and arduous initiation process–wrestling with spirits in the mountains, out on the barren tundra, or in deep, dark caves. The trance, and subsequent journey, was the essence of shamanic practice. The shaman's soul would journey to the spirit world to search for the souls of human beings who had been captured by malevolent spirits, or to bargain with the guardian of the animals (such as the Sea Woman) for animals to be sent to the human world to be hunted. In their journeys to the spirit world, shamans would often be assisted by a helping spirit, which often took the form of an animal, such as a polar bear.

THE HUNTER AND THE HUNTED

In the worldviews of indigenous peoples, animals are sentient beings and have souls that need to be treated correctly and respectfully once they have been hunted. Hunters depend on killing animals so that they and their families can survive. Animals, too, depend on the hunt and on being hunted. In this way, hunting is a contract between hunter and prey. Hunters and other members of the community must follow precise rules not only in terms of how they must kill, but also of how they deal with the kill,

share and consume the meat and utilize the fur. Among Inuit groups, ritual and ceremonial life is often devoted entirely to ensuring the souls of seals, whales, walrus, polar bear and caribou receive proper treatment and respect. Because of the extreme physical conditions and climate people must endure, the Arctic environment is a dangerous and uncertain one. As the rich mythology of Arctic peoples shows, this danger and uncertainty also arises from the fact that, because all human food consists of souls, maintaining balance between the human and natural worlds is often considered a matter of life and death. Hunters are obliged to see that animals are killed properly and their meat, bones and hide used in ways that will not offend the animal's guardian spirit. Hunting and consumption of an animal is an act of regeneration, both of human society and of the animal. If animals are not respected, either when alive or dead, they will not allow themselves to be hunted or 'give' themselves up to their hunter.

A **Siberian shaman** calls on the tribal spirits to heal a sick man. To cure the person, the shaman would go into a trance, assisted by the ritual beating of a drum, and travel to the spirit world. He would then try to find out what spirit was causing the sickness and why, thus being able to advise the ailing person of a cure.

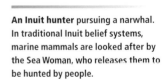

An **Inuit hunter** pursuing a narwhal. In traditional Inuit belief systems, marine mammals are looked after by the Sea Woman, who releases them to be hunted by people.

ANIMALS AND DREAMS

How can a hunter find a seal in a wide expanse of open sea, or amongst a tumble of ice floes? How can he track caribou through difficult mountain terrain, or know where to look for deer or moose in dense forest? Hunters must be knowledgeable as well as skillful, and how they acquire this knowledge and skill arises in part from the profound relationship between hunter and prey. Dene, Cree and Naskapi hunters often make contact with animals in dreams: a respectful hunter (and one who is also respected by animals) who has dream-power can leave his body at night and travel through the forest along dream-trails until he encounters an animal. Although it is mostly male hunters who have dreams, a woman, too, can occasionally dream of animals; she then relates the dream to the hunter – most likely her husband – who sets out to find the dream-trail she followed while asleep. On some dream journeys, the hunter is assisted by his helping spirit. The following day, or even several days later, the hunter locates the dream-trail and follows it until he comes across the animal he met in his dream. Because a contract based on mutual respect has been made between the hunter and the animal in the dream, the animal gives itself to the hunter as prey.

Landscape, Sky and the Underworld

For the indigenous peoples of the Arctic aspects of the natural world, the elements and the universe, such as lakes, rivers, the sun, the moon and so on, have souls just as humans and animals do. This shared spiritual essence between humans, animals and natural phenomena is a common theme of many myths, which act to remind human beings that they are not separate from the natural world, but part of a transcendent universe in which everything emanates from the same source.

Many features of the diverse Arctic landscapes of Siberia, Alaska, northern Canada, Greenland and northern Fennoscandia (Norway, Sweden, Denmark and Finland) are sacred places and sites of religious and spiritual significance, especially along animal migration routes and dream-trails, places in the landscape where animal spirits reveal themselves to humans, sacrificial sites, or places of initiation for shamans. The Athapaskan peoples of Alaska and Canada have rich and vibrant oral histories which describe how the features of the vast boreal forest were once human beings whose spirits are now embodied in the natural world.

In Siberia and Lapland, reindeer antlers are placed at sacred sites and adorned with gifts, while sacred stones which incarnate local spirits or deities are placed on mountain tops, on lakeshores and riverbanks. The Arctic is a homeland for indigenous peoples who name its features not just in a geographically descriptive sense, but in order to convey information about spiritual aspects, family and community history and mythological events.

The Saami
The Saami lived by hunting, fowling and fishing. Elk and bear were frequently hunted, and from the later prehistoric period reindeer were hunted, herded and even used for traction. Shamanism was the main Saami religion and animal sacrifices were often carried out next to unusual trees and stones.

The Saami

○ Site Location

Saami Culture

● Settlement
▲ Sacrificial Site
▼ Grave
■ Hunting Pit
◇ Rock Engraving
◆ Bear Grave

Time Scales

▬ 200 BC – AD 1200
▬ AD 1200 – 1700

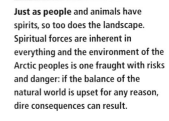

MOUNTAIN WANDERERS

Most Arctic peoples have stories and myths about mysterious, supernatural beings, spirits and ghosts that wander the landscape. Some of the most powerful and evocative stories come from Greenland and detail the activities of the *qivittoq* (pl. *qivittut*), mountain wanderers who left behind their home communities to live alone in the wilderness. Stories relate how this rejection of the world of family and friends was often due to personal pressures and difficult relations with other people. The most common explanation is that *qivittut* (who are originally mainly men) had been unlucky in love. Stories tend to focus on their solitary nature and habits. After some years living alone in the mountains, the senses of the *qivittoq* sharpen; his eyes, ears and nostrils grow larger to enable him to see, hear and smell animals, while his teeth and fingernails become long and sharp. Living alone in caves in winter, the *qivittot* moves down to the coastline in summer. During winter, people fear *qivittut* coming down to villages under cover of darkness to steal fish and dogs, they also peer through the windows of people's houses. For most of the year, however, they tend to keep themselves hidden in the mountains and shy away from human contact. When a *qivittoq* dies it is said to remain on earth as a ghost.

THE NORTHERN LIGHTS

For centuries, travellers in the Arctic – and far down in the North American continent – have marvelled at and been moved by the *aurora borealis*, the northern lights. These brilliant winter displays also occupy a prominent place in the mythology and spiritual beliefs of Arctic peoples. The Inuit believe that when people die, their souls ascend to the heavens to form part of the northern lights. In this way, the northern lights are comprised entirely of human souls waiting to be reborn on earth. Because the dead

do not wish to remain apart from the living, they communicate with them by whistling. A living person who hears this must reply with a soft whistle and the lights will come closer to earth. A recurring theme in Inuit myth is that the land of the dead is a land of plenty – the souls of those who go there feast and play ball with a walrus skull, and this appears as the aurora. Indeed, the Greenland Inuit call the northern lights *arsarnerit*, 'the ball players'. Variants in myths about the northern lights from Greenland and the Canadian Arctic relate how the souls of the deceased make a crackling sound as they run across the frost-hardened snow of the heavens.

Just as people and animals have spirits, so too does the landscape. Spiritual forces are inherent in everything and the environment of the Arctic peoples is one fraught with risks and danger: if the balance of the natural world is upset for any reason, dire consequences can result.

The aurora borealis, or northern lights, occur about 110 km (68 miles) above the earth's surface. The *aurora borealis* occupy a prominent place in the mythology and spiritual beliefs of Arctic peoples.

THE SOUL'S JOURNEY

Many different Arctic peoples have similar beliefs about the nature of the human soul. A person is comprised of three souls that, upon death, separate. One, the shadow soul, remains in the land of the living as a spirit or ghost. Another, the breath soul, which is able to leave a person's body during life, also remains on earth as a spirit or ghost, but some Siberian peoples believe it eventually journeys to the heavens. The third, the name soul, is called back to earth to reside in the body of a newly born child. In this sense, there are a finite number of persons who live, die and are reborn through their names. This belief in the profound spiritual nature of the name is especially powerful among the Inuit. The Inuit of east Greenland strongly believed that a person's name-soul could transmigrate through an animal, such as a seal, before it entered a new-born baby's body. This, along with their general belief in the souls of animals, meant that they treated the animals they hunted with great respect.

Creation Myths

North America has one of the world's richest collections of myths, due to the efforts of ethnologists, linguists and native storytellers who worked together in the late 1800s and early 1900s to record as many of the tales as they could. These records sparked a revival and, although there was a decline in the 1940s and 1950s, storytelling today is as vibrant as it was in the past. The stories are recited on many occasions: during winter storytelling sessions, as a part of ritual and ceremony and at inter-tribal powwows. There have been changes in the content of some of the tales, especially at powwows where they are often used to raise awareness of ethnic origin, but the old, traditional tales are still important and remain as a 'lived reality' for the majority of modern Native Americans.

This canvas altar is part of a Blackfoot Horse medicine bundle used during ceremonies intended to increase wealth in horses or as part of a horse doctor's secret rites. The red half was placed to the north to represent this direction and the day time; the black half symbolized the night. The four feathers symbolize the four directions and the sacred powers who govern these.

Creation tales are of particular importance, since these help define the distinctive character of Native American belief and help separate and protect it from the pervasive influences of Euro-American culture. Fundamental to this belief is the understanding that the world has always existed and was not brought into being for the benefit of its human occupants. As a result, there are no true creation myths in North American

North America on the Eve of European Conquest
Although the arrival of the europeans in America had an adverse effect on the myths and culture of the native American people, interest has recently revived and story telling now is almost as vibrant as it was in the past. The map shows the distribution of the native peoples of North America on the eve of the European conquest.

North America on the Eve of European Conquest:

- Arctic
- Sub-Arctic
- Northwest Coast
- Plateau
- Great Basin
- California
- Southwest
- Great Plains
- Northeast
- Southeast

mythology: most are tales of transformation which assume the existence of previous worlds. Many of these tales emphasize the unformed character of the previous worlds; these worlds are sometimes underwater, enclosed in darkness or have none of the features that the present world contains. The creator-transformer brings light by stealing the sun, creating lakes and rivers through his teardrops or forming mountains by stamping his foot.

The creator-transformer figure is often characterized as a trickster. Among the Blackfoot of Montana and Alberta he is credited with creating mountain mudslides simply because he wishes to have fun. Raven on the northwest coast creates rivers because he is being mischievous and thinks how pleasant it would be if the people had some water (although when they receive it they do not know what it is). In other Raven tales from the north-west coast he makes whirlpools because he wishes to drown an opponent who has stolen his wife. It is impossible to think of these characters as the equivalent of an omnipotent creator-god.

THE FIRST FLOOD

Floods are a common motif in mythology and in North America there are numerous pre-Christian tales that deal with the first flood. In a period before people are created, the creator-transformer often had a canoe or raft from which he would send his animal helpers to dive for mud. Such animals, usually four in number, demonstrate their successive diving skills until finally they bring up just sufficient mud for the transformer to roll in the palm of his hand. By scattering this and breathing on it, or sometimes by wishing things merely to be different, he is able to create the entire world. Typically, his action is almost always a self-centered one: he is bored sitting alone in his canoe and thinks it would be fun to make changes in order to see what happens.

EMERGENCE FROM OTHER WORLDS

Tales of the emergence from previous worlds are quite widespread, although they do not always include transformation and may assume that the present world exists in its current form but is simply unknown. Such tales are particularly important among Pueblo tribes of the south-west (New Mexico and Arizona), but numerous variants are found among tribes as widely separated as California and the Great Lakes. These describe a succession of different worlds through which the human-animal occupants have passed in order to reach their present condition.

Hopi stories, for instance, tell of five successive worlds in which various incidents have served to define the different characteristics of people and animals. They were once all the same, but as they emerged from one world to the next they became differentiated. Bat is blind because he came from the third world, which was one of darkness. Mouse is quiet and timid, because he was cautious about leaving the fourth world to go into the present. People are garrulous and argumentative because when they came into the present world they were unable to decide which way to travel, so all went off in different directions.

THE PRIMORDIAL WORLD

There are occasional tales in which there exists a primordial world that is unrelated to the present. The Zuni of the south-west call it *Awonawilona*, a name that it is impossible to translate. Perhaps the closest to the Zuni concept would be to think of *Awonawilona* as a nebulous energy source. From this source, which thought itself into being, came Awitelin Tsita (Mother Earth) and Apoyan Tachu (Father Sky), and from their tempestuous relationship grew all the things needed to sustain human populations. Other tribes claim similar energy sources, such as Wakan Tanka for the Siouan groups or Mahishsedah for the Crow, but only recognize their existence and tell no stories of them.

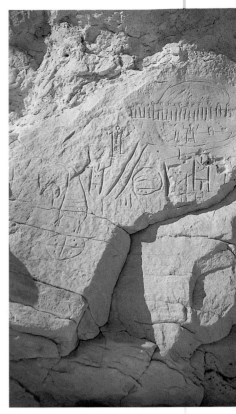

This rock engraving from Castle Garden in Wyoming is part of a prehistoric sacred site that contains a great number of carved images on rocks. Among them is a circle containing a cross, which symbolizes the Sacred Circle enclosing the Four Directions, Four Winds or Four Powers of Creation.

This carving is by Bill Reid, a contemporary Haida carver from the northwest coast. It is titled 'The Raven and the First Men' and shows the creator-god, Raven, releasing people into the present world.

A UNIFIED WORLD

North American myths emphasize the unity of the world and everything within it. All things, whether animate or inanimate, are said to possess a soul or spirit, and to have the power of reason and motivation. Existence in the present world is transitory, as it was in the previous worlds and will be in those still to come. At the time of the creation of the present world, people became separated from animals and were given the special responsibility of holding rituals and ceremonies that would help maintain harmony and balance. Many of these rituals are re-enactments of the origin stories and serve to remind people of the responsibilities they have.

Hero Myths

Distinct from, but merging into, the tales of the North American creator-transformer are hero myths. These differ from the transformation tales in that the world in which they take place resembles that of the present and that the hero, although not completely devoid of shape-changing ability, is essentially human. Many of the tales deal with attempts made to defeat the hero or test his abilities, and his efforts at overcoming these obstacles.

U nlike the transformation tales, most of the hero stories are set within or make reference to tribal organization and society. The hero is, nevertheless, frequently defined by his difference from others. Lazy Boy in Plains Indian stories is derided because he spends his time sleeping, and refuses to engage in the industrious pursuits of war and the chase suitable to young Plains warriors. It is only when the entire tribe is threatened by man-eating buffaloes that he wakes up, sets out alone to defeat the buffalo and then returns and goes back to sleep that the people recognize his extraordinary skills.

THE RELUCTANT HERO

Unpromising and reluctant heroes such as Lazy Boy are frequent in Plains tales, but also occur with regularity among tribes of the Plateau (the river-cut tablelands of central interior British

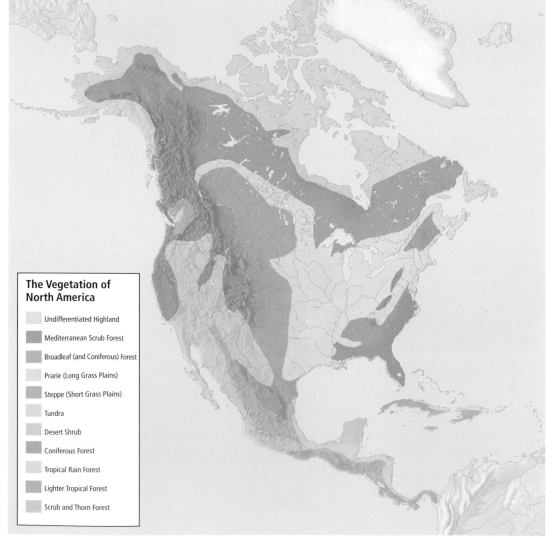

The Vegetation of North America

- Undifferentiated Highland
- Mediterranean Scrub Forest
- Broadleaf (and Coniferous) Forest
- Prarie (Long Grass Plains)
- Steppe (Short Grass Plains)
- Tundra
- Desert Shrub
- Coniferous Forest
- Tropical Rain Forest
- Lighter Tropical Forest
- Scrub and Thorn Forest

These house posts from the northwest coast represent sea lions and support a cross-beam in the form of Sisiutl, the double-headed serpent. Sisiutl is an important mythological figure who assists shamans during seances when they make out-of-body journeys to locate the source of an illness or to recover lost souls.

The Vegetation of North America
The geography and vegetation of North America had a strong influence on the kind of myths told in any particular region. In Plains Tales for example, the heroes are often uncompromising and reluctant, a reflection of the tough environment of the Plains.

Columbia, eastern Oregon and Washington) and among the Iroquois. Among the Okanagon on the Washington–British Columbia border he is Dirty Boy, who lives in a decrepit lodge of brush and bark at the edge of the camp and soils his bed. His only companion is his grandmother, whom the tales describe as a toothless old crone dressed in rags. Unknown to the people, the grandmother is Star and the boy is Sun. When the chief arranges a contest to select suitable marriage partners for his daughters, Dirty Boy wins all the contests but the chief and his elder daughter are reluctant to accept this filthy child as a son-in-law. The younger daughter, however, goes to Dirty Boy's lodge. In the morning, when a wealthy tribe arrive to celebrate the marriage ceremony of the pair, the grandmother emerges as a young woman in a skin dress sparkling with starlight and with stars in her hair, while so many stars shine around Dirty Boy that people are dazzled if they look at him. The younger daughter is bathed by the grandmother and also becomes covered in stars, but the jealous elder daughter has to go and live with the ravens (the myth does not specify why, but it is presumably due to the ravens' reputation for cheating, which becomes apparent in other tales).

THE TWIN HEROES

Such tales define the nature of the hero and carry a moral that things should not always be judged by their appearance. In other stories the heroes are often twins who suffer adversity but support each other. In Apache stories one of the twins is lame, the other blind. The tales tell of how the blind brother carries the lame one to give him legs and of how the lame twin acts as his brother's eyes.

Elsewhere the world is formed by arguments that occur between the twin heroes. The famous tales of Manabozho from the Menominee (a Great Lakes tribe) are characteristic of these. Manabozho is helped by a good manitou (a spirit or power that influences life) and it is from him that many stories of the Noble Savage have passed into the popular imagination and from whom, according to the Menominee storytellers, the tales

of Brer Rabbit derive. Manabozho had a twin, Naqpote, who could assume the form of a wolf, and whatever Manabozho did during the day, Naqpote would reverse at night. According to one tale, the twins decided to have a final contest. Manabozho called all his helpers – the thunderers (in Great Lakes mythology there was a division between the sky powers – represented by the thunderers – and the underwater powers – represented by the underwater panther). Thunderers are mythological creatures, associated with the thunderbird, whose eyes flash lightning and whose wing claps are thunder; his earthly counterparts are the eagles, the geese, ducks and pigeons. Naqpote set his assistants – the underground bear, snakes, otters, fishes, deer and other beasts of the field – against them. The contest was undecided. Naqpote now lives in a stone canoe in the north of the world and has threatened to return; Manabozho appears to people frequently as a little white rabbit with trembling ears who anxiously awaits the return of his twin.

MIRACULOUS BIRTHS

Hero tales often involve characters whose births are little short of miraculous. Among the Blackfoot, Blood-Clot Boy is born from a clot of buffalo blood and returns to rescue his aged parents from the tyrannical rule imposed on them by their son-in-law. The Crow Indians tell of Lodge Boy and Thrown-Away whose mother is killed by the evil Red Woman. Lodge Boy lives behind the curtain which lines his father's tipi, but Thrown-Away is cast into a spring where the animals succour him. When the two are finally reconciled with their father, they are found to have gained prodigious skills and perform magic to bring their mother back to life before setting out on adventures in which they overcome various giants and cannibals who threaten the people.

The thunderbird appears during the sacred Tsetseka winter season of the Kwaikutl tribes of Vancouver Island. It is readily recognized in this mask by the downturned beak and feathered horns. The thunderbird is closely associated with the major deities of the northwest coast, and has Eagle as his assistant.

MORALITY LESSONS

Native American hero myths set parables for what may happen in the future. They typically leave events undecided and often fail to distinguish between the heroes and their helpers. We do not know from the stories whether Lazy Boy and Dirty Boy are cosmological characters, and we are left with a lingering doubt that Manabozho, the great creator-hero, may be nothing more than a white rabbit. In modern retellings, the hero myths serve as reminders of the fragility of human existence and of the need to recognize and respect the qualities that other people possess.

Supernatural Journeys

Many North American tales deal with epic voyages. While some of these can be classed with the hero stories, they have a defining character in that the journeys inevitably mean travelling out of the realm of human beings and into other realms. Even when the journeys take place in the natural world they require feats of endurance or demonstrations of amazing abilities. In these tales there is a confusion of worlds. Sometimes the journeys are made to the sky or take place deep under water, or they may involve travelling to the tops of distant mountains or to the land of the dead.

Perhaps the best known of these stories is that of Sedna, a reluctant heroine of the Inuit (Eskimo – see p. 157). Married against her will to Storm Petrel, she is cast into the ocean to become the Mistress of the Animals. From her home at the bottom of the sea she capriciously wreaks vengeance on the people for her unhappy marriage by calling the animals to her and creating famines. It is only through a journey across razor-sharp bridges and over rivers of blood that Sedna can be reached and entreated to restore the animals to the people.

Tales of journeys to visit supernatural beings appear on the northwest coast, in British Columbia and southern Alaska, where the journey is to a place known only as the North End of the World. In the tales of the Kwakiutl, this is the home of Baxbakualanuxsiwae, the Cannibal Giant, whose insatiable appetite can only be satisfied with human brains supplied by his associate Hoxhok. Anyone travelling here is met by Kinqalala, a seductress who dances naked carrying a corpse but who promises status and wealth to those who succumb to her charms.

TRAVELS THROUGH TIME AND SPACE

Elsewhere the tales involve impossible leaps from one dimension to the next. Among the Apache, the journey means travelling from the top of each of four sacred mountains and covering the distance between each mountain in the space of a single day. The mountains are, however, so far apart that they define the limits of the known world and each part of the journey is fraught with difficulties. There are numerous monsters at every stage who attempt to trick the

This Assiniboine hand drum from the Great Plains area shows a horned figure with bat-like wings. Similar figures have been reported as being seen during hallucinatory visions brought on by weakness and partial delirium resulting from ritual fasting. Such fasts were used by Great Plains tribes to enable individuals to make contact with the spirit forces from whom protective power might be gained.

careless traveller into a false sense of security and it is only with supernatural help and insight that these difficulties can be overcome. The journey was thought to have been undertaken because the monsters dwelling in the mountains had threatened the people (although the journey was later supposedly undertaken by shamans as a test of their power).

JOURNEYS TO THE LAND OF THE DEAD

These journeys are equally as hazardous. A journey to the Land of the Dead was undertaken when a relative did not want to be parted from a loved one – the relative travelled to entreat the dead to return the loved one to the Land of the Living. Also, the souls of the recently departed were thought to travel to the Land of the Dead, from which they could be retrieved (usually by a shaman on a journey in pursuit of the soul) if this was done before they tasted the food of the ghosts. The journeys are frequently across four burning prairies and the traveller has only four containers of water. The temptation is to use most of the water during the early stages of the journey, but then the traveller will find he has no water left when the fourth prairie has to be crossed. Even when this part of the journey is successful, entrance to the Land of the Dead may be barred by a raging torrent where the only means of transportation is a canoe with holes in the bottom (a burial canoe). Other journeys involve a sky window, a rope or chain of arrows to the sky or a rainbow bridge. Sometimes, as in the south-west, the entrance to the other world is provided by Spider Woman, who spins a gossamer web that will successfully transport only those who show no doubt and who will follow her instructions faithfully – failure to do so means the web will break.

Throughout all these stories there is an underlying theme: prudence and a willingness to listen will provide success; greed and rashness will only bring disaster. The person who uses all the water to cross the burning prairies will have nothing left to enable a return.

Txamsen of the Tsimshian Indians of the north-west coast summarizes this moral with his visit to Chief Echo. Chief Echo repeated all Txamsen said, so that when Txamsen proclaimed his greatness he heard Chief Echo telling him he was right. He had made his journey and braved all the difficulties, and consequently felt very proud of himself. Listening to Chief Echo confirming his own opinion of himself convinced him he was right. He ate all the mountain-goat fat and gorged himself on crab apples mixed with grease and sat on the mat at the north of the house, which he had been told was the place for the Great Chief. But then he heard some women laughing at him from a corner of the house and he was frightened and ran away. A stone hammer hit him on the foot and some other people took away all the meat and fat he had tried to take with him. Since then Txamsen has had only poor food and now has to walk with a stick to support him.

This whale vertebrae, walrus ivory and hide carving was made by an Eskimo shaman from Point Hope, Alaska. It depicts the shaman undergoing transformation as his spirit leaves his bodily form to make a journey, under trance, to the other world.

UNDERTAKING SUPERNATURAL JOURNEYS

The tales of supernatural journeys emphasize that such journeys are only undertaken either by the foolhardy or the extremely wise. The foolhardy travel because they refuse to listen to sense and are dismissive of the dangers they will face; as a consequence they often suffer misfortune. The wise, who are usually shamans (medicine men or women), are fully aware of the dangers and thus able to protect themselves. In contemporary tellings, people are reminded of the disasters that can happen if one fails to listen to advice or attempts the impossible.

Animal Stories

Animal stories in North America generally fit into one of two general categories. The first is that which defines the behaviour or appearance of the animals and in these the animal character is clearly recognizable. The second type of tale deals with a time before the people and the animals were differentiated from one another and in these it can be difficult to tell whether the tale is dealing with an animal or a person.

Pottery bowl from the Mogollon culture of the Southwestern United States, dating from the tenth century AD. Such bowls were made exclusively as burial goods and were ritually 'killed' at burial with punctures to their base, which were believed to release the vessel's spirit into the next world.

Subsistence Patterns of Indigenous Americans.
The indigenous people of America lived in fine balance with nature. The map shows their general subsistence patterns.

In the first category the animal's behaviour or appearance often stems from involvement in other activities: Mouse's timidity as a result of his failure to lead the Hopi people into a strange new world during their tales of emergence is a classic of this kind. On the Plains we find Raven is made black by being held in the smoke hole of a tipi as a punishment after he refuses to give Buffalo to the people. In another Plains tale, Crow is black simply because he is so busy painting all the other animals and birds that when it is his turn to be painted there are no colours left.

In tales from La Push, in Washington, Snail originally has sharp eyesight but is so keen to exhibit this peculiarity of his vision that he lends his eyes to others. When he lends them to Eagle, Eagle keeps them and gives Snail only small stalks in return. A Cherokee story shows similar responses to conceited behaviour. Opossum used to have a fine bushy tail that he liked to show off. When invited to a dance he demanded a special place where everyone could see his tail, but Cricket decided his vanity was too much to endure. He offered to groom Opossum's tail for him, but his touch was so soothing that Opossum fell asleep and Cricket was able to nibble off all the luxurious growth.

ANIMAL WIVES AND HUSBANDS

The second category of animal stories often involves animal wives and husbands, and usually serves one of two functions. The stories either explain the powers that animals possess

Subsistence Patterns of Indigenous Americans

- Game
- Cultivated Plants
- Fish
- Balance of Game and Wild Plants
- Wild Plants

and teach the people to respect them, or they create a relationship between people and animals in which the animals offer themselves as food to help their human relatives.

The Blackfoot story of Beaver is typical of the first type of animal-marriage story. Beaver, who is Chief of Animals, entices away the wife of the chief and she lives with him in his den for four days (four years in the human world). When this illicit affair is discovered, Beaver offers magic gifts to the offended husband, explaining that with these gifts he will receive the power of the animal world. But, should he refuse the gifts, his wife will be lost to him forever.

The second type of animal-marriage can be demonstrated by way of an Arapaho tale. Splinter-foot Girl, like many of the culture heroes, had a miraculous birth, but she was abducted by Bone Bull, the Buffalo Chief. At this time the buffaloes ate people and humans were very afraid of them. The bravery of Splinter-foot Girl's brothers in finding and saving her from Bone Bull persuaded the man-eating buffaloes to become benevolent. Thereafter, the buffaloes and the people considered themselves related, and the buffaloes offered themselves willingly as food for the people in order to atone for Bone Bull's abduction of the young girl.

THE ANIMAL TRICKSTER

In other tales we find animals acting as humans, but generally with far greater power. Coyote is the supreme trickster throughout the Great Plains, in parts of the southwest and in California. His place is taken by Blue Jay on the northwest coast, and by Hare in the Woodlands and Great Lakes. In many of these stories the differences between human and animal elements are impossible to distinguish: Coyote, in fact, seems able to change his form at will. Even so, the tales emphasize that although Coyote may appear to be human, he is nevertheless beyond the social constraints that bind human societies.

Coyote is of particular interest in contemporary storytelling, since he appears today as an almost universal creator-trickster in every region of the continent. Modern storytellers refer to Coyote as a symbol of the relationship between people and nature, and of the consequences of allowing this to become out of control. All the animal stories nevertheless tend to reinforce a basic fact of Native American belief: a respect for animals and for animal behaviour. There are constant reminders that people and animals must live in a harmonious relationship, and that exploitation or excess will have disastrous results.

Buffalo was thought of as a life-giver and as the originator of time by tribes of the Great Plains. This skull, from the Arapaho or Blackfoot, was used as an altar and is painted with symbols that represent the duality of all living things: its symbolism encompasses numerous oppositions such as day and night, north and south and masculine and feminine.

Indians of the Great Plains considered the eagle to be the greatest of birds. It was renowned for its courage and its ability to strike its enemies swiftly and noiselessly but was also revered because 'it lived on the earth but could reach the sky'. War bonnets of eagle feathers, such as that shown here, were symbols of the outstanding warrior and a source of spiritual power and inspiration.

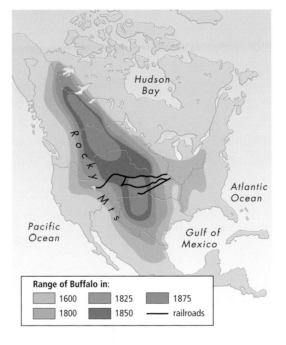

Range of Buffalo in:
1600 1825 1875
1800 1850 ——— railroads

The image of the buffalo often appears in Native American mythology. The economic and spiritual base of Native American culture was destroyed when the buffalo herds were cut in two by the transcontinental railroad (1869) and then slaughtered in a deliberate campaign to starve out the Sioux. By the 1890s, the buffalo, like the Native Americans, survived only on reservations.

THE HUMAN–ANIMAL SYMBIOSIS

There is a symbiotic relationship between people and animals in Native American myths. They typically address the animals as 'brothers', a term that implies a respect relationship rather than one of direct kin, and point out the advantages that can accrue when this relationship is honoured. This reflects a past when the cooperation of the animals was essential to the survival of Native American communities, but can also be seen today in a general abhorrence of the exploitation of the animal world. The tales emphasize that people and animals were created as equals and that the qualities that each possess should be recognized and respected.

Tales of Cultural Origins

A considerable number of North American myths deal with cultural origins. Although the majority of these are told as part of other story cycles, such as the tales of the creator-transformer, as animal stories, or within the series of stories relating the adventures of the culture heroes, they nevertheless share characteristics that give them an identity of their own.

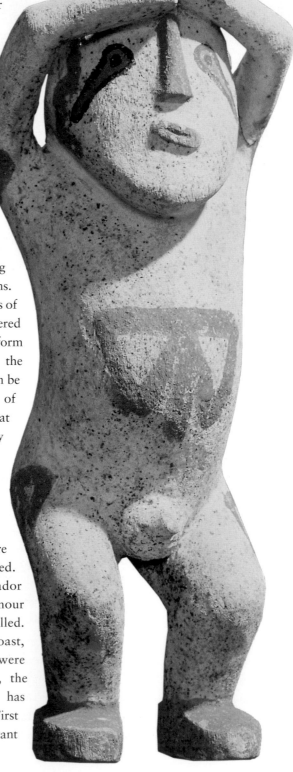

Tribes of the southwest US lived as agriculturists in a semi-arid desert environment. The onset of spring rains was important to them and their ancestors and deceased relatives were enshrined as Kachinas or rain-bringers. This Kachina, from Hopi Pueblo, is painted with phallic symbols that are intended to ensure the fertility of their crops.

A few generic story types deal with the origins of matters of widespread concern. Typical of these is the theft of fire, which among many tribes was said to have been kept from the people by Thunder. In some stories the fire is stolen from Thunder by people who send the smallest animal to Thunder's camp, and then begin a relay race back to their own homes when Thunder starts in pursuit. Since each animal-person in the relay is stronger than the last they are able to keep ahead of Thunder, although He remains angry and even today sends blasts of lightning to indicate his wrath.

NIGHT AND DAY

In a similar category is the origin of night and day, which results from inconclusive gambling between the birds – who want permanent day – and the animals – who want it to remain dark. Since neither side is able to prevail they reach a compromise in which half the day will be light and half dark. Other stories describe the origin of the stars or of the winds. In almost all of these tales there is an attempt to create a balance between extremes; much ritual activity was devoted to maintaining this harmonious relationship between the elements.

AGRICULTURAL ORIGINS

Other tales of cultural origin are specific to particular culture areas. In the south-west, where agriculture was practised in a semi-arid environment, the tales focus on the Kachinas, or Rain-Bringers, who descend from their mountain homes each spring to help the people. Here too, as well as in the south-east and Woodlands, are extensive stories that are concerned with the origin of corn and with the respect due to the Corn Mother. In many of these tales the corn is considered a relative, and the young corn plant is nurtured as if it were a beloved child. Thus the Kachin-Mana, or Corn

Maiden, of the Hopi Indians is carefully watched over until she matures and is reburied (planted) to be born again the following year.

HUNTING ORIGINS

With regard to hunting tribes, as on the Great Plains, the emphasis shifts to the origins of game animals and the introduction of hunting techniques and weapons. Frequently, as in the tales of the buffalo encountered previously, the animals form a relationship with the people in which they can be considered as kin; this, of course, is similar to that established with corn by the agricultural tribes. The relationships are rarely friendly at first, and it is only through promises of friendship and respect that they are ultimately maintained. The Naskapi of Labrador show reverence and honour when a caribou is killed. On the northwest coast, where the people were dependent on fishing, the origin of salmon has precedence and the First Salmon Rite is an important annual ceremony.

This Hudson Bay blanket has been embroidered with the figure of a double-headed eagle by the Kaigani Haida of Prince of Wales Island, British Columbia. In this modified form it became a ceremonial robe that was worn by a chief on important occasions. The eagle was an important clan crest that identified the lineage to which the chief belonged.

The separation of the people from the game animals is explained in a Cheyenne tale that is set in the period when the people and the animals were able to talk to each other. As befits the hunting ethos of the Cheyenne, the story unfolds as a competition between the buffalo and the people. The buffaloes, who were the biggest animals, failed to see why they should not be considered as equal to human beings and proposed a race to see who was the strongest. They were joined by the deer, antelope and elk, while the dog, eagle and hawk were to run with the people. Hawk won the contest by swooping ahead of the buffalo in the closing stages of the race and since then all the split-hoofed animals have lived apart from the people and are hunted for their meat and hides. The dog was honoured by becoming the constant companion of the humans, while both eagle and hawk were respected as warrior birds. Even today, the men's societies of the Cheyenne pay homage to the eagle and hawk as the greatest of the birds and the bravest of the brave.

Northwest-coast shamans relied on powers given to them by supernatural patrons via animal intermediaries. This Tlingit rattle is carved in the form of a salmon, the primary food resource on the northwest coast, but contains within it a miniature effigy figure of a shaman, which makes the relationship between man and animal unusually explicit.

CULTURAL IDENTITY

Tales of cultural origins are important in modern storytelling, since they stress the uniqueness of Native American cultures and help to maintain a sense of tribal identity. Indeed, many of the tales form the basis of rituals and ceremonies that are still carried out today. Of major importance among these are the First Salmon Rites of the northwest coast and the annual Kachina performances of many Pueblo tribes, including the Hopi, Zuni and some Rio Grande Pueblos.

Borrowed Stories

A final category of North American mythology that needs to be considered is those tales that have borrowed elements from other areas. In the past this happened frequently among tribes that came into contact with each other through warfare, trade or intermarriage. In areas where there was little cultural exchange, such as California or the north-west, the range of tale types is relatively small; on the Great Plains, which saw a merging of highly nomadic tribal groups from differing backgrounds, the borrowing has been extensive.

Myth elements were freely borrowed among the tribes of the Great Plains. Tales of the trickster, whether Napi of the Blackfoot or Iktomi of the Sioux, are remarkably similar in their overall content. So, too, is the importance of the buffalo, not only as the giver of life but also as the creator of time. Other stories of the Eye-Juggler, the Rolling Head and the Bungling Host have equally frequent currency. Tales like these were common, even among groups such as the Cheyenne, who had abandoned a sedentary agricultural life in the east and moved on to the Plains as nomadic hunters as late as 1700.

BORROWINGS FROM NON-INDIGENOUS SOURCES

The tales were never static entities, but were changed through subsequent retellings that incorporated matters of immediate concern and borrowed elements simply because these were what the audiences liked to hear the storytellers recount or because they had relevance at the time. Thus there are several tales from Canada that show French influence, there are Spanish elements in some south-west tales and Negro influences in stories from the south-east.

Navaho and Apache stories are replete with references to horses, although the Spanish only introduced horses to the south-west in the fifteenth century. The stories of the Horses of Creation and the Sun-String Bridle told by the Apache emphasize all the wonders of a magical world and

the sense of unbounded freedom encompassed in the Apache's desert homelands. These are often recited as origin tales, but it is apparent that in these stories the horse as a symbol of freedom has been incorporated within the structure of former tales that were concerned with a pedestrian, nomadic hunting economy.

CINDERELLA SOUTHWEST

The European tale, Cinderella, inspired the Zuni of the south-west to tell the story of Matsaki, a poor girl who herds the turkeys of wealthy families. She is tattered and dirty and does not

There was a large influx of Chinese on the northern part of the northwest coast in the 1870s and 1880s, when European-owned salmon canneries drafted in a Chinese workforce to replace seasonal Indian labour. Ideas and beliefs from these immigrant groups influenced the mythology of the area. A Chinese migrant is shown here in this carving by a Tlingit Indian.

The European Colonization of North America
European colonization had a profound effect on the indigenous population, wiping out a large proportion of them and changing their way of life forever. This map shows colonial settlements by 1776.

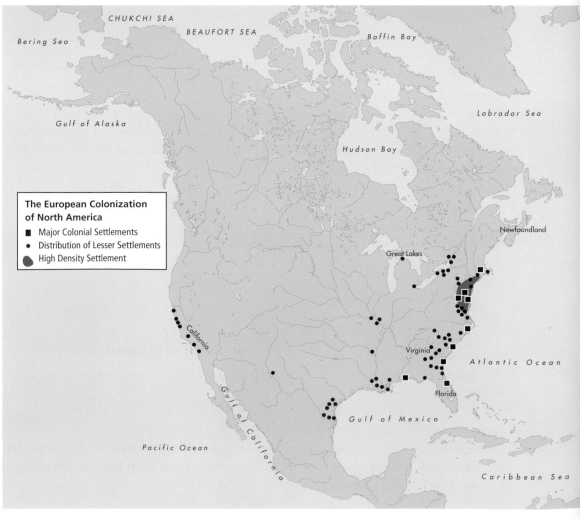

The European Colonization of North America
■ Major Colonial Settlements
• Distribution of Lesser Settlements
⬤ High Density Settlement

THE DEVELOPMENT OF AMERICAN CULTURE

AD 1000	Cahokia (Illinios) is the biggest town with 30,000 inhabitants
1607	English settlement founded at Jamestown, Virginia
1620	*Mayflower* reaches America and the Pilgrim Fathers found Plymouth, New England
1718	New Orleans is founded by the French
1776	American Declaration of Independence
1784	Iroquois League of six Native Indian nations disbanded
1849	California gold rush
1851–1876	Sioux resistance to the advance of white settlers, culminating in victory for the Sioux and Cheyenne at Little Big Horn
1861–1865	American Civil War
1890	Battle of Wounded Knee

This mask depicts a red-haired European sailor or trader, whose freckled face has been represented by inlaid glass. It was made by a Haida carver in the mid-nineteenth century and reflects the growing European influence on the north-west coast at this time.

own the good clothes needed to attend the Dance of the Sacred Bird. The turkeys take pity on her, furnishing her with the finest clothing imaginable, but she is carried away by the excitement of the Dance and fails to return in time. Her turkeys return to their wild haunts and she is left alone.

BIBLICAL STORIES

Other stories collected in the 1930s, when missionary activity among the tribes was intense, refer to Biblical incidents. Atam and Im of the Thompson Indians of the Plateau are equivalent to Adam and Eve, and the Choctaw have a story of the Tower of Babel. Their creator-god, Aba, originally made all people to speak the same language, but they became curious and started to build a pile of rocks to reach the sky. Each night the wind blew the rocks down, separating the people into different groups, until on the fourth day the people found they were unable to understand each other. They scattered to form the many North American tribes, each of which spoke a different language, and were thereafter in conflict with one another.

THE NEW ORDER

Apart from direct borrowings, many other myths incorporate non-native elements. These have become increasingly important with a resurgence of Native American story-telling as part of a revival of traditional values, although they are also apparent from the early reservation period. In one tale from the late nineteenth century, Saynday, the traditional Kiowa hero, meets a strange man on a horse coming slowly from the east. He is unable to understand the man's behaviour since the east is the direction of rebirth, and anyone coming from that direction should travel quickly. It is only when Saynday reaches him that he discovers the man is Death – in some versions referred to as Smallpox – and that he has come to count everything, because the white men always count things and the dominance of the white man is to be the new order in the world.

The indigenous horse became extinct in North America at the close of the Ice Age, but horses were reintroduced by the Spanish in the sixteenth centur, and quickly became an essential requirement for many tribes in hunting, war and transport. The horse effigy shown here was made by the Sioux and commemorates a war pony that was been wounded in battle.

STORYTELLING

Storytelling is fundamental to the expression of a Native American identity. Traditional stories are recited today, both as a reminder of cultural heritage and to express the belief that the values they encompass are relevant in a modern world, although appropriate adaptations are often made to the traditional characters to give them a contemporary relevance. At the same time, there is a vast body of Pan-Indian stories and poetry that addresses issues of poverty, racism, and ethnicity. Coyote, the trickster, may today drive a 'one-eyed Ford' and live on the Rez (reservation), but it is certain that his indomitable character has not been changed and that the old traditions of myth-making and storytelling are as alive today as they have ever been.

Mesoamerica
Mesoamerican Civilizations

The first human beings had reached Mesoamerica by at least 15,000 years ago. Agriculture appeared by *c.*5000 BC, and village life by 2000 BC. Common traits throughout the region led anthropologists to propose the idea of Mesoamerica – a cultural area whose diverse societies shared maize-beans-squash agriculture, monumental architecture, organized religion and a 260-day ritual calendar.

The first civilization in Mesoamerica appeared around 1250 BC on Mexico's tropical eastern coast. The Olmec (1250–200 BC) created many cultural traits, which featured throughout Mesoamerican prehistory. These included the rubber-ball game, monumental architecture and sophisticated pottery and jadework decorated with images of gods and supernatural beings. The two main Olmec centres were San Lorenzo and La Venta, whose sites were adorned with giant monolithic stone heads and zoomorphic sculptures. Between 500 BC and AD 700, the Zapotecs of southern Mexico's Oaxaca Valley flourished in their hill-top city of Monte Albán. The city housed perhaps 25,000 inhabitants at its peak between AD 500 and AD 700, with the elite building 20 pyramid-temples and a ballcourt around the great central plaza. In Zapotec religion, clouds represented

The 'Temple of the Inscriptions' at the Classic Maya city of Palenque was the terraced mausoleum of the city's founding ruler Pacal. Deep inside the temple pyramid, below ground level, is a highly decorated stone sarcophagus in which Pacal was laid to rest some time around AD 683.

The Peopling of the Americas
About 15,000 years ago, the first humans migrated to the Americas. As the Bering Strait emerged as dry land, so animals colonized the Americas. They were followed by humans, who gradually moved south as the ice melted and sea levels rose again. Migrations overland from Siberia, and, later by sea continued until about 3000 BC.

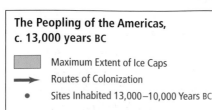

The Peopling of the Americas,
c. 13,000 years BC

☐ Maximum Extent of Ice Caps
→ Routes of Colonization
• Sites Inhabited 13,000–10,000 Years BC

transformed ancestors, and worship focused on Cociyo, god of lightning. As with other Mesoamerican gods, Cociyo was revered through ritual bloodletting and sacrifice carried out with obsidian lancets. Further north, in the Valley of Mexico, the great urban metropolis of Teotihuacán emerged around AD 100 and fluorished until around AD 700. Teotihuacán's great economic and ideological influence on Mesoamerica was due partly to its size and partly to its exploitation and trade in the dark volcanic glass obsidian, which was the 'steel' of prehistoric Mesoamerica. Covering *c*.20 sq km (7 sq miles), and housing *c*.200,000 people, the city of Teotihuacán was dominated by the Pyramid of the Sun, the Pyramid of the Moon, the ceremonial avenue known as the Street of the Dead and the great Palace of Quetzalcoatl, the 'Feathered Serpent'. Archaeological evidence indicates that Teotihuacán shared both trade links and cultural ties with the Zapotec city of Monte Albán.

THE CLASSIC MAYA

The Classic Maya civilization (*c*.AD 250–850) flourished in the tropical lowlands of modern Mexico, Guatemala, Belize and Honduras. The Maya were never a unified empire, but rather a series of autonomous city-states each ruled by a royal dynasty and a god-like king. They possessed Mesoamerica's most sophisticated glyphic writing system, a complex dual calendar and a vigesimal (base 20) counting system. The Maya built great ceremonial centres like Tikal and Palenque, whose astronomically aligned architecture was the backdrop for an elaborate ceremonial life, including ritual bloodletting and human sacrifice. Internal dissension, Teotihuacán's collapse and possibly climate change have all been suggested to explain the Maya collapse around AD 850.

THE AZTEC

Following the demise of Mesoamerica's Classic cultures, a new militaristic era began. It was the warrior society of the Toltecs at their capital of Tula (AD 950–1150) that set the scene for the tumultuous post-Classic period. Most significant were the Aztecs (1325–1521), Mesoamerica's last imperial civilization. Aztec society was hierarchical, ruled by a divine emperor and nobility. Long-distance trade by the Pochteca merchants (often doubling as spies), conquest and tribute (everyday and luxury items) constituted the backbone of their economic success. Aztec religion was dominated by the tribal war god Huitzilopochtli, the rain/fertility god Tlaloc and the supreme deity Tezcatlipoca, the Lord of the Smoking Mirror. Human sacrifices to these and other deities were considered debt payments to the gods whose acts of self-sacrifice had brought the present world into being.

The Great Aztec Temple, in Tenochtitlán (modern Mexico City) was built as the ceremonial centre for state rituals which included human sacrifice. Each enlargement buried its predecessor, and here stone statues were found laid against the steps that led to the summit.

TENOCHTITLÁN AND THE GREAT TEMPLE

The Aztec built their capital of Tenochtitlán (modern Mexico City) on an island in Lake Texcoco in the Valley of Mexico. Like Venice, it was built on reclaimed land, criss-crossed by canals and connected to the shoreline by great causeways. At its peak, the city housed up to 200,000 people. In myth, the city was founded around 1350 when Aztec priests saw an eagle perched atop a great cactus – a sign given by Huitzilopochtli. The Aztec expressed their imperial destiny by building the 'Great Temple' in the heart of Tenochtitlán. Temples were considered godhouses or *teocalli*, and embodied the Aztecs' cosmic essence and identity. The Great Temple had two shrines on its summit, dedicated to Huitzilopochtli and Tlaloc (representing blood and water), and thus materialized cosmic myths relating to both deities.

Rebuilt and enlarged by successive emperors, the Great Temple was a symbolic recreation of the mythic mountain Coatepetl and the human sacrifices which took place there recapitulated the cosmic victory of Huitzilopochtli over his sister, the moon goddess Coyolxauhqui. The presence of the shrine and offerings of jade and seashells to Tlaloc suggests that the temple was also conceived as a great mountain symbolizing water and fertility.

Myths of Origin

Mesoamerican myths placed society at the centre of the universe, legitimizing the social order and sanctifying the will of divine rulers. Myths gave sacred meaning to ideas of birth, marriage, war, sacrifice and death, interpreting them as re-enactments of previous events in a universe governed by cyclical time.

Aztec stone sculpture depicting a jaguar-shaped heart container (Tcuauhxicalli). In a cavity in the animal's back are carved images of the god Tezcatlipoca and the emperor Motecuhzoma II engaged in auto sacrificial bloodletting rites. The jaguar was Tezcatlipoca's alter ego, and Tezcatlipoca the patron of royalty.

In the highlands of Central Mexico, creation myths reflected a landscape where frost, drought, earthquakes and volcanoes threatened civilized life. The Aztecs believed that the universe was conceived in an elemental struggle between light and darkness, with cosmic principles being embodied in Ometeotl and Omecihuatl, the male and female lords of duality. Their four offspring, Xipe Totec, Huitzilopochtli, Quetzalcoatl and Tezcatlipoca were joined by Tlaloc, the rain god, and Chalchiuhtlicue, goddess of water, in a series of cosmic battles which saw successive worlds created and destroyed.

The Aztecs believed in five creations or 'Suns', each identified by the cataclysm which engulfed it. The first creation (Four-Jaguar), presided over by Tezcatlipoca, was destroyed when Quetzalcoatl knocked Tezcatlipoca into the primordial waters and the earth was consumed by jaguars. The second creation

The Aztec deity Xipe Totec (the 'Flayed Lord') in a page from the Codex Borbonicus. Xipe Totec was a god of springtime renewal and patron of goldsmiths and is shown here wearing the skin of a sacrificial victim. Facing him is an image of Quetzalcoatl (the 'Feathered Serpent').

(Four-Wind), was ruled by Quetzalcoatl, and ended when Tezcatlipoca cast Quetzalcoatl off his throne and destroyed the world with hurricanes. The third creation (Four-Rain), was governed by Tlaloc and destroyed by fiery rain sent by Quetzalcoatl. The fourth creation (Four-Water), belonged to Chalchiuhtlicue, and ended with a flood, its human inhabitants turned into fish. Tezcatlipoca and Quetzalcoatl then changed into two great trees, raising the sky above the earth. Quetzalcoatl created human flesh by mixing powdered bones with divine blood. The world remained buried in darkness, however, until the gods gathered at Teotihuacán to create the fifth, Aztec, world (Four-Movement). The deity Nanahuatzin hurled himself into the cosmic fire and was transformed into the rising sun, remaining motionless until his fellow gods sacrificed their blood to give him the energy for his daily journey across the heavens.

POPOL VUH, THE BOOK OF MAYA CREATION

In Mesoamerica's lowlands, Maya creation myths also embodied natural phenomena in epic tales of successive world eras. The *Popol Vuh*, the sacred 'book of counsel' of the Quiché Maya of Guatemala, is a unique masterpiece of Mesoamerican literature, preserving ancient creation stories which tell how the creator-gods Gugumatz and Huracan shaped the earth, dividing mountains from water and separating sky from earth. Their first world creation failed when the jaguars, deer, birds and serpents they made were unable to speak or praise their makers. Their second attempt also proved unsuccessful when, made from mud, the beings dissolved in the primordial waters. With the help of sorcerers, Gugumatz and Huracan tried a third time, carving their creations from wood so as to speak and look like real people. When the manikins forgot their makers, the vengeful gods turned the world upside down, forcing pots and grinding stones to turn against the unworthy creations. The fourth and final creation saw the gods fashion human flesh from multicoloured maize brought by the fox, coyote, parrot and crow. They transformed the maize into the first four men able to honour their makers – the mythic founders of the four Quiché Maya lineages. Jealous that their creations were too perfect and might one day be rivals, Gugumatz and Huracan diluted the mens' uniqueness by clouding their vision and inventing women with whom they could procreate.

Colossal Aztec stone sculpture of the monstrous earth goddess Coatlicue, mother of Huitzilopochtli. She is wearing a skirt of woven serpents, a human skull pendant, while her head is composed of two giant snakes representing the blood which gushes from her severed throat.

AZTEC ORIGIN MYTHS

One Aztec myth tells how the ancestors emerged from the sacred earth at Chicomoztoc, legendary mountain of 'the seven caves', and place of cosmic genesis for many Mesoamerican peoples. An alternative legend relates that the Aztecs took their name from an island called Aztlan in northwest Mexico, and began an epic migration south-east to the Valley of Mexico, in the year '1 Flint' (1116 or 1168). During the journey, the Aztecs were guided by a speaking idol of their war god Huitzilopochtli, who prophesied future greatness for his people, conquering all others and receiving tribute of gold, emeralds, quetzal feathers and *cacao* (chocolate). The Aztecs continued their wanderings to Coatepetl ('serpent mountain'), where, in a form of mythical rebirth, the god Huitzilopochtli was magically conceived by Coatlicue, the Earth Mother, from a ball of precious feather down. The unborn god was forewarned of an attempt by his jealous sister, the moon goddess Coyolxauhqui, and her 400 star brothers, the Huitznahua, to kill his mother and himself and retain their cosmic supremacy. Forestalling the murder, Huitzilopochtli was born in adult form, springing from his mother's womb as an invincible warrior. With a flaming fire-serpent, Huitzilopochtli cut off his sister's head, mutilated her body and scattered his star brothers to every corner of the sky. According to legend, the Aztecs then continued their journey southwards into the valley of Mexico and founded the city of Tenochtitlán.

The Sacred Calendar

Mesoamerican civilizations devised a dual calendar system which fused real and mythic time in two intermeshing calendars. Like interlocking cog-wheels, the sacred and secular calendars created a unique date every day for a 52-year period (i.e. 18,980 days) – the so-called 'Calendar Round'. Each day had a patron deity which exerted influence over people and events.

The Mesoamerican calculation of time integrated observable phenomena in the real world, such as cycles of growth and decay, and the movements of celestial bodies, with ideas of cosmic fate and mythological events. Time itself was cyclical; every physical action possessed a supernatural aspect. Everyday events and their consequences could be explained, enhanced or sometimes avoided by a precise and seemingly endless series of calculations based on knowledge contained within the dual calendar system.

THE MAYA CALENDAR

Maya mythology gave emphasis to the ritual significance of gods, signs and numbers, which marked the passage of time. The Haab or solar calendar had 18 'months' each of 20 days, with five unlucky days called *uayeb* added on to make a total of 365 days. Running in parallel, and intercalated with the solar year, was the sacred calendar, or Tzolkin, made up of 260 days divided into 20 'weeks' of 13 days. The origins of the Tzolkin may be as an approximation of the nine-month human gestation period. Each 'week' had its own deity or deities and every day its own god or goddess. The association of each day with its supernatural patron signified a specific symbolic value: the day Kan meant 'maize' and 'abundance'; and Caban meant 'earth' or 'earthquake'. The last day of each solar month

Ancient Mesoamerican ideas of cyclical time and ritual calendars survive today in the Dance of the Voladores (Fliers). Four men jump from a revolving platform atop a high pole, with thirteen revolutions bringing them to earth. 4 x 13 symbolizes the 52-year cycle of the sacred Calendar Round.

Mesoamerican Civilizations
By AD 250, Mesoamerica was dominated by Teotihuacán, the Maya and the Zapotecs. Three centuries later, new civilizations – the Totonacs, the Mixtecs and others – were emerging. From about AD 1000 another cycle began: the age of the Toltecs.

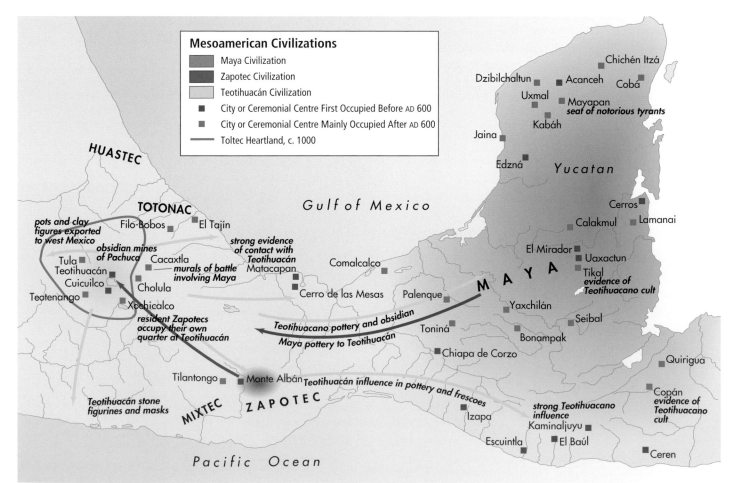

Mesoamerican Civilizations
- Maya Civilization
- Zapotec Civilization
- Teotihuacán Civilization
- ■ City or Ceremonial Centre First Occupied Before AD 600
- ■ City or Ceremonial Centre Mainly Occupied After AD 600
- — Toltec Heartland, c. 1000

was designated the 'seating of' the next month, whose supernatural influence could already be felt. Thus, the 'seating of' the month Pop preceded One Pop, and instead of Twenty Pop came the 'seating of Uo', the succeeding month.

THE AZTEC CALENDAR

The Aztecs possessed a similar but distinct calendrical system also composed of two intermeshing day-counts. The ritual calendar, or *tonalpohualli*, was a 260-day cycle composed of 20 'weeks' of 13 days (called trecenas), each with its own number and a glyphic name such as ocelotl (jaguar), cipactli (caiman) or tecpatl (flint). The cycle of 20 days rotates with 13 day numbers, giving a unique date to each of the 260 days in the calendar, such as One Acatl (One Reed) or Thirteen Ozomatli (Thirteen Monkey). This sacred day-count was recorded in the *tonalamatl*, books made from barkpaper, which served as ritual almanacs. Like modern astrological horoscopes, these were interpreted by professional diviners who foretold a person's fate according to the good or bad qualities associated with their date of birth. For example, Seven Rain was fortunate, but Two Rabbit was unlucky. If a birthdate was deemed inauspicious, it could be changed. The *tonalpohualli* was intercalated with the *xiupohualli* or solar year, which, like its Maya counterpart, was composed of 18 'months' of 20 days with the five unlucky days known as *nemontemi*. Each 'month', known in Central Mexico by the Spanish term *veintena*, possessed its own festival, which was closely associated with the agricultural year. Each Aztec year was named after the 'year bearer', one of the four possible day-name and number combinations of the *tonalpohualli* which occurred on the last day of the eighteenth month – and was either Rabbit, Reed, Flint or House.

The huge jaguar monster Tepeyollotl was the alter ego of the supreme Aztec deity Tezcatlipoca. In this page from the ritual almanac *Tonalamatl Aubin*, Tepeyollotl sits on a jaguar throne facing the god Quetzalcoatl, who is grasping a sacrificial victim by the hair.

The Great Aztec Calendar Stone is in fact a sculpture representing cosmological myth. The four previous eras or 'Suns' are shown as boxes around the central face, which represents either the Night Sun or Earth Monster. Beneath it are giant claws grasping human hearts.

COUNTING TIME, MAYA NUMBERS

The Maya developed the concept of zero, representing it as a shell. Their vigesimal (base 20) counting system increased from the bottom to the top in vertical columns, unlike our decimal (base 10) system, which progresses from right to left. From 1 to 19, they wrote numbers using a bar-and-dot system, in which the dot = 1 and the bar = 5. Using positional notation, the first position counted from zero to 19, the second position had units with a value of 20, the third had units worth 400, and so on. In this way, 1 kin = 1 day, 20 kins = 1 uinal, 18 uinals = 1 tun (360 days), 20 tuns = 1 katun (7,200 days) and 20 katuns = 1 baktun (144,000 days). This sophisticated system recorded calendrical, genealogical and mythological dates, sometimes encompassing millions of years. The Maya also invented a 'Long Count' of years whose mythical starting date was 3114 BC. This allowed time to be calculated in a linear fashion in basic units of 360 days (tuns). Correlating this with our modern calendar allows us to calculate historical dates for named Maya rulers, such as Yax Pac, king of Copán, who died on 10 February in AD 822.

Gods and the Spirit World

In Mesoamerica, gods and myths emerged from an Amerindian worldview, reflecting a natural philosophy where ideas concerning life and death were linked symbolically to the earth, sky and sea in a grand cosmic scheme. As civilization developed, ancient spirits became powerful deities, controlling every aspect of sacred and secular life.

In Mesoamerican worldview, the earth was sacred, the sea the 'mother of fertility' and the sky an untouchable realm of gods and spirits whose influence reached down to affect all earthly life. This was a universe ruled by cyclical time, where myth was a living reality and everyday life punctuated by ceremonies which recapitulated the legendary events of the past. In pre-Columbian times, and still today, the rhythms of nature and human life-cycles were united with social, economic and political life, and every part of the natural world was infused with spiritual force. The shimmer of lakes and rivers, the lustrous sheen of jade and pearls, the iridescence of bird feathers and the crimson glow of human blood, were manifestations of the fertilizing cosmic power that permeated all existence. Throughout Mesoamerica, gods were deifications of natural phenomena – sun, moon, rain and wind – and intimately associated with human concerns of birth, death, fertility and war.

THE NATURE OF GODS

At the heart of the Mesoamerican life was the symbolic equation of blood-for-water. Humans offered their blood to the gods and the gods reciprocated by forestalling drought, frost and, crucially, by sending rain to the earth to fertilize the crops. The daily worship of ambivalent but all-powerful deities was essential to keep the world in motion and the universe in balance. Exemplifying the uneasy relationship between Mesoamerican peoples and their deities was the supreme Aztec deity Tezcatlipoca, Lord of the Smoking Mirror. He was patron of royalty and

A skull rack ('tzompantli') in the Great Aztec Temple in Mexico City. The decapitated heads of sacrificial victims were placed on a huge wooden original, of which this is a smaller version carved from stone, and formed part of the Great Temple's ritual precinct.

The Aztec Empire
The Aztecs entered central Mexico from the north. In the course of the fifteenth century they built a large, tribute-based empire. The enormous appetite of the Aztec Empire for food, gold and sacrificial victims was the source of its strength and its eventual demise, explaining both its tentacular reach and its unsustainable consumption.

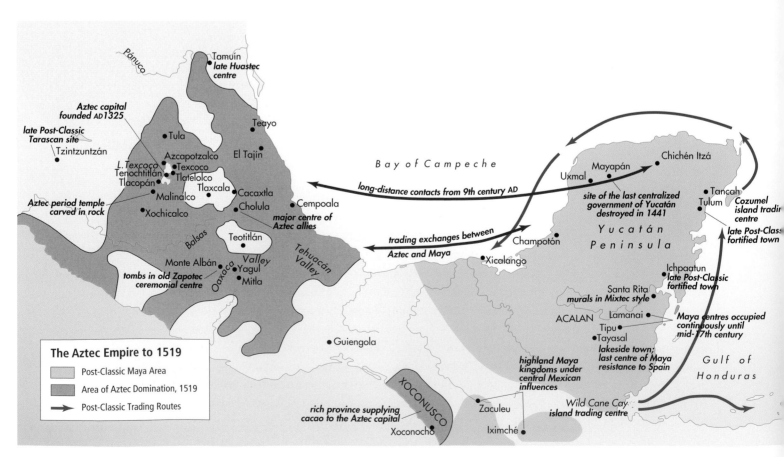

The Aztec Empire to 1519
- Post-Classic Maya Area
- Area of Aztec Domination, 1519
- → Post-Classic Trading Routes

Pánuco
Tamuín
late Huastec centre

Aztec capital founded AD 1325
late Post-Classic Tarascan site
Tzintzuntzán
Tula
Teayo
Azcapotzalco
L. Texcoco
Tenochtitlán · Texcoco
Tlacopán · Tlatelolco
Tlaxcala
El Tajín
Malinalco
Cacaxtla
Aztec period temple carved in rock
Xochicalco
Cholula
Cempoala
major centre of Aztec allies
Balsas
Teotitlán
Tehuacán Valley
Monte Albán
Oaxaca Valley
Yagul
tombs in old Zapotec ceremonial centre
Mitla

Bay of Campeche
long-distance contacts from 9th century AD
trading exchanges between Aztec and Maya

Uxmal
Mayapán
Chichén Itzá
site of the last centralized government of Yucatán destroyed in 1441
Yucatán Peninsula
Champotón
Xicalango
Tancah
Tulum
Cozumel island trading centre
late Post-Classic fortified town
Ichpaatun late Post-Classic fortified town
Santa Rita murals in Mixtec style
ACALAN
Lamanai
Tipu
Tayasal
lakeside town; last centre of Maya resistance to Spain
Maya centres occupied continuously until mid-17th century
Gulf of Honduras

Guiengola
highland Maya kingdoms under central Mexican influences
XOCONUSCO
rich province supplying cacao to the Aztec capital
Xoconocho
Zaculeu
Iximché
Wild Cane Cay island trading centre

warriors, master of human fate and inventor of human sacrifice through which he could be revered. Capricious by nature, cruel and generous by turns, he watched the world through his magical obsidian mirror, seeing into the very thoughts of his subjects. The Aztecs regarded themselves as his slaves, and their emperor as a living manifestation of the god. Equally bloodthirsty was Huitzilopochtli (Hummingbird of the South), the Aztec war and sun god, often depicted carrying his serpent-shaped spear-thrower. His association with war and death is reflected in his name, as hummingbirds were the souls of fallen warriors who accompanied their patron's solar image as it journeyed across the sky. Where these two gods sanctified the shedding of human blood, other Aztec deities were concerned with water and fertility.

Chief among these was Tlaloc, an ancient rain deity, worshipped throughout Mesoamerica under different names, such as Cociyo amongst the Zapotecs, and Chaak amongst the Maya. In Aztec belief, Tlaloc was associated with mountains where rain clouds gathered and mists lingered, and where young children were sacrificed to his cult – their tears an augury of the coming rains. So influential was Tlaloc that the lush and brilliantly coloured Aztec paradise or heaven was called Tlalocan. The god's consort was Chalchiuhtlicue (She of the Jade Skirt) who summoned hurricanes and was associated with the breaking waters which precede childbirth. Quetzalcoatl, Feathered Serpent, was also an ancient deity whose imagery is found in Olmec art and at Teotihuacán. During post-Classic times, the Maya knew Quetzalcoatl as Kukulkan (also Feathered Serpent), and the Aztec regarded him as a wind god, who announced the rains.

The Maya rain god Tlaloc was widely depicted as a grimacing toothy face with a large curling nose. Chaak masks, arranged in serried ranks, were used as architectural decoration on Maya temples, as here at the Maya city of Uxmal.

In an echo of ancient beliefs, modern day jaguar-men fight in the village of Acatlán. At the height of the dry season, human blood is spilt for the jaguar god, who repays the offering by sending rain to fertilize the maize.

BLOOD FOR RAIN AT ACATLÁN

Today, in remote parts of Mesoamerica, echoes of ancient blood sacrifices can still be heard. In villages like Acatlán, Zitlala and Ostotempa in the Mexican state of Guerrero, young men don jaguar costumes and helmets to fight or dance in honour of the supernatural jaguar. These ceremonies occur in early May, when the soil is parched. Although now Christianized as festivals of Santa Cruz (Holy Cross), they may be a survival of the springtime Aztec ceremony of Toxcatl, which celebrated the god Tezcatlipoca and his jaguar alter-ego, the monstrous Tepeyollotl. Most such events see the jaguar-men dancing or whipping each other with ropes, or a single jaguar-man being chased by villagers. But in Acatlán, where the Aztec language of Nahuatl is still spoken, events are more violent. Before dawn the villagers make a pilgrimage to the nearby summit of Cerro Azul (Blue Mountain), clear a sacred arena, then decorate a stone altar with blood-red and orange flowers. At midday, with the sun at its zenith, groups of jaguar-men engage in violent fist fights during which blood is spilt and contestants knocked unconscious. The villagers explain that only by shedding young and potent blood for the jaguar deity can he be persuaded to release his own blood in the form of fertilizing rains.

South America
Andean Civilizations

Human beings had reached the southernmost parts of South America at least 13000 years ago. These early hunters and gatherers flourished, adapting quickly to tropical rainforests, arid deserts and high Andean valleys. By around 2000 BC, huge cities were being built from carved stone and mud brick (adobe) and adorned with dazzling sculpture.

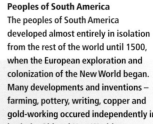

The Ponce Stela at the great pre-Inca city of Tiahuanaco on the shores of Lake Titicaca, Bolivia. Carved from a single block of granite, this statue may represent an historical or mythical ancestor of the city's rulers.

Peoples of South America
The peoples of South America developed almost entirely in isolation from the rest of the world until 1500, when the European exploration and colonization of the New World began. Many developments and inventions – farming, pottery, writing, copper and gold-working occured independently in both the Old and New Worlds.

In the Andes, a precocious civilization emerged at Chavín de Huántar and flourished between 700 and 200 BC. The site was a religious centre, its finely wrought stone architecture decorated with jaguars, eagles, caymans and supernatural fanged gods – images found also on pottery, textiles and goldwork. Inside a monumental, U-shaped building interior passages lead towards an impressive stone-carved image of a half-human, half-feline deity. Chavín culture exerted a powerful influence on many later civilizations, and remained a pilgrimage centre into Inca times.

On the coast, the Mochica civilization came to prominence between 200 BC and AD 650, and is famous for its pottery depicting everyday activities, mythological and religious scenes and superbly realistic effigies of human faces. The Mochica also built monumental architecture such as the Pyramid of the Sun, composed of some 100 million adobes. Recently, a wealth of spectacular gold artefacts has been discovered by archaeologists excavating the tombs of Mochica priest-rulers. Around the same time (AD 100–650), on Peru's south coast, the Nasca people were making huge desert drawings – long, straight lines, geometrical shapes

and gigantic animal images such as the condor and monkey – etched into the desert's surface. Between AD 400 and 800 in the highlands, the Huari civilization innovated road-building, agricultural terracing and bronze-working. The

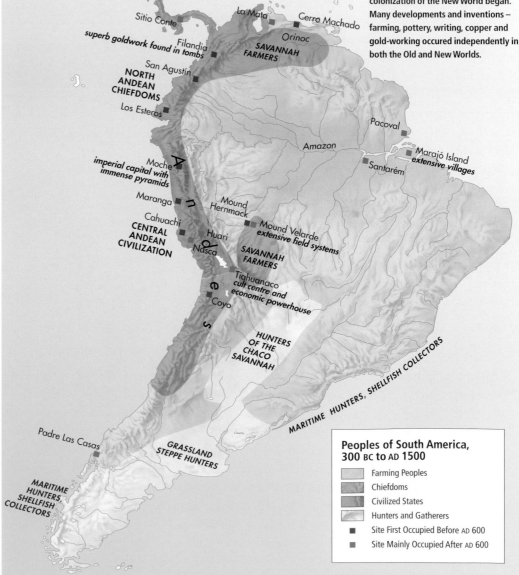

Sitio Conte
superb goldwork found in tombs
Filandia
San Agustín
NORTH ANDEAN CHIEFDOMS
Los Esteros
La Mata
Cerro Machado
Orinoc
SAVANNAH FARMERS
Pacoval
Amazon
Marajó Island
extensive villages
Santarém
Moche
imperial capital with immense pyramids
Maranga
Cahuachi
CENTRAL ANDEAN CIVILIZATION
Nasca
Mound Hernmack
Huari
Mound Velarde
extensive field systems
SAVANNAH FARMERS
Tiahuanaco
cult centre and economic powerhouse
Coyo
HUNTERS OF THE CHACO SAVANNAH
Padre Las Casas
GRASSLAND STEPPE HUNTERS
MARITIME HUNTERS, SHELLFISH COLLECTORS
MARITIME HUNTERS, SHELLFISH COLLECTORS

Peoples of South America, 300 BC to AD 1500
- Farming Peoples
- Chiefdoms
- Civilized States
- Hunters and Gatherers
- ■ Site First Occupied Before AD 600
- ■ Site Mainly Occupied After AD 600

Huari also invented the Andean equivalent of the European writing systems such as Latin, Spanish, French and English – through multi-coloured knotted strings known as *quipu* which they used for communication and record-keeping.

At the same time, the city of Tiahuanaco was built on the southern shores of Lake Titicaca, with temples constructed of stone slabs fitted together with metal clasps. Tiahuanaco boasts the 'Gateway of the Sun', a giant doorway carved from a single slab of stone. The last great pre-Inca civilization was the Chimú Empire which arose in the old Mochica region between AD 1000 and 1476. The Chimú capital of Chan-Chan covered some 20 sq km (7 sq miles), and had some 30,000 inhabitants. It was composed of giant compounds which served as royal palaces during a ruler's lifetime and as his mausoleum after death. The Chimú and their god-like rulers fell in 1476 to invading Inca armies under the emperor Tupac Yupanqui.

THE INCA EMPIRE

Originally just one of many small groups in the Valley of Cuzco region, the Incas began their rise to imperial power in 1438, when they defeated their highland Chanca enemies. The victorious Inca leader took the title Pachacuti (Cataclysm), became the first emperor, and together with his son Tupac Yupanqui, created a vast empire known as Tahuantinsuyu, the Land of the Four Quarters. Over the next 90 years, the Incas built 30,000 km (18,642 miles) of roads, tying together an area of 1 million sq km (621,400 sq miles) and controlling the lives of over 12 million people in pre-Columbian America's largest multi-ethnic empire. The Incas transformed the landscape by constructing canals, bridges and agricultural terracing, kept detailed bureaucratic records on the *quipu*, and re-worked ancient myths and traditions of ancestor worship to create an imperial religion based on the sun god Inti and the living emperor as his divine representative.

Above: A polychrome mural of the Mochica culture showing the Great Priestess attended by several helpers dressed in animal masks, disembodied heads and a cat-like snake. This is a replica of the now destroyed original on the North coast of Peru.

The sacred heart of Cuzco was the Coricancha, the temple of the Inca sun god Inti. Fine Inca masonry rises up from the original golden garden and is now surmounted by the seventeenth-century colonial Spanish church of Santo Domingo.

CUZCO, THE SACRED CITY

For the Inca, their imperial capital of Cuzco was the 'navel of the world' – the place where the earth, sky and rivers met. Surrounded by sacred, snow-capped mountains, Cuzco was more than a city: it was the embodiment of Inca myth, history and cosmic identity, and was regarded as the 'mirror of heaven'. Built on a grand scale by Pachacuti, the city was laid out in the shape of a giant puma, the symbol of Inca royalty. Divided into two halves or *moieties*, upper and lower Cuzco, it housed temples, shrines and the palace-mausoleums of past emperors, whose mummies were the focus of a royal cult. From the Coricancha – the temple of the sun god Inti – 41 lines of invisible power (the *ceques*) radiated out like the spokes of a wheel. Each *ceque* had sacred places or *huacas* distributed along its length. Some of the *huacas* were identified with geographical features, such as caves or springs, while others were more ideological, such as the 'House of the Puma', a sanctuary where the mummy of Tupac Yupanqui's wife was preserved and young children were offered as sacrifices. Criss-crossing the city, the *ceques* fanned out beyond the horizon, imposing spiritual order on the everyday and religious lives of the people.

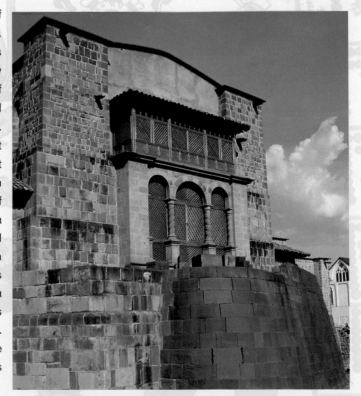

Myths of Origin

For Andean peoples, mythology was a living reality. In vivid and memorable language, myths provided a framework for living, explaining the mysteries of life and death. Epic stories told of magical ancestors shaping the landscape, creating order from chaos, light from darkness, and infusing the world with spiritual essence.

Lake Titicaca, the world's highest navigable lake, was the mythical place of emergence for Inca and pre-Inca peoples. Today, mixed blood Uros and Aymara Indians still live on the lake, sail traditional reed boat, and live precariously through tourism.

The Inca Empire 1438-1525
The Inca Empire expanded rapidly in the fifteenth century. From Cuzco, the Inca emperor exerted rigid control over this extensive territory by means of a highly trained bureaucracy, a state religion and an advanced communications network.

Andean mythologies are as diverse as the region's many civilizations, yet share common themes. At their heart, myths express the spiritual unity of people and landscape, the vitality of sacred places and the cosmological importance of magical journeys made by gods and humans. Throughout the Andes, in the highlands and on the coast, myths sanctified the social order and gave a spiritual dimension to ethnic identity. They accounted for the origins of human beings and described how ancestors had emerged from caves, lakes or the sea, and how rocks had turned into heroes and back again. By re-enacting mythical events in their ritual lives, Andean peoples sought to guarantee the well-being and fertility of land, livestock and themselves. Sacrifices, worship, offerings and pilgrimages were ways by which the universe was kept in balance.

INCA CREATION MYTHS

Inca mythology drew inspiration from the spectacular Andean scenery and traditions of their neighbours and predecessors. Older beliefs were woven into a grand imperial design sanctifying the propaganda that it was the Incas and their gods which created the world and brought civilization to it. These varied influences are apparent in the cycle of creation myths which featured Lake Titicaca as a place of emergence, a metaphor for spiritual rebirth associated with the Pacific Ocean as the mother of fertility. A common theme emphasizes the gods' repeated attempts to perfect their handiwork by successive creations. One myth tells how the god Viracocha first created a world of darkness inhabited by a race of great stone giants. When the giants ignored his wishes, he punished them by sending a great flood to destroy the world. Everything perished, except for one man and one woman who were magically saved. Viracocha tried a

second time, making people out of clay, painting onto them the clothes whose varied designs and colours distinguished one nation (or ethnic group) from another. He also gave each group its own language and customs. Then Viracocha blew his

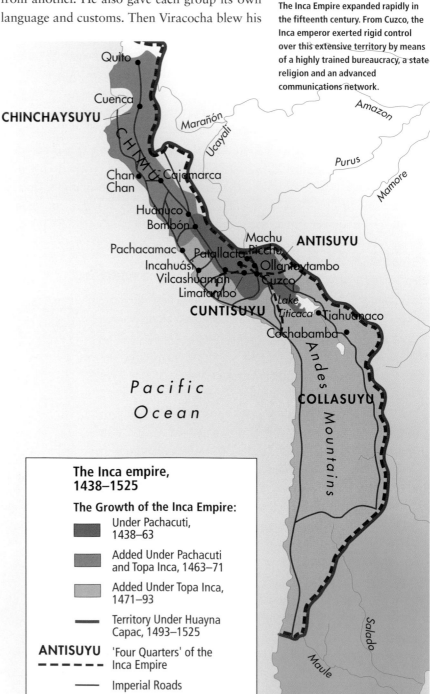

The Inca empire, 1438–1525

The Growth of the Inca Empire:

Under Pachacuti, 1438–63

Added Under Pachacuti and Topa Inca, 1463–71

Added Under Topa Inca, 1471–93

Territory Under Huayna Capac, 1493–1525

ANTISUYU 'Four Quarters' of the Inca Empire

Imperial Roads

divine breath into them, thereby bringing his models to life. He sent them to the earth and commanded them to emerge from the natural features of the landscape – caves, lakes and mountains. At each place of emergence they were told to honour their maker by building shrines for his worship.

A variation of this myth tells how three brothers and three sisters, the ancestors of the Incas, came into the world from three caves at the place known as Pacariqtambo (Inn of the Dawn). One brother, Ayar Cachi, angered the others by performing great feats of strength, hurling his magic slingstones and thereby shaping the Andean landscape. Jealous of this display, his brothers tricked him into returning to Pacariqtambo, whereupon they sealed up the cave behind him. Ayar Cachi escaped, telling his brothers they should wear golden earrings as a sign of their royal status. He then turned himself and a brother into stone. The remaining brother, Manco Capac, then founded the Inca city of Cuzco on the site later occupied by the temple of the sun god Inti.

Above: The Inca shrine of Kenko near Cuzco. On the left are the semi-circular walled remains of the shrine, which originally incorporated the sculpted rocky outcrop. Kenko has been identified as Patallacta, the place where the emperor Pachacuti Inca died.

Snow-capped Andean peaks had long been sacred places. Here, in an early seventeenth-century drawing by the chronicler Guaman Poma, is a depiction of mountain shrines, Inca offerings to their idols and the supernatural jaguar called Otorongo.

MYTH OF THE MAGIC BIRDS

The Cañari people of Ecuador tell a creation myth of magical birds and a great deluge. Two brothers avoided a great flood by escaping to the summit of the mountain Huacayñan, which magically rose in height every time floodwaters threatened to engulf it. Each time the waters receded the brothers went in search of food. One day, they returned to find a meal and *chicha* (maize beer) laid out to eat. For 10 days this happened until the elder brother hid to see who was bringing the food. He spotted two macaws fly into the hut and begin to prepare the meal. He came out of hiding when he saw the birds had the faces of women, whereupon the birds became angry and flew away without leaving any food. When the younger brother returned and found no meal he decided to hide and watch. Three days later the birds returned. When the food had been cooked he slammed the hut door, trapping the smaller bird while the larger one escaped. He lived with the macaw for many years and it bore him six sons and daughters. The Cañari believe that they are descended from these mythical children and that is why they revere macaws and regard Huacayñan as a sacred mountain.

Andean Gods

In their dazzling shapes and powers, Andean gods expressed the relationships between human society, the forces of nature and the spirit realm of ancestors. Drawing on ancient traditions, Inca deities were powerful sky gods who symbolized a world infused with spirituality, and crisscrossed by invisible lines of supernatural power.

Viracocha was the supreme Inca god – an ever-present creator-deity who remained remote from the everyday affairs of men and women. So distant was he from humankind that he had no name – 'Viracocha' was merely a term of respect. Having set the Universe in motion by breathing his magical breath into the humans, animals, plants and lesser gods that he had fashioned, Viracocha journeyed through the Andes, performing miracles and shaping the world before retiring into the cosmic background.

THE ROYAL SUN

Viracocha delegated the affairs of everyday life to more active deities who presided over the heavens and the earth. Ancient beliefs in the life-giving power of the sun were adapted by the Inca who made Inti, their sun god, into the divine ancestor of the Inca royal dynasty. Represented as a golden disk surrounded by sun rays and with a human face, Inti was

Machu Picchu, 'the lost Inca city', was only rediscovered in 1911 by Hiram Bingham. Strategically located overlooking the Urubamba River, it had originally been a military outpost. Later, it became a summer palace of the emperor and a centre of imperial Inca ritual.

celebrated in elaborate ceremonies which took place in his golden temple, the Coricancha, in the Inca capital of Cuzco. His shimmering solar image was flanked by the mummies of dead emperors and surrounded by walls covered in sheets of hammered gold – the sacred 'sweat of the sun'. Outside, in the Coricancha's sacred garden, was a precious miniature landscape in which every kind of life known to the Incas was modelled from gold, silver and gems. Butterflies, serpents, jaguars, llamas and human beings – even the soil itself – were all fashioned from these precious materials. They were regarded as the spiritual prototypes of all earthly forms of life, bathed in Inti's light and protected by the emperor, himself considered the 'son of the sun'.

THE SKY GODS

While Inti reigned supreme in the Inca pantheon, other sky gods sent rain, hail, lightning, drought and earthquakes to afflict the land. These elemental deities embodied the forces of nature and dwelt in the sky or atop snow-capped mountain peaks. The powerful

An Inca emperor's mummified body adorned with fine clothing and a golden death mask is paraded during a festival in Cuzco. The presence of the sun and moon in the sky symbolizes the royal dynasty's spiritual relationship with these celestial deities.

weather god Ilyap'a controlled the rains which the Incas saw as the god shattering a huge jug of water with a slingshot in the form of a lightning bolt. Thunder was the crack of his slingshot, and lightning the sparkle of his brilliant clothing as he advanced across the sky. Mama Kilya was the moon goddess, the sister-wife of Inti, and mother of the Inca race. The relationship between these two cosmic deities served as a sacred prototype for brother-sister marriage practised by the Inca emperor.

Mama Kilya was responsible for the passage of time and for regulating the many religious festivals of the ritual calendar. During a lunar eclipse the Incas believed a great serpent or mountain lion was trying to devour the moon and so they made as much noise as possible in order to scare the creature away. Mama Kilya's symbolic associations with Inca nobility mirrored those of her brother-husband Inti. Her image in the Coricancha was flanked by mummies of previous Inca queens or Coyas, and the shrine itself was covered in silver – the colour of the moon in the night sky.

INCA WOMEN OF THE SUN

Young Inca maidens were selected at the age of 10 to serve the state cult of Inti, the sun god. Known as *acllas* or 'chosen women', they were picked for their outstanding beauty and physical perfection. They lived cloistered lives in convents known as *aclla huasi*, where they were supervised by elder matrons, the *mama cunas* or 'mothers'. They were expected to tend the royal mummies of past emperors and queens as well as satisfy the needs of the present royal family. While some engaged in making clothing, others prepared food or brewed the maize beer known as *chicha* for the royal household and for state occasions. Others took

a vow of chastity in honour of the sun god and to these fell the symbolic duty of guarding the sacred flames for the deity's important festival, known as Inti Raymi. The high priestess of these chosen women was of royal blood and regarded officially as the sun god's consort on ceremonial occasions. The *acllas* combined religious, ideological and political duties. While some were selected as concubines for the emperor, others were a tool of imperial policy – given to foreign dignitaries with whom the Inca wished to forge political marriage alliances.

The carved rock known as *inti huatana* or 'hitching post of the sun' at Machu Picchu. An important feature of Inca religious architecture, the *inti huatana* links the sacred earth with the movements of the celestial bodies, especially the sun and moon deities.

EL DORADO, THE SPIRIT OF GOLD

In South America, gold possessed supernatural qualities as an incorruptible metal infused with cosmological power. Often mixed with copper and known as *tumbaga*, its transformation into sacred images by metalsmiths was regarded as a magical process which recombined the mystical elements of life. The most enduring myth of gold is that of El Dorado, the 'gilded man', which originated among the Muisca people of Colombia, and soon became a fantasy of unimaginable wealth for European explorers. The El Dorado myth was grounded in historical reality. Muisca rituals took place at Lake Guatavita, in a ceremony celebrating the appointment of a new chief. After a period of seclusion, the ruler-to-be arrived at the lake, was stripped of his clothing and his body was smeared with sticky resin onto which was blown a glittering layer of gold dust. Accompanied by four lesser chiefs adorned with golden jewellery, the gilded man sailed out into the lake on a raft, itself richly adorned and bearing four braziers smoking with incense. Those left behind on the shore blew flutes and trumpets and sang. On reaching the centre of the lake, silence fell, and the new chief cast his gold into the lake, with his companions doing likewise. The offerings made, they returned to the shore, where the chief was received as the new ruler.

Myth and Spirits of the Amazon

The power of Amazonian myth stems from its use of a magical worldview of supernatural forces to account for the events and experiences of everyday life. Where outsiders see endless jungle, Amazonian Indians perceive a landscape rich in symbol and metaphor which provides a framework for the mythic relationships between people, animals, plants and the world of ancestors.

I n the shape-shifting universe of Amazonian societies, people transform to animals, wind is the breath of the spirits and every feature of the jungle is invested with spiritual essence. Enshrined in myth, such ideas are perhaps a philosophical acknowledgement of cycles of rapid growth and decay in a lush tropical environment. In Amazonia, landscape is living

myth, a place of memory, kinship and sorcery. The Tukano, who live in the Vaupes region of Colombia's Amazonian rainforest, see lightning as the result of a shaman hurling magical quartz crystals at an enemy, and the shimmering surface of lakes as boundaries between the natural and supernatural worlds. Rivers are likened to umbilical cords, and rapids seen as the spirit

This sixteenth-century depiction of tribal South American Indians by Theodore de Bry is uncharacteristically accurate. Drawn from sailors' verbal accounts, not life, it shows Brazilian Tupinamba shamans blowing magical tobacco smoke over Indian warriors in a war dance.

Cultures of the Amazon
The vegetation of the Amazon Basin ranges from wet tropical forest to savanna grassland. Both the savanna lands and the river flood plains were suitable for cereal cultivation and were settled, with dense populations and sophisticated hierarchical societies, from the time of Christ to the European conquest in the 16th and 17th centuries.

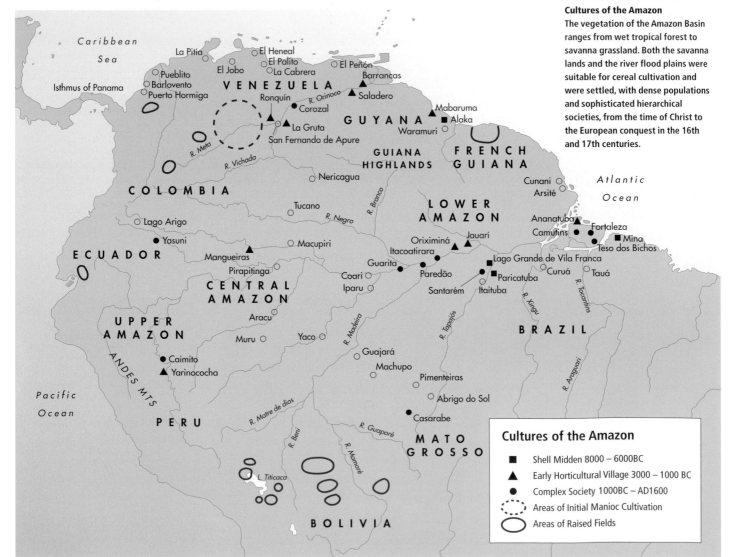

Cultures of the Amazon

- ■ Shell Midden 8000 – 6000BC
- ▲ Early Horticultural Village 3000 – 1000 BC
- ● Complex Society 1000BC – AD1600
- ⬭ Areas of Initial Manioc Cultivation
- ◯ Areas of Raised Fields

dwellings of fish. Among the Yekuana, who live between the rivers Orinoco and Negro in Venezuela, roundhouses are microcosms of the universe, linked to mountains regarded as spirit houses. Symbolic landscapes become symbolic houses, eventually traced through the family to the formation of life in the womb.

The preparation and eating of food is one example of an everyday activity guided by myth and surrounded by ritual behaviour. Some plants and animals are considered dangerous and are subject to taboo, while safe foods require a shaman to blow purifying spells over them. The buzzard, a carrion eater, aids the shaman in purifying food and curing illness by devouring the malign spirits of disease. Among the Barasana, who live near the Tukano, the earth itself is seen as a great ceramic griddle used to bake the staff of life, cassava bread.

FIRST SHAMAN, FIRST WORLD

In Barasana mythology the first shaman was a virgin woman named Romi Kumu (Woman Shaman). She created the world, embodying the diurnal changes of jungle life. With a magic beeswax gourd she changed her skin, appearing young and beautiful in the morning and old and ugly in the evening. Romi Kumu held fire in her vagina and her urine was the rain. At the dawn of time she gathered clay and created a cosmic griddle which was the sky and made mountains to support it. On lighting a fire beneath, the supports broke, and the griddle fell to the earth, pushing it down to become the underworld. The griddle was now lodged in-between as the earth's surface. A third griddle became the sky. Romi Kumi then flooded the world, and inside the first cosmic house all items turned into fierce animals and began to eat the people she had created. The manioc-beer trough and coca sieve became

THE PEOPLES OF CENTRAL AND SOUTH AMERICA

c.3000 BC	Maize first cultivated in Mesoamerica
c.300 BC	Rise of the Maya civilization in Mesoamerica
AD 100	Rise of Teotihuacán
700	Teotihuacán destroyed
AD 900	Emergence of the Toltecs
c.AD 990	Expansion of the Inca Empire in Peru
c.1160	Fall of Tula, capital of the Toltecs
1325	The rise of the Aztecs and foundation of Tecnochtitlán
1438	Start of the Inca Empire
1492	Christopher Columbus reaches the Americas
1519	Cortés begins his conquest of the Aztecs
1532	Pizarro begins his conquest of the Inca Empire

anacondas, a housepost a cayman and pottery fragments piranhas. Only those who made a canoe survived. Landing safely on the top of a mountain, the survivors began eating each other as there was no food. Eventually, the rains stopped, the floodwaters receded and the sun rose high in the sky. As everything became dry, so the earth caught fire and all was destroyed. Although Romi Kumu had no husband she made two daughters, and also created the He People – the ancestral spirit-beings of the world, whom she turned into creatures resembling women. Such myths focus on the shaman's role in recreating society, rendering it safe through spells and receiving his typically male powers from a mythical woman shaman who is herself sexually ambiguous.

Tribal peoples of lowland Amazonia still possess a deep knowledge of, and respect for, their tropical rainforest environment despite a rapidly encroaching modern world. Here a Yanomamo Indian family pose confidently for a photograph before the husband goes hunting with his bow and arrow.

THE JAGUAR SPIRIT

A potent image in Amazonian mythology is the jaguar (*Panthera onça*), America's largest feline. Native Amazonian peoples view the cat's appearance and behaviour as the epitome of physical and supernatural qualities shared by shamans, chiefs and warriors. Beautiful but deadly, the jaguar evokes powerful human emotions. Its strength, agility and razor-sharp claws make it a paragon of male virtues. Its stealth and ability to see in the dark identify it with sorcery and magic – the alter ego of shamans who transform into supernatural jaguars in drug-induced trances. By virtue of its ability to hunt on land, up trees and in water, the jaguar is a boundary crosser, widely regarded in myth as the Master of Animals. The jaguar's roar announces the rains and its pelt, fangs and claws are worn by shamans who intercede with the spirit realm. The jaguar's most significant role in myth is its possession of fire with which it cooked its food at a time when humans ate their food raw. The myth tells how a culture hero stole the jaguar's fire, thereby acquiring culture for humankind and leaving the jaguar to eat its food raw. Today, the reflection of the jaguar's lost fire can be seen in its mirror-like eyes.

The Caribbean World

A string of islands stretching from Trinidad in the south and northwards in an arc through Puerto Rico and Hispaniola to Cuba, the Caribbean was home to a diversity of prehistoric cultures. From around 4000 BC to a Christopher Columbus's arrival in 1492, the indigenous Caribbean peoples developed a distinctive world of myth and supernatural beings.

The Caribbean islands offered many different landscapes and resources to early human settlers. The first evidence for human occupation in the region comes from around 5000 BC in Trinidad, and 4000 BC in the Dominican Republic and Cuba. Most of the Amerindian settlers (from present-day Venezuela) came through Trinidad from where they passed northward by sea-going canoes to Tobago, Grenada, Martinique and beyond. These intrepid explorers probably saw the region as a unique blend of sea, land and sky – different in reality and myth from the riverine, grassland and forest landscapes of their South American homeland. Around 300 BC, a new wave of people from the Orinoco river in Venezuela arrived, bringing with them a settled village life, agriculture and a shamanic religion typical of Amazonian societies. These first farmers grew manioc (cassava), sweet potato, cotton and tobacco. They introduced pottery-making in the form of distinctive white-on-red painted ceramics known as Saladoid, often decorated with zoomorphic designs and appliqué figures. By AD 300, Saladoid peoples had colonized the Caribbean. The sea still played an important role in the everyday and religious lives of these peoples, with canoe travel linking islands and maintaining contact with South America.

THE TAÍNO

When Columbus arrived in 1492, the Caribbean was occupied by two main indigenous groups – the Taíno (Arawak) in the Greater Antilles and the Carib in the Lesser Antilles. Despite controversy about names, ethnic identities and languages, their worldviews were all but identical. Taíno society had evolved out of Saladoid culture and

A typical Caribbean landscape of sand, sea and palms. Beneath this Tobago beach, as throughout the Island Caribbean, archaeologists have discovered pottery, stone tools, and bones – the remains of an ancient settlement and its human burials.

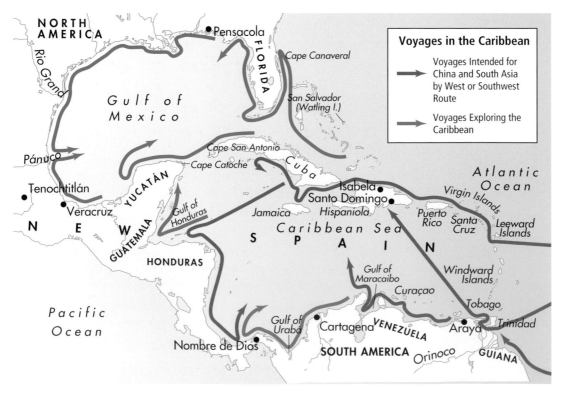

Voyages in the Caribbean, 1492–1519
In 1492 Columbus arrived in the Caribbean and ended a period of over 5000 years of isolation in which the indigenous people of the Caribbean had been able to develop their own distinctive world of myth and supernatural beings. Spanish expeditions explored the Caribbean, searching for a seaway to China and India. When they found it landlocked they took to slaving and plundering instead.

Voyages in the Caribbean

→ Voyages Intended for China and South Asia by West or Southwest Route

→ Voyages Exploring the Caribbean

was based on manioc cultivation, which supported large villages ruled by chiefs (*caciques*) and shamans (*behiques*). In Hispaniola (modern Haiti and Dominican Republic), and Puerto Rico especially, they played a ball-game called *batey* in great stone-lined courts. Teams could have between 10 and 30 players and the idea, as in Mesoamerica, was to move the heavy rubber ball to the opponents' end using neither hands nor feet. Sometimes games were between different villages and wagers were made.

TAÍNO WORSHIP

Taíno religion, like its Amazonian forebears, was based on ancestor worship, with shamans contacting the spirit world by snuffing the hallucinogenic powder *cohoba* while seated on elaborately carved wooden stools known as *duhos*. In magical flight they journeyed to the spirit realm to cure illness and divine the future.

Sacred images of stone, wood and cotton were cult objects known as *zemís*, representing powerful supernatural beings including their two major deities, Yúcahu (Spirit of Cassava) and Atabey (goddess of human fertility). They also worshipped the goddess Guabancex (Lady of the Winds), who sent devastating hurricanes. Animals such as bats, frogs and various species of bird played an important role in Taíno myths as they were believed to possess magical powers. Their likenesses were carved as ritual objects in wood, bone and semi-precious stones. Taíno chiefs valued the gold-copper-silver alloy known as *guanín*, trading it widely across the Caribbean and wearing it as sacred jewellery. This glittering metal was regarded as a symbolic link between heaven and earth, and a physical expression of the bright fertilizing energies of the sun.

This uniquely preserved Saladoid effigy bottle was discovered underwater off the coast of Trinidad in 1990. Its origins are unknown, maybe it was lost overboard from an Amerindian canoe, or perhaps thrown into the sea as a votive offering to the spirits of the deep.

Ceremonial plazas, used for dancing and/or the ball game *batey*, were an important feature of Taíno social and ritual life. This dance court, at the site of Caguana on Puerto Rico, is lined with stones decorated with images from Taíno mythology.

COLUMBUS, CARIBS AND CANNIBALS

In 1492, Christopher Columbus stumbled into the Caribbean, encountering a native world governed by chiefs and shamans, and alive with ancestral spirits and the power of myth. In Medieval Europe, strange and foreign places such as the Caribbean were believed to be inhabited by exotic creatures such as Amazons and cannibals. Columbus quickly came to regard the Taíno as docile and peaceful allies and the Carib as warlike enemies, savage eaters of human flesh. The Taíno saw the Spanish as powerful allies against their Carib enemies and accused the latter of eating their men and stealing their women. These accusations appeared to be supported by Columbus's observations on the Carib islands of Dominica and Guadeloupe when he rescued captured Taíno women and encountered human bones hanging inside Carib houses. By accident or design, the Spanish misunderstood ancient Amerindian customs of respect for the dead and humiliation of defeated enemies, attitudes which involved the ritual display of human bones and the drinking of manioc beer mixed with powdered human bone. The 'evidence' for such bestial behaviour suited Columbus's desire to attack, then enslave, the Caribs and gain continued royal patronage for further voyages of exploration. Carib and cannibal became synonymous and the region soon became known as the Caribbean or 'caribe-an', which literally means the 'seas in-between the Carib islands'.

Caribbean Creation Myths

The mythologies and religions of indigenous Caribbean peoples originated in South America and share many features with their counterparts in lowland Amazonia. The spiritual worldview of Amazonian peoples spread throughout the Caribbean, adapting to local island conditions in a mosaic of beliefs, myths and rituals, which were fundamentally Amerindian yet distinctively Caribbean.

The island geography and dramatic weather of the islands of the Caribbean imposed physical, social and economic constraints on the everyday, mythic and religious lives of the Taíno and Carib peoples. Yet both groups retained elements of their South American origins. This was apparent in the view that ancestor spirits were ever present and that every feature of the physical world – from mountains, rivers, hurricanes and animals – was infused with a supernatural force. Trees, for example, were symbolic ladders, bridging the divide between heaven and earth, providing raw materials for voyaging canoes, magical carved *zemí* images and coffins for the dead. In a similar vein, the souls of the dead were believed to hide from the sun, only emerging at night to seek out and eat the sweet guava fruit.

TAÍNO MYTHS OF ORIGIN

According to Taíno mythology, the universe was created in five stages. The first era began when the Supreme Spirit, Yaya, killed his rebellious son and placed his bones in a gourd which he hung inside his house. One day, Yaya and his wife noticed the bones had transformed into fish, which they ate. A variation of this myth tells how the four sons of Itiba Cahubaba,

Throughout the Caribbean, waterfalls and rivers were sacred places where powerful and often dangerous spirits dwelt. Such locations, like this one on the Carib island of Dominica, were widely seen by Amerindians as spiritual thresholds between the natural and supernatural worlds.

came the less numerous people of the Caribbean and other groups who did not share the customs of the Taíno. This second era ended when Guahayona called forth those remaining in the cave in order to populate the islands of the Caribbean.

The third era saw humans become civilized and women created as sexual partners for men. During the fourth era, the Taíno spread throughout the Caribbean, perfected cassava agriculture and preparation, lived in well-ordered villages and developed a sweet-sounding language in which to converse. They lived this way until the fourth era ended upon Columbus's arrival in 1492. The calamitous fifth era witnessed the extermination of the Taíno by European maltreatment, disease and assimilation.

Sacred ancestors or supernatural spirits? These mysterious figures are carved on a boulder high in the Northern Range mountains of Trinidad. Throughout the island, Caribbean petroglyphs and cave paintings depict strange anthropomorphic beings from the world of Amerindian mythology.

the Earth Mother, who had died giving birth to them, arrived in Yaya's garden. One brother retrieved the gourd and they all gorged themselves on the fish it contained. Hearing Yaya return, they replaced the gourd, but in their haste it broke, spilling water full of fish which covered the earth and became the ocean. The brothers fled to their grandfather's land but when one of them asked for some cassava bread, the old man became enraged and spat on the boy's back. This spittle transformed into the narcotic *cohoba* which all Taíno shamans used henceforth as a gateway to the spirit world.

The second era of Taíno cosmogony saw the creation of the first people. In one myth, the Taíno emerged from one of two caves on the island of Hispaniola. When one man neglected his guard duties at the mouth of the cave he was turned to stone by the sun. The others were soon captured by the sun and turned into trees. One of these, called Guahayona, washed himself with the *digo* plant, sneaking out before sunrise. The sun caught him and changed him into a bird which sings at dawn. From the second cave

First contact. Theodore de Bry's imaginative sixteenth-century depiction of Christopher Columbus's meeting with Caribbean Amerindians in AD 1492. Such momentous and ultimately tragic encounters saw Europeans exchanging Christianity and, unwittingly, disease, for Taíno treasures of pearls and guanín.

BRILLIANT MYTHS

For the Taíno, as for Mesoamerican and South American peoples, sunlight, moonlight and shiny objects represented the sacred power that energized the world, promoted fertility and symbolized élite status. The importance of such beliefs is indicated by their being enshrined in creation myths and materialized in the shimmering ornaments worn as status symbols by chiefs and shamans. One legend tells how the culture hero Guahayona rescues the woman called Guabonito from the sea. In return, she cures him of sexual disease and places him in isolation at a place called Guanara. Another version tells how the grateful Guabonito gave Guahayona many *guanines* so that he could wear them suspended around his arms and neck. The *guanine* gifts were made from an alloy of gold, copper and silver, known today by the term *guanín*. Taíno myth suggests that *guanín* was also regarded as an iridescent rainbow-bridge which connected the sky and underworld – a view supported by the discovery of distinctive crescent- or rainbow-shaped *guanín* objects in Taíno archaeological sites. These myths may be a sacred charter for the social status of chiefs, who could claim their shiny metal jewels as power objects conferred on Guahayona by Guabonito in primordial times.

Culture, Food and Symbolic Relationships

In Taíno mythology, stories about humans, food, society and shamanism are characterized by symbolism taken from the rhythms of the natural world. Animals play key roles in expressing Taíno ideas of the origins of cultural life, particularly in issues concerning marriageable women – a vital issue for small and widely scattered Caribbean societies.

The symbolic relationships between everyday food, like cassava, and spiritual sustenance such as tobacco and the shaman's hallucinogenic *cohoba* snuff, is embodied in a complex Taíno myth which tells of the gift of bread and the acquisition of fire and thus civilized life. In this myth, Deminán Caracaracol, one of the four sons of Itiba Cahubaba, the Earth Mother, asks the old man Bayamanaco (in fact, his grandfather) for some cassava bread which he sees in the old man's house. The offering of cassava and *cohoba* snuff was common etiquette for the Taíno. At this request, the old man put his hand to his nose, and threw some *guanguayo* (tobacco juice spittle) onto the boy's back. This act, in which *guanguayo* is identified as the shaman's saliva which stimulates the narcotic effects of *cohoba*, is interpreted as a mythic invocation of a person's grandfather – a form of ritual divination and communion with ancestors. Deminán's discovery of baked cassava bread in his grandfather's house is also a mythic rendering of the discovery of fire for cooking, a common metaphor for the acquisition of culture.

GODS OF FERTILITY

The pervasiveness of food-related imagery in Taíno mythology and religion is seen in the deification of particular aspects of agricultural

This Taíno *zemi* ritual statuette is kept in native houses and worshipped.

Main Areas of Carribean Religion
Afro Caribbean religions such as Voodoo in Haiti, Shango in Trinidad and Santería in Cuba stemmed from African religions brought over by slaves, mixed with Roman Catholicism and the remnants of Taíno spiritual beliefs.

Main Areas of Caribbean Religion

- Santeria
- Voodoo
- Shango

FLORIDA
Miami
THE BAHAMAS
Havana
CUBA
HAITI
DOMINICAN REPUBLIC
PUERTO RICO
Caribbean Sea
Caracas
COLOMBIA
VENEZUELA
TRINIDAD

fertility and the staple crop cassava. The supreme Taíno deity, Yúcahu, (Spirit of Cassava), was an invisible god of fertility on land and sea. In his *zemí* images, Yúcahu is shown with an open mouth, ready to eat away the soil and thereby make room for the sprouting cassava tubers. Yúcahu's female counterpart was Atabey (Mother of Waters), associated with freshwater streams and ponds and the rain needed to fertilize the cassava crops. Together, these deities symbolize a concept of fertility which extends from the natural to social and spiritual worlds, with images of both gods being buried in cassava fields to encourage growth, and also invoked to ensure successful childbirth.

Human fertility, the origins of sexuality and the incorporation of both into society are also enshrined in myth. One legend tells how one day men, anxious to possess women, went to bathe in the river. They saw strange, asexual creatures fall from the trees and gave chase. However, they were unable to catch them due to the creatures' slippery skin. The men asked their chief for the help of four men, known as *caracaracol*, who had rough hands and who could grip the slippery creatures easily. After the creatures had been caught, the men discussed how to make them into women. They sought out the bird known as Inriri (a woodpecker) renowned for making holes in trees. The men bound the hands and feet of their asexual captives and attached the woodpecker to them. Believing them to be trees, the woodpecker bored holes in the creatures' bodies where today a woman's sexual parts are found. In this way, women were first made for Taíno men. This story, which may be a mythic version of women's puberty rites, links human life to ancestral trees, menstruation and the magical intercession of a spirit bird.

Cassava bread being baked on a griddle over an open fire. A staple food for native Caribbean peoples, cassava featured in many Taíno myths, and was important enough to be identified with the supreme Taíno deity, Ycahu, the 'Spirit of Cassava'.

VOODOO – AFRO-CARIBBEAN GENESIS

European conquest and diseases soon decimated indigenous Caribbean peoples. To provide labour for the new plantation economy, Europeans began importing African slaves in the seventeenth century. These people brought their own animistic religions, gods and myths to the Caribbean where they took root, mixing with Roman Catholicism and the remnants of Taíno spiritual beliefs. Thus were born Afro-Caribbean religions such as Voodoo (Vodoun) in Haiti, Shango in Trinidad and Santería in Cuba. In Haiti, Vodoun rites conjured up zombies who wandered the countryside as the 'living dead', though in reality they were social outcasts shunned by a superstitious peasantry.

The gods of Vodoun, the *loa*, are spirit-masters of crossroads, cemeteries, the sea and the dead. Vodoun priests – both male (*oungans*) and female (*mambos*) – raise the *loa* through song and prayer. Falling into trance, the *loa* possess them and are asked for favours to resolve life's problems. Each *loa* has its own sanctuary or *bagi*, containing an altar, flowers and plates of food and drink with which they fortify themselves. Through their destruction of the Taíno and Carib worlds, European conquest created new spiritualities and mythologies which live on today in the once-sacred landscapes of the original Caribbean peoples.

Origins of the World

In a continent as vast as Africa, myths vary naturally with geography – weather and desert, tropical rainforest, grassy plain, snowcapped mountain or sea, lake and river. Some peoples believe in sky-dwelling gods, others in sea, lake or forest gods and yet others in mountains and in desert gods. Moreover, unlike the structured myths of Greece and Rome, with their family of gods and told in a single language, African myths are mostly unstructured and recounted in over a thousand languages.

What makes African myths hard to trace to original rituals and beliefs is the evolving communion with Christianity and Islam during colonial times. This is a pity as man is believed to have originated in Africa thousands of years ago, and so the range of mythologies developed would have been vast. Where authentic religions are still alive – mainly in tropical areas, as among the Yoruba of Nigeria and the Ashanti of Ghana – myths may give us an idea of the earliest human beliefs. A further paradox is that while storytelling is one of the greatest arts, some of the most deeply held beliefs cannot be talked about, especially to strangers. Good storytellers pass on tales handed down over generations; they know the tribe's customs and the importance of passing on traditional beliefs and history; they also know the power of the gods and spirits who can punish the tribe by famine or drought if secrets are divulged.

Bottom left: The myths of Africa are as diverse as the landscapes of the countries that make up this vast continent. However, despite over 1000 languages and a huge variety of widely differing cultures, there are some common threads that bind the mythologies of these lands together, such as creation myths, for example.

African Languages
African myths are mostly unstructured. They are told in over a thousand languages. The analysis of language provides vital evidence for the reconstruction of African history.

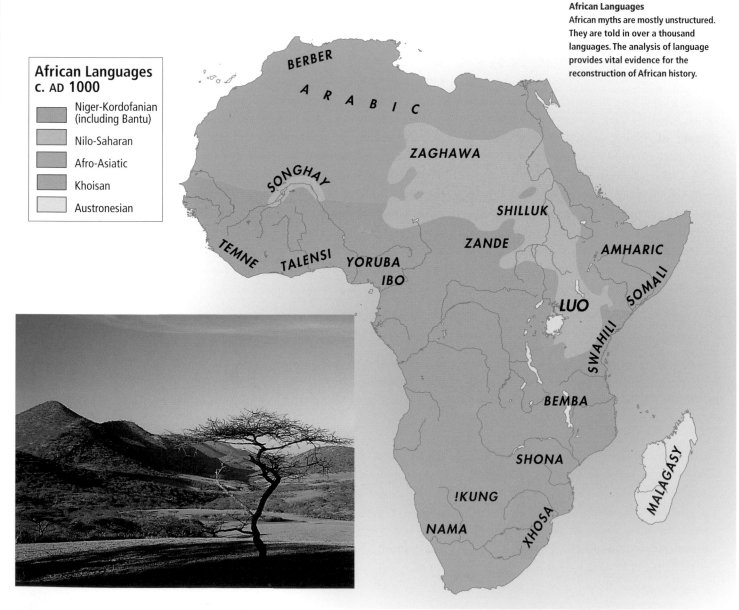

African Languages
C. AD 1000

- Niger-Kordofanian (including Bantu)
- Nilo-Saharan
- Afro-Asiatic
- Khoisan
- Austronesian

SUPREME GOD

Despite its rich diversity, many African myths contain related themes, including gods and the origin of the world and humans. Most peoples in tropical and southern Africa share the hazy notion of a supreme sky god who originally lived on earth, but moved up to the sky by means of a spider's thread when humans started misbehaving. Earth and water are invariably goddesses. For the Yoruba, Ile is the goddess of earth and mother of all creatures; Yemoja is the goddess of water – her messengers are crocodile and hippopotamus and her daughter Aje is goddess of the Niger river from which Nigeria takes its name.

THE GREAT SERPENT

Given the prevalence of dangerous snakes in many parts of Africa, it is hardly surprising that several peoples talk of creation in terms of a huge serpent, usually a python, out of whose body the world and all creatures came. In northern areas, the sky god first made the cosmic serpent, whose head is in the sky and whose tail is in underground waters. In central and southern regions, the primordial

serpent Chinawezi is identified with the rainbow. Whatever shape God's intermediary took, it is common for God to create sky and earth first, then fire and water, thunder and lightning. After these elements, the supreme being made the first living beings: a human, an elephant, a snake and a cow. In other legends, the supreme god first sent rain, lightning, locusts and then twins. Twins are often referred to as the 'children of heaven' and in some parts thought lucky, in others very unlucky and in the past have even been killed.

FIRST MAN AND WOMAN

A widespread belief among the Zulus is that the first man and woman burst out of a reed; others say from a tree, yet others from a hole in the ground to the west of Lake Nyasa in Malawi. Many peoples do not speculate on the creation. The Masai of Kenya and Tanzania have a story about a time when meat hung down from the sky for people to eat. When it moved out of reach, people built a bamboo tower to the sky. To their surprise, sky messengers came down with three gifts: a bow to shoot the new wild animals in the bush, a plough with which to till the land in the new seasons of wind, rain and sun and a three-stringed fiddle to sing to in their leisure time. Other tales talk of earth and sky being connected by a rope by which gods sent down cattle.

In other creation stories, the world passed through three ages. First was an ideal or golden age when gods, humans and animals lived in harmony in a sort of celestial nirvana. Then came the age of creation in which the supreme god separated sky and earth, with the latter intended to mirror the harmony of the former age, and humans formed in the gods' image. But it did not work out, for humans were fallible and caused destruction, so introducing death: the Ashanti say humans set fire to the bush, so killing each other. The third age is the modern age where gods and humans live separately and people have lost their divine virtue of immortality completely. Through their myths and rituals, people are constantly trying to recreate the long-lost golden age.

Nigeria Yoruba dancers, West Africa. The mythologies of the Yoruba are some of Africa's most complex and well-preserved, with stories and gods that equal Mesoamerica and India in their richness and complexity.

The creation of the first man and first woman is one theme in common to most of the myths from around the continent. While the details vary widely, the main beliefs are centred around a great creator-serpent, a remote creator-god, the motif of twins or a cosmic egg.

ORIGIN OF DIFFERENT-COLOURED PEOPLE

With the arrival of people of different-coloured skins, new myths arose to explain colour. According to the dark-skinned people of the Sudan, God created all humans from earth. For white, he took white loam, for dusky, light-brown clay and for black he took the fertile black soil of the banks of the River Nile. In other versions, told by lighter-skinned people, God baked the first people in an oven: some were not properly ready, some got burned, but the third were perfectly golden-brown. According to a Cameroon myth, God gave Africans long legs so they could run like flamingoes when fishing, long arms to swing hoes like apes who swing sticks for nuts, eyes to see food, mouths to eat and ears to hear.

Witchcraft and Sorcery

Sorcery has always played a big part in mythology all over Africa. Just as the difference between gods and spirits is blurred, so is the distinction between witchcraft and sorcery as conscious crafts. All that can be distinguished is the good or evil intent on the part of the person working the magic. The term 'doctor' (as in witch doctor) basically denotes a person skilled in any art or knowledge. So the doctor may be a diviner, herbalist, sage, storyteller, conjurer or dancer.

Some tribes claim that the 'doctor' is someone who develops special powers after a serious illness, during which time he communes with the spirits, having come close to death. Thereafter he is able to see spirits that are invisible to ordinary mortals. After apprenticeship to a professional and an initiation, he becomes skilled at dancing, singing and chanting, and is called upon to perform at funerals and other ceremonies.

The trance is a familiar phenomenon among many tribes. It is induced by doctors either spontaneously or by chewing certain hallucinatory herbs, inhaling their smoke or drinking a concoction which gives them superhuman strength and power to know and see things others cannot. The trance state may be caused, people believe, by a person's spirit leaving his body, travelling off into unknown regions and being possessed by spirits of the dead, so that when he returns he begins to speak in a strange way, telling of the wonderful things he has seen. It is the possessing spirits that

A Turkana witch doctor from the shores of Lake Turkana, Kenya. The belief in spirits, both good and evil, and the profound effect they have on day-to-day life is central to African mythology. Doctors are believed to be able to commune with the spirit world and are consulted on a wide variety of matters, from fertility to sickness, and perform rites and rituals, such as funerals.

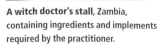
A witch doctor's stall, Zambia, containing ingredients and implements required by the practitioner.

enable him to cure an illness, bring rain or luck in hunting.

Such spiritual doctors have often had an exotic, even unkempt, appearance, letting their hair grow, smearing it with oil and ochre and adorning it with shells, feathers and charms – the insignia of their profession. They may have a magic wand in the form of a zebra tail on a stick which they wave about during exorcisms or other operations. The fly whisk carried by some African leaders is a remnant of this fusion of chieftainship and magic.

SORCERERS AND WITCHES

Sorcerers and witches are naturally evil and perform black magic out of a hatred for people. Their tools are the spirits they control and they can enslave people by causing their death, before reviving them as the living dead – zombies (from the Congo word *zombi*, meaning 'enslaved spirit'). They also make fetishes possessed by servant spirits which fly through the air and attack victims. Often a victim dies of fright merely by seeing such a monster approaching.

Witches can change into animals at night or have animals as their familiars, especially baboons, hyenas, leopards or owls, and they can be seen flying through the air at night with fire coming out of their backsides. Their aim is to devour human bodies, dead or alive. But they can also change others into animals to

be at their service. Mostly they brew poison, put it in the victim's food and enslave his or her spirit. The *muloyi* (or *mulaki, murozi, ndozi, ndoki* – all of which translate approximately to 'sorcerer') of Central Africa creates an *erirogho* (magic) mixture from the ashes of dead bodies, does a ritual dance around it and then mixes it with the victim's food or beer. Sometimes he adds the victim's fingernails, hair or earth from his footsteps to the *erirogho*, wrapping it in leaves or burying it beside the victim's house. The victim's spirit will be forced to go and live in the *erirogho* while his body decays. Often the *muloyi* can be heard laughing in the darkness.

THE FOREST

Other Central African peoples regard the forest as being the other or spirit world inhabited by dwarf-demons or imps, the *elokos*, who feed off human flesh. Anyone entering their world must perform certain rituals. Sorcerers carve a fetish or piece of wood taken from the spirit world (which therefore possesses magical properties) and use it to kill their enemies. Every tree has its spirit, which survives in the wood even after it has been chopped down and made into a hut, drum or boat. Without the spirit's goodwill, the carved item will bring only bad luck.

Fetishes contain spirits controlled by the sorcerer. As the spirit serves the sorcerer, it will obey his every wish, and the sorcerer may thus be able to rule whole villages by the terror the fetish invokes. The sorcerer may also use the fetish to kill his victims. This wooden fetish is from the Congo.

FORETELLING THE ARRIVAL OF EUROPEANS

More than one witch doctor is said to have foretold the coming of Europeans to Africa. A certain prophet, Mulengo of Ilala (Zaire), foretold that, 'There will come people who are white and shining with bodies like locusts'. Another, Podile, a chief of the Bapedi (South Africa), prophesied the arrival of the Boers: 'Red ants will come and destroy our land.... They will have baskets (hats) on their heads. Their feet will be like those of zebras (boots). Their sticks will give out fire. They will travel with houses drawn by oxen.' Missionaries in the early nineteenth century left reports of seers who made their prophesies during a trance or illness. One missionary, Reverend E. W. White, referred to the prophet Mohlomi, who died in 1815, as 'the greatest figure in Basuto history'; Mohlomi said he saw 'a cloud of red dust coming out of the east, consuming our tribes'.

Animal Myths

Animals play a key role in mythology – and not only in Africa. African slaves took their stories around the world, often as fables, and adapted them to their new environments. The Uncle Remus stories of America's southern states (Brer Rabbit was originally the hare; Brer Terrapin was originally the tortoise) came from West Africa, as did the Aunt Nancy (Kwaku Anansi) spider tales of the Caribbean, originally told by the Ashanti, Yoruba, Ibo and Dahomey. It is believed that the Greek slave Aesop originally came from Ethiopia.

In the oldest versions of African myths, the characters are mostly animals, such as the serpent involved in the world's creation. At this stage they are deities of supernatural size and strength. Anansi the spider can climb up to the heavens to commune with Nyame, the sky god (Ashanti); Simba the lion is a potent god from whom several African chiefs traced their ancestry (such as Haile Selassie, the Lion of Judah). Similarly, some Zulu chiefs have claimed descent from the python. Some clans bow before a python

and address it as 'Your Majesty', offering it sacrifices of goats. In Mozambique there are traces of the worship of Sangu, the hippopotamus, a goddess who rules an underwater realm of lush, flowering meadows; she protects pregnant women and has to be sacrificed to by fishermen.

In the northwestern regions (Mali, Guinea), the sky god Faro sent down the antelope to teach the Bambara

The one-time Emperor of Ethiopia, Haile Selassie, here pictured in a jewelled, gold headdress in 1930, believed that he was a descendent of the lion god, Simba. The titles he gave himself included Lion of Judah and Conquering Lion of the Tribes of Judah. The lion as king of beasts symbolizes royal authority.

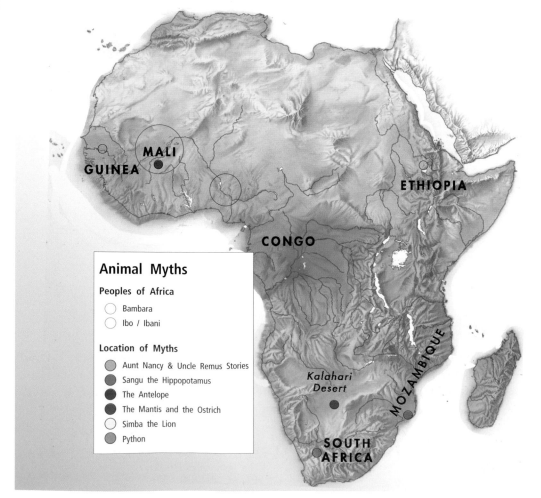

Animal Myths

Peoples of Africa
- ○ Bambara
- ○ Ibo / Ibani

Location of Myths
- ● Aunt Nancy & Uncle Remus Stories
- ● Sangu the Hippopotamus
- ● The Antelope
- ● The Mantis and the Ostrich
- ○ Simba the Lion
- ● Python

Animal Myths
Animals play a very important part in African mythology. Many of these myths have since been exported to other countries by African slaves. The Uncle Remus stories of America's southern states, for example, came from West Africa as did the Aunt Nancy stories told by the Ibo. The sky god Faro sent down the antelope to teach the Bambara people farming skills. The map shows where the myths come from and the location of the people that were affected by them.

people farming skills; hence the many wooden carvings of the sacred antelope. According to the Bushmen of the Kalahari Desert, the mantis stole fire from the ostrich and passed it on to humans. The mantis is also credited among the Khosians of southwest Africa of inventing language through which animals and humans can converse.

HALF-HUMAN ANIMALS

As myths evolved, animals became half-human, half-animal characters who can be either good or evil, depending on their whim or veneration. They can take either form and foster human children, often coupling with human beings. Such children display both human and animal characteristics, so they can catch prey and speak animal languages. The human offspring of lions are particularly gifted: they can hunt at night and they know the bushlore and power of putting a spell on game (since no animal dies without the gods willing it). Ordinary mortals fear such half-human offspring, for they are brave, fierce warriors possessing magic and charms. Women love lion-men, who often become great rulers. As for lion-women, they grow up to be irresistibly attractive to men, who fall in love with them; the men, however, can end up being eaten by their wives. Lions are so potent that even a lion's eyelash can give a woman power over her husband, so that she can have children merely by instructing his mind to do so.

TRICKSTERS

At the third stage of evolution of myths, animals lose their divine qualities and take their animal shape, but act as humans do, with their own characteristics. Two particular animals stand out

The lion holds a central place in African mythology. As well as being a symbol of kingship, people fear and admire it for its strength and warrior-like qualities.

as tricksters who use cunning to outwit more powerful beasts: the hare and the tortoise. In parts of Africa where there are no hares or tortoises (the Congo River basin), the trickster is the little water antelope, the jackal or the turtle. The lion, elephant and especially the hyena are the foils, their brute force and stupidity being no match for the nimble wits of the hare or the slow, patient wisdom of the tortoise. Even the hare (in the famous race) is overcome by the tortoise's quiet, dogged determination. A person of exceptional intelligence among the Ibo is referred to as *Mbai* and among the Ibani is *Ekake*, both meaning 'tortoise'. Not only is the tortoise harmless, eating only fallen fruits of the forest, he is practically immune from attack and his silent nature implies mystery and veiled purpose – qualities valued in the human world.

This wooden Suku mask-helmet from Zaire features an antelope; in some mythologies the antelope is the culture hero responsible for introducing agriculture to people on earth.

THE MAGIC TREE

There is a story found as far afield as Nigeria and the Transvaal about a magic tree bearing ripe, tempting fruit. As they search for food during a famine, the animals come upon the tree but, not knowing its name, they cannot get at the fruit. So they send various animals to the tree's god. One after the other, the animals – lion, elephant, jaguar, python – seek out the god but forget the name before their return. This is because either they trip over an anthill and spill the name out of their head, or they disobey the god's command not to look back. All is saved by the tortoise (sometimes the hare or gazelle) who remembers the name: Uwungelema (in Lamba). At once the fruit falls and the animals can eat. So grateful are they that they proclaim Kudu the tortoise as their chief in place of the lion or python.

Sacrifice and Offerings

All around people are spirits who have to be appeased and gods who have to be placated; in the past this could mean anything up to and including sacrifice. Since life is based on a balance in nature, there must be as much giving as receiving – someone has to die in order that others may live. If rain does not come, sacrifices and offerings must be made to induce the rain god to end a drought. Every tribe and region has its rituals and special doctors, priests and diviners who know exactly what offering must be made.

In many clans, it is the traditional duty of the eldest son to sacrifice to the clan spirits – those of his father and grandfather. Without such sacrifices the people could die and the sacrifice must be gladly offered, otherwise it is not acceptable. The common purpose of sacrifice is to create, celebrate or restore good relations with the deity of ancestral spirits. Usually the gods will be satisfied with nothing less than the slaughter of an animal (normally chicken, goat or lamb). The Dogon people of Mali, for example, have a special sacrificial rite called *bulu* (meaning 'to revive'), restoring the community's relations with the universe of life. The living sacrifice has a soul (*kikinu*) and vital force (*nyama*). As the victim's blood flows into the earth, it carries its *nyama*. The deity, thus nourished, has the will to give *nyama* back into the sacrifice's liver, which is eaten by the priest in a ritual meal, thereby consuming the divine energy. These sacrificial rituals were transported with slaves to the Caribbean, especially Haiti, where the sacrifices (usually of chickens) come under the name voodoo/vodoun.

MEDIUMS

Another sacrifice common to Mali is intended to induce the rainbow god, Sajara (a multicoloured serpent) to send rain. A white ram is sacrificed by a forked tree and has its blood sprinkled over the

If the right offerings and rituals are performed, it is believed that the spirits may grant the people what they ask for; here, people in Nigeria are taking part in a festival to ask the rain god to send the rains.

tree as dancers circle the tree. The sky gods take possession of some of the dancers and speak through their mouths. These oracles or mediums often become 'possessed' women who speak in a strange voice they do not understand and which has to be interpreted by a priest. Besides inducing rain, people consult them on sickness in the family or in domestic animals, sterility, floods or drought – even about marital problems.

DIVINATION

When the deity does not speak through a medium, it may give signs or omens which can be read only by trained diviners who will make offerings or sacrifices to reveal knowledge that is concealed from ordinary mortals. That also includes advice on the best time for hunting, sowing, harvesting, fishing, migration or performing sacrificial rituals. For divining they may read the stars, throw lots, study lines in the soil or sand or examine the entrails of the sacrificed animal. Some diviners have a divining board on which they cast palm nuts or stones. The diviner also has to be consulted on sacrifice in the case of sickness and after a funeral to remove the contagion of death.

Another occasion for special offerings and sacrifices is when going hunting or gathering in the forest, which is inhabited by terrifying spirits,

monsters and ghosts. Among the Ashanti of Ghana, the forest spirits are called the *mnoatia* and the forest ogre, Sasabonsam, is a hairy giant with large blood-red eyes and enormous feet that trip up unwary travellers. The hunter has to be on good terms with all these horrifying creatures. He needs special offerings for them all, as well as charms and fetishes to ward off evil.

In the past it was not unknown for soccer teams (notably in southern Africa) to offer sacrifices to the gods to let them win or to place fetishes in the goal of the opposing team, hoping their spirits would let goals in.

A voodoo priest in Togo, West Africa, making an offering to a god. The belief that appeasing the spirits will provide the solution to a problem, or cure an affliction, remains very strong in many parts of the continent.

Divining is a practice used by mediums to read the will of the gods; in various parts of Africa it is also used as a way to detect witches. Pictured is a divining bowl from Sierra Leone, together with other objects used for witch-finding, including a bell and an alarm clock.

IFA AND ESHU

Among the Yoruba people of southern Nigeria, sacrifices are often made to two contradictory gods simultaneously: Ifa and Eshu. Ifa is the god of wisdom, knowledge and divination. At the time of the creation, he came down to earth with the other deities to establish order. He settled on earth, married and had eight sons, all of whom became chiefs of the provinces of Yorubaland. Eshu had been sent into the world by Olodumare, the supreme god, to test people and examine their real characters. One day Ifa felt insulted by his sons and went to live in heaven, so leaving the mischievous god Eshu to cause quarrels, make women barren and trick people into insulting the gods, for which they had to pay sacrifices. In despair, Ifa's sons went to heaven to beg their father's help. He refused to return, but he did give each son a divining board and set of 16 palm nuts as divination tools. It is through these palm nuts that Ifa conveys the will of the gods to people.

Death

Three vital questions concern all African cultures: how did death come into the world; why do people die and what happens after death? Despite the wide disparities in cultures, there is general agreement on the answers to these questions.

Death was not part of the original scheme of things in African myth: it came later, typically as a result of a blunder, a mistaken message or late delivery of a message. A common myth is that from southern Africa about the moon goddess who returns after dying; she originally decided on life and death, promising that people would be restored to life. The message is sent to earth with the chameleon or mantis, as well as the hare. The hare is first to arrive, but gives a garbled message, thus depriving humans of immortality, since gods can never revoke a message once delivered. The Ibo have a similar tale, with a message sent by the great spirit Chuku; here the dog dawdles and the sheep muddles the message.

ORIGIN OF DEATH

Some myths put the blame for the coming of death on women. The Baluba and Chaga say a girl disturbed her grandmother as she was discarding her old skin, so breaking a secret ritual. The Ganda people to the north of Lake Victoria blame the supreme god's daughter Nambi who married a mortal, but went back for grain to feed her chicken and was overtaken by her brother Walube (Death), who then accompanied her to earth. The Dinka, herders of southern Sudan, tell that the supreme god gave a grain of millet to an earthly couple, but the woman Abuk was too greedy and accidentally hit the god with the end of her hoe, after which he sent a bird to cut the rope of life linking heaven and earth.

WHY PEOPLE DIE

In a continent where mortality is high, the cause of death, especially premature death, is often attributed to evil spells cast by agents of misfortune. The all-pervading fear of death provides work for diviners, witch doctors, shamans and makers of charms, amulets and fetishes. Dead ancestors, too, play an important role. Often when someone falls ill, it is supposed that an ancestral spirit has been offended and sent the sickness, or that some

human enemy has put a spell on the victim. In either case, the result is more work (and remuneration) for the various doctors.

AFTERLIFE

It is a commonly held belief that death is not the end of existence, but instead that it is merely the moment when a person can no

A wooden fetish from Zaire, West Africa, stuck with nails (the purpose of the nails driven into the fetish is to anger the spirit inside it). The fear of evil spirits causing great harm, or even death, is very real in many parts of Africa.

longer dispose of his body, except as a ghost or spirit in someone or something else's body, whether animal, tree, plant, river or wind. The living sometimes see and talk to the dead in their dreams or receive messages through omens or mediums. The spirits of the dead usually remain near their funeral place for a time – whether under their hut (usually for chiefs), in forest or river, or even inside hyenas, who frequently devour corpses. After a while the spirits depart for the land of the dead.

It is the duty of the spirit's descendants to serve ancestors by erecting a shrine where they regularly place offerings of food and drink. If the rites are neglected, the ancestors will blight their descendants' lives for several generations. In Tanzania, family spirits (those of father, grandfather and maternal uncle) are called *makungu*. These spirits are venerated for three generations, after which time they merge with the host of spirits called *vinyyamkela*.

THE UNDERWORLD

Many peoples believe that the dead live in the bowels of the earth, very much as they did on earth, tending plentiful herds of speckled cattle.

AFRICAN CIVILIZATIONS

c.4000 BC	Copper first used in Egypt
4000–3000 BC	Desiccation of the Sahara, once a fertile region, commences
2686–2181 BC	The Egyptian Old Kingdom, when hieroglyphic script was invented and the famous pyramid tombs built
1152 BC	Death of Ramses III, last great pharaoh of Egypt
c.AD 700	Rise of Islam and decline of Aksum (northern Ethiopia)
c.1200–1400	Rise of kingdoms of Mali and western and central Sudan
1498	Arrival of the Portuguese in eastern Africa
1957	Ghana becomes the first black sub-Saharan country to gain independence from European rule
1994	Nelson Mandela inaugurated as president of South Africa

To the Ibo people, the earth goddess Aje is also goddess of the underworld, where she rules over many deities as well as the ancestors buried in her womb. Sometimes when she is angry, she moves forests, mountains and rivers if the relatives of the deceased have not made proper offerings to her when burying the corpse. In a Fon tale from West Africa, the rainbow serpent Aido-Hwedo, who supports the earth in the ocean, will one day run out of food; he will then chew on his tail and cause the whole earth to topple into the sea.

The Dahoman people believe that in the underworld social status remains unchanged: the chieftain continues to rule and the slave to serve forever. The Basutos believe that the dead wander silently and dully about their green valleys, called *mosima* ('the abyss'), with no emotions of joy or sorrow. The Swahili name for this spirit land is *kuzimu*. On the other hand, in the underworld there is no retribution for earthly sins, and no distinction between heaven and hell.

Dogon masqueraders from Mali here perform a ceremony known as a *dama* in which the souls of the honoured dead are drawn away from the village, bringing prestige to their families.

PATHS TO THE UNDERWORLD

The land of the dead can be reached through caves or holes in the ground. The Bapedi of the Transvaal claim that the gateway to *mosima*, the underworld, lies on their land and can be entered by anyone sufficiently daring. Myths say that two people go together, holding hands as they enter the pass and shout, 'Spirits, clear the way or we'll throw stones at you!', and they pass by without difficulty. Many are the adventures of living beings who accidentally stumble into the underworld. They often follow a porcupine or some other burrowing animal they are hunting into its hole. This happened to a hunter, Mpobe, in Uganda and to a Zulu hunter, Uncama. The hunters return unharmed to tell the tale, but never find their way back down again.

The Dreamtime

Humans settled Australia during a period when it was linked to the islands of what are now Indonesia and Papua New Guinea by a land bridge, and earliest evidence of humans dates to almost 40,000 years before the present. Because of the former physical link between Australia and Melanesia, there are similarities between the mythologies of the two areas, although it appears that the movement of mythical themes went from Australia to New Guinea, rather than the other way around.

The Dreamtime, or Dreaming, is the most significant and distinctive religious-mythological concept throughout Australia. It refers to a primordial time when ancestor beings travelled across the land and sea, making the species that walk the land today, as well as its distinctive landmarks and topographical features.

ALCHERINGA

The Aranda people of the central desert region refer to the epoch of ancestral primordial creativity as *Alcheringa*. During this time, everything that is of importance to present-day humans was created. Although this creativity occurred in the remote ancestral past, its power and influence on human life is ongoing. It can be accessed or made visible through the performance of the proper ritual techniques. The practice of these rituals becomes present-day human beings' effort to recreate ancestral acts of inauguration and to tap into this power for contemporary purposes – ensuring health, fertility and abundant supplies of foodstuffs for people today. Aboriginal people all over Australia remark that it was during the Dreamtime that the law regulating all human behaviour was established, and that present-day human beings are merely following the law set down by their ancestors.

In the Aranda concept of the Dreamtime, the governing view is that the earth and its creatures were originally an undifferentiated, featureless mass. There was neither day nor night. The Supernatural Beings woke from their sleep and emerged through the surface of the earth. It was at this time that birthplaces became infused with their sacredness, becoming places of life and creative sacred power. The Beings proceeded to carve the undifferentiated mass up into its distinct and separate forms – the animals of the earth and human beings. Before this time, humans existed only as a formless collection of

A petroglyph incised in the rock at an Aboriginal sacred site. These designs are often thought to have been made by ancestral beings who also formed the rest of the landscape during the creative period or Dreamtime. Other rock art is avowedly man-made.

Pleistocene Man in the Greater Australian Continent
The map shows the land bridge between New Guinea and Australia, across which Pleistocene man was able to travel into Australia.

Pleistocene Man in the Greater Australian Continent

▲ Excavated Pleistocene Site (Older than 10,000 Years)

— Maximum Extent of the 'Greater Australian Continent'

— Modern Coastline

NEW GUINEA

Arnhem Land

AUSTRALIA

Tasmania

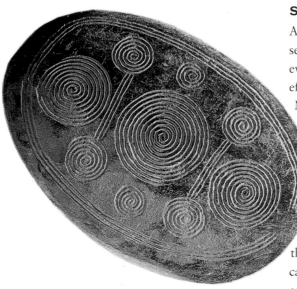

SEARCHING FOR SIGNS

Although the original creation of the world may seem to have been a singular mythico-creative event, humans keep ancestral power alive and efficaceous through their various ritual activities. Moreover, although much of the creation story is known to humans and forms the basis of their current religious life, this knowledge is still incomplete. There is always the possibility that a hitherto unrevealed site of ancestral action, with its attendant myth, artistic design and secret language, may become known to modern human society. Humans are therefore always inspecting the landscape with care, alert to the possibility of the revelation of ancestral knowledge. Under such conditions, it is difficult to separate the divine from the mundane characteristics of the physical world.

A *tjurunga* from Central Australia. It was believed that Creator Beings and their weapons became these sacred discs, each disc representing a Being's immortal spirit, while the design is a totemic pattern of the associated sacred site. Such objects could only be viewed by initiated men and had to be handled with the correct ritual songs.

Water hole at an Aboriginal sacred site associated with ancestral beings, New South Wales. Permanent water holes in Queensland and New South Wales are often identified as places of residence of the mythical serpents, the Carpet Snake or the Rainbow Snake.

individuals, without orifices or bodily shape. The Supernatural Beings sliced the individuals apart, giving them fingers, toes and limbs, carving openings into their heads and bodies, so creating man and woman in their current form.

When the Creator Beings had finished their work, they returned either to the holes in the ground from which they had emerged, or turned into rocks, trees, other natural features or *tjurunga* objects. *Tjurunga* are objects made of stone or wood, incised with ancestral patterns, and represent the material residue or remains either of the ancestral beings themselves or of some act of their first creation. The places where the Creator Beings assumed their final resting place became important sacred sites. These sites can only be approached by fully initiated men – children and women are still forbidden from approaching them upon pain of death.

EVIDENCE OF ANCESTRAL BEINGS

'Living as a human being is itself a religious act,' said Mircea Eliade, a famous scholar of world religions, when considering the *Intichiuma* rituals of the Aranda of the central desert region of Australia. In the *Intichiuma*, the travels and actions of ancestral Creator Beings are recounted. It is not sufficient that the ancestral beings created the world once and for all – it is the responsibility of contemporary humans to maintain this power and assure its continuing potency. An ancestral being may have created a species or landmark through the shedding of his blood, or the excision of part of his body tissue. This may have caused an abundance of certain species at that place today. This is why present-day humans take powdered rock from that particular sacred place and deposit it in other areas where they wish a similar flourishing of animal species to occur.

Among the Bardi of the Kimberley Coast in Western Australia, the Supreme Being Djamar is thought to have made everything. He inhabits the saltwater under a rock, and where the water bubbles, there Djamar is thought to live. Young Bardi initiates are shown the stony, creek bed-mouth and the holes where Djamar is said to have inserted his bull-roarer. (The bull-roarer is an elliptical piece of wood with a hole on one end through which string is threaded; this is then whirled round the head to produce a loud whirring drone, which is the voice of the spirit.) The old men emphasize how strong the power of Djamar and his *tjurunga* were by pointing out how barren the surrounding hills are, a landscape that was permanently damaged when Djamar swung his bull-roarer.

Initiation

Life renewal through ritual is regarded as a continuation of ancestral power by human means, and is also thought to give new powers of creativity to the young people who undergo the experience. The most important way this is done is by transforming children into adults. The imagery of symbolic death and rebirth thus becomes very important throughout Australian initiation ceremonies.

Throughout the countryside of eastern Australia, in the states of New South Wales and Queensland, numerous remains of bora rings can be found. The largest ones are about 70 m (230 ft) in diameter with a path connecting them to a smaller circle. Among the Kamilaroi of the northern New South Wales–Queensland border, a number of figures were drawn on the ground on either side of the path, or clay effigies were placed alongside it. The largest of these figures represents Baiami, the Supreme Sky Being. The uninitiated novices were not permitted to view the effigy of Baiami. The bora ground represents Baiami's first camp, and the initiates themselves represent those young men who were with Baiami in that first camp. The initiates relive the original creative period during which the bora ceremony was held for the first time.

INITIATION RITUALS

The ritualized separation of boys from their mothers and, in fact, from all things female, is an integral part of their transition to male adulthood. Among the Yolngu of northeast Arnhem Land, Northern Territory, women cried and tried to resist the men who were taking their sons to the initiation camp. In general throughout Australia, initiates are segregated from the main camp in specially isolated parts of the bush. At this camp it is revealed to them the objects and secrets they would have to control as men. A ritual washing or cleansing at the finale of the initiation ceremony is designed to remove all traces of their sacred sojourn in the ceremonial ground and to prepare them for their return to the ordinary camp life.

Circumcision and sub-incision of the penis has been widely practised throughout Australia. The Walbiri of the central desert region explicitly related this circumcision to symbolic death. The bull-roarer, itself a phallic object, is shown to the boys immediately before their operation. The bull-roarer is said to be the voice of the Creator Being. The detachment of the boys' foreskin is therefore associated with the symbolic detachment of the Creator Being's power, lodged in the bull-roarer, the phallic voice. Among the Yolngu of north-east Arnhem Land, the boys' circumcision is equated with their being swallowed by Yurlunggor, the giant

This bark painting from north-east Arnhem Land depicts mythical spirit figures with sacred serpents. In some parts of Australia, the initiation ritual consists of adolescent boys being symbolically consumed by the creator serpent, and reborn as the first humans.

Painted wooden Aboriginal figure of a woman from Arnhem Land. Figures such as this represent named sacred beings as described in clan mythology; they are also used in dances and are shown to youths in training. Each section of the design on the figure has a different local interpretation, such as flowers, rain, blood, etc.

creator-snake. The boys themselves represent the first humans to be born from the ancestral Djanggawul Sisters, who were also swallowed by Yurlunggor during the creation period.

During these rituals, the novice discovers a world of religious and mythological meaning previously undisclosed to him – it is, in fact, a rebirth into a new world. Among the Aranda, at the end of the young men's instruction, they are taken to the cave where the *tjurunga* are kept. The older initiated men explain the significance of these objects to the neophytes, and the novices take turns in holding the objects and pressing them to their bodies. It is then revealed to the neophytes that the *tjurunga* are the bodies of the ancestral Bandicoot Men who lived at Ilbalintja Soak, a sacred Aranda site. This is the great secret that the men keep to themselves. As a source of power, the young men are also taught the real name of the great chief of the Ilbalintja sacred storehouse. It is believed that knowledge of names is key to the meaning of myth.

Indian Head and beach, Fraser Island. This is the site where hundreds of Aborigines were driven by European settlers over the nearby cliffs to plunge below to their deaths in the late nineteenth century. As the most prominent massacre site on Fraser Island, it is now considered a sacred site. The island also contains sites where initiation, both male and female, takes place.

FEMALE INITAITION

Women, too, have their own ceremonial responsibilities in different parts of Australia. The rise of feminist social science has caused some female anthropologists to look for women's ceremonies so as to correct the overwhelming male bias which they feel characterizes much early analysis of Aboriginal religious life. A ceremonial complex was reported for central Australian women, and distinct men's and women's myths and stories have been reported for Aboriginal groups from South Australia through to Queensland. Fraser Island, off the coast of central Queensland, is the location of sites of both men's and women's initiation, according to present-day Butchulla people. In 1995, the Ngarrindjeri of the Lower Murray River area of South Australia became embroiled in a Royal Commission to defend their claim of secret women's business around the site of a proposed bridge to Hindmarsh Island in the mouth of the Murray. Their claim was alleged to be linked to an elaborate and still-functioning system of transmission of women's secret cosmological knowledge. Throughout Australia, the transmission of both men's and women's knowledge to people of younger generations depends upon the perceived abilities, sensitivities and interest of the younger person seeking such knowledge.

Fertility

The preoccupation with fertility – of humans, of animals and of plants for hunter and gatherer societies such as Aboriginal Australians – can readily be understood. Because they do not till the earth, they are more subject to the natural reproductive potential of these species. They therefore attempt to influence and augment such reproductive potential by appealing to the creative power of Dreamtime beings and agents.

The most dramatic fertility cults are found among the Yolngu of north-east Arnhem Land, Northern Territory, of which the most famous is the *Gunabibi* (or *Kunapipi*). They are linked to the very important myth cycle of the Wawilak (or Wagilak) Sisters and Yurlunggor the giant python.

THE WAWILAK SISTERS

Essentially, the Wawilak were two sisters who originated somewhere south of Arnhem Land, probably near the Roper River. Before they departed this place, the elder sister had incestuous intercourse with a clansman of hers and became pregnant. The two sisters wandered northwards, trapping animals and consuming them along the way. Presently, the elder sister gave birth to a daughter. They continued travelling north and came to the vicinity of the sacred well, Muruwul, the home of Yurlunggor the Python. They made a fire and tried to cook their animals, but their food jumped out of the fire and ran into the well, as did the plants the sisters also tried to cook. Yurlunggor sensed the birth blood of the elder

Fertility is a central concern in Aboriginal religion, and myths concerning the regeneration of the cosmos are widespread. There are a variety of Creator Beings, both male and female, in different parts of Australia, each with its own associated fertility cult. In some parts of the continent, it is a serpent which has the most important part in the fertility cult; portrayed here is the Rainbow Serpent, which is associated with fertility rites throughout the Central Desert and Northern Territory.

female. As a male it is phallic, but as a female it is womb-like, in that it swallows the women and 'gives birth to them' once more by regurgitating them. Ronald Berndt, a famous West Australian anthropologist who provided the first full-length account of the *Gunabibi* ceremony, said that his Yolngu informants explained that the act of Yurlunggor swallowing the women 'is like a penis going into a vagina, only we put it the other way around' – that is, it is the phallus which acts as a uterus in the myth. In this way, the Yolngu present to themselves the possibility that male reproductive power is superior to that of women, even though they know 'it is the other way around'.

The Wawilak myth is, in many ways, a story of the origin of sexual reproduction – the Yolngu say that if the Wawilak Sisters had not 'done wrong' in their own country – copulated incestuously and then menstruated in the well of Yurlunggor – all the creatures would have 'walked around' by themselves. There would have been no copulation and thus no children. The rise of Yurlunggor also depicts the dramatic alteration between the wet season and rising water, and the dry season and receding water, which dominates life in this region of Australia.

sister, which was polluting his well – the sister should not have approached it. Angry and attracted by the smell of the elder sister's blood, Yurlunggor raised his head and emerged from the well. The younger sister tried to dance to force the python to withdraw; this dance is that which is re-enacted during the *Gunabibi* ceremony.

The sisters, unsuccessful in warding off Yurlunggor, took refuge in a hut they had built. However, Yurlunggor pursued them and swallowed both of the women and the child. Yurlunggor later regurgitated them, where they were revived by biting ants, but were swallowed by the python once more.

The symbolism of the myth is striking, first, because Yurlunggor the Python is both male and

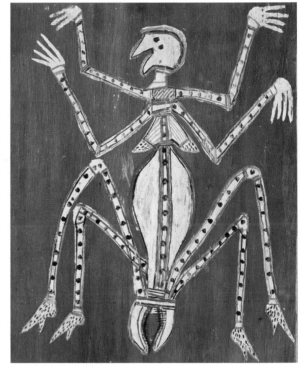

Aboriginal bark painting of pregnant female spirit from Croker Island, Northern Territory. The depiction of female procreative power is a central theme of myth and art throughout the Northern Territory. Cave and bark paintings were adjuncts of ritual activity throughout most of Aboriginal Australia. The designs were clan property and only certain persons with authority were allowed to paint them.

RITUALS

Increase ritual was a type of ritual performance designed to promote fertility of the species upon which Aboriginal people subsisted and depended. It is still practised today. The most famous of these were the *Intichiuma* rituals of the Aranda and their neighbours of the Central Desert. In one part of the ritual, men open veins in their arm and allow blood to flow on the ground. Sacred designs are drawn using the blood and allowed to dry. The sign of the emu totem is also drawn using clay, ochre and charcoal, in preparation for the older men to decorate themselves with *tjurunga* and impersonate the emu ancestors. Each totemic group performs a similar ceremony for the species with which it is associated, and thus no two *Intichiuma* are the same. As Ronald and Catherine Berndt remarked, 'All increase sites or objects, along with the ritual acts which are carried out, are associated with mythological and totemic characters.' The persons who perform these rituals must be members of the totemic group, for they are literal descendants of the totemic Creator Being and are reincarnations of that Being. Blood, symbolizing the flow of life and its animation, is a significant element in these rituals.

Medicine Men

Termed 'Aboriginal Men of High Degree' by noted anthropologist
A.P. Elkin in his eponymously named book, the so-called doctor men
or doctor sorcerers played an important role in Aboriginal society
throughout Australia. These men were possessed of extraordinary
knowledge, not infrequently linked with powers to heal, to foretell the
future, to travel through space and to kill their enemies with sorcery.

In Queensland, these men were called gundir
or gundil, and the institution of the so-called
'clever man' in southern Queensland
remained extremely powerful and resilient
throughout the colonial period and into the
latter part of the twentieth century. Many people
today can recall such men still practising in their
lifetimes, which means that the last of the
Queensland clever men were alive in the 1950s,
perhaps even later. They had intimate knowledge
of sacred places that was not known to other
men, and often went on their own into the bush
to commune with spirit familiars, ancestors and
to make medicines and potions. The Wakka
Wakka of the Burnett River Valley in southeast

Queensland were especially noted for
their gundir, as were the neighbouring
Kabi Kaba – the category of Miva Men
from the area near what is now
known as the Sunshine Coast
were especially noted for their
magical and medicinal
knowledge.

In the Great Victorian Desert, Aboriginal
people distinguish between the *baramambil*, the
sorcerer, and the *baramambin*, the healer; in this
area, these functions are separate skills. Here,
power is thought to reside in stone objects called
maban. Two main waterholes in that region are
associated with the training of these men of high

An Aboriginal man from Central
Australia wearing corroborree dress. In
Central Australia, men possessed of
great knowledge impersonated
mythical figures and re-enacted certain
critical productive and creative events
in the Alcheringa, or Dreamtime.

**The European Settlement and
Development of Australia**
The spread of European settlement
from 1820 had a catastrophic effect on
the Aboriginal way of life. Extensive
mineral discoveries have led to a high
standard of living, but many of these
are on lands which are now subject to
Aboriginal land claims.

**The European Settlement and
Development of Australia**

	Native Land Rights Claims, Jan. 1997
	More Than Two Persons Per Square Mile 1961 (by Statistical Division)
	No Significant Use, c. 1960
■ Penal Settlements	● Settlements

Railways

—— Before 1881	----- 1901–1920		
—·— 1881–1900	········ After 1920		

Minerals

Gold		Tin		Zinc	
Copper	U	Uranium	▲	Oil	
Lead	⊕	Blast Furnace	N	Nickel	
Natural Gas		Iron Ore	A	Alumina/Bauxite	
T Tungsten		Silver	M	Manganese	

degree. They are both linked with Wonambi, the Rainbow Serpent. As was the case with the Wawilak complex in northeastern Arnhem Land (see p. 210–213), the Rainbow Serpent is said to swallow the initiate whole, and then later regurgitate him in the shape of a small baby.

ASSESSING SUITABILITY

Among the Wiradjuri of northern Victoria and New South Wales, a man must have shown promise as possessing exceptional power from a very young age before he becomes apprenticed to a practitioner. After he has received training, the boy's father or grandfather will perceive the deity Baiami, the Supreme Sky Being, in a dream, who will let the practitioner know that he is willing to impart secrets to their son or grandson.

Among the Dieri of northern South Australia, the *gudji* spirit assumes the shape of a bird or animal. A person aspiring to become a clever man is led into the desert by the *gudji* and undergoes a period of isolation and meditation. During a trance state, the *gudji* enters him and replaces his human consciousness with that of the *gudji* spirit. The aspirant is reborn as a spirit himself, having been given gifts of certain powers by the *gudji*.

SPECIAL POWERS

In western Arnhem Land, Northern Territory, (in a manner reminiscent of Papua New Guinea), Aboriginal doctors receive their power and instruction mainly from spirits of the dead. One or more of these spirits may become particularly close to the doctor, to which the man may turn for oracular advice or other information. The ghost of the dead person is usually that of a close

deceased relative of the doctor. Some of these ghosts are said to be more powerful than others. A man who has much power can pursue the soul of an afflicted person and persuade it to return to its owner, thus healing the ill person.

Bark painting from western Arnhem Land depicting a seated woman. Designs of this type were often associated with love magic. Aboriginal doctors would be consulted on all kinds of matters, including fertility; it was believed that the doctor received his knowledge and power from one or more spirits.

SIGNIFICANCE OF CRYSTALS

Wiradjuri men can become clever men by inheriting the knowledge from their fathers, being recognized as having a calling or special talent or by undertaking a personal quest in search of power. In *Native Tribes of South-East Australia* (1904), the early anthropologist Howitt reported a young man retelling the story of his own initiation. His father pressed two quartz crystals against his breast, where they melted into his body. The boy also drank a liquid that he thought contained quartz crystals. Later, he was taught to produce a crystal from inside his body at will by the older men with healing knowledge. The crystals figure in the invocation of Baiami, whose material form is thought to be impressed upon the crystal formations themselves.

The use of such crystals extended all along the eastern coast into Queensland; to this day, Aboriginal people maintain that the ownership, use and physical incorporation of these crystals is the mark of the clever man or medicine man. In this way, the sorcerer-healer becomes a literal repository of the rock of his own country, fused corporeally with the life-giving ancestral spirits who themselves created and were a part of the country. Thus, as is the case with virtually all of Aboriginal myth, spirituality, significance and power always go back to the land and country itself.

The Art of Myth

Today, Aboriginal mythology remains most alive and visible in the flourishing art forms that have become famous throughout the world as emblems of Australian Aboriginal creativity. Noted Aboriginal artists' work now commands high prices in all the world's major auction houses.

Throughout Queensland, in such spectacular sites as Canarvon Gorge in central Queensland, Aboriginal artists left paintings in caves. The Canarvon Gorge in central Queensland is particularly significant, as it is between the headwaters of the two major watersheds; to the west water flows into the Murray–Darling system, and to the east various rivers, such as the Fitzroy, empty into the sea. The site was therefore a place of great cultural exchange and transmission between inland desert, coastal and peri-coastal populations.

BARK PAINTINGS

The bark painting of the Northern Territory, especially that of Arnhem Land, is a significant means of visual representation of important mythical episodes. These mythic designs are represented both in abstract and realist modes.

The knowledge of these designs is highly restricted, being the property of certain men who alone have the right to produce the images and instruct others.

The paintings, though not intended to be permanent (most were destroyed after their ritual use was over) were nevertheless incarnate representations of the spiritual figures and objects that were the subjects of important life-creating myths. The paintings and other objects served as the media through which the Creator Beings could continue to exert their life-enhancing and life-forming powers in the present-day world.

Bark paintings are most famously associated with Arnhem Land in the Northern Territory. In western Arnhem Land, they favour the X-ray style is favoured, where the interior of any animal or being is displayed, and realistic images

Cave painting of a Wandjina spirit. The Wandjina are venerated as Creator Beings in the Kimberley Region of Western Australia: each spirit was responsible for forming part of the landscape before painting a picture of themselves and disappearing underground. As each painting is believed to be an incarnation of a Wandjina spirit, they continue to be sacred to present-day Aboriginal people.

The Art of Myth
Evidence of Aboriginal mythology can be found in many examples of aboriginal art throughout Australia. For example the bark paintings of the Northern Territory, the cave paintings of Central Queensland and the dot and circle art of the Central and Western Desert.

An X-ray-style bark painting from western Arnhem Land depicting a kangaroo and a hunter. The X-ray technique in which the internal anatomy of an animal is depicted in great detail may have been used so as to show which parts of the animal are edible. The cross-hatching that appears on the painting serves to associate it with an individual clan and to endow the objects with spiritual force.

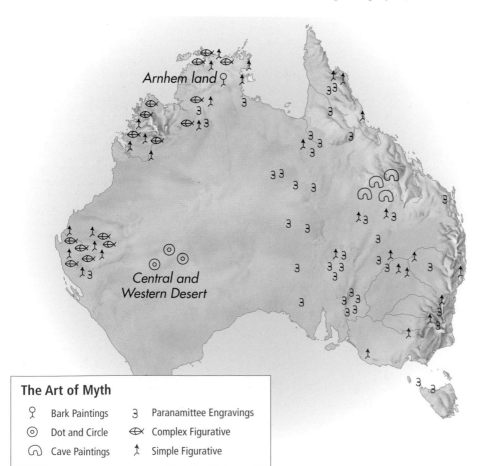

The Art of Myth

⚲	Bark Paintings	ꝫ	Paranamittee Engravings
⊙	Dot and Circle	⊕⤬	Complex Figurative
⌒	Cave Paintings	⏀	Simple Figurative

of animals and people are the dominant motif. In eastern Arnhem Land, on the other hand, geometric and abstract patterns with more attention paid to in-fill and background are favoured, rather than foregrounded figures. Action in these paintings is depicted through a series of smaller scenes that are figured against the background. The careful and fine cross-hatching that fills in much of the background of eastern Arnhem Land painting is designed deliberately to produce a shimmering or brilliant effect, suggesting vibration and movement, which enhances the religiosity and ritual efficacy of the painting.

THE DOT-AND-CIRCLE MOTIF

The other major school of Aboriginal art is associated with the central and western desert regions of the country. This style of art, originally done on shields, weapons and the human body, uses a dot-and-circle motif, and lines of dots to suggest tracks of movements. The dot and circle motif can represent many things – a waterhole, a camp, a ceremonial ground, an animal or bush – and the tracks depict the geographical position of these objects as encountered by Creator Beings, as related in the myths of the Dreamtime. Today, many famous central Australian painters use acrylic paints on canvas and it is in this form that central and western desert paintings have entered the international art scene.

The contemporary problem of copyrighting such designs is a pressing one – since the images convey important and restricted cosmological knowledge whose circulation must be controlled, the idea of intellectual property rights is of key concern for many Aboriginal groups, for whom art has a very serious ritual–religious function.

THE HISTORY OF AUSTRALIA

*c.*50,000 BC	First settlement of Australia from Southeast Asia
1769–1770	Englishman James Cook first maps east coast of Australia
1788	First British penal colony established in Sydney Cove
1840s	First European colonization of Australia
1850s	Australian gold rush
1901	Commonwealth of Australia established
1974	Dismantling of the White Australia policy
1992	Maboo judgement resulting in the restoration of land to Aboriginal ownership

An Aboriginal bark painting of funeral ceremony with a kangaroo by Melangi de Milingibi, which has been used on an Australian banknote. Mortuary ceremonies are in symbolic respects, a reversal of the spiritual procreation of the person and involve the proper disposition of the deceased's spirit and totemic creative force.

ART IN CONTEMPORARY SOCIETY

Not all contemporary Aboriginal art follows the ancestral patterns. Many Aboriginal artists have experimented with modern techniques, photography and other forms to depict the history of Aboriginal–European contact and the destructive effects upon indigenous Australian religion and Aboriginal spirituality wrought by colonialization. The Butchulla artist Fiona Foley uses materials from her native Fraser Island to create montages depicting the dispossession of the Butchulla people from their land and myths. In several paintings and lithographs, she has made use of black cockatoo feathers and the image of the nautilus shell – both totemically important animals for the Butchulla – as a way of reminding viewers of the central role totemic affiliation continues to play in Butchulla country. The Ngarrindjeri weaver Yvonne Koolmatrie uses rushes from her traditional country along the Coorong Penninsula in South Australia to create new forms of Ngarrindjeri baskets, but she has also fashioned aeroplanes and other relics of colonial society using the same materials. Albert Namatjira began what is now known as the Hermannsburg School of Central Australian art. He used watercolours to produce fairly Western-style landscape paintings of scenes from his Central Desert home, fusing Western and Aboriginal ways of imagining country and its spiritual significance.

Papuan Hero Tales

The connection between Australia and Papua New Guinea is an intimate one, both geologically and historically. Although it is nearly 4,000 km (2,486 miles) away, myths from the centre of Australia have found their way into the interior of Papua New Guinea, by way of the Torres Strait Islands. As is the case with Australian Creator Beings, Papuan heroes wandered the landscape, creating notable features and giving creatures and humans their present-day form.

A painted child from New Guinea. Throughout Melanesia, children embody the wealth and creativity of their parents and their clan groups. They are often given prominence in collective displays of clan vitality.

The coastal societies of southern New Guinea and west New Guinea (now part of Indonesia and known as Irian Jaya) share the origin stories of a giant Creator Being who wandered across the landscape, creating its features. Among the Kiwai Islanders, natives from an island just off the southwest coast of Papua New Guinea, he is known as Sido. Further west, among the Marind-anim, a tribal people who inhabit the coast of west New Guinea, he is called Sosom. Sosom was a giant and he is credited with inseminating the landscape and making it fertile; he was also responsible for the origin of the practice of insemination of boys in order to make them mature and become men. Sosom tried to force himself onto a woman, but she cut his penis off. This later became the bull-roarer, which is used in the male initiation cults of traditional Marind-anim society.

In the Torres Strait, through which these myths undoubtedly entered New Guinea from the south, a series of myths involve the characters Sida, Said, Soida or Soido. According to A.C. Haddon, an anthropologist who collected myths and ethnographic data during the famous Cambridge expedition to the Torres Straits at the end of the nineteenth century, Sido taught people language, stocked the sea and reef with valuable shells and introduced cultivars to humans.

Sido and Sosom are responsible for bringing vegetable food to other parts of New Guinea and thus for the practice of horticulture. In Kiwai, Sido eats vegetable food which passes directly into his penis. During an act of copulation with a woman, the vegetables are released, introducing cultivated plants to human beings. These myths are important in that they link the activity of gardening

Creator Beings
The map shows the location of the Creator Beings of Papua New Guinea.

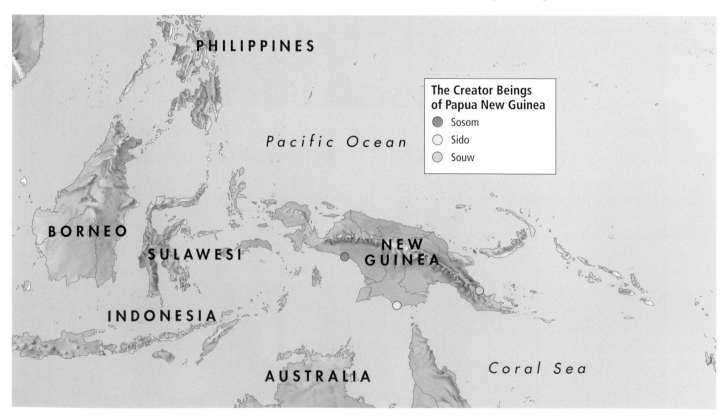

The Creator Beings of Papua New Guinea
- Sosom
- Sido
- Souw

PHILIPPINES

Pacific Ocean

BORNEO

SULAWESI

NEW GUINEA

INDONESIA

AUSTRALIA

Coral Sea

with a more general male–female sexual complementarity that governs subsistence activities in this part of the world.

A HERO IN SERPENT FORM

Further inland, among the Daribi of the southern Simbu Province of Papua New Guinea, this figure is known as Souw, and is credited with creating many prominent features of the landscape. Here, the Sido–Souw character has changed somewhat – he is identified with a serpent or python, perhaps revealing the eventual origin of this myth in the Australian Aboriginal myth of the brown python. The hero is considered immortal – he merely sheds his skin and becomes young again. According to the anthropologist Roy Wagner in his book, *The Curse of Souw* (1967), in a Souw myth from Bumaru in Daribi country (Simbu

Province, Papua New Guinea) a young woman and a widow live at a place called Orouwa. A bird in the bush would cry out often, indicating it had sighted a snake. As long as the older widow went in response to the bird, everything went well. But one day the young girl went out and saw that it was the penis of Souw. She cried out in alarm, and Souw became ashamed and cursed humans with the present-day institutions of warfare, death and sorcery, feuding and mourning customs; as a result, human life is always filled with trouble.

In another version, Souw is able to take his skin off and become young again. During his episode of shame, Souw discarded his own skin. Had humans claimed it they, too, would have become immortal. But instead, the snakes found it with the result that snakes do not die, they just shed their skins and become young again.

Wooden, decorated masks from the Sepik River region of New Guinea representing events and ancestral culture heroes. The function of masks such as these was to serve a ritual purpose, and as ritual objects were not made of durable materials because they were not designed to endure for posterity.

THE HABU CEREMONY

The Daribi Habu ceremony follows directly on from the message of the Souw myth. In times of sickness or death, people perceive that a ghost is responsible. The Habu men must therefore go out into the bush and repatriate the ghost so that it ceases its destructive effects on living society. They follow the cry of the rufous shrike-thrush who, as did the bird in the Souw myth, alerts men's attention to game animals drawn to the kava plant (which grows in the South Pacific; and is used to make a mildly intoxicating drink, known as kava). The men hunt and smoke game in the bush for a period of time, and then bring the meat back to the village in the hope that the smell will force the ghost to accompany them. The ghost returns to the village, following the smell and is reassimilated into human society and the threat ended. The Habu ceremony demonstrates that such myths serve as a template for the most important cosmological rituals in these interior New Guinea societies.

Myths of Kinship

Many Papua New Guinea myths deal with dilemmas and conflicts of blood and marriage relations – between brothers, between fathers and sons, between in-laws – that are resolved in various ways. It has long been a truism of psychological anthropology that such myths make visible structural tensions in such relationships and suggest solutions to them in the world of the imagination that real life cannot permit.

The most well-known cluster of what could be called the Two-Brother myths are those concerning the brothers Kilibob and Manup from the Huon Peninsula–Vitiaz Strait–West New Britain area of central north New Guinea. Kilibob is the industrious brother, a carver of wood, while Manup, a fisherman, mistreats his wives. Kilibob makes trouble with his brother by saving Manup's wives from mistreatment by their husband. Kilibob carves a design on his brother's wife's thigh in return for finding an arrow of his with the same design. In another episode, after fleeing up a tree from Manup, Kilibob throws leaves onto Manup's wives' breasts, making them pregnant. In all these episodes, the adulterous appropriation of a brother's wives is the point of conflict between the two men.

Among the interior of New Guinea, Two-Brother myths are very common. The elder brother is moral, industrious, honest and a good hunter. The younger brother is lazy, treacherous and envious of his elder sibling. The elder brother goes to inspect his traps, or fires an arrow at a bird, whereupon the bird he thought he caught turns into a beautiful woman. The younger brother nags him for the secret of this transformation but in his impatience, neglects to listen carefully – he traps or catches an ugly black bird which turns into an ugly wife, much to his anger. The theme of the good elder brother and the inattentive and unpleasant younger brother is retold in many variations throughout central New Guinea.

A mask from the Sepik River region, New Guinea, made from mud and decorated with cowrie shells. Cowrie shells are both a form of ceremonial wealth and a decoration for objects and human bodies in Melanesia. In interior Papua New Guinea, cowries are sewn onto long ropes and traded in this form.

COMMON THEMES

Women are commonly tricked by men in New Guinea myth – for instance, a woman either comes across or is approached by a decrepit old man. She treats him with kindness and takes care of him, whereupon he reveals himself to be a handsome young man in disguise. Other myths take the opposite tack – a young man approaches a woman and causes her to fall in love with him; he then reveals himself as a treacherous, ugly, old man. The woman then escapes with the help of another, virtuous, young man. Women also find themselves married to spirits or ghosts; again, these are non-human beings who approach the women in human form and trick them into joining them in the Sky World or the Land of the Dead.

The Greek theme of Orpheus finds numerous parallels in the mythology of central New Guinea. A man loses his wife to death and goes to the Land of the Dead to find her. He is allowed to bring her back so long as he observes certain conditions. Like Orpheus, he fails to heed the instructions and loses his wife a second time.

In these myths, the almost universal male dilemma of keeping a wife is given expression and symbolic elaboration.

This door panel from northwestern New Guinea features an X-ray drawing of a pregnant woman. The similarity between this image and depictions of the Wawilak Sisters myth from northeast Arnhem Land, Australia, is striking, due in part to the regular and important contact between Aboriginal Australians and the people of New Guinea.

PREGNANCY AND FERTILITY

These are themes that find many mythological variations in New Guinea. In a Foi myth, a small boy turns into an insect and hides in a bamboo tube of drinking water. After drinking the water, a young woman finds herself pregnant. In a Daribi myth, a woman's menstrual blood accidentally falls onto the ground and red yams grow from that spot.

In the Foi myth of sexual complementarity, the first woman originally had no genitals. Her brother notices her sliding up and down against a palm tree. He inserts a stone blade and when next she slides against the trunk, she cuts herself, furnishing herself with a vagina. The brother and sister copulate and give birth to the human race.

Certain implements – such as women's string bags, men's tools and musical instruments – literally become parts of bodies in myths throughout New Guinea. The female string bag, worn by women as an all-purpose carrying implement, is intimately linked to her 'internal bag' (her uterus) and a few myths detail how a string bag can gestate a human infant by itself. In some myths, a man's drum is his voice and organ of procreation; in others, men go in search of their drum that has been lost or stolen.

Cargo Cult Mythology

Melanesia is noted for its syncretistic use of Western characters and imagery. Melanesian mythic patterns are used to comment on the often incommensurable worlds of the West and Melanesia: the scientific and the magical. Many such myths hypothesize, for example, on the magical source of the Westerners' seemingly vast supplies of material wealth, or the kinship relations that must surround the institution of the British monarchy. Cargo cults rely very heavily on the use of imagery.

The arrival in Oceania of the Europeans and their wealth of material goods triggered the formation of the cargo cults in Melanesia. The islanders hoped to gain the same knowledge of magic and ritual that the newcomers must surely have possessed in order to have amassed such apparent wealth and riches. One of the most important and well-documented cargo cult myths is from the Rai Coast of Madang District, on the north coast of New Guinea. Yali was a man of the Ngaing people from the Rai Coast. The Ngaing and other people had by 1947 already gone through a number of cargo cults. They decided that the missionaries held the secret cult knowledge of the Westerners' material wealth, so most of them

accepted the missionaries' preaching enthusiastically and became 'Christians'. It soon became apparent that mere conversion was not enough; the people believed the missionaries were holding onto vital secrets of cargo. Dissatisfaction that the administrators and missionaries were not releasing the secrets they held grew, though oddly enough, the missionaries were not blamed; people thought that the administrators were preventing the missionaries from disclosing the secret.

Yali was a member of the police when the Japanese invaded New Guinea in 1942. He helped evacuate people from the Rai Coast, and when Lae fell, he made his way with an Australian captain to Finschhafen, on the northeast coast of Papua New

The Journey of Yali
Yali was from the Rai Coast of New Guinea. Although he was originally profoundly impressed by a journey that he made to Australia in 1942 he ultimately concluded that his people had been deceived by the Europeans and embarked on a full scale revival of his traditional religion. The map shows the route of Yali's journey.

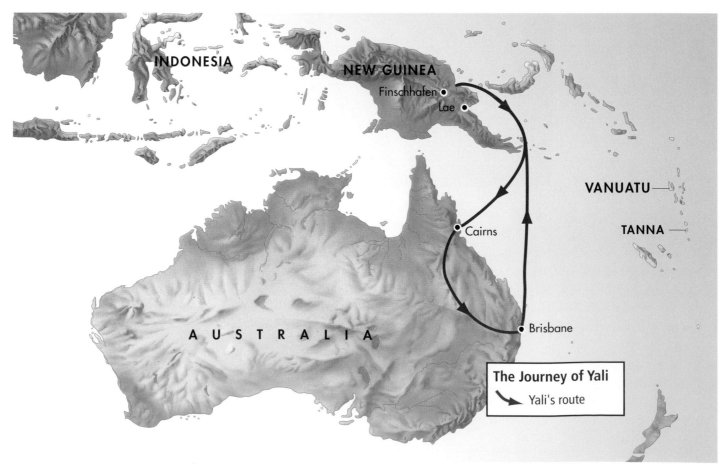

INDONESIA

NEW GUINEA

Finschhafen
Lae

VANUATU

TANNA

Cairns

AUSTRALIA

Brisbane

The Journey of Yali
Yali's route

EUROPEAN TOTENISM

Two other things greatly impressed Yali when he was in Australia. The first was his reaction to the theory of evolution, when he was shown pictures of the great apes and depictions of man's relationship with his hominid forebears. Like all New Guineans, Yali had thought that the missionaries' story of creation represented the only cosmogonic theory the white man had. Yali thus proceeded to interpret his discovery in the only way he could, and look at it in terms of his own society's beliefs. He concluded that 'one specific group of Europeans claimed descent from the joint totem Adam-and-Eve, while another entirely discrete group claimed descent from the totem "monkey"' [Lawrence, *Road Belong Cargo*, p. 175].

This discovery of European totemism was taken even further by Yali after his visit to Brisbane Zoo and his learning of the white custom of keeping apparently useless pets in their houses. Yali concluded that his

Just as everyday life in Melanesia is influenced by new arrivals (as in this Papua New Guinean Hiri Hanemo beauty contest in which a participant holds a model of the *hiri laketoi*, the canoes used by traders from the south coast), so is its mythology. With the arrival of the Europeans and their civilization, existing myths were altered and new ones created in an attempt, for example, to understand the secret behind the Europeans' wealth.

Guinea. His subsequent visit there had a profound impact on him. He was impressed with the orderliness and tidiness of Brisbane and Cairns. Compared with their evident prosperity, his own remembered village was ridiculous and pathetic. He finally saw the true source of *kago*: the canneries and factories, and more importantly, he came to realize that *kago* was only produced through the labour of white people. Compared with the industriousness of Australians, the work habits of his own people seemed deficient and contemptible.

people had been thoroughly and systematically deceived by the missionaries all along. They had discouraged the pagan rituals to the gods and the ceremonies honouring the spirits of the dead when all along they knew that their own people practised such rituals. At the same time, they had withheld the secret of the efficacy of their own Christian ritual. Yali thus embarked on a full-scale revival of the traditional pagan religion among the Ngaing, urging people to abandon both legitimate Christianity and the pseudo-Christian cargo cult.

Prince Philip, husband of Queen Elizabeth II, is at the centre of a cargo cult on the island of Tanna, in the south of Vanuatu.

THE JOHN FRUM MOVEMENT

In 1940, a stranger appeared on the island of Tanna in the south of Vanuatu, a group of islands formerly known as the New Hebrides, east of Papua New Guinea, whose inhabitants wore European clothing and healed the sick. The rumour spread that the god Karapanemum had appeared among humans – the god that the missionaries had labelled an evil devil. The stranger revealed his name to be John Frum. He announced that the whites would be ejected from Tanna and Erromango Islands, that European currency would be flung into the sea and that people would resume their traditional customs and lifestyle. John Frum had come to purify the island and return people to *kastom* (all traditional things). The John Frum Movement gathered force and people stopped going to church. In 1941, the British district administrators arrested 11 people, burned John Frum's healing hut that had been built for him and banned the utterance of his name. Nevertheless, the John Frum Movement survived for many years and continues to be a part of Tannese custom and practice today, though in a more routine manner.

Hawaiian Mythology

In keeping with most Polynesian mythology, that of Hawaii emphasizes an initial period where there was nothing but a formless void. The work of the gods was to insert discontinuities and contrasts into this primordial chaotic void. The realm called Po was a vast, empty land, a dark abyss where only one life form dwelled: Keawe.

Keawe opened his great gourd and threw the lid into the air; as it unfolded, it became the canopy of the sky. He then drew an orange disc from the gourd and this was the sun, which he hung in the sky. Next, Keawe took the form of Na Wahine, a female divinity considered to be his daughter. In addition, he became Kane, his own son, also known as Eli, the male generative force of creation. Na Wahine and Kane mated and begot a divine family, who became additional primary gods. According to the original mythology, three sons, Ku, Lono and Kanaloa, along with Kane, became the four major Hawaiian gods. Kane became the god of natural phenomena, such as the earth, stones and fresh water. Most importantly, Ku as Kukailimoku was god of war. Kanaloa became responsible for the sea and as such was god of seamen and fishermen. Lono, god of the sun and of knowledge, caused the earth to bear fruit. When Captain James Cook arrived in Hawaii in November 1778, he inadvertently ushered in the the period of Lono's ascendency (a time of renewal), at the end of the Makahiki festival.

Oahu Beach, Honolulu, Hawaii. In pre-colonial times, Hawaii possessed a rich and complex mythology, as well as one of Oceania's most developed societies. The arrival of Western civilization and resulting developments has meant that Hawaii's cultural identity and indigenous language is now all but lost.

Colonization of Hawaii
A map of Hawaii showing the route of Captain Cook's last, fateful journey to the island, as well as the location of various archaeological sites.

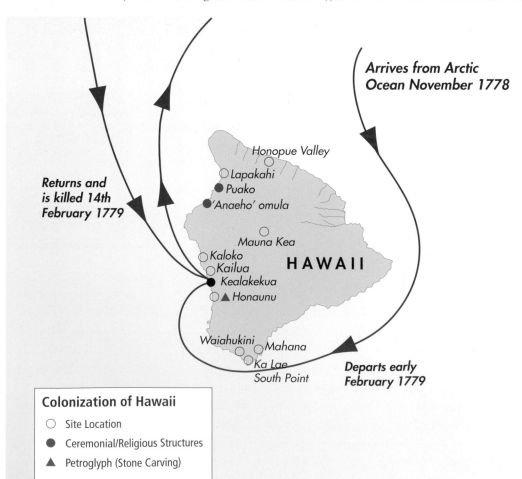

Arrives from Arctic Ocean November 1778

Returns and is killed 14th February 1779

Honopue Valley
Lapakahi
Puako
'Anaeho' omula

Mauna Kea

Kaloko
Kailua
Kealakekua

HAWAII

Honaunu

Waiahukini
Mahana
Ka Lae
South Point

Departs early February 1779

Colonization of Hawaii

○ Site Location

● Ceremonial/Religious Structures

▲ Petroglyph (Stone Carving)

GODS AND MEN

Each Hawaiian man worshipped a deity, or *akua*, that held sway over his occupation. Gods existed for bird-snarers, canoe-makers, robbers, tapa-makers, fishermen and others involved in different occupations. Gardeners gave obeisance to Lono, who was considered a benign god. When crops ripened, gardeners performed religious rituals to the gods by building a fire to honour whichever god they worshipped, be it Ku, Kane, Lono or Kanaloa. During the ceremonies, food was cooked and distributed to each man. These men sat in a circle around a statue of the particular god they were worshipping.

The old gods were disavowed by the nobility as a consequence of the arrival of Christian missionaries in 1820. Temple idols were pushed over and destroyed, but as commoners still feared the power of the gods, they were faced with the problem of what to do with the stone images representing various gods, since neglect of those idols might cause unknown disasters.

Illustration showing Captain Cook being killed in Hawaii, February 1779. Many people believe that Cook lost his life after unknowingly flouting Hawaiian cosmic protocol. The details of his arrival had fulfilled a local legend, which stated that Lono would arrive at the end of the Makahiki festival and circle the island in a clockwise direction. However, the locals became angry after Cook departed and then returned to the island from the wrong direction, in contradiction of the local myths. (See *Foreign Influence*, below).

Mt Haleakala, Maui, Hawaii. The island of Maui is believed to have been created when Maui, an Oceanic culture hero, was out fishing in his canoe and pulled out a fish, which became the island. On top of the island's highest mountain, Mt Hikurangi, is thought to rest the canoe Maui used on this fishing trip.

Kane and Na Wahine had daughters as well as sons. Among them, Laka was the goddess of hula; Hina was the mother of Maui who pulled the Hawaiian islands from the ocean and Kapo was the goddess of the South Pacific, who was largely worshipped on Maui. Among the major divinities was the goddess Papa, queen of nature, and the man she married, Wakea; Papa also recurs in Maori mythology. In legend, Papa and Wakea's first child was born deformed as a taro root (a plant indigenous to the Pacific region). From the child's grave, the first taro plant grew to furnish sustenance to the rest of the human race, which had its origins in this first couple.

FOREIGN INFLUENCE

Hawaii is well known for stories of foreign gods who came from distant lands and usurped the powers of indigenous deities. The legend of Paao is perhaps the most important in this respect, according to Marshall Sahlins, an anthropologist who has written extensively on the topic of Captain Cook in Hawaii. Paao left his home after a quarrel with his elder brother. He set sail with a number of men, and in some versions, with the god Kukailimoku. When he arrived safely in the Hawaiian Islands from his home in some invisible lands across the sea, Paao instituted the custom of human sacrifice. He also installed the new chief, Pilikaaiea, to whom Kamehameha, the chief at the time of James Cook's arrival, could trace a connection back 20 generations.

Cook arrived at the time when Lono was due to return to Hawaii at the end of the Makahiki festival in a particular direction. Hawaiians, seeing Cook's ship, which was carrying out precisely such a clockwise circumnavigation of the island, thought he was Lono and escorted him to the temple where he was persuaded to perform the ritual gestures. Cook then departed Hawaii in the correct (anticlockwise) direction, ushering in the period of Lono's ascendancy over Makahiki. When Cook returned, however, he threw the ritual sequence into disarray, and was killed by Hawaiian nobles, angry at the god's disavowal of cosmic protocol.

Angan Cosmologies

According to the Iqwaye, a group of Yagwoia tribesmen of the central Angan area (Morobe and the Eastern Highlands Provinces in Papua New Guinea) who have been studied by the anthropologist Jadran Mimica, the body of Omalyce, the first man, *was* the cosmos in its entirety.

This is an abbreviated form of the primal Iqwaye myth of creation, from Mimica's ethnography:

'At the time of darkness, the sky and the earth were conjoined. The earth was impregnated with water. These elements [of cosmos] were Omalyce himself [the creator of the cosmos who is also the first man]. They were his body. The sky, the earth and water were bound together because Omalyce had his penis in his mouth. The penis was his umbilical cord. The water was his semen. It was going into his mouth, then into his body, and in there it circled through all the regions of his body which encompassed the whole cosmos. Then from his body, semen was going into his penis, then into his mouth, and so on. Omalyce's fingers and toes kept his body locked, and with his penis, held the sky, the earth and water within it. The vital clench was the conjunction of mouth and penis, i.e. the umbilical cord. When Omalyce severed his umbilical cord to take a breath, in that moment the sky and the earth went asunder, and thus the world [cosmos] came into being. Omalyce's eyes ascended into the sky. They became the sun and moon. Ever since they appear in the sky paralleling the alternation of day and night. Omalyce vomited semen and blood. As he was vomiting, he created all things in this world.'

MEANING OF THE MYTH

In this myth are found the implications for all of the Iqwaye's social forms in their cosmological significance. The figure of Omalyce was the cosmos, envisioned as a self-copulating, self-perpetuating being who is neither male nor female and yet is both at the same time. It is an act of autosexual creation, of autogenesis, where Omalyce both inseminates and feeds himself at one and the same time. He needs neither a mate nor someone to provide him with food. In this myth, the cosmos is pictured as a totally self-sealed and self-reproducing structure. Of course,

Carved wooden figure of a woman with two hornbills, as found on a spirit house from the Maprik region of northeast New Guinea. This figure may be a composite male/female symbol; the hornbills' beaks can be regarded as phallic, and therefore male, while the woman's figure represents the female aspect.

in this form it is a totally ahuman structure since it does not allow the possibility of interpersonal relationships; indeed Omalyce is not a person in any real sense at all.

The primordial condition of the self-perpetuating Omalyce depicts the original condition of unity that characterized the Iqwaye universe. Everything is united into one self-sustaining whole. When Omalyce severed his own penis/umbilical cord, he gave birth to himself and to the cosmos as a spatial realm all at once. Omalyce was also responsible for the separation into opposites of sky and earth, blood and semen, day and night, sun and moon – in other words, all of the dualities upon which the present-day cosmos is founded.

The themes of parthenogenesis and autogenesis, of self-creation within a closed cycle, are common to both Australia (as in the Wawilak and Yurlunggor myth and the Aranda account of creation in the *Alcheringa* or Dreamtime) and Melanesia. The Adam and Eve story in Western Judaeo-Christian cosmology is also an account of autogenesis, of the creation of duality and multiplicity out of a primal monism. These themes must be profoundly and deeply located within the human pysche.

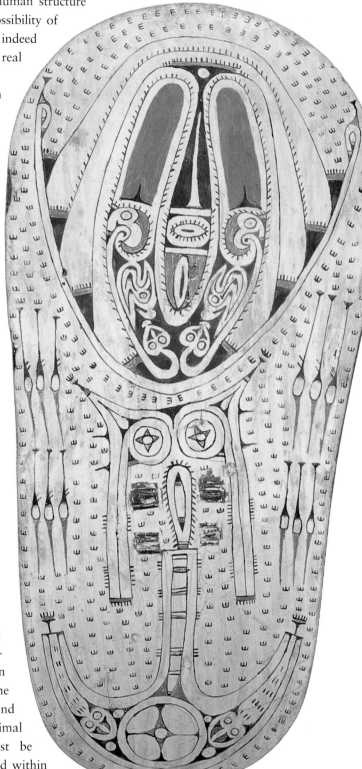

Painted wooden shield from the Trobriand Islands, Papua New Guinea, with a design representing a stylized vulva, a symbol of procreation and fertility. Mythological themes, such as fertility, creation, death and rites of passage are all found in the major myth cycles of most of Oceania's island groups.

OMALYCE'S OFFSPRING

In another mythic fragment, Omalyce creates his own sons by fashioning five lumps of earth – one for each finger of one hand – and then making them into true human men by inseminating them through their mouths. Omalyce had not yet fashioned genitals for the fifth son and, after ingesting Omalyce's semen, the son became pregnant. Because he had no way to deliver a child, his brothers shot him with arrows and, having turned into a cassowary (a flightless bird) the son had his womb split open by the arrows and a red marsupial-man emerged. The cassowary thus became the first woman. In a strict sense, Omalyce was identical to his sons since they were created totally by him out of his own substance. The critical fact to remember, however, is that even though a unity of the two sexes was achieved in the body of Omalyce itself, this unity was only possible in the body of the male sex; females are a sub-set of male unity.

Common Themes

Although the mythologies described in this volume encompass a diverse range of cultures and timespans, there are various elements that are common to many of them. Described below are just a few of these themes.

Agriculture *see* **Nature**

Animals: Gods and goddesses often appear as animals and are associated with the quality of the creature whose guise they take. For example, Egypt's cow goddess Hathor is associated with fertility and India's elephant god Ganesha with wisdom. In some mythologies, including Maori, animals are the ancestral people, while many African and North American myths refer to a time when all creatures, including humans, lived together in harmony and shared the same language.
Bear: A symbol of new life as well as perseverance and strength; associated with rites of passage.
Carp: Revered in Japan and Korea as the symbol of youth, bravery, perseverance, strength, and self-defence.
Deer: Often associated with the tree of life. In Siberia, where deer masks were sometimes worn by shamans to promote good hunting, deer can be regarded as the essence of the soul.
Jaguar: In Aztec mythology it symbolizes the powers of darkness and in Mexican myth, it is the messenger of the forest spirits. It is a form often taken by shamans.
Lion: Often associated with solar deities, in Egyptian mythology with Ra and in Roman mythology with Apollo.
Monkey: Usually associated with transformation and trickery.
Serpent: Particularly common in Oceanic, African and South American myths, serpents are associated with immortality and rebirth as well as fertility and water.
Spider: In North American mythology, the spider is sometimes the creator-deity. Spiders are also associated with the Mother Goddess as weavers of destiny.
Tiger: Associated with strength and impetuosity.

Creation: The created world can emerge from a great void (Norse mythology), from a primal ocean (Sumerian mythology) or from a cosmic egg (Chinese and Egyptian mythology). Sometimes the world is sung, spoken, woven or thought into existence. A Navajo myth tells how creation emerged from sacred chants while in the American southwest, Spider Woman spins life from the threads in her belly. In Mayan mythology, thought creates the first being and in Hindu mythology, it creates the primordial egg.

Cycles, World: Many mythologies (for example Hopi, Aztec and Hindu) see the world as undergoing successive cycles of creation and destruction or successive ages. The end of a particular world era is usually signalled by a cataclysm such as the chaos of Ragnarok, the 'last days' of Norse mythology.

Death and disease: Death often arrives as a result of humans turning away from the gods; according to an Inuit myth, however, it was introduced to prevent the world from becoming overcrowded. In some mythologies deities are associated with particular illnesses: in Africa, for example, Sagbata is the god of smallpox while in Greek mythology it is the mortal woman Pandora who unwittingly introduces disease to the world.

Deities: The gods who succeed the giants usually take increasingly human shape. They may be associated with features in the landscape such as mountains or lakes, with specific functions such as archery or agriculture or with natural phenomena such as thunder, lightning or volcanoes. In Irish mythology, the race of gods known as the Tuatha de Danaan destroyed the rule of the giant Fomorians, and in Greek mythology the Olympians succeeded the Titans.

Demons: Although daemon means simply 'supernatural being', demons usually oppose the gods and are regarded as malevolent. In Hindu mythology the demon king Ravana leads the evil Rakshas; in Japan there are the Awabi and Oni, in Southeast Asia the Jin and in Persia the Daevas.

Earth: Often the Great Mother, the universal nourisher; in China, it is the feminine yin priniciple.

Family and ancestors: Many myths seek to account for and enforce the status of individuals and groups within society. The Japanese tale of Izanagi and Izanami justifies women's alleged inferiority to men and in Greek myth a woman – Pandora – is held responsible for loosing countless ills on humanity. Japan's emperors gained prestige and authority by tracing their lineage back to the goddess Amaterasu while the pharaohs of Egypt claimed descent from Isis and Osiris. Ancestor worship has a prominent place in many mythologies, particularly in China where great emphasis is placed on respect for elders. In Australian aboriginal mythology, the ancestors are said to have travelled across the country in the Dreamtime, shaping the landscape and determining the nature of society.

Fire: Gods of fire usually symbolize purification and transformation (for example, the Indian fire god Agni). In North American mythology fire is often regarded as the home of the Great Spirit.

The Flood: A great flood or deluge appears in numerous mythologies including Mesopotamian, Yoruban,

Aztec, Dayak, Greek and Hindu. The flood is often sent down to punish humanity for turning away from the divine. Usually a flood hero is instructed to build a boat or ark so that he will survive the deluge and go on to repopulate the earth.

Food: Foods essential to survival are often regarded as divine. In Southeast Asia, rice is said to provide supernatural nourishment while in Greek and Roman mythology corn symbolizes fertility and rebirth. Bread is widely regarded as the food of both body and soul while apples are symbols of fertility, knowledge and magic.

Giants: Primordial giants appear prior to the gods in several mythologies. In Greek mythology there are the Titans, in Scandinavian mythology the original giant Ymi and in Irish mythology the Fomorians.

Great Spirit or Absolute: In many mythologies a Great Spirit or pervasive power lies behind the created world. In India, for example, there is Brahma (the Absolute), while in North American Indian mythology there is Wakan.

Heroes: Sometimes immortal, sometimes human, sometimes semi-divine, heroes usually undergo trials of strength and often undertake a quest in order to find a sacred treasure or kill a terrifying monster. Notable heroes include the Polynesian Maui, the Greek Herakles and the Indian Arjuna.

Moon: Usually associated with wisdom and fertility and represented as the Mother Goddess. Sometimes, however, the moon is the male principle. In Egyptian mythology, the crescent moon symbolizes Isis; in Japan it is the male god Tsukiyomi.

Mythical creatures: Many mythical creatures appear as half human, half divine. In Greek myths the Sirens have the bodies of birds and heads of women while the Sphinx of Egyptian mythology, associated with the sun god Ra, sometimes has the head of a woman. Other mythical animals include the unicorn, associated with the feminine principle and good luck, and the dragon. In Chinese mythology, the dragon is associated with good luck and wisdom, whereas in Mespotamian mythology it can be associated with the power of evil.

Nature/Agriculture: Many myths concern the cycle of nature and the agricultural year. For example, the Greek goddess Demeter is a symbol of both agriculture and fertility; her annual sojourn in the underworld symbolizes winter, and her appearance in spring coincides with the growth of crops. While the plough is sometimes an attribute of agricultural deities, for nomadic peoples it can symbolize a violation of the body of Mother Earth.

People, origins of: Humans are sometimes fashioned by a deity from mud or clay as in the Egyptian tale of Khnum, the Chinese story of Nu-gua and the Inca tale of Viracocha. In some North American and African myths, humans crawl to the surface from beneath the earth. A Zulu myth tells how the great sky god makes humans out of grass while, according to a Yoruba tale, humans were made in heaven and sent down to earth on a spider's web.

Sky: Usually an omnipotent male creator-deity who transcends the created world. In African mythology, the sky deity is often androgynous (for example, Mawu Liza).

Spirit beings: Countless lesser spirit beings populate the world's mythologies. The Nymphs of Greek myth (female powers associated with fertility and nature) are similar to the Apsaras of Hindu mythology and the Najada of the Slavic peoples. Among the many other types of spirit being are the Awakkule, playful dwarves which appear in North American mythology.

Tricksters: Known for their capacity for cunning and mischief, tricksters are often creative forces, breaking boundaries and challenging the status quo. They include the Scandinavian Loki, Native American Coyote and Hanuman, the trickster monkey god of India who uses his wit to rescue Sita from the demon king Ravana.

The underworld: The underworld often lies across a stretch of water such as the River Styx of Greek mythology. Once at their destination, the dead may be judged before being consigned to a particular region or they may at some time be reborn on earth. Dying and rising gods are a feature of many mythologies, for example Osiris (Egyptian), Tammuz (Babylonian) and Adonis (Greek).

Structure of the Universe: In many mythologies, the universe is regarded as divided into layers. For some cultures there are three levels: the upper world (heaven), the middle world (the everyday world) and the lower world (the underworld); for others (for example the Kedang of Southeast Asia) there are as many as seven levels above the Earth and five below. Sometimes, however, heaven is situated on the same plane as Earth: in Slavonic myth it is situated in the east while in Celtic mythology it lies to the west. The different vertical worlds are sometimes united by a world axis or *axis mundi*, for example a world tree such as Yggdrasil of Norse mythology or a sacred mountain. The centre of the world or cosmic centre (sometimes known as the omphalos or navel) is usually regarded as the home of the gods. It might be a sacred mountain such as Mt Meru (India) or Olympus (Greece) or it might be represented by a ritual space, for example the North American Lodge.

Water: The divine source, undifferentiated experience. Water is usually associated with the female principle, fertility and new life (for example, the Mesopotamian Tiamat).

Pantheon

Africa
PRINCIPAL AFRICAN DEITIES

Abassi (Nigeria/Efik): Creator who placed the first couple on Earth.

Abuk (Sudan/Dinka): The first woman; she emerged from a pot with her husband Garang.

Adu Ogyinae (Ashanti): The first man; he led people to the surface of the earth.

Ala (Nigeria/Ibo): Supreme mother goddess; daughter of Chuku.

Amma (Mali/Dogon): Supreme god who created the sun and moon.

Anansi (West Africa): Trickster spider.

Cagn (Southwestern/Bushmen): The supreme creator.

Chuku (Nigeria/Ibo): Supreme being and creator-deity.

Deng (Sudan/Dinka): Sky god; bringer of rain and fertility.

Efik (Kenya/Abaluyia): Creator-god; father of the sun and moon.

Gawana (Southwestern/Bushmen): Leader of the spirits of the dead; opponent of Cagn.

Gu (Dahomey/Fon): Smith god; son of Mawu-Liza.

Kintu (Sudan/Dinka): The first man and founder of the Dinka.

Lebe (Mali/Dogon): The first ancestor to die, thereby bringing life to mankind.

Mawu-Liza (Leza) (Dahomey/Fon): The first deity; either androgynous or male and female twins.

Nana Buluku (Dahomey/Fon): Primeval creator-god who engendered Mawu-Liza.

Ngewo (Sierra Leone/Mende): Primal deity present in natural phenomena.

Nummo (Mali/Dogon): Primeval man and woman produced by Amma.

Ogun (Nigeria/Yoruba): God of iron and war.

Olokun (Nigeria/Yoruba): Sea god who caused a deluge.

Olorun (Nigeria/Yoruba): The supreme creator-deity.

Osun (Nigeria/Yoruba): The power of love and sensuality.

Sagbata (Dahomey/Fon): God of smallpox.

Sogbo (Dahomey/Fon): God of thunder, lightning and fire; son of Mawu and brother of Sagbata.

Unkullunkulu (Southern Africa/Zulus): Supreme deity who created the first people from grass.

Yemonja (Nigeria/Yoruba): Great goddess; daughter of the sea.

Ancient Near East
PRINCIPAL NEAR EASTERN DEITIES

Adad (Babylonian): God of wind, storm, thunder and flood.

Anu (Babylonian): Supreme deity and father of the gods.

Ashur (Assyria): Chief deity and national god of Assyria.

Dumuzi/Tammuz (Sumerian/Babylonian): Vegetation and harvest god; husband of Innana/Ishtar.

Enki/Ea (Sumerian/Babylonian): God of waters and wisdom.

Enlil (Sumerian): God of air and weather who punished humanity with a flood.

Ereshkigal (Babylonian): Queen of the underworld and wife of Nergal.

Innana/Ishtar (Sumerian/Babylonian): Queen of heaven and goddess of love, war and death.

Marduk (Babylonian): Supreme god who defeated the monsters of chaos.

Nabu (Sumerian/Babylonian): Babylonian god of knowledge; son of Marduk.

Nanna/Sin (Sumerian/Babylonian): Moon god associated with wisdom.

Nergal (Sumerian/Babylonian): War god who became ruler of the underworld.

Ninhursag (Sumerian): Earth goddess; consort of Enki.

Utu/Shamash (Sumerian/Babylonian): God of justice and the sun.

SUMERIAN NAME	BABYLONIAN NAME
An	Anu
Enlil	Ellil
Enki	Ea
Nanna	Sin
Inanna	Ishtar
Utu	Shamash
Ninlil	Mullitu, Mylitta

PRINCIPAL PERSIAN DEITIES

Ahriman/Angra Mainyu: Principle of darkness, in opposition to Ahura Mazda.

Ahura Mazda: Supreme god and principle of light.

Anahita: Goddess of water and fertility.

Apaosha: Demon of drought defeated by Tishtrya.

Mithra: God of light and fertility who killed the divine bull.

Rapithwin: God of the noon-day heat.

Tishtrya: God of water.

Vayu: God of the wind and rains.

Arctic
PRINCIPAL INUIT DEITIES

A'akuluujjusi: Great creator-mother.

Adlivun: Home of Sedna where the dead are purified.

Akycha/Malina: The sun.

Anguta: Supreme being who takes the dead to Adlivun.

Idliragijenget: God of the sea.

Igaluk/Aningan: God of the moon, brother of the sun whom he chases across the sky.

Irdlirvirisissong: Demon cousin of the moon.

Nanook: God of bears.

Pinga: Goddess of game, the hunt, medicine and people.

Sedna: Greatly feared goddess of the sea and sea-creatures.

Sila: Divine ruler; universal energy.

Tekkeitserktock: Earth god and master of hunting.

PRINCIPAL SIBERIAN DEITIES

Ai Tojon (Siberia/Yakut): Eagle-headed creator-deity.

Ajysyt (Siberia/Yakut): Mother goddess who gives children souls.

Anky-kele (Siberia/Chukchi): Sea god who governs human lives.

Buga (Siberia/Tungu): Supreme god; creator of the world and the first two humans.

Ec (Siberia/Yenisei): Supreme god; husband of Khosadam.

Erlik (Siberia/Altaic): King of the dead; enemy of Ulgan.

Khadau (Siberia/Amur): Creator-god who makes the souls of shamans.

Khosodam (Siberia/Yenisei): Wife of Ec forced from the sky for having an affair with the moon.

Kutkinnaku (Siberia/Koryak): Beneficent raven god.

Maidere (Siberia/Altaic): Saviour sent to protect people from Erlik.

Main (Siberia/Evenk): Hero who rescues the sun from a great elk.

Mamaldi (Siberia/Amur): Wife of Khadau.

Picvucin (Siberia/Chukchi): God of hunting and wild animals.

Pon (Siberia/Yakagir): Supreme sky god.

Sacred Fireboard: Regarded as a protective deity.

Tengri (Siberia/Buriat): Spirit beings and also realms which form the cosmic tree.

Ulgen (Siberia/Altaic): Supreme sky god who sent Maidere to Earth.

Caribbean

PRINCIPAL CARIBBEAN DEITIES

Agaman Nibo (Haiti/Vodoun): Goddess of the dead; mother of Baron Samedi.

Anacacuya (Taino): Brother in law of Guayahona.

Annency/Ti Malice (West Indies): Trickster and spider; known as Ti Malice in Haiti.

Atabei (Cuba): Earth goddess.

Ayida Wedo (Haiti/Vodoun): Rainbow snake goddess; wife of Damballa.

Baron Samedi (Haiti/Vodoun): Chief deity; god of death, magic and the underworld.

Corocote (Taino): Guardian of sexual pleasure and romance.

Damballa/Damballa Wedo (Haiti/Vodoun): Serpent god associated with fertility and fresh water; leader of the loa.

Ghede (Haiti/Vodoun): God of the dead. A wise man, represented as an undertaker.

Guabancex (Taino): Goddess of storms, wind and water.

Itiba Cahubaba (Taino): The Taino earth mother who gave birth to two sets of male twins, the fathers of humanity.

Legba (Haiti/Vodoun): God of the sun who offers protection from evil spirits.

Lemba (Haiti): A deity, of Congo religion, worshipped in the African cults of Haiti and Brazil.

Loa (Haiti/Vodoun): Group of divinities led by Damballa. Some protect cemeteries or crossroads.

Maman Brigitte (Haiti/Vodoun): Wife of Ghede who protects graves in cemeteries.

Maquetaurie Guayaba (Taino): Lord of the Dead, master of sweetness and delight.

Obtala (West Indies): Sky goddess. (Also the name of a male deity.)

Odduda (West Indies): Wife of Obatala, the male god.

Opiel Guabiron (Taino): Guardian of the underworld.

Oshun (West Indies): Goddess of love and fertility.

Yaya (Taino): Supreme god and origin of creation.

Celts

PRINCIPAL CELTIC DEITIES

Belenus (Gaul): God of light: 'The Shining One'.

Brigid (Ireland): Goddess of healing and fertility.

Cernunnos (Gaul): God of fertility, animals, wealth and the underworld: 'The Horned One'.

Children of Don (Wales): The powers of light, opposed to the Children of Llyr.

Children of Llyr (Wales): The powers of darkness.

Dagda (Ireland): Leader of the Tuatha de Danann; son of Danu.

Danu (Ireland): Mother-goddess; founder of the Tuatha de Danaan.

Don (Wales): Mother-goddess; equivalent to Danu.

Epona (Gaul): Horse goddess who accompanied the soul on its final journey.

Goibniu (Ireland): Smith god, son of Danu.

Llyr (Wales): Sea god; father of Bran, Branwen and Manawydan.

Lugh (Ireland): Sun god and lord of arts and crafts.

Lugos (Gaul): Equivalent of Lugh.

Morrigan (Ireland): Queen of battle, strife and fertility. She helped the Tuatha de Danaan.

Nantosuelta (Gaul): Protective goddess of water.

Ogma (Ireland): God of eloquence and learning; son of Danu and Dagda.

Ogmios (Gaul): Patron of scholars.

Pwyll (Wales): Lord of Dyfed set tasks by Arawn, king of the underworld.

Rhiannon (Wales): A version of the horse goddess Epona. She bore Pwyll a son and after his death married Manawydan.

Sucellos (Gaul): God associated with fertility.

Taranis (Gaul): The thunder god.

Tuatha de Danann (Ireland): A race of gods founded by the goddess Danu.

THE CHILDREN OF DON

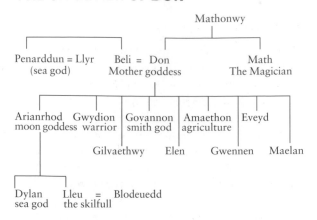

THE CHILDREN OF LLYR

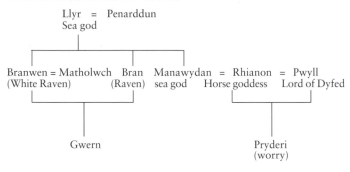

Central and Eastern Europe
PRINCIPAL SLAVIC DEITIES

Dazhbog: Sun god; son of Svarog and brother of Svarozhich.

Mokosh: Earth goddess who spins the web of life and death; wife of Perun.

Perun: Thunder god and creator-deity.

Rod: Early god of fertility.

Rozhanitsy: Mother and daughter goddesses of fertility. The mother was both consort and mother of Rod.

Stribog: God of the winds.

Svantovit: War god, sometimes regarded as the supreme deity.

Svarog: Sky god, smith and giver of fire.

Svarozhich: Fire god; son of Svarog and brother of Dazhbog.

Veles: God of music, art, poetry and animals; sometimes associated with the underworld.

Central and South America
CHIEF CENTRAL AND SOUTH AMERICAN DEITIES

Ah Puch (Maya): God of death who rules the lowest underworld.

Ayar (Inca): Four legendary brothers from whom the Inca rulers traced their descent.

Chac (Maya): Rain god; lord of thunder, lightning and fertility.

Chalchihuitlicue (Aztec): Goddess who unleashed the deluge; wife of Tlaloc. Ruler of the fourth world.

Chicomecoatl (Aztec): Goddess of maize and plenty.

Coatlicue (Aztec): Bloodthirsty earth goddess; mother of Huitzilopochtli.

Ek Chuah (Maya): Fierce war god.

Huacas (Inca): Features of the landscape credited with sacred power.

Huehueteotl (Aztec): Ancient god of fire.

Huitzilopochtli (Aztec): 'Hummingbird of the South. God of war; son of Coatlicue.

Ilyap'a (Inca): God of weather.

Inti (Inca): Sun god; son of Viracocha and father of Manco Capac.

Itzamna (Maya): Chief god; son of Huntab.

Ixchel (Maya): Storm goddess, feared as the sender of floods.

Ixtab (Maya): Goddess of suicide.

Jaguar Sun God (Maya): During the day he is Kinich Ahau; at night he becomes the fearsome Jaguar God.

Kilya (Inca): Goddess of the moon; wife of Inti.

Kukulchan (Maya): Wind god and culture hero.

Manco Capac (Inca): Mythical founder of Cuzco; one of the Ayar.

Mictlantecuhtli (Aztec): God of death and ruler of Mictlan, the underworld.

Quetzalcoatl (Aztec): The 'plumed serpent', creator sky-god and ruler of the second and fifth worlds.

Tezcatlipoca (Aztec): God of war and night; ruler of the first world.

Tlaloc (Aztec): Rain god; ruler of the third world.

Viracocha (Inca): The supreme creator-deity.

Xipe Totec (Aztec): The 'flayed lord'. God of agriculture and human sacrifice.

Xochiquetzl (Aztec): Goddess of flowers and fruits who rules over beauty, love, happiness and youth.

AMAZON BASIN
PRINCIPAL DEITIES OF THE AMAZON

Iae (Mamaiuran): God of the Moon who, with Kuat, stole light from Urubutsin.

Kanassa (Kuikuru): Creator-deity.

Kuat (Mamaiuran): Sun god who stole light from the king of the birds.

Mavutsinim (Mamaiuran): Creator-god who turned a shell into a woman and begot the first man.

Nyami Abe (Tukano): Moon god banished by Page Abe.

Page Abe (Tukano): Sun god who created the earth.

Sinaa (Juruna): Cat-like ancestral god; son of a gigantic black jaguar and a mortal woman.

Uaica (Juruna): Great magician and medicine man.

Urubutsin (Mamaiuran): Vulture god; king of the birds, lightening and fire; son of Mawu and brother of Sagbata.

Unkulunkulu: Supreme ancestors created by sky god Umvelinqangi from reed.

China
PRINCIPAL CHINESE DEITIES

Chang O: Woman who became the moon goddess; consort of Yi.

Chu Jung/Zhu Rong: Fire god and wise ruler of the universe.

Di Jun: Great god of the eastern sky, father of the ten suns; husband of Xi He.

The Five Elements: The world is said to be composed of Wood, Fire, Soil, Metal and Water. Each element is associated with one of five seasons and five cardinal directions (each including a centre) and a planet.

Wood	Spring	East	Jupiter
Fire	Summer	South	Mars
Soil	Centre	Centre	Saturn
Metal	Autumn	West	Venus
Water	Winter	North	Mercury

The Five Mountains regarded as particularly sacred by Chinese rulers:

Hengshan (Northern Peak and Southern Peak)
Huashan (Western Peak)
Songshan (Central Peak)
Taishan (Eastern Peak).

Taishan, the birthplace of Confucius, is the most important. Its god is the 'Great Divine Ruler of the Eastern Peak'.

Fu Xi: Ancient creator -god transformed into the mythical first emperor; husband of Nu-gua.

Gong Gong: Water god who caused numerous floods; opponent of Zhu Rong.

Kuan-yin: Goddess of compassion who evolved from the Indian bodhisattva Avalokitesvara and protects women, children and sailors.

Long Dragons: Benevolent water gods associated with the emperor.

Nu-gua: Creator-goddess who fashioned the first humans; wife of Fu Xi.

Pa Hsien: Good men who became the Eight Immortals of Taoism.

Pan Gu: Primordial giant born from the cosmic egg and from whom all creation arose.

T'ien: The supreme being or principle; worshipped as Yu Huang.

Tripitaka: Monk who journeys west to bring the Buddhist scriptures back to China.

Xi He: Solar goddess; mother of the ten suns.

Xi Wangmu: Goddess of immortality known as the Queen Mother of the West. Personification of the female principle (yin); her husband Mu Gong personifies the male principle (yang). Daughter of Yu Huang.

Yi: Archer who saved the world by shooting down nine suns.

Yu: Legendary first mortal ruler who contained the waters of the deluge and founded the Xia Dynasty

Yu Huang: The Jade Emperor; supreme ruler of heaven.

Zao Chun/Tsao Chun: Popular kitchen deity; protector of the family.

Egypt
PRINCIPAL EGYPTIAN DEITIES

Aapep: Serpent who preyed on Re.

Amun: Ram-headed god and national deity.

Amun-Re: An assimilation of Amun and Re, worshipped as father of the pharaohs.

Atum-Re: An assimilation of Atum, the primeval creator-deity, and Re.

Anubis: Jackal-head funerary god and guardian of the underworld.

Apis or Hapi: Sacred bull; creator-deity of Memphis.

Aten: Worshipped by the pharaoh Akhenaton as the supreme creator-god.

Bast/Bastet: Cat goddess and daughter of Re.

Bes: Household god who protects children and families.

Buto: Ancient snake goddess who helped to protect Horus.

Geb: Earth god; consort of Nut and father of Osiris, Isis, Nephthys and Seth.

Hapi: River god who sent the annual flooding of the Nile.

Hapi (2): Son of Horus who protected the dead.

Harpokrates: Horus the child, sometimes regarded as a fertility god.

Hathor: Sky goddess depicted as a cow; mother of Horus.

Horus: Sky god equated in early times with the king.

Imhotep: Architect and doctor later worshipped as god of healing.

Isis: Egyptian mother goddess.

Khepra: A creator-deity associated with the scarab beetle.

Khnum: Ram-headed creator-god.

Khons: Moon deity and god of healing.

Maat: Goddess of truth and justice; daughter of Re.

Meshkent: Goddess who assisted in the birth of babies and in assigning their destinies.

Mnevis: The sacred 'bull of Heliopolis'; an agent of fertility.

Nepthys: Sister of Isis and Osiris and both consort and sister of Seth. Associated with death.

Nun: The primeval waters and source of creation.

Nut: Sky goddess raised by Shu above Geb.

Osiris: Dying and rising god; ruler of the underworld.

Ptah: Ancient god associated with creation.

Re/Ra: Ancient sun god and creator deity.

Renenutet: Goddess of agriculture, harvest and motherhood.

Sebek: Crocodile god.

Sekhmet: War goddess; wife of Ptah.

Serapis: State god of Egypt during the Macedonian occupation (305–30 BC); associated with fertility and the underworld.

Seth: Brother and opponent of Osiris.

Shu: God of air, created by Atum.

Tauret: Hippopotamus goddess; guardian of children and childbirth.

Tefnut: Goddess of moisture, created by Atum.

Thoth: Patron of learning and magical arts who recorded the weighing of souls when they entered the underworld.

HELIOPOLIS ENNEAD, OR NINE GODS OF HELIOPOLIS

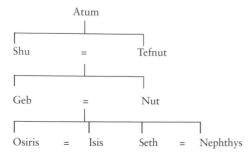

Atum
Shu = Tefnut
Geb = Nut
Osiris = Isis   Seth = Nephthys

Greece
PRINCIPAL GREEK DEITIES

Titans: Godlike giants, offspring of Ge and Ouranos: Kronos, Rhea, Iapetus, Themis, Okeanos, Tethys, Hyperion, Theia, Crius, Mnemosyne, Coeus and Phoebe.

Olympians: The gods who lived on Olympus, both heaven and a mountain in northern Greece. Led by Zeus, they ruled the universe after overthrowing the Titans.

Aphrodite: Goddess of love, beauty and fertility; daughter of Zeus and Dione.

Apollo: God of light, prophecy, medicine and learning. Son of Zeus and Leto; brother of Artemis.

Ares: God of war; son of Zeus and Hera.

Argos: Son of Zeus and the mortal Niobe.

Athene: Goddess of crafts and war; daughter of Zeus and Metis.

Artemis: Virgin goddess of the hunt; daughter of Zeus and Leto and sister of Apollo.

Demeter: Goddess of agriculture; sister of Zeus and mother of Persephone.

Deukalion: Survivor with his wife Pyrrha of the deluge; son of Prometheus and Clymene.

Dionysus: God of wine; son of Zeus and the mortal Semele.

Eileithyia: Goddess associated with childbirth; daughter of Zeus and Hera.

Ge/Gaea: Earth goddess born from the void; mother of Pontus, Ouranos, and many more supernatural beings.

Giants: Children of Ge.

Graces: Goddesses of charm and beauty; daughters of Zeus and Eurynome.

Hades: God of the dead; brother of Zeus and Poseidon.

Hebe: Goddess of youth; daughter of Zeus and Hera.

Helen: Daughter of Zeus and the mortal Leda; sister of Castor, Polydeuces and Clytemnestra: Her relationship with Paris sparked the Trojan War.

Hephaestus: God of fire and crafts; son of Zeus and Hera.

Hera: Wife of Zeus and Queen of the Olympians.

Herakles: Hero who performed the Twelve Labours; son of Zeus and the mortal Alcmene.

Hermes: Messenger of the gods and guide of souls to the Underworld; son of Zeus and a mountain nymph.

Hestia: Goddess of the hearth.

Horae (the Hours): Goddesses of the seasons, order and nature.

Iapetus: Son of Ge and Ouranos; father, by either Clymene or Asia, of Menoetius, Atlas, Prometheus, Epimetheus, and Hesperus.

Kronos: Son of Ge and Ouranos; brother and husband of Rhea. He became leader of the Titans.

Kyklopes: One-eyed giants who built Olympus for the gods; sons of Ge.

Lakedaemon: The son of Zeus and Taygete, one of the Pleiades.

Metis: Goddess of wisdom; daughter of Okeanos and first wife of Zeus.

Minos: Legendary king of Crete; son of Zeus and Europa.

Muses: Goddesses who presided over the arts and sciences.

Okeanos: Personification of the river that circles the earth; son of Ge and Ouranos.

Ouranos: Son and consort of Ge and father of the Titans.

Persephone: Daughter of Zeus and Demeter; abducted by Hades.

Perseus: Son of Zeus and Danae. He killed the gorgon Medusa.

Polydeuces: Son of Zeus and the mortal Leda; twin brother of Castor.

Pontus: Sea deity; son of Ge and Aether.

Poseidon: God of the sea, earthquakes and horses; brother of Zeus and Hades.

Prometheus: The wisest Titan; he gave fire to mankind.

Rhea: Wife of Kronos.

Zeus: Supreme god of the Olympians; youngest son of the Titans Kronos and Rhea.

GREEK-ROMAN PARALLELS

Roman	Greek
Jupiter	Zeus
Juno	Hera
Minerva	Athene
Apollo	Apollo
Diana	Artemis
Ceres	Demeter
Bacchus	Dionysus
Mars	Ares
Venus	Aphrodite
Neptune	Poseidon
Mercury	Hermes
Vesta	Hestia
Liber	Dionysus
Saturn	Kronos
Dis Pater	Hades
Faunus	Pan

Cupid	Eros
Vulcan	Hephaestus
Aesculapius	Asklepios
Castor and Pollux	Castor and Polydeukes

GREEK PRINCIPAL DEITIES

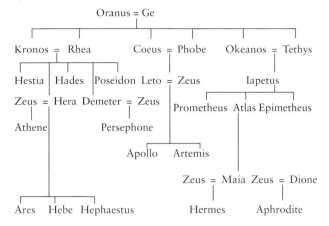

GODDESSES

Mother	Children
Calliope	Corybantes
Demeter	Persephone
Dione	Aphrodite
Eurynome	Graces
Hera	Ares, Eileithyia, Hebe, Hephaestus
Leto	Apollo, Artemis
Maia	Hermes
Metis	Athene
Mnemosyne	Muses
Semele	Dionysos
Taygete	Lakedaemon
Themis	Horae, Moerae

MORTALS

Mother	Children
Aegina	Aeacus
Alcmene	Herakles
Antiope	Amphion, Zethus
Callisto	Arcas
Danae	Perseus
Electra	Dardanus, Emathion, Harmonia, Iasion
Europa	Minos, Rhadamanthys, Sarpedon
Io	Epaphus
Laodamia	Sarpedon
Leda	Polydeuces, Helen
Niobe	Argos, Pelasgus
Pandora	Graecus, Latinus

India
PRINCIPAL INDIAN DEITIES

Aditi: Mother goddess usually regarded as the mother of Vishnu.

Adityas: Offspring of Aditi who offer salvation from all ills.

Agni: God of fire; a chief deity of the Rig Veda.

Ananta/Shesha: The coiled serpent of infinite time.

Ashvins: Twin horsemen, offspring of the sun.

Asuras: Supernatural beings at war with the Devas (gods).

Brahma: The creator and the personification of Brahman, the 'absolute' behind creation.

Buddha Gautama: the founder of Buddhism. Regarded as an avatar of Vishnu.

Durga: Terrifying mother goddess; wife of Shiva.

Dyaus: Sky god of the Vedic religion.

Gandharvas: Nature spirits associated with fertility.

Ganesha: Elephant-headed god of wealth and learning; son of Shiva and Parvati.

Ganga: Goddess of the river Ganges; associated with fertility.

Garuda: The half-eagle, half-human mount of Vishnu and Lakshmi.

Gauri: A form of Durga.

Gopis: Cow girls; consorts of the young Krishna.

Hanuman: Monkey god.

Hari-Hara: A synthesis of Shiva and Vishnu.

Himalaya: Mountain god; father of Ganga.

Indra: King of the gods.

Jyeshtha: Goddess of bad luck.

Kali: Terrifying aspect of the great mother goddess; wife of Shiva.

Kama: God of desire, sometimes said to have initiated creation.

Karttikeya: God of war; also called Skanda and Kumara.

Krishna: The divine hero, an avatar of Vishnu.

Lakshmi: A consort of Vishnu and goddess of beauty, pleasure and prosperity.

Manasha: Goddess of snakes.

Manu: The first man, saved from the flood by Matsya.

Mitra: God of light; son of Aditi.

Nagas: Semi-divine snakes associated with fertility.

Nandi: The white bull; a form and mount of Shiva.

Nataraja: A form of Shiva who dances out the creation of the world.

Parashurama: A human incarnation of Vishnu.

Parvati: Consort of Shiva and aspect of the mother goddess.

Prajapati: Lord of gods and demons and master of created beings.

Prithivi: Vedic earth goddess; consort of Dyaus.

Purusha: Primordial man from whose dismembered body the cosmos was made.

Radha: Krishna's favourite gopi.

Rama: Avatar of Vishnu who killed the demon Ravana.

Rudra: Vedic god of storms and disease.

Sati: First wife of Shiva.

Shakti: Female energy, the creative force of Shiva.

Shashti: Goddess who protects children and women in childbirth.

Shatala: Goddess of smallpox.

Shiva: Creator and destroyer; sometimes worshipped as the supreme deity.

Skanda: A warrior god, sometimes known as

Kartikkeya.

Soma: The vital life-force regarded as both a sacred drink and a deity.

Surya: God of the sun.

Tvashtar: Craftsman of the gods.

Uma: Another name for Shiva's consort.

Ushas: Goddess of the dawn and bringer of life.

Vach (Hindu): Goddess of speech.

Varuna: Great (though remote) sky god who oversaw the moral order.

Vishnu: The most widely worshipped Hindu god

Vivasvat: God of sunrise.

Yama: Lord of death and guardian of hell; son of Vivasvat.

THE TEN AVATARS OF VISHNU

Matsya: Fish who protects Manu, the first man.

Kurma: Turtle who supports Mount Mandara on his back during the churning of the ocean.

Varaha: Boar who rescues the earth from the ocean.

Narasimha: Man-lion who kills the demon Hiranyakashipu.

Vamana: Dwarf who saves the world from the demon Bali.

Parashurama: The Brahman who kills Arjuna.

Rama: Hero who kills the demon king Ravana.

Krishna: Hero whose words of encouragement to the warrior Arjuna form the *Bhagavad-Gita*.

The Buddha: The corrupter of demons.

Kalkin: Saviour, yet to come, who will establish a new era.

THE FIVE GREAT GODS

Vishnu

Shiva

Devi

Surya

Ganesha

Japan

PRINCIPAL JAPANESE DEITIES

Amasuhiko (Shinto): Son of Hikohohodemi and husband of Tamayori Hime.

Amaterasu (Shinto): Sun goddess and traditional founder of Japan; daughter of Izanagi.

Ame-no-oshiho-mimi (Shinto): Son of Amaterasu.

Amida (Buddhist): Deity to whom the dying turned.

Benten (Buddhist): Goddess of good fortune, love, wisdom and water.

Daikoku (Buddhist): God of wealth and happiness and patron of farmers.

Dainichi-Nyorai (Buddhist): Bodhisattva known as 'The Great Sun Buddha'.

Emma-O (Buddhist): Lord of the underworld.

Fugen Bosatsu (Buddhist): Bodhisattva of perfect beauty.

Hikohohodemi (Shinto): 'Fireshade'; great-grandson of Amaterasu and brother of Honosuseri.

Honinigi (Shinto): Grandson of Amaterasu and father of Honosuseri and Hikohohodemi.

Honosuseri (Shinto): 'Fireshine'; brother of Hikohohodemi and eldest son of Honinigi.

Hosho Nyorai (Buddhist): The element of fire; also called 'The Gem-Birth Buddha'.

Ida-ten (Buddhist): God of law and monasteries.

Izanagi (Shinto): The primordial sky god who together with Izanami created the world.

Izanami (Shinto): Earth goddess and sister of Izanagi. She later ruled the underworld.

Jimmu Tenno (Shinto): The first emperor and legendary founder of the imperial dynasty.

Jizo Bosatsu (Buddhist): Buddha of great compassion.

Kannon Bosatsu (Buddhist): The bodhisattva to whom childless women turn for help.

Kishi Mojin (Buddhist): Patron goddess of little children, originally a demon.

Kono-hana-sakuya-hime (Shinto): Wife of Honinigi.

Kusa-nada-hime (Shinto): The 'Rice Paddy Princess' whom Okuninushi rescued from a monster and married.

Miroku Bosatsu (Buddhist): Boddhisatva who will save the world of the future.

Okuninushi (Shinto): God of magic and medicine: son of Susano.

Rakan (Buddhist): A perfect saint, worshipped as a god.

Susano (Shinto): God of the winds, storms, and ocean; born from Izanagi's nose.

Suseri-hime (Shinto): Daughter of Susano and wife of Okuninushi.

Tamayori Hime (Shinto): Wife of Amasuhiko.

Toyotama-hime (Shinto): Wife of Hikohohodemi.

Tsuki-yomi (Shinto): God of the moon, born from Izanagi's right eye.

Watatsumi-no-kami (Shinto): God of the sea whose daughter married Hikohohodemi.

Ya-gami-hime (Shinto): Princess who married Okuninushi.

Yakushi-nyorai (Buddhist): Buddha of meditation and healing.

JAPAN: DESCENDANTS OF IZANAGI

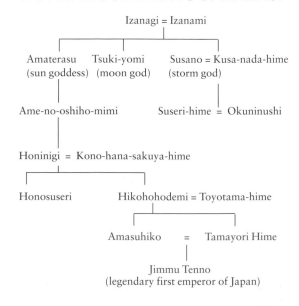

Korea
PRINCIPAL KOREAN DEITIES

Aryong Jong: Goddess of rainfall.

Chumong: Legendary founder of the Koguryeo kingdom in 37 BC; son of Haemosu and Yuhwa.

Habaek: Water deity; father of Yuhwa.

Haemosu: Sun god; father of Chumong.

Hwanin: Supreme god of heaven and earth.

Hwanung: Founder of the City of the Gods on Mount Tíaebaek; son of Hwanin.

Kim Suro: Traditional founder of the Kaya kingdom in the first century AD; said to have descended from heaven in a gold chest.

Kud: Personification of darkness and evil.

Palk: Founder of the realm of light.

Seok Tíalhae: Fourth king of Shilla, said to have hatched from an egg.

Songyang: Original king of Koguryeo; defeated by Chumong.

Tangun: Traditional founder of Choson, the first Korean kingdom; son of Hwanung.

Ung-yo: A bear who transformed into a beautiful woman, married Hwanung and gave birth to Tangun.

Yuhwa: Abducted by Haemosu, she laid an egg from which Chumong emerged; daughter of Habaek.

North America
PRINCIPAL NORTH AMERICAN DEITIES

Awonawilona (Pueblo/Zuni): Chief creator-deity.

Bears (widespread): A race with human form but who wear their bear coats in public.

Buffalo (widespread): Appear in many rituals; the White Buffalo represents wisdom.

Coyote (Southwestern Indians, but known in other areas): Creator, trickster, messenger and/or culture hero.

Dzoavits (Shoshonean): Ogre.

Enigorio and Enigonhahetgea (Northeastern tribes): Spirits of the woodland peoples.

Evening Star (Pawnee): Evil spirit who drives the sun out of the sky.

Kachinas (Hopi): Ancestral spirits, intermediaries between humans and the gods.

Kitcki Manitou (Algonquin): The Great Spirit.

Michabo (Algonquin): The 'great hare' and creator of the earth.

Morning star (Pawnee): Heavenly power who leads the sun into the sky.

Nanabozho (Ojibwa/Chippewa): Trickster hare.

Nanabush (Algonquin): Trickster hero; grandson of Nokomis.

Nokomis (Algonquin): Mother Earth.

Power of the Shining Heavens (Haida): The ultimate force in the universe.

Raven (Northwestern tribes): Trickster, culture hero or creator-deity.

Shakura (Pawnee): Sun god for whom the Pawnee

performed their famous Sun Dance.

Sin (Haida): Chief deity, a sky god.

Spider Man and Spider Woman (widespread): Usually beneficial, sometimes creators or tricksters.

Tawa (Pueblo): Spirit of the sun and creator of humans.

Thunder Beings (widespread): Powerful beings who sometimes help humans.

Thunderbird (widespread): A chief sky god, sometimes with the power of creation and destruction.

Tirawa (Pawnee/Nebraska): Creator of the heavens and earth.

Underwater panthers (widespread): Malevolent though wise gods of water and healing.

Wakan Tanka (Lakota): Great Spirit or Mystery.

Windigo (Ojibwa, Chippewa, Algonquin): Giant cannibals who feed upon humans when food is scarce.

Northern Europe
PRINCIPAL NORTH EUROPEAN DEITIES

Balder (Norse) Son of Odin and Frigg.

Bragi (Norse) God of eloquence. Son of Odin; married to Idun.

Donar (Germanic) God of sky and thunder.

Freyja (Norse) Goddess of witchcraft and fertility; leader of the Valkyries.

Freyr (Norse) Twin brother of Freyja; married to the giantess Gerd.

Frigg (Norse) Sky goddess; wife of Odin and mother of Balder and Hoth.

Heimdall (Norse) Watchman of the gods.

Hoenir (Norse) God known for his indecisiveness.

Holler (Norse) God of death and destruction.

Idun (Norse) Goddess of spring and eternal youth; wife of Bragi.

Loki (Norse) Trickster god.

Nehalennia (Holland) Goddess of vegetation, dogs and the sea.

Nerthus (Norse) Mother of Frey and Freyja.

Njord (Norse) God of the wind and the sea. Father of Freyr and Freyja by his sister, Nerthus; husband of Skadi.

Odin (Norse) Supreme god of wisdom, poetry, magic and war; father of the Aesir.

Thor (Norse) God of thunder and lightning, eldest son of Odin and Jord, the earth goddess.

Tiwaz (Germanic) God of law.

Tyr (Norse) God of war and justice; son of Odin and Frigg, brother of Thor.

Ull (Norse) God of hunting; stepson of Thor.

Wodan (Germanic) Alternate name for Odin.

SOME PRINCIPAL NORSE DEITIES

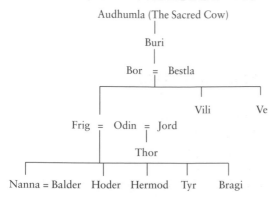

PRINCIPAL AESIR, THE RACE OF GODS WHO LIVED IN ASGARD

Odin (leader of the Aesir)
Balder
Bragi
Forseti
Freyja (originally a Vanir)
Freyr (originally a Vanir)
Frigg
Heimdall
Hodr
Idun
Loki
Njord (originally a Vanir)
Sif (possibly originally a Vanir)
Thor
Tyr
Ve
Vidar
Vili

PRINCIPAL VANIR, THE RACE OF GODS WHO LIVED IN VANAHEIM

Frejya
Freyr
Gerd
Gullveig
Kvasir
Nerthus
Njord
Sif
Skadi

Oceania

PRINCIPAL OCEANIC DEITIES

Haumia Tiketike (Polynesia): God of wild food; brother of Rongo.
Hina (Hawaii): Mother of Maui.
Kanaloa (Hawaii): God of the sea.
Kane (Hawaii): Male force of creation.
Ku (Hawaii): God of war, crops and craftsmen.
Lejman (Marshall Islands): The first woman who emerged with Wulleb, the first man, from the leg of Loa.
Loa (Marshall Islands): Creator-deity; father of Wulleb and Lejman.
Lono (Hawaii): Lord of the heavens.

Luk (Caroline Island): Chief deity.
Maui (Polynesia): Trickster god.
Na Atibu (Gilbert Islanders): Son of Nareau; with Nei Teukez, he gave birth to the gods.
Nareau (Gilbert Islands): Lord Spider, the creator of the universe.
Olofat (Caroline Islands): Son of Lugeilan who brought fire to earth.
Papa (Hawaii/Maori): 1. The Hawaiian earth goddess who married Wakea the first chieftain. 2. In Maori myth, consort of the sky god Rangi and mother of all creatures.
Pele (Hawaii): Goddess of the volcano.
Rangi (Maori): Sky god who fell in love with Papa.
Rongo-ma-Tane (Polynesian): God of peace and cultivated foods.
Taíaroa (Tahiti): Supreme god who emerged from the cosmic egg.
Tane-Mahuta (Maori): Lord of the forest; son of Rangi and Papa.
Tangaroa (Polynesia): Lord of the ocean who created all gods and people; son of Rangi and Papa.
Tawhiri-Matea (Maori): God of storms; son of Rangi and Papa.
Tu Matavenga (Maori): Warrior god; son of Rangi and Papa.

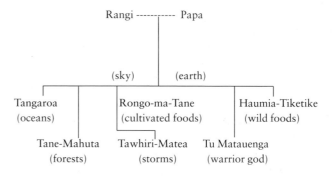

Rome

PRINCIPAL ROMAN DEITIES

Aeneas: Son of Anchises and Venus; mythical ancestor of the Romans.
Bacchus: God of wine and intoxication.
Bellona: Goddess of war, associated with Mars.
Bona Dea: Fertility goddess; daughter of Faunus.
Ceres: Goddess of grain and agriculture; daughter of Saturn and mother of Proserpina.
Dido: Queen of Carthage who fell in love with Aeneas.
Dis Pater: Ruler of the Underworld.
Janus: God of gates and doors.
Jupiter: Supreme sky god, son and consort of Juno.
Juno: Queen of the gods. Daughter of Saturn and consort of Jupiter; mother of Jupiter, Mars and Vulcan.
Liber: Ancient god of fertility.
Magna Mater: Roman name for the Phrygian mother goddess Cybele.
Mars: God of war; father of Romulus and Remus.
Ops: Earth goddess; sister and wife of Saturn.
Quirinus: Ancient deity later associated with Jupiter.

Rhea Silvia: The Vestal virgin who became, by Mars, the mother of Romulus and Remus.

Roma: Goddess of the city of Rome.

Romulus and Remus: Founders of Rome; twin sons of Mars and Rhea Silvia.

Saturn: God of agriculture; husband of Ops.

Sol: Sun god. Sol Invictus became god of the state.

Tellus: Goddess of the earth.

Terminus: God of boundaries; associated with Jupiter.

Venus: Goddess of vegetation, later of love and beauty.

Vesta: Goddess of the hearth.

Vulcan: God of fire and craftsmanship.

Southeast Asia
PRINCIPAL SOUTHEAST ASIAN DEITIES

Ara (Borneo/Dayak): Bird deity who formed the sky from an egg floating on the primordial ocean.

Au-Co (Vietnam): Goddess from the 36th heaven who married Lac Long Quang and bore 100 children.

Batara Kala (Bali): God who rules the underworld cave.

Boru Deak Paradjur (Indonesia/Sumatra): Daughter of Batara Guru.

Dewi Shri (Bali): Rice goddess; ruler of the underworld and moon.

Drestarata (Java): Blind king who fathered the Korawas.

Guriang Tunggal (Java/Sundanese): The supreme god; father of Guru Minda.

Guru Minda (Java/Sundanese): 'Black Monkey'; son of Guriang Tunggal and Ambu Dewi.

Hainuwele (Indonesia/Ceram): Goddess who provided humanity with cultural artefacts.

Ho Dong Dinh (Vietnan): Water goddess; mother of Lac Long Quan.

Irik (Borneo/Dayak): Bird deity who formed the earth from an egg floating on the primordial ocean.

Kinh Duong Vuong (Vietnam): Mountain god; father of Lac Long Quan.

Korawas (Java): The 100 wicked sons of King Drestara.

Manuk Patiaraja (Sumatra/Batak): Wife of Mulajadi na Bolon; mother of Batara Guru, Soripada, and Mangala Bulan.

Moyang Melur (Malaysia/Ma'Betisek): Spirit who guards the rules of civilized behaviour.

Mulajadi na Bolon (Sumatra/Batak): Supreme god.

Nagas (Southeast Asia): Serpents or dragons, rulers of the Underworld.

Naga Padoha (Sumatra/Batak): Great sea serpent who sought to destroy the first solid land.

Po Yan Dari (Cambodia): Goddess of disease.

Preas Eyn (Cambodia): Khmer thunder god.

Preas Eyssaur (Cambodia): Khmer god of death and new life.

Preas Prohm (Cambodia): Primeval god of the Khmer.

Pulang Gana (Borneo/Dayak): Earth spirit who ensures plentiful rice.

Raksasa (Indonesia): Demon of the wilderness.

Tadaklan (Philippines/Tinguian): God of thunder.

Tingang (Borneo/Dayak): Sky god who created the world tree.

Tibet
PRINCIPAL TIBETAN DEITIES

Ancient Kings (Bon): Seven rulers who descended from the sky and at the end of their reigns returned by a rope. The last cut the rope.

bDud (Bon): Heavenly spirits.

Beg-tse (Bon): God of war.

Brag-srin-mo (Bon): Goddess who gave birth to the first Tibetans.

bTsan (Bon): Demons who attack humans.

Chenrezi (sPyan-ras-gzigs) (Buddhist): Bodhisattva of compassion, equivalent to Avalokiteshvara.

Dhyani Buddhas (Buddhism): Five Buddhas usually identified as Vairocana, Aksobhya, Ratnasambhava, Amitabha, and Amoghasiddhi.

dMu (Bon): Group of country gods.

Drag-shed (Buddhist): Terrifying though benevolent deities; protectors of the dharma.

Gesar (Buddhist): Mythical king regarded as god of war and wealth.

gNyan (Bon): Spirits who live in trees and stones and send disease and death on mankind.

gShen-Lha-od-Dkar (Bon): God of white light who gave rise to all other gods.

gShen-Rab (Bon): Traditional founder of the later form of Bon religion.

Khadromas (Buddhist): Low-ranking goddesses usually represented as naked women who fly through the sky. (Skt = Dakini.)

Krodhadevatas (Buddhist): Terror-inspiring gods.

Lha (Bon): General term for deities.

Lhamo (Bon/Buddhism): Fierce goddess or demon.

Myal ba nag po (Black Misery) (Bon): Creator-deity. When he merged with White Radiance, five elements appeared: hardness, fluidity, heat, motion and space.

Padmasambhava: Legendary Indian mystic said to have brought Buddhism to Tibet in the eighth century AD.

Sa-bdag (Bon): Spirits who inhabit springs, fields, lakes and houses.

Tara (Buddhist): Female deity associated with compassion.

Vajra (Buddhist): 'Thunderbolt Sceptre'.

Yidam (Buddhist): Tantric tutelary deities who assist individuals' transformation.

Glossary

AETIOLOGY The use of natural events as part of religious ceremonies and rituals in primitive cultures. Today the term is also applied to the study of causation and natural phenomena.

AFTERLIFE The place where the spirit is believed to go after death. The Afterlife is known by many names across different cultures and religions, including the Underworld, Paradise, Hades and Heaven.

AGES OF MAN In Greek mythology the dawn of time was followed by five clearly-defined eras, known as the ages of man. These were the Golden Age, characterized by perfection and innocence; the Silver Age, an era of hardship and decay; the Brazen Age, a period of war and strife; the Heroic Age, when the world was populated by demigods and heroes; and the Iron Age, in which life was all toil and degradation, lacking in virtue and ideals.

ALCHEMY An early form of chemistry, dating from medieval times, which sought to transform base metals into gold; it was also concerned with creating an elixir which would prolong life or even render the drinker immortal.
See also Elixir

ALLEGORY A story, poem or picture which has both a literal and underlying meaning; allegory, a way of describing one thing as another, was often used in storytelling to teach a moral lesson.

AMAZONS In Greek mythology, a race of female warriors believed to live in Scythia; in the legend of Hercules one of his labours was to obtain the girdle of the Amazonian queen Hipployta.

ANCESTORS The first humans, from whom all members of a tribe or clan are descended, and who continue to watch over their progeny. Often regarded as creator-beings, ancestors are frequently deified and worshipped as the masters and controllers of a particular race.

ANDROGYNOUS A state in which a person or deity has both male and female characteristics.

ANIMISM The belief that spirits inhabited natural objects such as trees, stones and rivers; often applied by cultures or societies that lived closely with nature, and used to explain their movement and changing forms.
See also Transformation

ANTHROPOLOGY The academic study of human origins, evolution and the differences in global cultures and lifestyles which arose after the publication of Darwin's theories in the nineteenth century.

ANTHROPOMORPHISM The state in which a deity, animal or inanimate object takes on human form and characteristics.

ASCETICISM A central practice in religions such as Theravada Buddhism and Jainism, by which the follower abstains from all worldly pleasures and indulgences and exerts strict self-discipline.

ASSYRIA One of the kingdoms of ancient Mesopotamia in the area that is now northern Iraq. It arose in the second millennium BC and reached its height in the eighth century BC, by which time its empire extended as far as Egypt. Assyria was subsumed into the Babylonian Empire in 612 BC.

AUTOCHTHONY The ancestry and associated spiritual connection with the Earth which is a common belief in many indigenous and aboriginal societies.

AVATAR From the Sanskrit word avatara ('descent'). In Hinduism, deities are believed to descend to Earth whenever there is an increase in evil; the incarnation of a deity in human or animal form is called an avatar. Krishna, for example, is an avatar of the god Vishnu.

AZTECS A Central American civilization, centred on the advanced city of Tenochtitlán, which grew up around Mexico from the twelfth century AD; characterized by sun worship, human sacrifice and control by despotic rulers. The Aztecs were conquered by the Spanish in 1532.

BABYLONIA An ancient civilization in Mesopotamia, on the banks of the Euphrates river, present-day Iraq. It was formed from the assimilation of the Sumerian and Akkadian Empires in the second millennium BC. Babylonia eventually became part of Assyria and was conquered by the Persian Cyrus the Great in 539 BC.
See also Assyria, Persia, Sumer

BODHISATTVA In Mahayana Buddhism, an enlightened person who delays his final liberation through nirvana to remain on Earth and help others.
See also Buddhism

BON An extremely ancient religion indigenous to Tibet, in which the region was represented as a eight-leafed lotus plant. Bon takes the swastika as its symbol, standing for permanence and indestructability.

BRAHMAN In Hinduism, a member of the highest caste, the priesthood; also in Hinduism, the concept of the Universal Being and the absolute reality.

BUDDHA Name applied specifically to Siddharta Gautama (c.563–c.460 BC), the Indian founder of Buddhism, who renounced material possessions to become an ascetic and later achieved enlightenment. The name has subsequently been given to other humans who have reached this state.
See also Buddhism

BUDDHISM The philosophical and religious following derived from the teaching of the Buddha, Siddharta Gautama in the sixth century BC. Buddhism is based on the principles that worldly suffering can be brought to an end by the abandonment of material possessions, overcoming greed, hatred and desire and through this the cycle of karma, which will lead to the attainment of nirvana, a state of enlightenment. Buddhists worship no gods and the central tenets are the Four Noble Truths and the Eightfold Path. The two major Buddhist traditions are Theravada, which focuses on asceticism and meditation, and the less austere Mahayana, which values outward practices as well as inward meditation.

CANAANITES Peoples from the biblical areas of Syria and Palestine, known as Canaan, which they occupied during the second millennium BC after their exodus from Egypt. Canaanite gods were closely associated with nature and fertility.

CANNIBALISM The practice of eating human flesh, found in some ancient and primal religions.

CARGO CULT Name given to any Melanesian religious movement, mostly originating in the nineteenth century, which follows the belief that the new millennium will bring forth the spirits of the dead carrying goods to be shared amongst its people; adherents look forward to this as a golden age when they will be reconciled with their ancestors.

CELTS The pre-Roman people inhabiting ancient Gaul, Spain and Britain. The Celtic civilization originated in the Bronze Age and reached its height in the fifth century BC. The Celts were eventually overrun by the invading Romans and later the Germanic peoples of northern Europe. They were an artistic people, with a social hierarchy led by the Druid priests.

CHRISTIANITY One of the great monotheistic religions, along with Judaism and Islam, and today the most widespread, with more than a billion followers largely divided between the three main denominations: Roman Catholic, Protestant and Eastern Orthodox. Christianity is based on the life and teachings of Jesus Christ, believed to be the Son of God, who came to Earth, suffered persecution and was crucified, but rose again and ascended into heaven. The life of Christ is recounted in the New Testament of The Bible, Christianity's holy book.

CLAN A social grouping of families descended from a common ancestor; in some primal religions this is believed to be a spirit ancestor.
See also Kinship

CONFUCIANISM An Eastern religion based on the teachings of the Chinese philosopher Confucius (551–479 BC), emphasizing moral values, the importance of family, and a striving for social order, peace and harmony. His ideas are collected in the *Analects of Confucius.*

COSMIC EGG A key part of the Creation myth in some cultures, wherein the pre-Creation universe was contained within a cosmic egg, symbolizing birth and reproduction. From this was created the Earth and all the objects in it.

COSMOGONY The academic study of the origin of the Universe.

COSMOLOGY The academic study of the origin and nature of the Universe.

CREATOR-GOD In many Creation myths, the world was formed by a supreme and omnipotent being or beings. Sometimes this was thought to be an ancestor, sometimes an intangible force. Often creator-gods were believed to control human destinies and to wield the power of life and death, happiness and suffering.

CULTURE HERO A mythological protagonist who either creates or saves the Earth from disaster, thus preserving a culture and allowing for its continued development.

DEGENERATION The corruption of myths through the infiltration and influence of different cultures and religions. Eventually, through the process of degeneration, the original mythology is lost completely.

DEITY Generic term for any god or goddess.

DEMIGOD A term used either to refer to a lesser god in a pantheon or to a being who is part god, part human.

DIVINATION The practice of finding out about the future supposedly through supernatural methods.

DOPPELGÄNGER From the German ('double-goer'), an apparition or duplicate of a living person.

DREAMTIME Part of the Australian Aboriginal Creation myth, the time when the Earth was formed and inhabited by ancestral beings, who roamed all over it, creating humans, trees, rivers and other natural elements, giving names to places and tribes.

DUALISM The belief in two opposing universal powers: good and evil. Also used in Christian theology to explain the two co-existing – human and divine – natures embodied in Jesus Christ.

ECOGEOGRAPHICAL SYSTEM The geographical and environmental position of a civilization or people, which often combined to influence their mythology and culture.

ELIXIR A magical (and mythical) potion sought by medieval alchemists that was capable of transforming base metals into gold and prolonging human life. *See also Alchemy*

ENLIGHTENMENT In Buddhist belief, the final release from the endless cycle of death and reincarnation, when the soul is awakened to the reality of itself, the human and spiritual worlds. *See also Buddhism, Meditation*

FERTILITY DEITY A god or goddess believed to have powers over reproduction in the human and natural world. Fertility deities were often worshipped in communities that depended on agriculture for their survival.

FETISH An inanimate object believed to be possessed of supernatural powers or inhabited by a member of the spirit world and thus having religious or magical significance.

FOUNDATION MYTH Any myth concerned with the creation of the Earth, humans and their system of beliefs. Foundation or Creation myths are to be found in most religions and civilizations.

GAULS The peoples who inhabited the region of Europe known as Gaul, which comprised much of modern-day France, Belgium and the Netherlands. The Gauls were slowly overcome by the Romans over a period of 250 years from around 222 BC.

GENEALOGY The continuous line of descent that can be traced from one ancestor.

GERMANIC PEOPLES The name given to the tribal peoples who spread and settled across northern Europe after the decline of the Roman Empire. They are defined by the Germanic language they spoke in contrast to Celtic, Slavic or Latin-speaking peoples. Their religion and mythology is based on a large pantheon of gods and human-like creatures, and the opposing forces of good and evil.

GOD Specifically (used with an upper-case G), the name given to the Creator and Supreme Being in Christian, Jewish and Islamic theology, the universal power and source of moral authority. More generally the term is used (with a lower-case g) to refer to any divine or supernatural being who exercises some form of control over the human world.

GOLDEN AGE The name given by Classical poets to the dawn of time, the first period in history, when humans lived in an idyllic state characterized by peace and prosperity, before evil invaded Earth.

GUARDIAN SPIRIT A protective spirit who safeguards humans against disaster and evil, often seen as an angel or the soul of a tribal ancestor. Belief in guardian spirits was widespread in ancient and indigenous cultures.

HEADS In many civilizations, such as that of the Celts, the cult of the head was significant. It was believed that a person's soul resided in their head and often captured enemies would be beheaded in order to possess the soul. Heads are a frequent symbol in ancient art and sculpture.

HEAVEN In Christianity, the place where God resides and where the good go when they die to be with Him for eternity; traditionally depicted as a realm above the sky. In other cultures, heaven refers to the home of the gods.

HELL In Christianity, the place where the wicked go when they die, representing a total and eternal separation from God; traditionally depicted as a realm below the Earth. In other cultures hell is seen as a place of suffering and evil, often depicted as a kingdom of fire.

HINDUISM Major polytheistic religion founded in India, developed from the ancient Vedic tradition and comprising a number of different cults with a common belief in a vast pantheon of deities, reincarnation, and a social structure based on the caste system. Hinduism has no ecclesiastical structure and draws on several sacred texts for its philosophy, including the *Vedas*, the *Upanishads* and the *Bhagavad Gita*.

HITTITE An ancient empire in Asia Minor and Syria which reached its peak between 1700 and 1200 BC.

ICONOGRAPHY The worship of icons – symbolic objects such as the crucifix, which have a particular significance to a religion of culture. Especially popular in Eastern Orthodox Christianity where they are used as devotional aids.

IMMORTALITY A state in which a being will never decay or die.

INCAS A Central Andean civilization established in around AD 1100 and centred on Peru. The Inca religion was based on divination, ritual and sacrifice. A technologically advanced civilization, the Incas were conquered by the Spanish in 1532, but their descendants still survive in parts of Peru.

INCANTATION The chanting of words or sounds during a religious or magical ritual by either an individual or a group, often to cast spells.

INCARNATION The manifestation of a deity in human form. In Christianity, the doctrine that God became human in the form of Jesus Christ. In Hinduism the embodiment of gods in human or animal form is known as an avatar.
See also Avatar

INDIGENOUS Originating and belonging naturally to a certain country or area.

INITIATION A ceremony in many religions and cultures by which boys (and sometimes girls) undertake a number of tests and lessons as a rite of passage to adulthood.

ISLAM One of the great monotheistic religions, along with Christianity and Judaism, and today with nearly one billion adherents, the Islamic religion is based on the teachings of the seventh century AD Muhammad, the Prophet of Allah and last in a line of Prophets that included Abraham, Moses and Jesus. The teachings are to be found in the Islamic holy book, the *Qur'an*, which details the revelations granted to Muhammad by Allah. Islam emphasizes the omnipotence of the one God and the importance of daily worship. The two major Islamic traditions are Sunni and Shi'ite.

JAINISM Ancient Indian religion founded in the sixth century BC by the Jina Vardhamana Mahavira. Jainism is non-theistic and is based on the principles of compassion for all living creatures, the attainment of salvation through reincarnation and most notably for its asceticism. It is still practised in some areas of India.

JUDAISM One of the great monotheistic world religions, along with Christianity and Islam, Judaism originated from the religion of the ancient people of Israel and the roots of its theology are based in God's covenant with Abraham and the word of God as revealed to Moses. Worship was once centred on the Temple in Jerusalem, but since its destruction in AD 70 the home and synagogue have become focal points for Jewish ritual. Jews observe the Sabbath and many holy days, including Yom Kippur, Hannukah and Passover. The sacred texts are the *Torah* and the *Talmud.*

KINSHIP Relationships formed by family or marriage within clans and tribes; these relationships were often characterized by common cultural rules and customs.
See also Clans

MAORIS The indigenous peoples of New Zealand, whose population was threatened by the arrival of European settlers, but which has since experienced a revival.

MATRIARCHAL SOCIETY A society or culture of which the female is head and in which ancestry is traced through the female line, or one which worships female deities.
See also Patriarchal society

MAYAS A Central American civilization centred on the city of Yucatán, but whose empire stretched to parts of southern Mexico and Guatemala at its height between AD 300 and 900. The importance of ceremony to the Mayas can be seen in the remains of the stone pyramidal temples and their religion comprised many gods and ritual human sacrifice.

MEDITATION An act of deep spiritual contemplation performed by an individual with the aim of achieving inner peace or self-knowledge, particularly important in Buddhist practices. In other cultures, a shaman might induce a state of meditation in order to communicate with the spirit world.

MESOAMERICA The term used to define the parts of Central America where various civilizations shared common religious and cultural features. Mesoamerican civilizations include the Olmec, Aztec and Mayan.

MESOPOTAMIA A large region of southwest Asia, situated between the rivers Tigris and Euphrates in modern Iraq. Mesopotamia was home to some of the greatest of the ancient civilizations, including Assyria, Sumer and Babylon, and was established in around 3500 BC.
See also Assyria, Babylonia, Sumer

METAMORPHOSIS The transformation of one animate or inanimate object into another, encompassing a complete change of physical form or substance, often through spiritual means or intervention.

MONOTHEISM A belief in only one God, Creator or Supreme Being. Of the world religions Christianity, Islam and Judaism are monotheistic.

MUMMIFICATION The practice of preserving human or animal bodies after death in the belief that they will be needed in the Afterlife. The ritual was particularly significant to the ancient Egyptians and involved removing and separately preserving the internal organs, embalming the body and hen wrapping it in bandages before burial.

MUSES In Greek mythology, the name given to the nine daughters of the god Zeus and Mnemosyne, who were the protectors and embodiment of the arts and sciences. The Nine Muses were Calliope (epic poetry), Clio (history), Euterpe (flute playing), Terpsichore (dancing and song), Erato (lyre playing and lyric poetry), Melpomene (tragedy), Thalia (comedy and verse), Polyhymnia (hymns), Urani (astronomy).

MYSTERY RELIGIONS In ancient Greek and Roman times, the name given to the secret rituals of the pagan cults that dominated the empire. The term is also used more generally to describe any religion focussing on secret or mystical rites.

NATURE SPIRITS Spirits, often thought to be those of ancestors, which were believed to inhabit natural features such as trees and rivers; common in animist cultures.
See also Animism, Transformation

OCEANIA The collective name for the Pacific islands, usually divided into three main regions: Melanesia, the collection of larger islands above Australia; Micronesia, the scattered islands inhabited by peoples of Asian origin; and Polynesia, encompassing Hawaii, New Zealand and Easter Island.

ORAL TRADITION Fundamental to many tribal societies, oral tradition is the passing down of myths and histories in the form of stories or narratives through the generations. Mainly used in cultures without a written tradition, the oral tradition was typically perpetuated by the tribal elders or sometimes the shaman.

PAGANISM A term used since the fourteenth century AD to describe anyone who did not follow one of the world's major religions, in particular those who resisted Christianity. Paganism was associated with superstition, magic and secret ritual.

PANTHEON The collective name for the gods of a particular polytheistic culture or religion.

PATRIARCHAL SOCIETY A society or culture ruled by men and in which the lines of ancestry are traced through the males.
See also Matriarchal society

PERSIA A country in southwest Asia, now Iran. The great Persian civilization grew up under the Achaemenid kings in the sixth century BC, reaching its peak under Cyrus the Great. The empire fell to Alexander the Great in 330 BC.

PHALLIC SYMBOL A representation of the penis in carving or art, often the focus for worship in patriarchal societies and used to pray to the gods for male fertility.
See also Patriarchal society

PLURALISM The presence in a particular society of a number of diverse ethnic or religious groups, characterized by tolerance and harmonic co-existence.

POLYTHEISM A belief in more than one god, with each member of the pantheon often having a specific area of rule over human life. Hinduism is an example of a polytheistic religion.

PROPHECY A prediction of the future or a message in which God's will is revealed, usually through a soothsayer, seer or prophet, in whom this is a special gift.

REINCARNATION Implicit to many cultures and religions, the belief that when a human dies their soul is reborn in another form, either animal or human. Many religions believe in a cycle of reincarnation in which a person's behaviour in this life dictates their form in the next and which is a continual process only ended when a state of true self-awareness and goodness is attained.

RESURRECTION In Christian theology, the rising of Christ on the third day after his crucifixion; also the rising of the dead on the Day of Judgement in Christian, Jewish and Islamic doctrine. Many ancient cultures also believed in resurrection and rebirth.

RITUALS Religious ceremonies comprising a series of actions played out in a fixed order. These often include dancing, singing and incantations, and are performed on occasions of significance such as births and deaths.

SAGA Originally a Scandinavian oral tradition, which began to be recorded in the eleventh century, consisting of prose narratives dealing with heroic adventures or royal family histories, usually from Norway or Iceland.

SAKTISM One of the major sects in the Hindu religion, characterized by worship of the Sakti – the divine energy.

SHAMANISM The oldest-known form of organized religion, originating in Asia, but now disseminated worldwide, based on a belief in spirits who are either good or evil, and who can be communicated with or controlled only by the priests or shaman.
See also Shamans

SHAMANS The powerful priests of the ancient Shamanic religion; they were believed to transcend the human and spiritual worlds, belonging to neither completely. They were often visionaries, practising supernatural powers through means of trance and ritual, whereby they could communicate with the spirit world and perform acts of healing.
See also Shamanism

SHAPE-SHIFTING The ability of a spirit or deity to transform from one shape to another, human, animal or natural.
See also Animism, Transformation

SHINTO A religion exclusively practised in Japan and characterized by ancestor worship and a belief in the sacred power of kami, which manifested itself in both animate and inanimate objects. For many years Shinto was the state religion of Japan, but this was abandoned in 1945.

SUMER A region of southwest Asia, now Iraq, which was part of ancient Mesopotamia. Sumer was divided into a number of city-states which were eventually subsumed by the Babylonian Empire.
See also Babylonia

SUPREME BEING The life force, often the creator, of the human and natural worlds. The Supreme Being takes different forms and is given different names in a variety of cultures but is an almost universal concept.

SYNCRETISM The absorption and combination of a number of different ideologies and their associated myths and beliefs to form a new religious or philosophical tradition.

TABOO A religious – and more recently social – custom which prohibits or restricts certain rituals or practices; these vary from culture to culture but often include behaviour such as incest or iconoclasm. The word comes from the Polynesian tabu, meaning 'that which is forbidden'.

TANTRISM In Hinduism and Buddhism, a method by which a person can increase their psycho-sexual energy through concentrating on a series of focal points called chakra.

TAOISM An ancient Chinese philosophy, later developed into a religion, based on the teachings of Lao-tsu and taking the Tao Te Ching as its central text. Taoism is based around the principles of leading a simple, humble and honest life characterized by religious piety and a union with nature, in order to achieve the Tao ('way'). By the third century AD Taoism had assumed many aspects of the Buddhist faith, including a monastic system

THERIOMORPHIC From the Greek therio ('beast') and morphe ('shape'); the process of a deity taking the form of an animal on their descent to Earth. Although frequently depicted physically in paintings and carvings, it can also be emotional or spiritual.

TOTEM Any emblem or symbol that is deemed sacred to a clan or tribe. Most famous are the carved totem poles of the North Americans and other tribes, but a totem could take the form of an animal, plant or other natural object.

TRANCE A state of being, often induced by drugs, in which a person is unable to act of their own free will; shamans often fell into trances in order to better act as intermediary between the human and spiritual worlds.
See also Shamans

TRANSFORMATION The metamorphosis of one object – animate or inanimate – into another, frequently human to animal.
See also Animism

VOODOO A black religious cult practised in the West Indies, particularly Haiti and Jamaica, parts of the African coast and the southern United States. Voodoo is based around ancestor worship, sorcery and superstition, taking the form of magical rites and ceremonies.

WITCH-DOCTOR In tribal societies, a man believed to possess supernatural powers of harm and healing. Both feared and revered, the witch-doctor would be approached to cure the sick, put curses on enemies and offer protection.

WORLD TREE In Norse mythology the World Tree, Yggdrasill, was the axis of the Universe; home to many creatures, including a wise eagle and an evil serpent, the World Tree was their source of life and would never wither or die. It represents the separation of the Earth from the sky and is often seen as a microcosm of the Earth.

YIN AND YANG Two of the main principles of Chinese philosophy about the Universe. Yin is the female principle, passive, negative, dark and cold; Yang is the male principle, active, positive, bright and warm. The interplay between these two complementary principles is key to the doctrines of Confucianism.

ZOROASTRIANISM Ancient Persian religion founded by the Prophet Zoroaster in the sixth century BC and still followed in parts of Iran and India. Zoroastrians (or Parsees) believe in one God, Ahura Mazda, who gave birth to the twin spirits of good and evil. The principles of the religion are founded in the continual struggle between these two concepts.

Bibliography

GENERAL

Campbell, Joseph, *The Masks of God*, Harmondsworth, 1982

Dundes, Alan (ed.), *The Sacred Narrative: readings in the theory of myth*, Berkeley, 1984

Elide, Mircea, *Cosmos and History: the Myth of the Eternal Return*, New York, 1955, rep. 1985

Lévi-Strauss, Claude, *Myth and Meaning*, London, 1978

Maranda, Pierre, *Mythology: selected readings*, Harmondsworth, 1972

Propp, Vladimir, *Morphology of the Folktale*, Austin, 1968

ANCIENT NEAR EAST

Black, J. and A. Green, *Gods, Demons and Symbols of Ancient Mesopotamia: An Illustrated Dictionary*, London, 1992

Boyce, Mary, *Zoroastrians, their Beliefs and Practices*, London, 1979

Brandon, S. G. F., *Creation Legends of the Ancient Near East*, London, 1963

Clifford, R. J., *Creation Accounts in the Ancient Near East and in the Bible*, Washington, 1994

Dalley, S., *Myths from Mesopotamia, Creation, the Flood, Gilgamesh and Others*, Oxford and New York, 1989

de Moor, J. C., *An Anthology of Religious Texts from Ugarit*, Leiden and New York, 1987

Gershevitch, I., *The Avestan Hymn to Mithra*, Cambridge, 1959

Gibson, J. C. L., *Canaanite Myths and Legends*, Edinburgh, 1978

Gray, J., *Near Eastern Mythology*, London, 1969

Gurney, O., *Some Aspects of Hittite Religion*, Oxford, 1977

Hinnells, J. R., *Persian Mythology*, London, 1973

Kovacs, M. G. *The Epic of Gilgamesh*, Stanford, 1989

Kramer, S. N., *Sumerian Mythology* (revised edn.), New York, 1961

Leick, G., *A Dictionary of Ancient Near Eastern Mythology*, London, 1991, 1999

Olmstead, A. T., *History of the Persian Empire*, Chicago, 1948

Ringgren, H., *Religions of the Ancient Near East*, London/Philadelphia, 1973

Saggs, H. W. F., *The Greatness that was Babylon*, London, 1962

EGYPT

A Dictionary of Egyptian Gods and Goddesses, London, 1986

Clayton, Peter A., *Egyptian Mythology*, London, 1998

Faulkner, R. O. (ed. C. Andrews), *The Ancient Egyptian Book of the Dead*, London, 1985

Hart, George, *Egyptian Myths*, London, 1990

Lichtheim, M., *Ancient Egyptian Literature*, 3 vols., Berkeley, 1973, 1976, 1980

Quirke, Stephen, *Ancient Egyptian Religion*, London, 1992

Rundle Clark, R. T., *Myth and Symbol in Ancient Egypt*, London, 1959

Shafer, B. (ed.), *Religion in Ancient Egypt: gods, myths and personal practice*, London, 1991

Spencer, A. J., *Death in Ancient Egypt*, Harmondsworth, 1982

Thomas, A. P., *Egyptian Gods and Myths*, 1986

GREECE AND ROME

Bremmer, Jan and Nicholas Horsfall, *Roman Myth and Mythography*, London 1987

Blake Tyrrell, W. and Frieda Brown, *Athenian Myths and Institutions*, Oxford, 1991

Carpenter, T. H., *Art and Myth in Ancient Greece*, London, 1991

Dodds, E. R., *The Greeks and the Irrational*, Berkeley, 1951

Donaldson, I., *The Rapes of Lucretia: a myth and its transformations*, Oxford, 1982

Easterling, P. E. and J. V. Muir (eds.), *Greek Religion and Society*, Cambridge, 1985

Gordon, R., L. (ed.), *Myth, Religion and Society*, Cambridge, 1981

Gransden, K. W., *Virgil, the Aeneid*, Cambridge, 1990

Kerenyi, C., *The Heroes of the Greeks*, London, 1974

Morford, Mark and Robert Lenardon, *Classical Mythology*, New York, 1991

Ogilvie, R. M., *The Romans and their Gods*, London, 1969

Perowne, S., *Roman Mythology*, Twickenham, 1983

Powell, Barry, *Classical Myth*, New Jersey, 1998

Scullard, H. H., *Festivals and Ceremonies of the Roman Republic*, London, 1981

Stanford, W. B., *The Ulysses Theme*, Oxford, 1963

Vernant, J.-P. (trans. Janet Lloyd), *Myth and Society in Ancient Greece*, New York, 1990

Wardman, A., *Religion and Statecraft at Rome*, London, 1982

Wiseman, Peter, *A Roman Myth*, Cambridge, 1996

THE CELTS

Cotterell, Arthur, *Celtic Mythology*, England, 1997

Delaney, Frank, *Legends of the Celts*, England, 1989

Green, Miranda J., *Dictionary of Celtic Myth and Legend*, London 1992

James, Simon, *Exploring the World of the Celts*, England, 1993

Jarman A. O. H., *The Legend of Merlin*, Cardiff, 1960

Loomis, R. S. (ed.), *Arthurian Literature in the Middle Ages. A Collective History*, Oxford, 1959

Mac Cana, Proinsias, *Celtic Mythology*, England, 1996

MacKillop, James, *Dictionary of Celtic Mythology*, England, 1998

McCone, Kim, *Pagan Past and Christian Present in Early Irish Literature*, Maynooth Monographs 3, 1990, rep. 1991

Nagy, Joseph Falaky, *The Wisdom of the Outlaw. The Boyhood Deeds of Finn in Gaelic Narrative Tradition*, Berkeley/London, 1985

Ross, Anne, *Pagan Celtic Britain. Studies in Iconography and Tradition*, London, 1967

CENTRAL AND EASTERN EUROPE

Afanasiev, Alexander, *The Poetic Interpretations of Nature by the Slavs*, 3 vols., St Petersburg, 1865–9

Afanasiev, Alexander, *Russian Folk Tales*, 8 vols., St Petersburg, 1855–67

Chadwick, H. Munro and N. Kershaw, *The Growth of Literature*, vol. II, pt. i 'Russian Oral Literature', pt. ii 'Yugoslav Oral Poetry', Cambridge, 1936

Ivanits, Linda J., *Russian Folk Belief*, New York/London, 1989

Oinas, Felix J., *Essays on Russian Folklore and Mythology*, Ohio, 1989

Perkowski, Jan L., *Vampires of the Slavs*, Cambridge, Mass., 1976

Popovic, Tatyana, *Prince Marko. The Hero of the South Slavic Epic*, Syracuse, N.Y., 1988

Riordan, James, *Tales from Central Russia*, Harmondsworth, 1976

Warner, Elizabeth, *Heroes, Monsters and Other Worlds from Russian Mythology*, London, 1985

NORTHERN EUROPE

Auden, W. H. and P. B. Taylor, *Norse Poems*, London, 1981

Davidson, H. R. Ellis, *Gods and Myths of Northern Europe*, London, 1964

Hutton, R., *The Pagan Religions of the Ancient British Isles: Their Nature and Legacy*, Oxford, 1991

Jones, G., *A History of the Vikings*, Oxford, 1984

Owen, G. R., *Rites and Religions of the Anglo-Saxons*, Newton Abbot, 1981

Simek, Rudolf, *Dictionary of Northern Mythology*, Cambridge, 1993

Todd, M., *The Early Germans*, Oxford, 1992

Turville-Petre, E. O. G., *Myth and Religion of the North*, London, 1964

SIBERIA AND THE ARCTIC

Bogoras, W. G., *The Chukchee*, New York, 1975 [1904–9]

Damar, D., *Handbook of North American Indians: Arctic*, Washington, 1984

Dioszegi, V. and M. Hoppal (eds.), *Shamanism in Siberia*, Budapest, 1978

Fienup-Riordan, Ann, *Eskimo Essays*, London, 1990

Kleivan, I. and B. Sonne, *Eskimos: Greenland and Canada*, Leiden, 1985

Lowenstein, T., *The Things That Were Said of Them:*

Shaman Stories and Oral Histories of the Tikigaq People, Berkeley, 1992

Merkur, D., *Powers Which We Do Not Know: the Gods and Spirits of the Inuit* Moscow, Idaho, 1991

Nelson, Edward, *The Eskimo about Bering Strait*, Washington, 1983

Rasmussen, Knud, *Intellectual Culture of the Hudson Bay Eskimos*, Copenhagen, 1929

Ray, Dorothy Jean, *Eskimo Masks: Art and Ceremony*, Seattle, 1967

Spencer, Robert, *The North Alaskan Eskimo*, Washington, 1959

Weyer, Edward, *The Eskimos*, New Haven, 1932

INDIA AND SRI LANKA

Bhaktivedanta Swami, A. C., *Srimad Bhagavatam*, Los Angeles, 1975

Daniélou, Alain, *Hindu Polytheism*, London, 1964

Dowson, J., *Classical Dictionary of Hindu Mythology*, London, 1961

Ions, Veronica, *Indian Mythology*, London, 1967

Jones, John Garrett, *Tales and Teachings of the Buddha*, London 1979

Kinsley, David, *The Sword and the Flute: Kali and Krishna*, Berkeley, 1975

Kuiper, F. B. J., *Ancient Indian Cosmogony*, New Delhi, 1983

Mahabharata, trans. and ed. J. A. B. van Buitenen, vols. 1–3, Chicago, 1973–78

O'Flaherty, Wendy, *Hindu Myths*, London 1975

Prime, Ranchor, *Ramayana, A Journey*, London 1997

Puhvel, Jaan, *Comparative Mythology*, Baltimore, 1987

Rajan, Chandra, *The Pancatantra*, London 1993

Shulman, David Dean, *Tamil Temple Myths*, Princeton, 1980

Stutley, Margaret and James, *A Dictionary of Hinduism: Its Mythology, Folklore and Development, 1500 BC–1500 AD*, 1977

Zimmer, Heinrich (ed. Joseph Campbell), *Myths and Symbols in Indian Art and Civilization*, Washington D. C., 1946

TIBET AND MONGOLIA

Altangerel, D., *How Did the Great Bear Originate? Folktales from Mongolia*, Ulaanbaattar, 1988

Berger, Patricia and Terese Tse Bartholomew, *Mongolia: The Legacy of Chinggis Khan*, London, 1995

Campbell, Joseph, *The Way of the Animal Powers: Historical Atlas of World Mythology, vol. 1*, London, 1983

Heissig, Walther (translated from the German by Geoffrey Samuel), *The Religions of Mongolia*, Berkeley, 1980

Project, Yeshe De, *Ancient Tibet*, Berkeley, 1986

Snellgrove, David, *Indo-Tibetan Buddhism*, London, 1987

Stein, R. A., *Tibetan Civilisation*, London, 1972

Tucci, Giuseppe, *The Religions of Tibet*, London, 1980

CHINA

Birch, C., *Chinese Myths and Fantasies*, Oxford, 1961

Birrell, Anne, *Chinese Mythology: an Introduction*, London, 1993

Christie, A. H., *Chinese Mythology*, 1968

Ke, Yuang, *Dragons and Dynasties: an Introduction to Chinese Mythology*, London, 1993

Loewe, Michael, *Divination, Mythology and Monarchy in Han China*, Cambridge, 1994

Palmer, Martin and Xiaomin, Zhao *et al*, *Essential Chinese Mythology*, London 1997

Waley, Arthur, *Ballads and Stories from Tun-huang*, London, 1960

Watson, W., *China*, London, 1961

Werner, E. T. C., *Myths and Legends of China*, London, 1922

JAPAN AND KOREA

Aston, W. G., *Nihongi: Chronicles of Japan, London and New York*, 1956

Choi, In-hak, *A Type Index of Korean Folktales*, Seoul, 1979

Grayson, James Huntley, *Myths and Legends from Korea*, Sheffield, 1998

Ilyon, Samguk yusa: *Legends and History of the Three Kingdoms of Ancient Korea* translated by Tae-Hung Ha and Grafton K. Mintz, Seoul, 1972

Jensen, Adolf E. (trans. Marianna Tax Choldin and Wolfgang Weissleder) *Myth and Cult among Primitive Peoples*, Chicago, 1963

Kidder, J. E., *Japan*, London, 1959

Lee, Peter H., *Sourcebook of Korean Civilization* 2 vols., New York, 1993 (vol. 1, *From Early Times to the Sixteenth Century*)

Philippi, Donald L., (trans.), *Kojiki*, Tokyo, 1968

Walraven, Boudewijn, *Songs of the Shaman: The Ritual Chants of the Korean Mudang*, London, 1994

SOUTHEAST ASIA

Coedes, G., C. Archaimbault, and T. W. R. Davids (eds.), *Buddhist Birth Stories, or, Jakata Tales*, London, 1980

Davis, R. B., *Muang Metaphysics: A Study of Northern Thai Myth and Ritual*, Bangkok, 1984

Hallam, Elizabeth, *Gods and Goddesses: over 130 deities and tales from world mythology*, London, 1997

Izikowitz, K.-G., *Fastening the Soul. Some Religious Traits among the Lamet*, 1941

Mus, Paul, *Barabudur*, New York, 1978

Trankell, I.-B., *Cooking, Care and Domestication. A Culinary Ethnography of the Tai Yong, Northern Thailand*, Uppsala, forthcoming

Whittaker, Clio, *An Introduction to Oriental Mythology*, London, 1997

OCEANIA

Beckwith, Martha, *Hawaiian Mythology*, Honolulu, 1982

Best, Elsdan, *Maori Religion and Mythology*, Wellington, 1982

Finney, Ben and Among, Marlene *et al*, *Voyage of Rediscovery: A Cultural Odyssey Through Polynesia*, Berkeley, 1994

Gifford, E. W., *Tongan Myths and Tales*, Bernice P. Bishop Museum, 1924

Gillison, Gillian, *Between Culture and Fantasy, a New Guinea Highlands Mythology*, Chicago, 1993

Grey, Sir George, *Polynesian Mythology*, London/Christchurch, 1965

Handy, E. S. C., *Marquesan Legends*, Bernice P. Bishop Museum, 1930

Knappert, Jan, *Pacific Mythology*, London, 1992

Landtman, G., *Folktales of the Kiwai Papuans*, Helsinki, 1917

Lawrence, P., *Road Belong Cargo*, Manchester, 1964

Lawrie, M., *Myths and Legends of Torres Strait*, Queensland, 1970

Lessa, W. A., *Tales from Ulithi Atoll*, Folklore Studies 13, Berkeley, 1961

Luomola, K., *Maui-of-a-thousand-tricks*, Bernice P. Bishop Museum, 1949

Malinowski, B., *Magic, Science and Religion*, 1954

Powdermaker, H., *Life in Lesu*, 1933

Young, M., *Magicians of Manumanua*, Berkeley, 1983

AUSTRALIA

Layton, R., *Uluru: an Aboriginal history of Ayers Rock*, Canberra, 1986

Morphy, H., *Journey to the crocodile's nest*, Canberra, 1984

Mudrooroo, *Aboriginal Mythology an A-Z Spanning the History of the Australian Aboriginal People from the Earliest Legends to the Present Day*, London, 1994

Neidje, B., *Kakadu Man*, Sydney, 1985

O'Brien, M., *The Legend of the Seven Sisters*, Canberra, 1990

Poignant, Roslyn, *Oceanic and Australian Mythology*, Feltham, 1985

Rutherford, Anna, *Aboriginal Culture Today*, Sydney, 1991

Sienkewicz, Thomas J., *World Mythology an Annotated Guide to Collections and Anthologies*, London, 1996

Turner, David H., *Australian Aboriginal Culture*, New York, 1987

Utemorra, D. and others, *Visions of Mowanjum*, Adelaide, 1980

Warlukurlangu Artists, *Kuruwarri: Yuendumu Doors*, Canberra, 1987

Western Region Aboriginal Land Council, *The story of the Falling Star*, Canberra, 1989

AFRICA

Beattie, John, *Bunyoro, An African Kingdom*, New York, 1960

Callaway, Henry, *The Religious System of the Amazulu*, London, 1870

Cosentino, Donald, *Defiant Maids and Stubborn Farmers: tradition and invention in Mende story performance*, Cambridge, 1982

Davidson, Basil, *Old Africa Rediscovered*, London, 1959

Evans-Pritchard, Evan Edward, *Nuer Religion*, Oxford, 1956

Ezekwuga, Christopher U. M., *Chi: The True God in Igbo Religion*, Alwaye, 1987

Finnegan, Ruth, *Oral Literature in Africa*, Oxford, 1970, rep. 1976

Forde, Daryll (ed.), *African Worlds: studies in the cosmological ideas and social values of African peoples*, London, 1954

Iloanusi, Obiakoizu A., *Myths of the Creation of Man and the Origin of Death in Africa: A Study in Igbo Traditional Culture and Other African Cultures*, Frankfurt, 1984

King, Noel Q., *African Cosmos: An Introduction to Religion in Africa*, Belmont, 1986

Mbiti, John S., *African Religions and Philosophy*, London 1969

Okpewho, Isidore, *Myth in Africa: a study of its aesthetic and cultural relevance*, Cambridge, 1983

Parrinder, Geoffrey, *West African Religion: A Study of the Beliefs and Practices of Akan, Ewe, Yoruba, Ibo, and Kindred Peoples*, London, 1949

Quarcoopome, T. N. O., *West African Traditional Religion, Ibadan*, 1987

Sawyerr, Harry, *God, Ancestor or Creator? Aspects of Traditional Belief in Ghana, Nigeria and Sierra Leone*, Harlow, 1970

Willis, Roy, *There Was a Certain Man: spoken art of the Fipa*, Oxford, 1978

THE CARIBBEAN

Ann, Martha and Dorothy Myers Imel, *Goddesses in World Mythology*, Santa Barbara, 1993

Derkx, J., *Caribbean Studies*, Leiden, 1998

Ferguson, *Eastern Caribbean a guide to the people, politics and culture*, London, 1997

Malinowski, S. and Shhets, A. *et al*, *The Gale Encyclopedia of Native American Tribes*, Detroit, 1998

Spence, Lewis, *Introduction to World Mythology*, London, 1994

NORTH AMERICA

Boas, F., *Tsimshian Mythology*, New York, 1970

Brown, J. E., *The Sacred Pipe*, Harmondsworth, 1971

Burland, C. A. and M. Wood, *North American Indian Mythology*, London, 1985

Campbell, J., *The Way of the Animal Powers*, London 1984

Curtin, J., *Seneca Indian Myths*, New York, 1923

Dooling, D. M. (ed.), *The Sons of the Wind*, San Francisco, 1992

Erdoes, R. and A. Ortiz (eds.), *American Indian Myths and Legends*, New York, 1988

Feldmann, Susan, *The Storytelling Stone: Traditional Native American Myths and Tales*, New York, 1965

Haile, B., *Navajo Coyote Tales*, Lincoln, 1984

Mariott, A. and C. K. Rachlin, *American Indian Mythology*, New York, 1968

Parsons, E. C., *Pueblo Indian Religion*, Chicago, 1939

Radin, P., *The Trickster*, New York, 1956

Riordan, James, *The Songs My Paddle Sings. Native American Legends*, London, 1995

Tooker, E., *Native American Spirituality of the Eastern Woodlands*, New York, 1979

Turner, F. W. III, (ed.), *Portable North American Indian Reader*, Harmondsworth, 1977

Walker, J. R., *Lakota Myth*, Lincoln, 1983

Wright, Ronald, *Stolen Continents: The Indian Story*, London, 1992

CENTRAL AND SOUTH AMERICA

Bray, Warwick, *The Gold of El Dorado*, London, 1978

British Museum, *The Hidden Peoples of the Amazon*, London, 1985

Carrasco, David, *Ancient Mesoamerican Religions*, New York, 1990

Chagnon, Napoleon A., *Yanomamo: The Fierce People*, New York, 1977

Coe, Michael D., Elizabeth P. Benson and Dean Snow, *Atlas of Ancient America*, Oxford, 1985

Fagan, Brian, *Kingdoms of Jade, Kingdoms of Gold*, London, 1991

Hadingham, Evan, *Lines to the Mountain Gods*, London 1987

Harner, Michael, *The Jivaro*, London, 1973

Miller, Mary and Karl Taube, *The Gods and Symbols of Ancient Mexico and the Maya*, London, 1993

Mosely, Michael E., *The Incas and their Ancestors*, London, 1992

Pasztory, Esther, *Aztec Art*, New York, 1983

Saunders, Nicholas J., *People of the Jaguar*, London, 1989

Schele, Linda and Mary E. Miller, *The Blood of Kings*, Fort Worth, 1986

Stevens-Arroyo, A. M., *Cave of the Jaqua: the Mythological World of the Taínos*, Albuquerque, 1988

Sullivan, Lawrence E., *Icanchu's Drum: An orientation to Meaning in South American Religions*, London, 1988

Tedlock, Dennis, *Popul Vuh: The Definitive Edition of the Mayan Book of the Dawn of Life and the Glories of the Gods and Kings*, New York, 1985

Townsend, Richard, *The Aztecs*, London, 1992 Urton, Gary (ed.), *Animal Myths and Metaphors in South America*, Salt Lake City, 1985

Index

Picture Credits

Academy for Korean Studies: 72,73

AKG: 75

Art Archive: 5, 32, 38, 65, 77(r), 108, 106, 136 (b), 179, 203(t), 219; Album/Joseph Martin: 87(t); Archaeological Museum Milan/Dagli Orti (A) 116; Archaeological Museum Naples/Dagli Orti (A): 97(b), 101; Archaeological Museum Spina Ferrara/Dagli Orti (A): 87(b); Archaeological Museum Venice/Dagli Orti (A): 117 (t); Biblioteca Nazionale Marciana Venice/Dagli Orti (A): 199(b); Bibliotheque des Arts Decoratifs Paris/Dagli Orti (A): 89(t); British Library: 41(r), 43, 45, 55(t); British Museum: 59(l), 118, 119, 122; British Museum/Jacqueline Hyde: 21(b), 25(t); Christies/Eileen Tweedy, 27(b); Civiche Racc d'Arte Moderna Pavia/Dagli Orti (A): 103; Dagli Orti: 14(t), 20, 22, 23(b), 27(t), 29,105(t), 115(t); Dagli Orti (A): 18(t), 37; Egyptian Museum Cairo/Dagli Orti: 24; Egyptian Museum Cairo/Dagli Orti (A): 15(r), 17(b), 18(b), 23(t), 19; Eileen Tweedy: 80, 135; Ethnographical Museum Gothenbarg Sweden/Dagli Orti: 201; Galleria Borghese Rome/Dagli Orti (A): 5; Galleria degli Uffizi Florence/Dagli Orti (A): 110, 117(b);Hermitage Museum Saint Petersburg/Dagli Orti (A): 147(t); Historiska Museet Stockholm/Dagli Orti (A): 130, 133, 137(t); Hittite Museum Ankara/Dagli Orti: 35(b); Jan Vinchon Numismatist Paris/Dagli Orti (A): 114; Jarrold Publishing: 124; Kizhi Museum/Nicolas Sapieha: 147(b); Lucien Biton Collection Paris/Dagli Orti (A): 69(b); Marco Polo Gallery Paris/Dagli Orti (A): 42; Miramare Paris Trieste/Dagli Orti (A): 88; Musée Ceramique Sevres: 107; Musée des Antiquites St Germain en Laye/Dagli Orti: 126; Musée des Arts Africains et Oceaniens/Dagli Orti (A): 203b, 213(r), 217, 220; Musée Guimet Paris/Dagli Orti: 41, 50 (t), 66,67; Musée Guimet Paris/Dagli Orti (A) 39(b):Musée du Louvre de Paris/Album/Joseph Martin: 113; Musée du Louvre de Paris/Dagli Orti: 28, 33(l), 41(l), 66(b), 67; Musée du Louvre de Paris/Dagli Orti (A): 39(b); Museo de America Madrid/Dagli Orti: 196; Museo Capitolino Rome/Dagli Orti (A): 89(b), 99,100; Museo del Prado Madrid: 86; Museo del Prado Madrid/Album/Joseph Martin: 36; Museo della Civilta Romana Rome/Dagli Orti: 105(b); Museo Provincale Sigismondo Castromediano Lecce/Dagli Orti (A): 93; National Gallery London: 10, 95(b); National Museum Athens/Dagli Orti: 95(t), National Museum Palermo/Dagli Orti: 97(t); National Science Academy Kiev/Dagli Orti (A): 98, 151(b), 151(t); Navy Historical Service Vicennes France/Dagli Orti: 158 (t); Nicolas Sapieha: 146; Oriental Art Museum Genoa/Dagli Orti (A): 84; Oriental Museum Genoa/Dagli Orti (A): 77(l); Palazzo Barberini Rome/Dagli Orti (A): 109(t); Prehistoric Musem Moesgard Højbjerg Denmark/Dagli Orti: 140; Private Collection Paris/Dagli Orti: 81, 154(t); Rijksmuseum voor Volkenkunde Leiden/Dagli Orti: 51 Royal Library Stockholm/Dagli Orti: 160; Staatliche Glypothek Munich/Dagli Orti (A): 115(t); Tate Gallery London/Eileen Tweedy: 102, 128; Victoria & Albert Museum London/Eileen Tweedy: 44, 47

Christie's Images: 157(t)

Collection Kharbine-Tapbor: 149(t)

Impact: Thierry Bouzac: 198; Keith Cardwell: 63; A J Deane: 40; Alain le Garsmeur: 59(r); Ken Graham: 157(b); 163(b); Mark Henley: 49(b), 64, 65; Christopher Joyce: 225(b); Susie Moberly: 204; Neil Morrison: 211, 224; Caroline Penn: 205(t); David Reed: 200(b)

Kobal: Kobal Collection, Hammer: 155

Mary Evans: 15(l),16,121(t), 13(l), 13(r), 134, 145(b), 149(b), 154(b), 156, 159(b), 161(b), 161(t), 225(t), 25(b), 30, 31(b), 31(t), 33(r), 39(t), 60(b), 60(t), 62(t), 91(r), 92, Mary Evans/ Edwin Wallace, 91(l), 96

Courtesy of Kojiki Nikonshoki (Shinchosa,1991): 83(t)

NJ Saunders: 110, 165(b), 166, 176, 177, 178(b),178(t), 180, 181(b), 181(t), 182, 183(b), 183(t), 184, 185(b), 185(t), 186, 187(b), 187(t), 188(b), 188(t), 189, 190(b), 191, 192, 193(b), 193(t), 194, 195(b), 195(t), 197

Tadeusz Skorupski: 68, 69(t)

Still Pictures: B & C Alexander: 159(t), Marek Libersky: 152; Oliver Gillie: 153; Richard West: 223(l)

Graham Stride: 45, 46, 48, 49(t), 55(b), 56, 57(b), 57(t)

Topham Picturepoint: 8, 12, 17(t), 21(t), 34, 35(t), 53(b), 62(b), 71(b), 79,112, 123(b), 125(b), 125(t), 131(t), 136 (t), 139(l), 141(r),150, 199(t), 200(t), 202, 205(b), 206, 212, 214, 216(t), 218, ; UNEP: 163(t)

Val/Artephot G.Mandel: 61

Werner Forman Archive: 9, 78, 83, 85, 141(l), 120, 127, 165, 174, 207, 208, 209(r);Anchorage Museum of History and Art: 169; H G Arnold Collection, Cody, Wyoming, USA: 171(l), Central History Musem, P'Yongyang: 71(t); Dakota USA: 175(b); Denpasar Museum, Bali: 54;Dorset Natural History and Archaeological Society: 123(t); Glenbow Museum, Calgary, Alberta: 164; P Goldman Collection, London: 52, 66(t), 226; Joslyn Art Museum, Omaha, Nebraska: 175(t); Manx Museum, Isle of Man: 144; Musees de Rennes: 121(b), Museum fur Volkerkunde, Berlin: 171(r); Museum of Anthropology, University of British Columbia, Vancouver: 167; National Museum, Copenhagen: 120, 127(t),129(b), 137(b);National Museum of Ireland: 127(b); National Museum of Man, Ottawa, Ontario, Canada: 173(t); Peabody Museum, Harvard University, Cambridge, MA: 170,172, 227; Plains Indian Museum, BBHC, Cody, Wyoming, USA: 168; Private Collection: 50(b), 53(t), 210(t), 213(l), 215: Private Collection, New York: 210(b); Private Collection/Prague: 216(b); Mr & Mrs John A Putnam: 173(b); Rijksmuseum voor Volkenkunde, Leiden: 221; Statens Historiska Museum, Stockholm: 131(b), 139(r), 142–3(t), 143(b), 145(t);Tara Collection, New York: 209(l); Thjodminjasafn, Reykjavik, Iceland: 138